VOLUME 08

The Amazing Spider-Man

Spider-Man's First Hunt

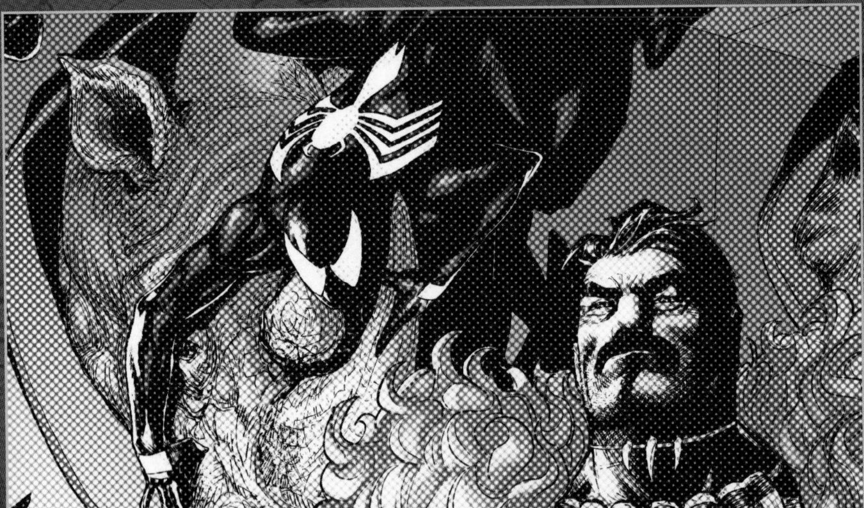

SPIDER-MAN

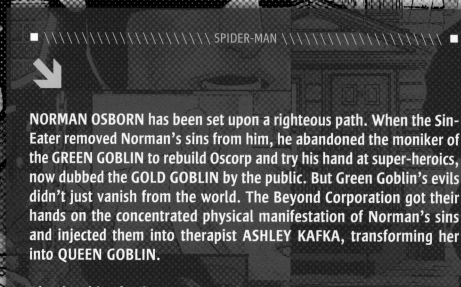

NORMAN OSBORN has been set upon a righteous path. When the Sin-Eater removed Norman's sins from him, he abandoned the moniker of the **GREEN GOBLIN** to rebuild Oscorp and try his hand at super-heroics, now dubbed the **GOLD GOBLIN** by the public. But Green Goblin's evils didn't just vanish from the world. The Beyond Corporation got their hands on the concentrated physical manifestation of Norman's sins and injected them into therapist **ASHLEY KAFKA**, transforming her into **QUEEN GOBLIN**.

Blaming him for her metamorphosis, Queen Goblin set out on a mission to systematically destroy Norman. In a final confrontation, Gold Goblin was forced to kill Queen Goblin to save Spider-Man's life. But Peter and Norman are about to be reminded — goblins don't stay dead for long.

Jennifer Grünwald COLLECTION EDITOR

Daniel Kirchhoffer ASSISTANT EDITOR

Lisa Montalbano ASSOCIATE MANAGER, TALENT RELATIONS

Jeff Youngquist VP PRODUCTION & SPECIAL PROJECTS

Jay Bowen BOOK DESIGNER

Adam Del Re MANAGER & SENIOR DESIGNER

David Gabriel SVP PRINT, SALES & MARKETING

C.B. Cebulski EDITOR IN CHIEF

AMAZING SPIDER-MAN BY ZEB WELLS VOL. 8: SPIDER-MAN'S FIRST HUNT. Contains material originally published in magazine form as AMAZING SPIDER-MAN (2022) #32-38. First printing 2023. ISBN 978-1-302-95344-7. Published by MARVEL WORLDWIDE, INC., a subsidiary of MARVEL ENTERTAINMENT, LLC. OFFICE OF PUBLICATION: 1290 Avenue of the Americas, New York, NY 10104. © 2023 MARVEL No similarity between any of the names, characters, persons, and/or institutions in this book with those of any living or dead person or institution is intended, and any such similarity which may exist is purely coincidental. **Printed in the U.S.A.** KEVIN FEIGE, Chief Creative Officer; DAN BUCKLEY, President, Marvel Entertainment; DAVID BOGART, Associate Publisher & SVP of Talent Affairs; TOM BREVOORT, VP, Executive Editor; NICK LOWE, Executive Editor, VP of Content, Digital Publishing; DAVID GABRIEL, VP of Print & Digital Publishing; SVEN LARSEN, VP of Licensed Publishing; MARK ANNUNZIATO, VP of Planning & Forecasting; JEFF YOUNGQUIST, VP of Production & Special Projects; ALEX MORALES, Director of Publishing Operations; DAN EDINGTON, Director of Editorial Operations; RICKEY PURDIN, Director of Talent Relations; JENNIFER GRÜNWALD, Director of Production & Special Projects; SUSAN CRESPI, Production Manager; STAN LEE, Chairman Emeritus. For information regarding advertising in Marvel Comics or on Marvel.com, please contact Vit DeBellis, Custom Solutions & Integrated Advertising Manager, at vdebellis@marvel.com. For Marvel subscription inquiries, please call 888-511-5480. **Manufactured between 12/8/2023 and 1/16/2024 by SEAWAY PRINTING, GREEN BAY, WI, USA.**

10 9 8 7 6 5 4 3 2 1

■ /////////////////////// VOLUME 08 ///////////////////////// ■

the AMAZING SPIDER-MAN

Spider-Man's First Hunt

Zeb Wells WRITER

AMAZING SPIDER-MAN #32-35

Patrick Gleason ARTIST

Marcio Menyz WITH
Erick Arciniega (#35) COLOR ARTISTS

John Romita Jr. &
Scott Hanna WITH
Morry Hollowell (#32) &
Marcio Menyz (#33-35) COVER ART

AMAZING SPIDER-MAN #36-38

Ed McGuinness PENCILER

Mark Farmer (#36-38),
Wade Von Grawbadger (#37-38)
& **Ed McGuinness** (#37-38) INKERS

Emilio Laiso INTERLUDE ARTIST (#37-38)

Marcio Menyz WITH
Erick Arciniega (#37-38) COLOR ARTISTS

Ed McGuinness &
Marcio Menyz COVER ART

VC's **Joe Caramagna**
LETTERER

Kaeden McGahey
ASSISTANT EDITOR

Tom Groneman
ASSOCIATE EDITOR

Nick Lowe
EDITOR

SPIDER-MAN CREATED BY
STAN LEE & STEVE DITKO

■ /////////////// THERE MUST ALSO COME GREAT RESPONSIBILITY /////////// ■

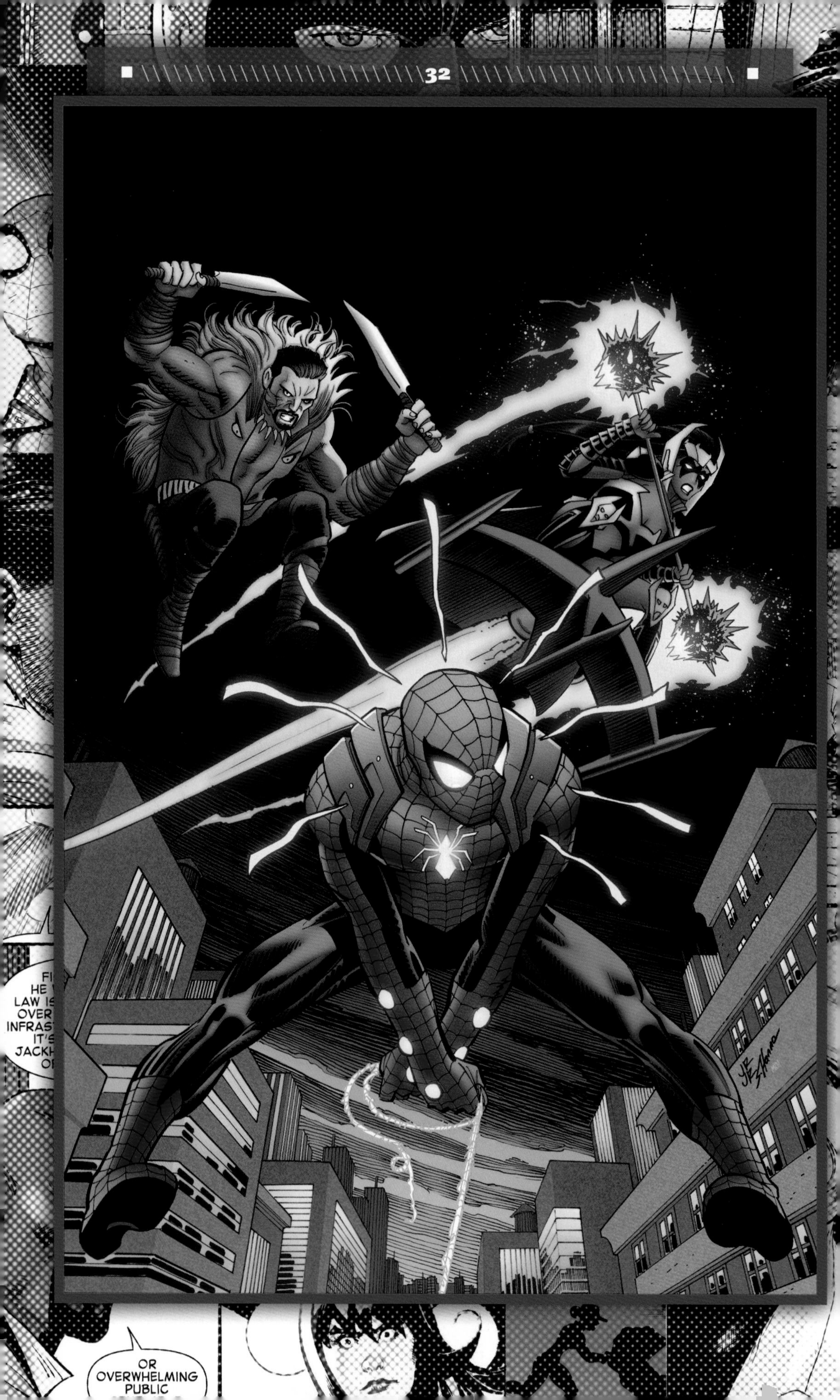
OR
OVERWHELMING
PUBLIC

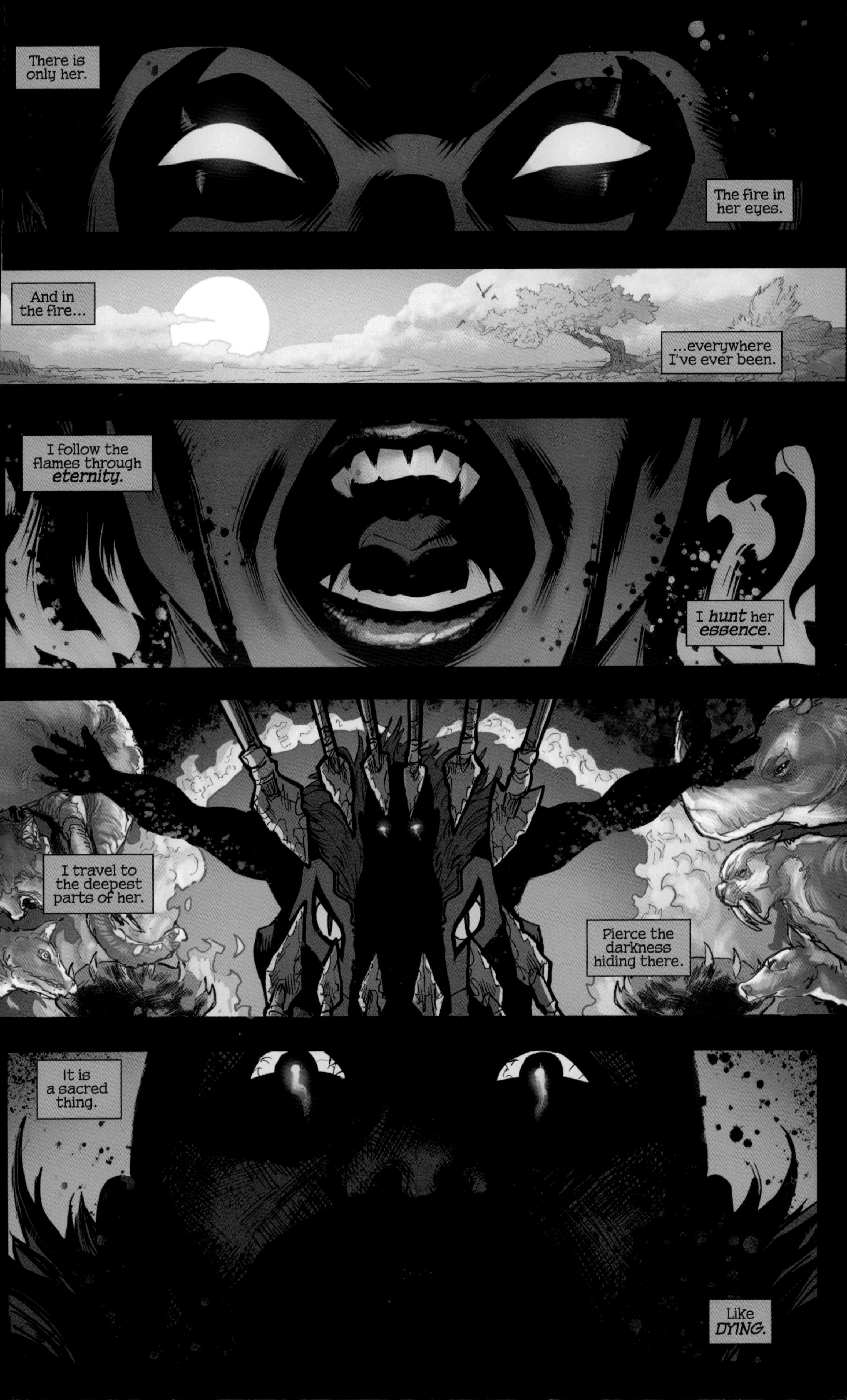
There is only her.
The fire in her eyes.
And in the fire...
...everywhere I've ever been.
I follow the flames through *eternity*.
I *hunt* her *essence*.
I travel to the deepest parts of her.
Pierce the darkness hiding there.
It is a sacred thing.
Like *DYING*.

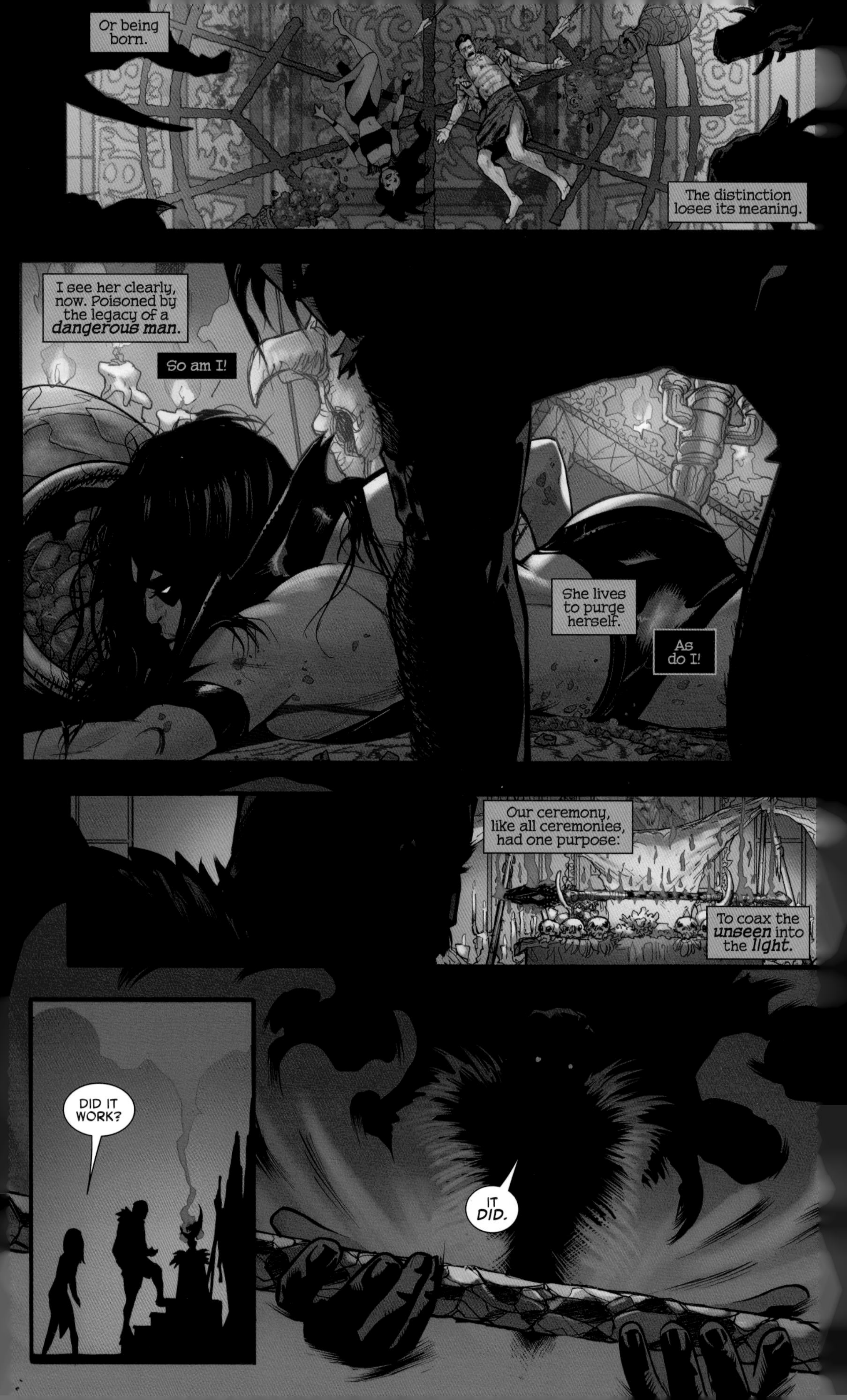
Or being born.
The distinction loses its meaning.
I see her clearly, now. Poisoned by the legacy of a dangerous man.
So am I!
She lives to purge herself.
As do I!
Our ceremony, like all ceremonies, had one purpose:
To coax the unseen into the light.
DID IT WORK?
IT DID.

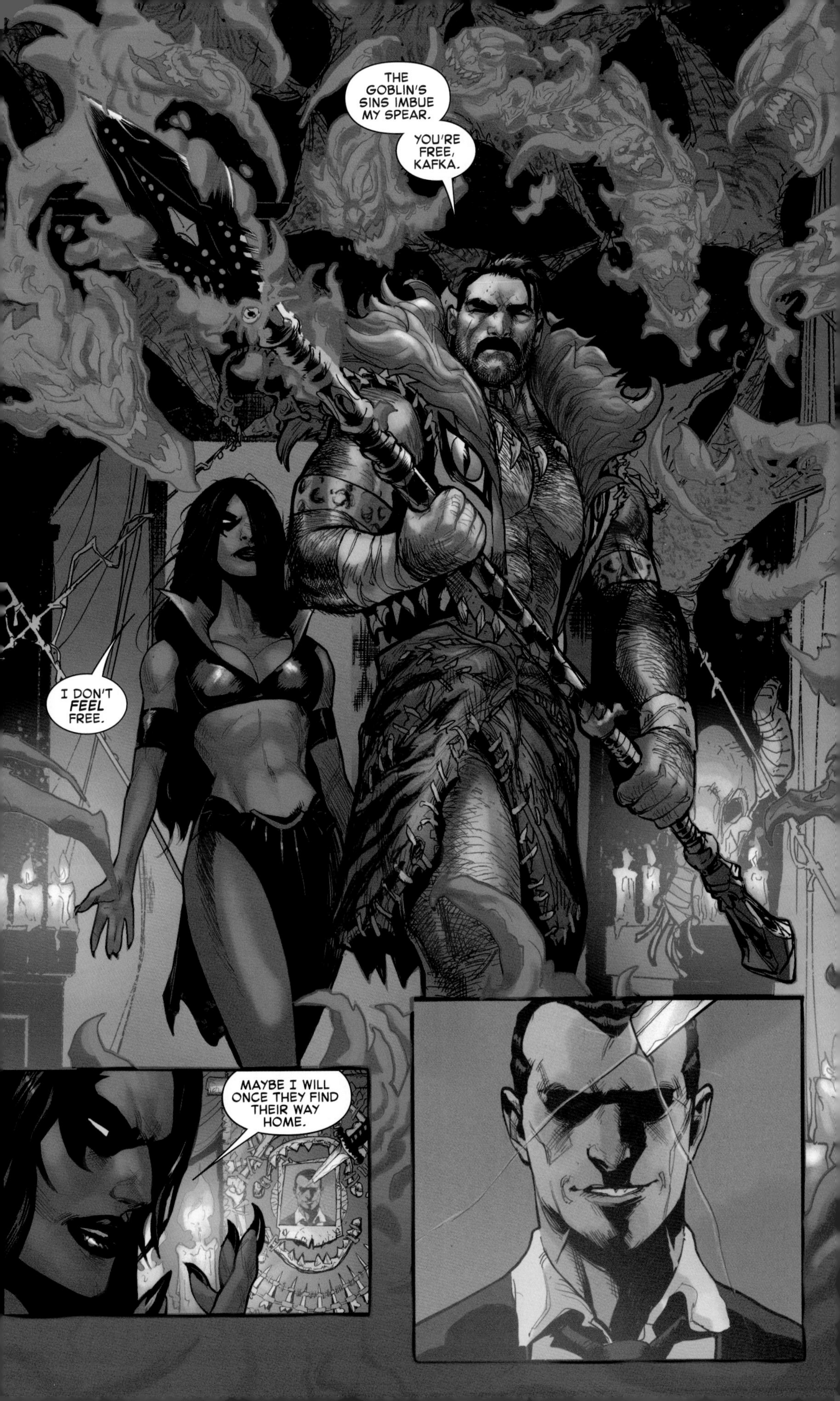
THE GOBLIN'S SINS IMBUE MY SPEAR.
YOU'RE FREE, KAFKA.
I DON'T *FEEL* FREE.
MAYBE I WILL ONCE THEY FIND THEIR WAY HOME.

NEW YORK CITY.

NORMAN?

PETER? YOU'RE CALLING LATE. I THOUGHT YOU HAD PLANS TONIGHT.

JUST WANTED TO MAKE SURE YOU'RE NOT STUCK WORKING AT THE OFFICE.

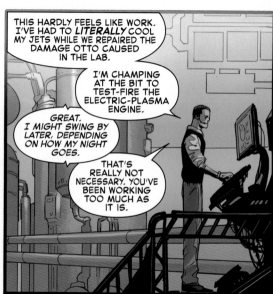

THIS HARDLY FEELS LIKE WORK. I'VE HAD TO *LITERALLY* COOL MY JETS WHILE WE REPAIRED THE DAMAGE OTTO CAUSED IN THE LAB.

I'M CHAMPING AT THE BIT TO TEST-FIRE THE ELECTRIC-PLASMA ENGINE.

GREAT. I MIGHT SWING BY LATER, DEPENDING ON HOW MY NIGHT GOES.

THAT'S REALLY NOT NECESSARY. YOU'VE BEEN WORKING TOO MUCH AS IT IS.

I KNOW, BUT--

OOPS, GETTING ANOTHER CALL. GOTTA GO.

SEE YOU *TOMORROW.* AND NOT A SECOND EARLIER--

TEK

FELICIA?

HEY, PETER. CHECKING IN. BEEN A FEW WEEKS SINCE WE BROKE UP, SO I WANTED TO SEE HOW THE INEVITABLE DRAWN-SHADES, DEPRESSED-SHUT-IN THING WAS GOING--

WAIT, WHERE ARE YOU?

I'M MEETING JANICE'S FRIEND MICHELE.

HOLD ON, THE LAWYER?

YOU KNOW HER?

I'VE *MET* HER. IS THIS A DATE?

WHAT? NO. RANDY AND JANICE AREN'T DOING WELL. I DON'T THINK THEY'VE *TALKED* SINCE THE WEDDING... OR *ATTEMPTED* WEDDING.

WE'RE GONNA COMPARE NOTES. SEE IF WE CAN HELP. WAIT--

WHY DID YOU ASK IF IT WAS A DATE?

WHY DO YOU THINK, PETER?

BECAUSE SHE'S *HOT.*

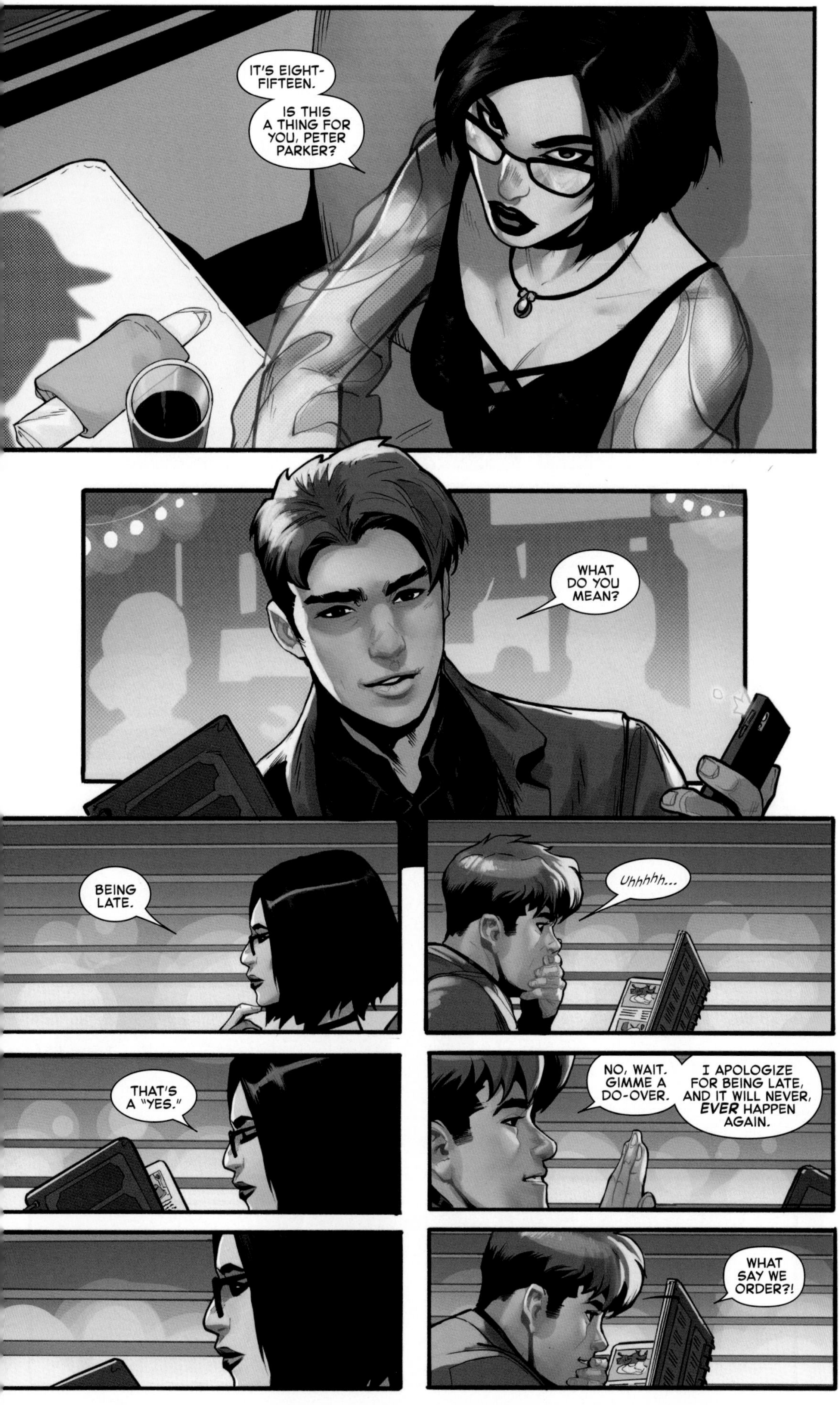
IT'S EIGHT-FIFTEEN.
IS THIS A THING FOR YOU, PETER PARKER?
WHAT DO YOU MEAN?
BEING LATE.
Uhhhhh...
THAT'S A "YES."
NO, WAIT. GIMME A DO-OVER.
I APOLOGIZE FOR BEING LATE, AND IT WILL NEVER, *EVER* HAPPEN AGAIN.
WHAT SAY WE ORDER?!

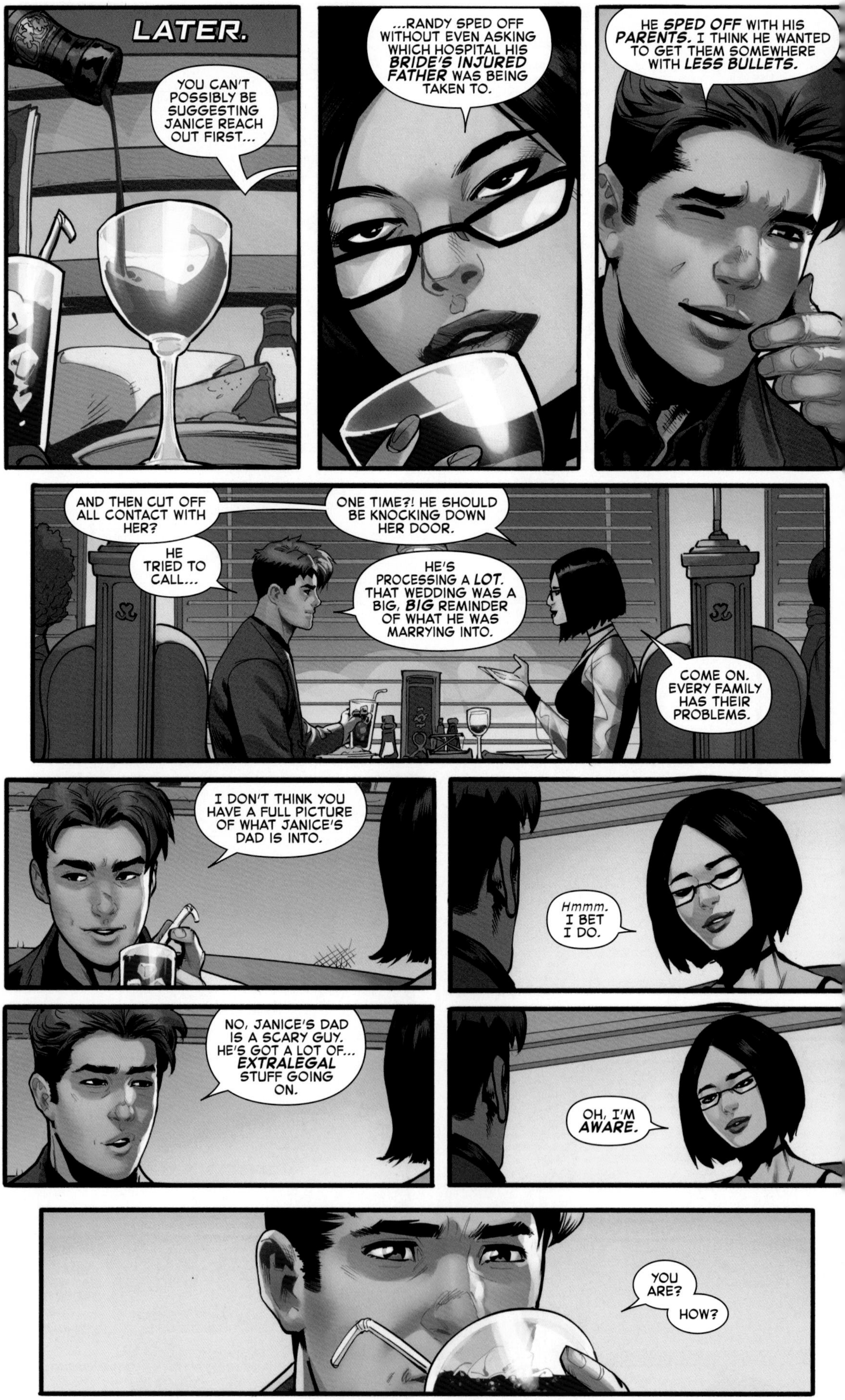

LATER.
YOU CAN'T POSSIBLY BE SUGGESTING JANICE REACH OUT FIRST...
...RANDY SPED OFF WITHOUT EVEN ASKING WHICH HOSPITAL HIS BRIDE'S INJURED FATHER WAS BEING TAKEN TO.
HE SPED OFF WITH HIS PARENTS. I THINK HE WANTED TO GET THEM SOMEWHERE WITH LESS BULLETS.
AND THEN CUT OFF ALL CONTACT WITH HER?
HE TRIED TO CALL...
ONE TIME?! HE SHOULD BE KNOCKING DOWN HER DOOR.
HE'S PROCESSING A LOT. THAT WEDDING WAS A BIG, BIG REMINDER OF WHAT HE WAS MARRYING INTO.
COME ON. EVERY FAMILY HAS THEIR PROBLEMS.
I DON'T THINK YOU HAVE A FULL PICTURE OF WHAT JANICE'S DAD IS INTO.
Hmmm. I BET I DO.
NO, JANICE'S DAD IS A SCARY GUY. HE'S GOT A LOT OF... EXTRALEGAL STUFF GOING ON.
OH, I'M AWARE.
YOU ARE?
HOW?

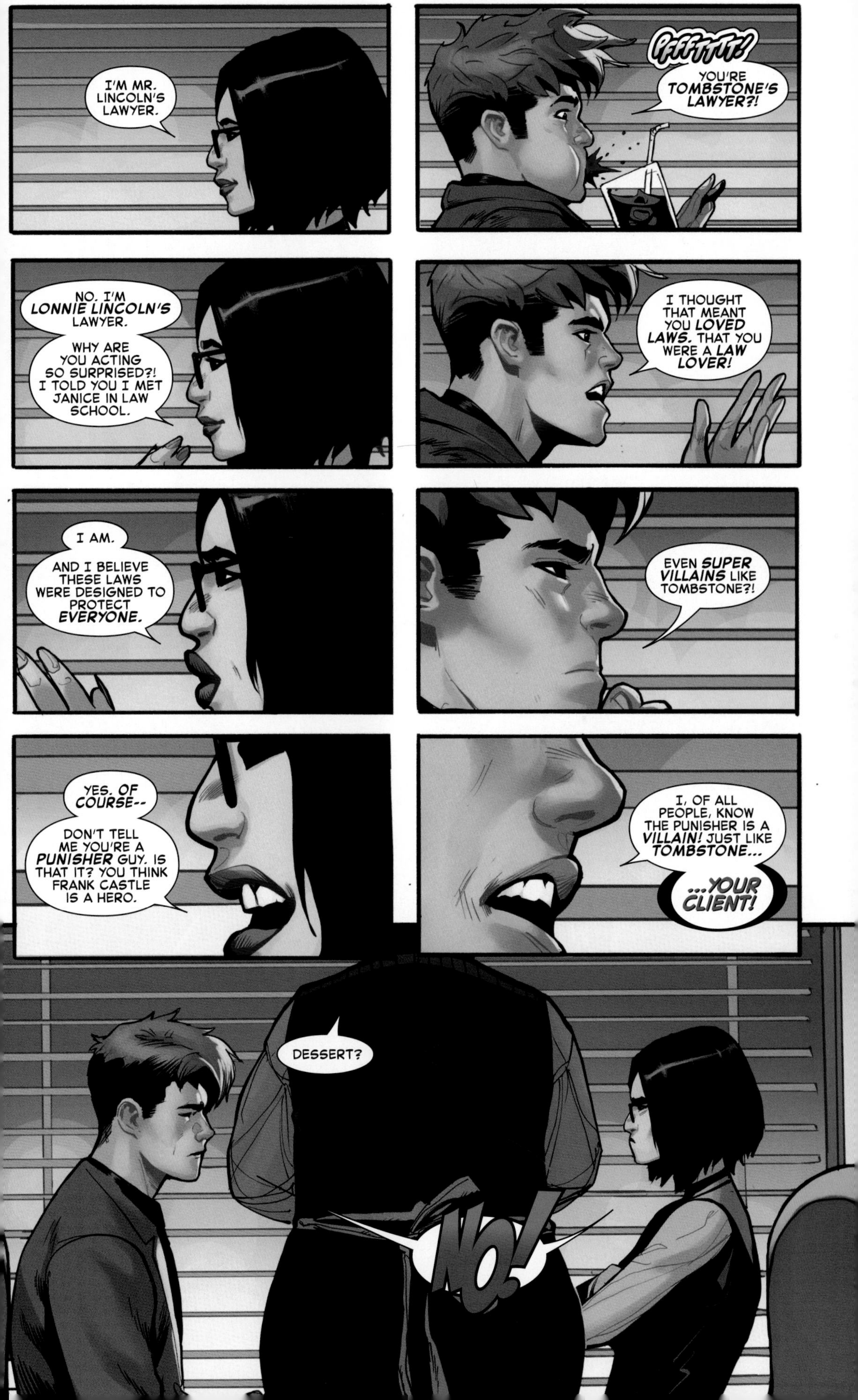
I'M MR. LINCOLN'S LAWYER.
PFFFTTTT!
YOU'RE TOMBSTONE'S LAWYER?!
NO. I'M LONNIE LINCOLN'S LAWYER.
WHY ARE YOU ACTING SO SURPRISED?! I TOLD YOU I MET JANICE IN LAW SCHOOL.
I THOUGHT THAT MEANT YOU LOVED LAWS. THAT YOU WERE A LAW LOVER!
I AM.
AND I BELIEVE THESE LAWS WERE DESIGNED TO PROTECT EVERYONE.
EVEN SUPER VILLAINS LIKE TOMBSTONE?!
YES. OF COURSE--
DON'T TELL ME YOU'RE A PUNISHER GUY. IS THAT IT? YOU THINK FRANK CASTLE IS A HERO.
I, OF ALL PEOPLE, KNOW THE PUNISHER IS A VILLAIN! JUST LIKE TOMBSTONE...
...YOUR CLIENT!
DESSERT?
NO!

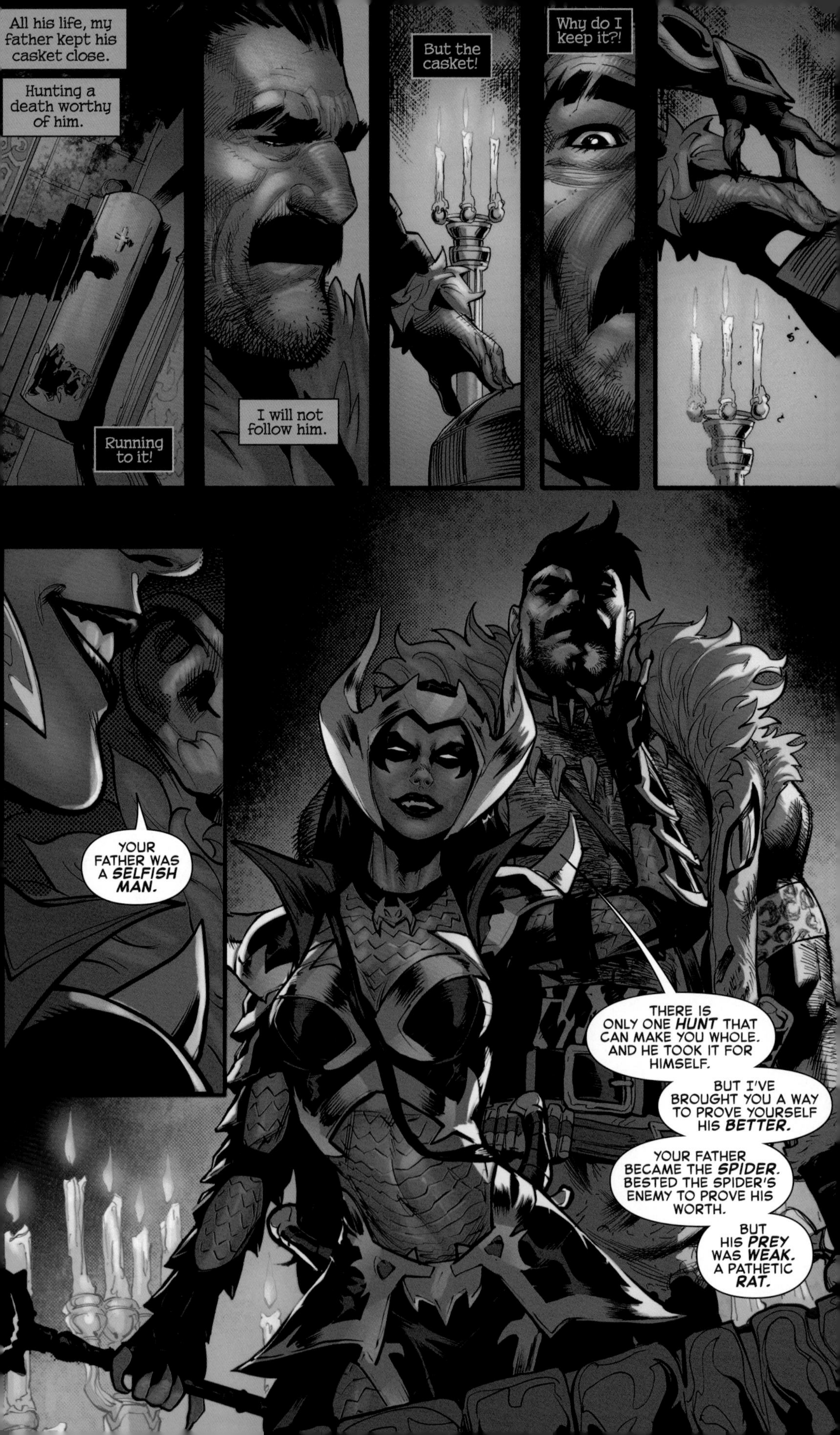
All his life, my father kept his casket close.
Hunting a death worthy of him.
Running to it!
I will not follow him.
But the casket!
Why do I keep it?!
YOUR FATHER WAS A SELFISH MAN.
THERE IS ONLY ONE HUNT THAT CAN MAKE YOU WHOLE. AND HE TOOK IT FOR HIMSELF.
BUT I'VE BROUGHT YOU A WAY TO PROVE YOURSELF HIS BETTER.
YOUR FATHER BECAME THE SPIDER. BESTED THE SPIDER'S ENEMY TO PROVE HIS WORTH.
BUT HIS PREY WAS WEAK. A PATHETIC RAT.

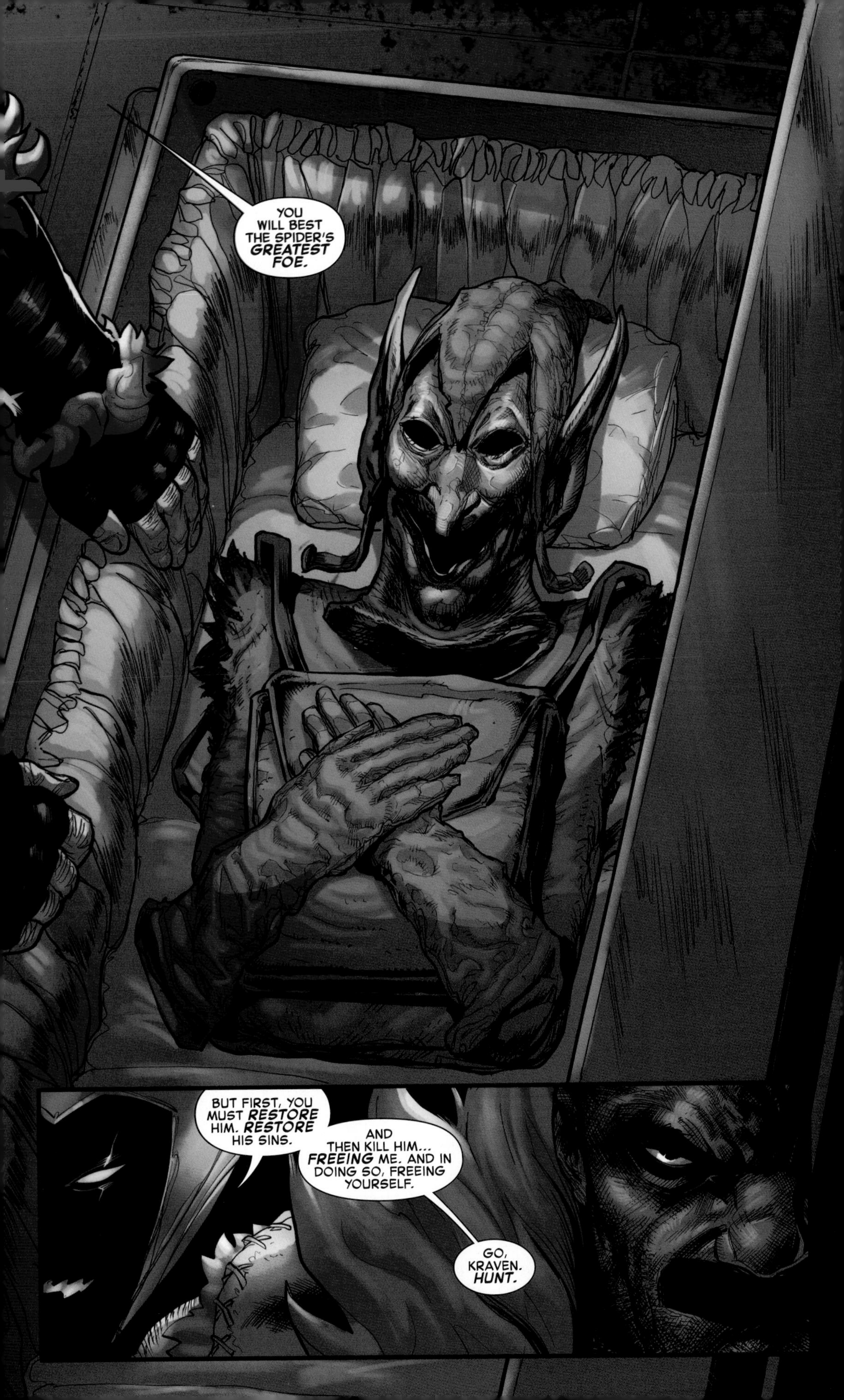
YOU WILL BEST THE SPIDER'S GREATEST FOE.
BUT FIRST, YOU MUST RESTORE HIM. RESTORE HIS SINS.
AND THEN KILL HIM... FREEING ME. AND IN DOING SO, FREEING YOURSELF.
GO, KRAVEN. HUNT.

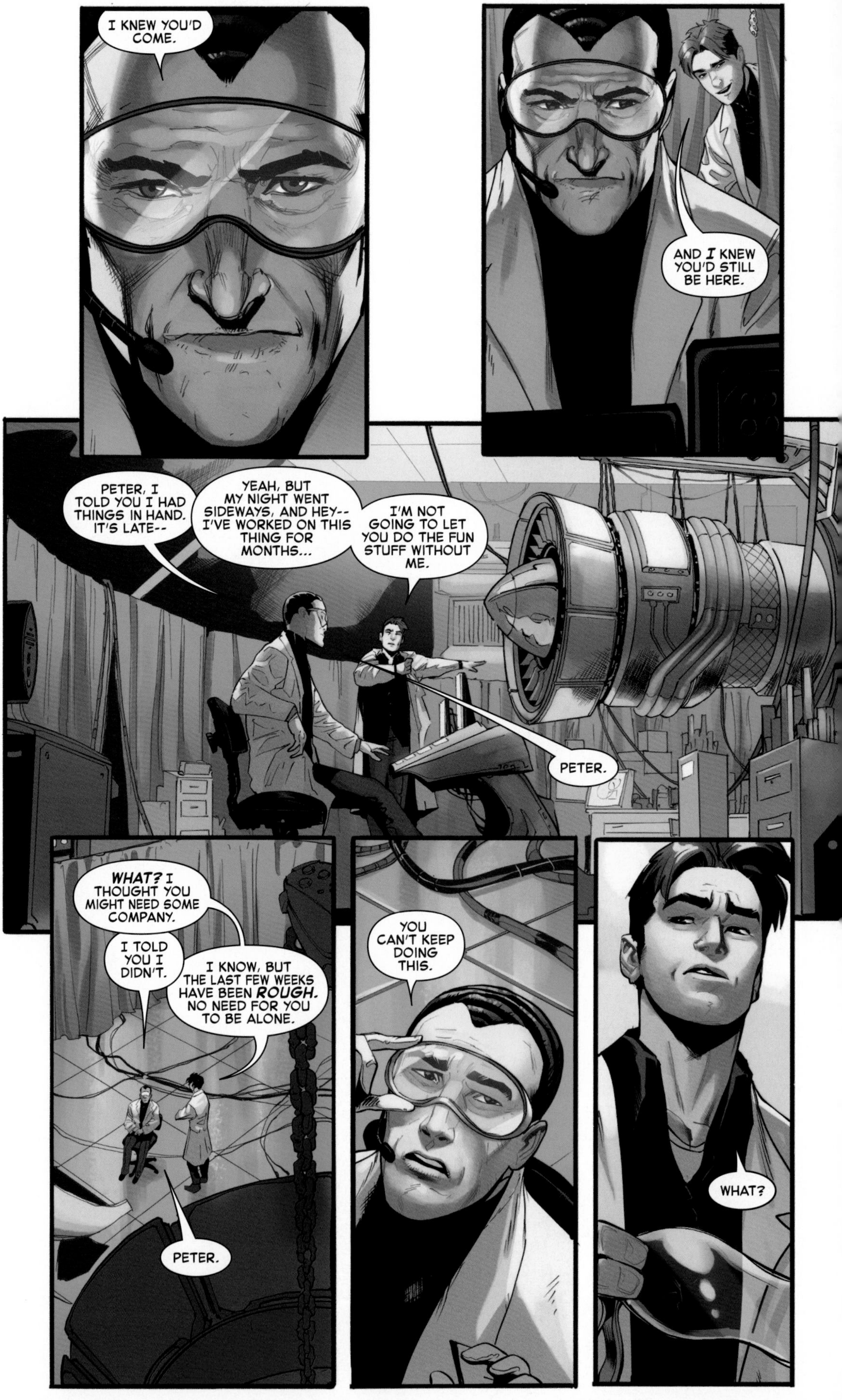

I KNEW YOU'D COME.
AND *I* KNEW YOU'D STILL BE HERE.
PETER, I TOLD YOU I HAD THINGS IN HAND. IT'S LATE--
YEAH, BUT MY NIGHT WENT SIDEWAYS, AND HEY-- I'VE WORKED ON THIS THING FOR MONTHS...
I'M NOT GOING TO LET YOU DO THE FUN STUFF WITHOUT ME.
PETER.
PETER.
WHAT? I THOUGHT YOU MIGHT NEED SOME COMPANY.
I TOLD YOU I DIDN'T.
I KNOW, BUT THE LAST FEW WEEKS HAVE BEEN *ROUGH.* NO NEED FOR YOU TO BE ALONE.
YOU CAN'T KEEP DOING THIS.
WHAT?

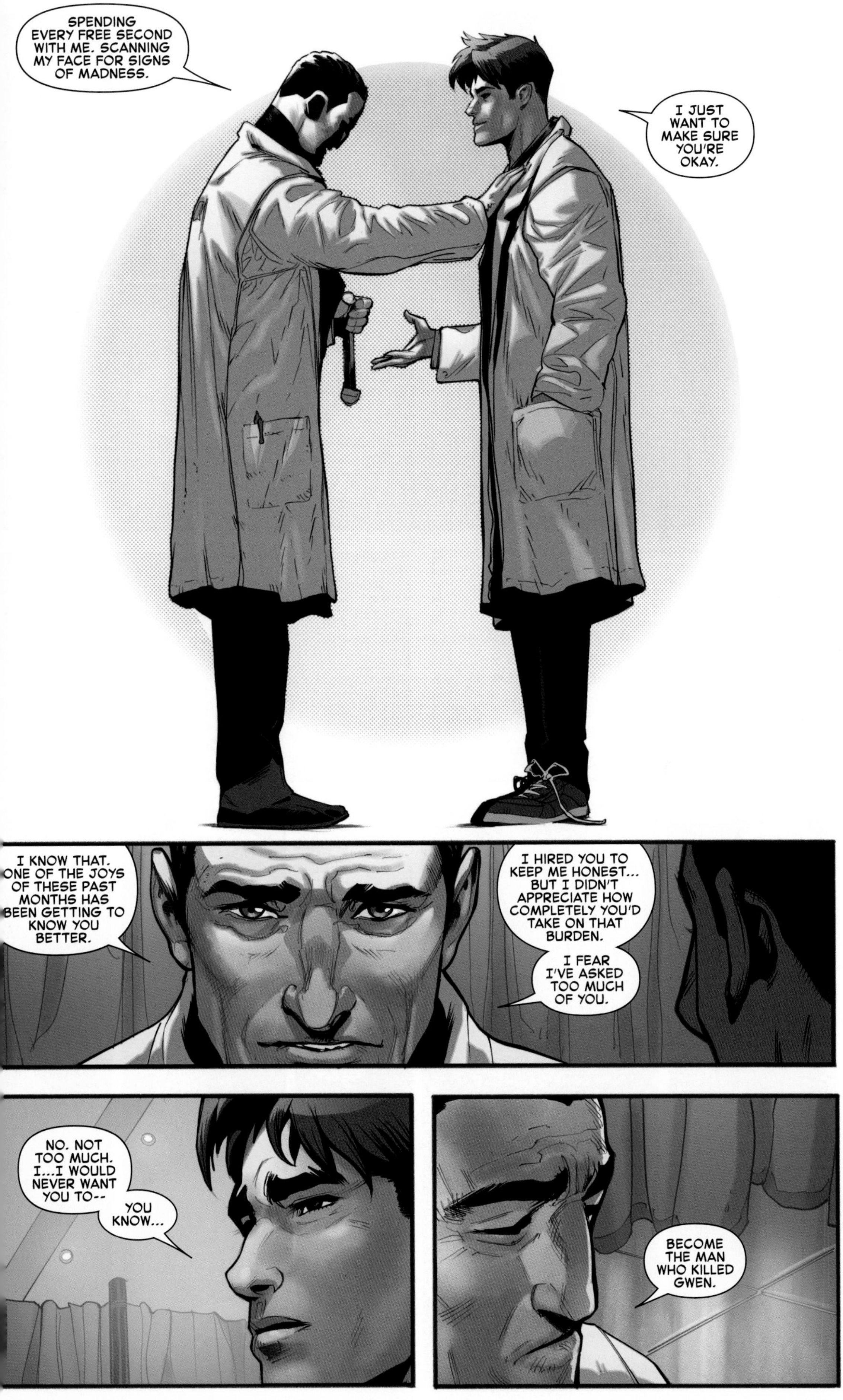
SPENDING EVERY FREE SECOND WITH ME. SCANNING MY FACE FOR SIGNS OF MADNESS.
I JUST WANT TO MAKE SURE YOU'RE OKAY.
I KNOW THAT. ONE OF THE JOYS OF THESE PAST MONTHS HAS BEEN GETTING TO KNOW YOU BETTER.
I HIRED YOU TO KEEP ME HONEST... BUT I DIDN'T APPRECIATE HOW COMPLETELY YOU'D TAKE ON THAT BURDEN.
I FEAR I'VE ASKED TOO MUCH OF YOU.
NO. NOT TOO MUCH. I...I WOULD NEVER WANT YOU TO--
YOU KNOW...
BECOME THE MAN WHO KILLED GWEN.

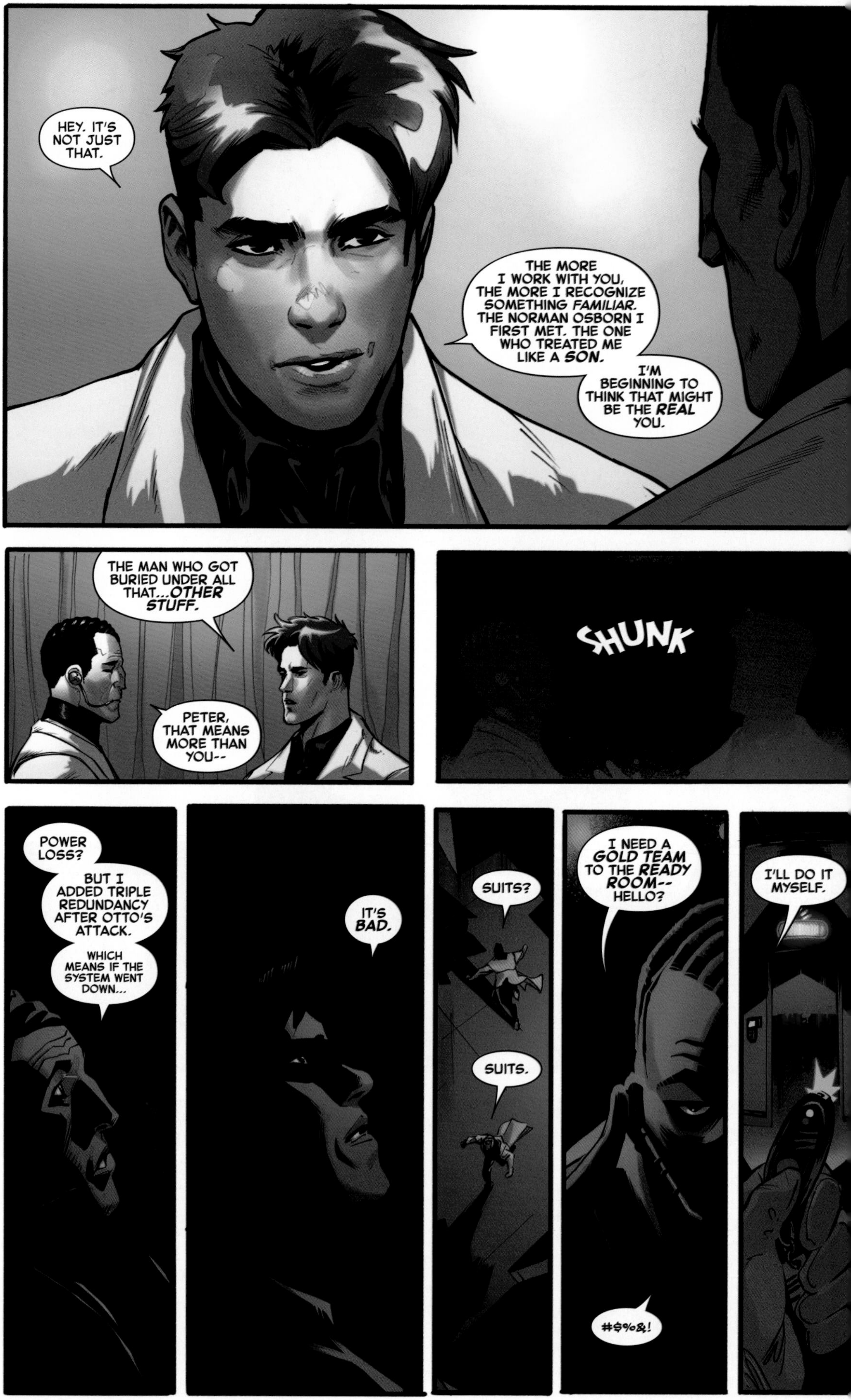
HEY. IT'S NOT JUST THAT.
THE MORE I WORK WITH YOU, THE MORE I RECOGNIZE SOMETHING FAMILIAR. THE NORMAN OSBORN I FIRST MET. THE ONE WHO TREATED ME LIKE A SON.
I'M BEGINNING TO THINK THAT MIGHT BE THE REAL YOU.
THE MAN WHO GOT BURIED UNDER ALL THAT...OTHER STUFF.
PETER, THAT MEANS MORE THAN YOU--
SHUNK
POWER LOSS?
BUT I ADDED TRIPLE REDUNDANCY AFTER OTTO'S ATTACK.
WHICH MEANS IF THE SYSTEM WENT DOWN...
IT'S BAD.
SUITS?
SUITS.
I NEED A GOLD TEAM TO THE READY ROOM-- HELLO?
#$%&!
I'LL DO IT MYSELF.

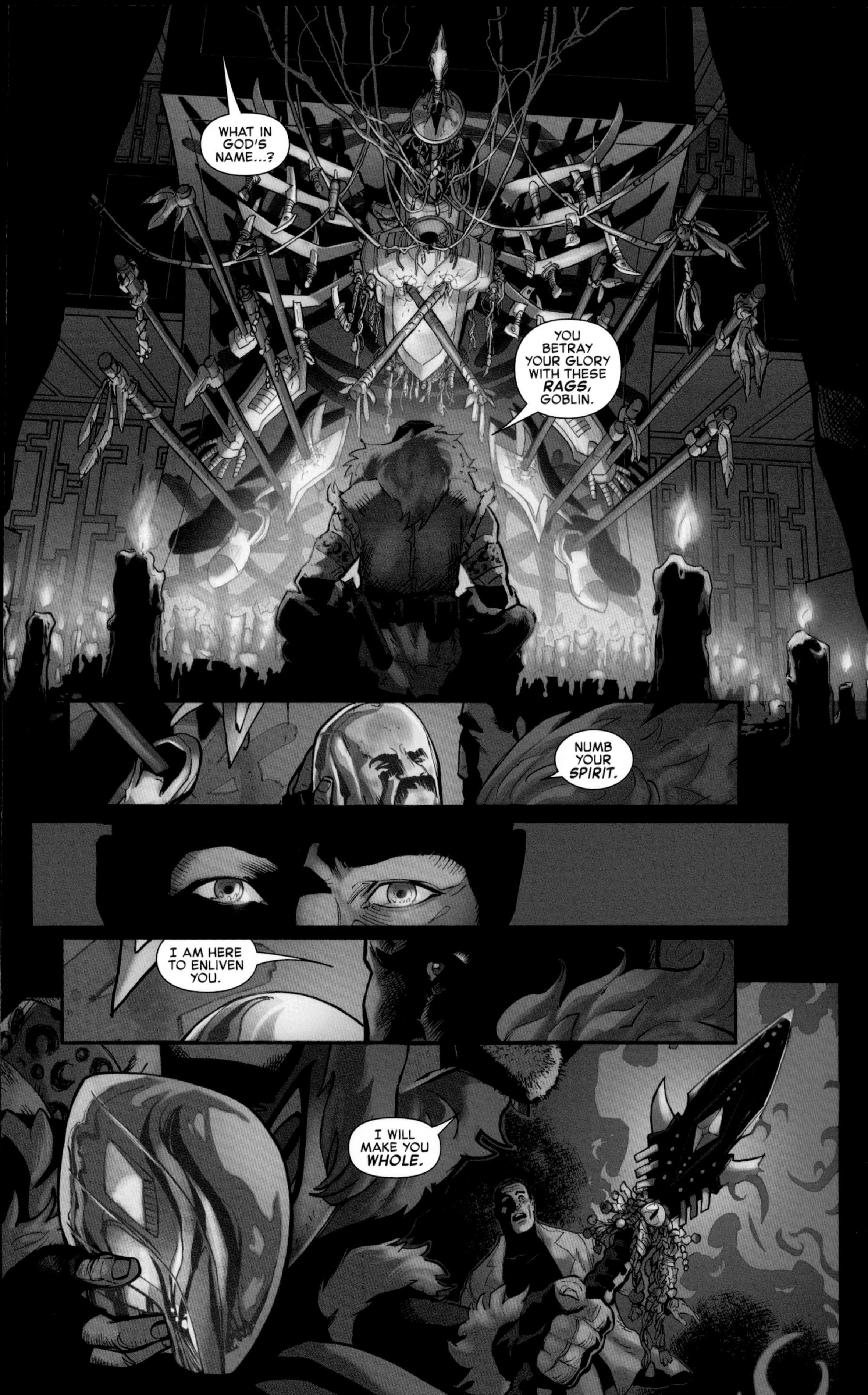
WHAT IN GOD'S NAME...?
YOU BETRAY YOUR GLORY WITH THESE RAGS, GOBLIN.
NUMB YOUR SPIRIT.
I AM HERE TO ENLIVEN YOU.
I WILL MAKE YOU WHOLE.

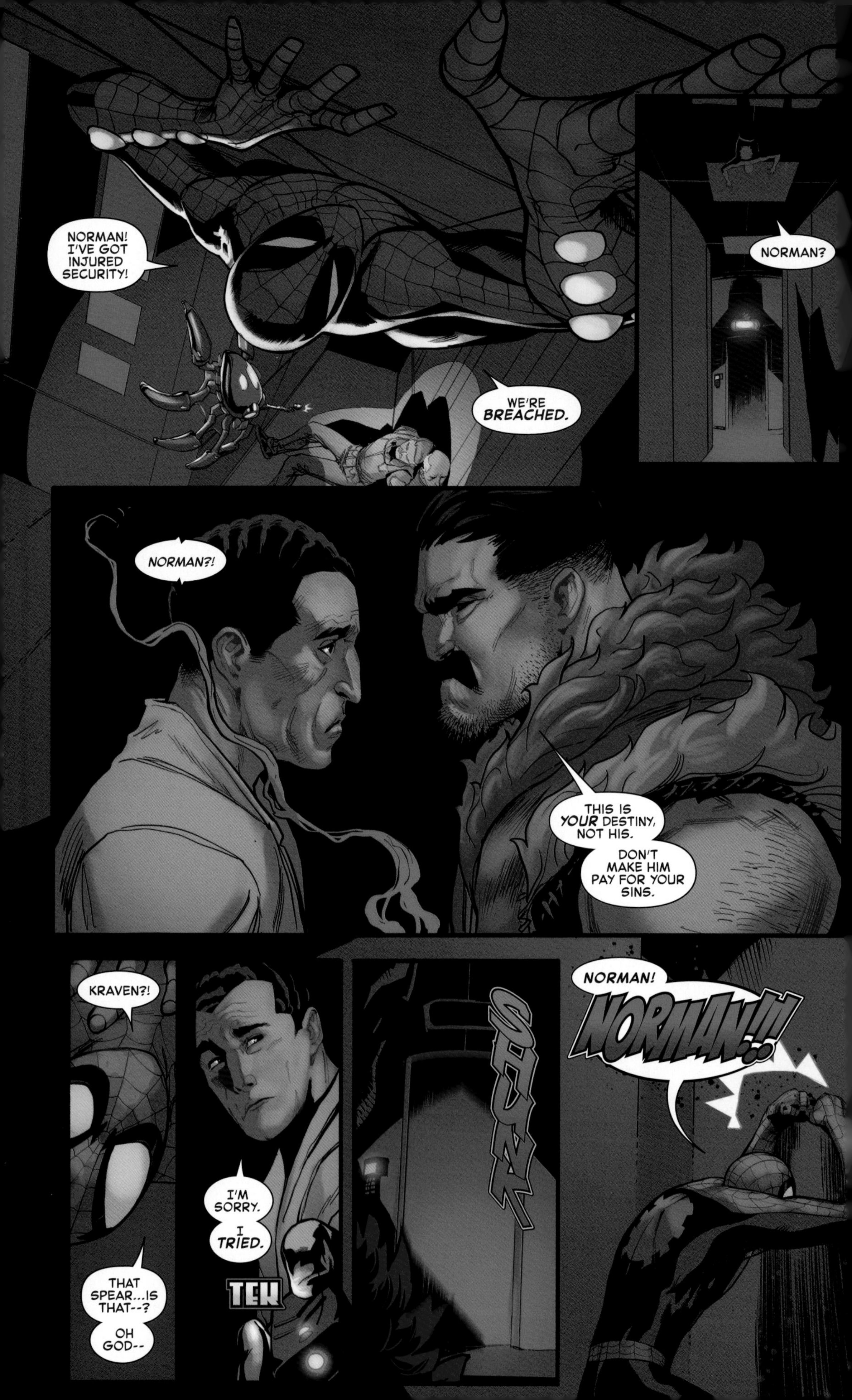

NORMAN! I'VE GOT INJURED SECURITY!
WE'RE BREACHED.
NORMAN?
NORMAN?!
THIS IS YOUR DESTINY, NOT HIS.
DON'T MAKE HIM PAY FOR YOUR SINS.
KRAVEN?!
THAT SPEAR...IS THAT--?
OH GOD--
I'M SORRY.
I TRIED.
TEK
SHUNK
NORMAN!
NORMAN!!!

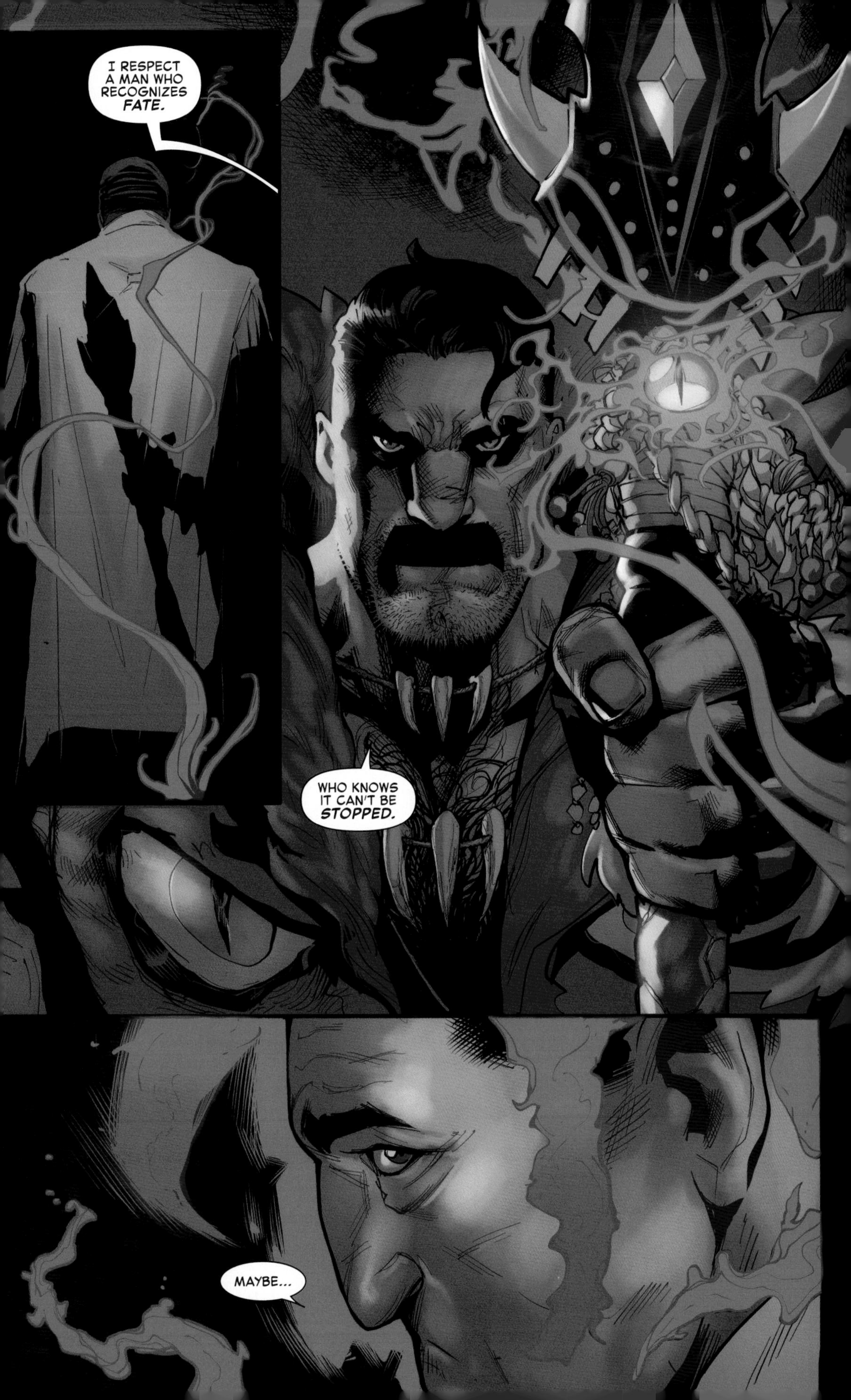
I RESPECT A MAN WHO RECOGNIZES FATE.
WHO KNOWS IT CAN'T BE STOPPED.
MAYBE...

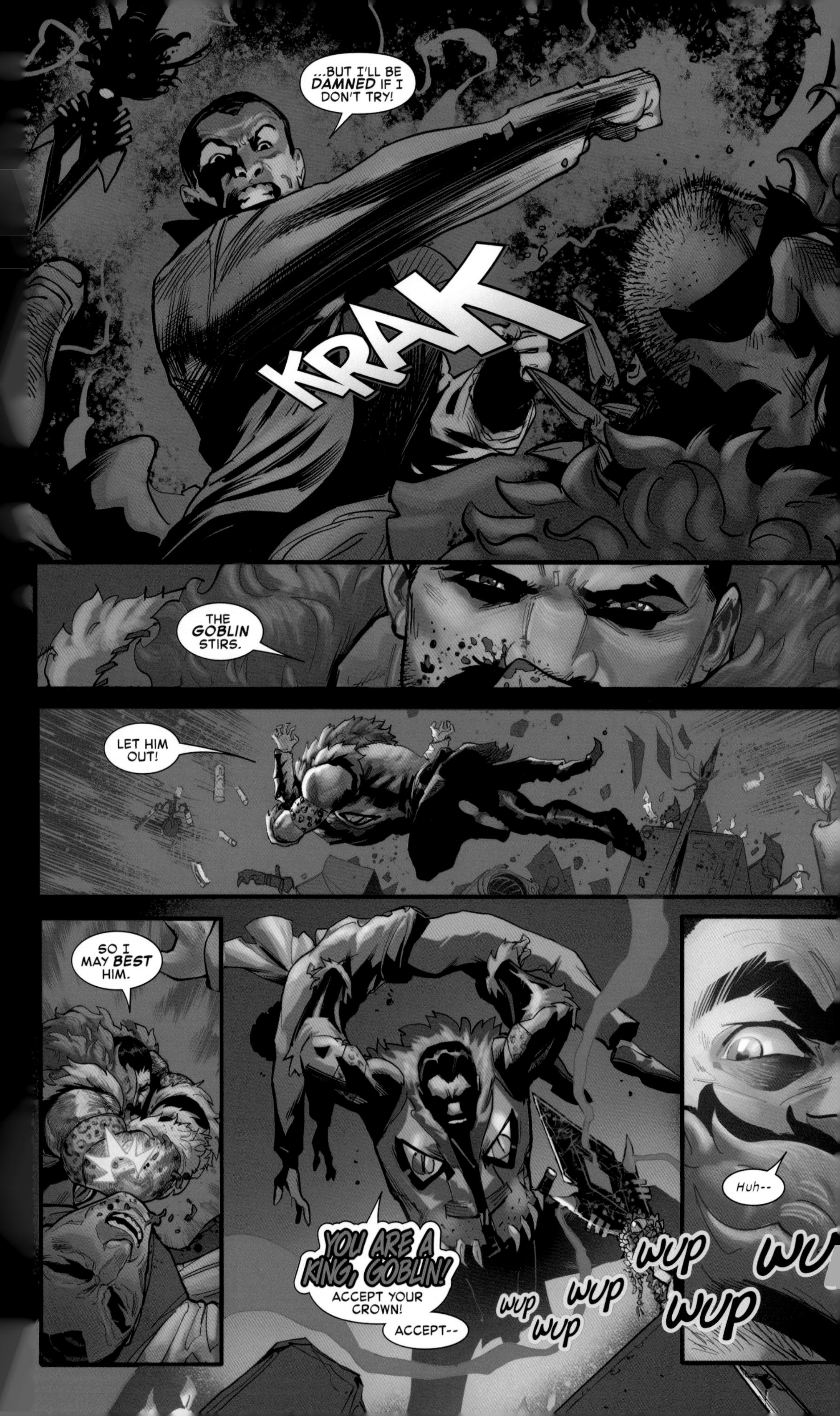
...BUT I'LL BE DAMNED IF I DON'T TRY!
KRAK
THE GOBLIN STIRS.
LET HIM OUT!
SO I MAY BEST HIM.
YOU ARE A KING, GOBLIN! ACCEPT YOUR CROWN!
ACCEPT--
WUP WUP WUP WUP WUP
Huh--

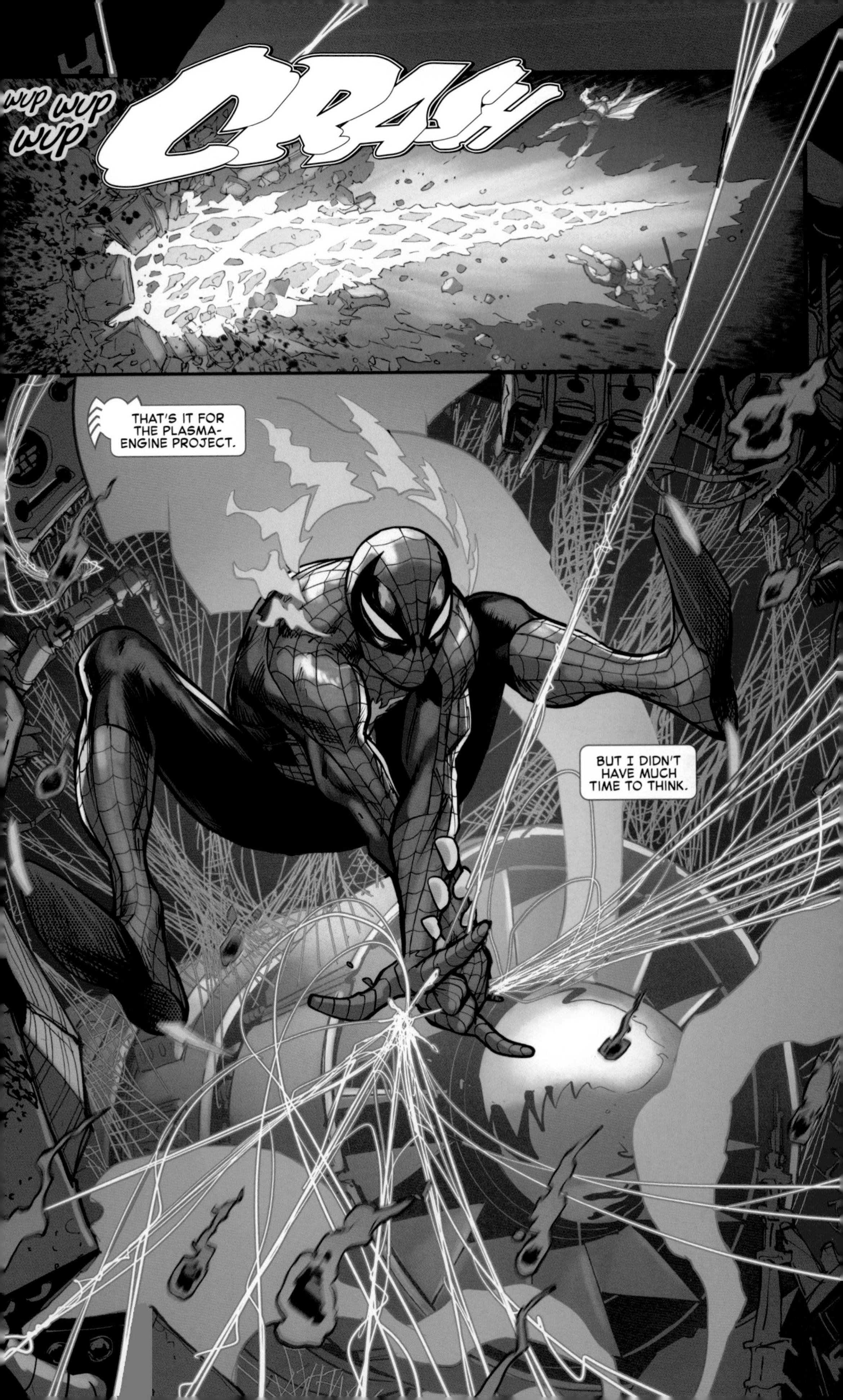
WUP WUP WUP
CRASH
THAT'S IT FOR THE PLASMA-ENGINE PROJECT.
BUT I DIDN'T HAVE MUCH TIME TO THINK.

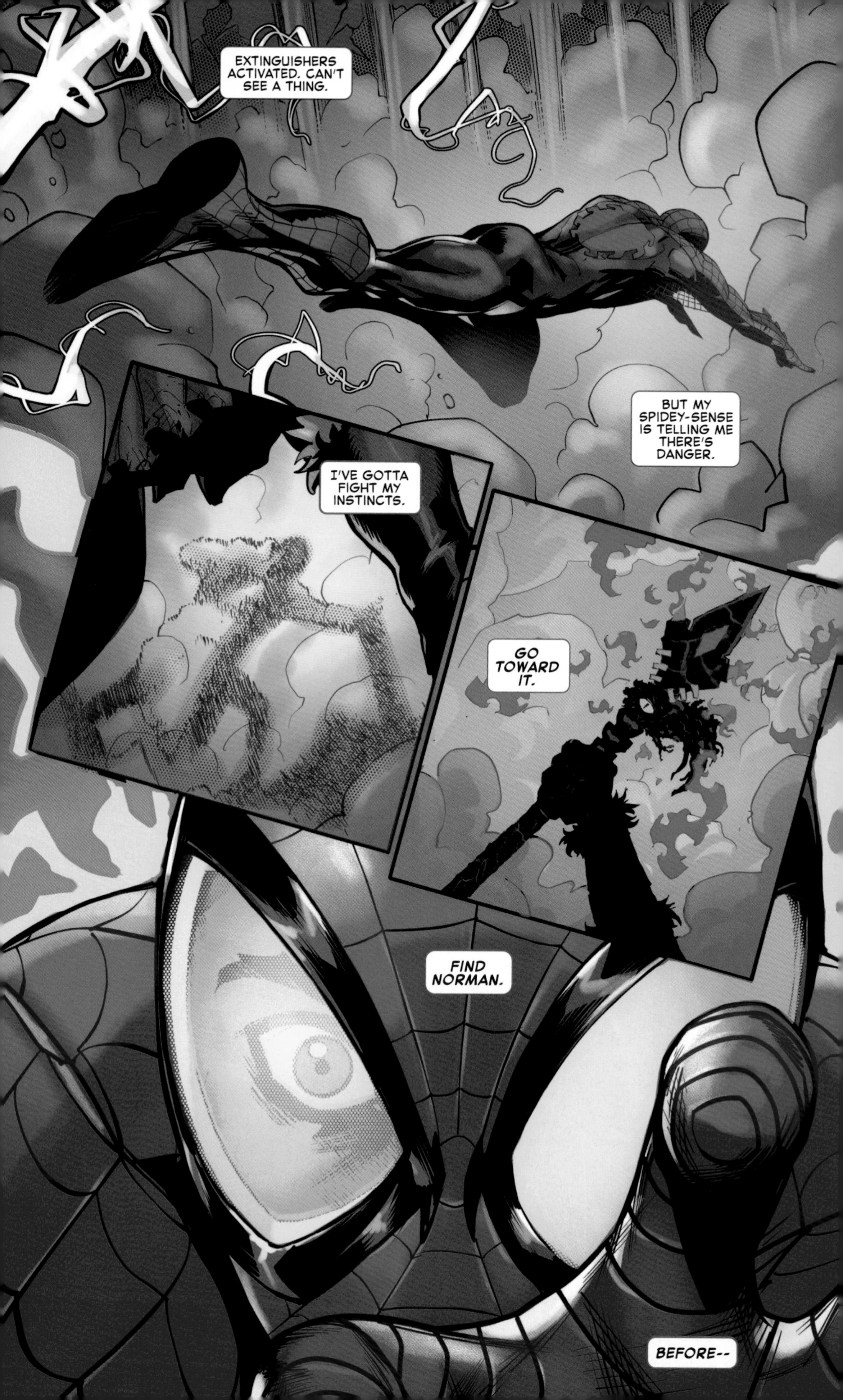
EXTINGUISHERS ACTIVATED. CAN'T SEE A THING.
BUT MY SPIDEY-SENSE IS TELLING ME THERE'S DANGER.
I'VE GOTTA FIGHT MY INSTINCTS.
GO TOWARD IT.
FIND NORMAN.
BEFORE--

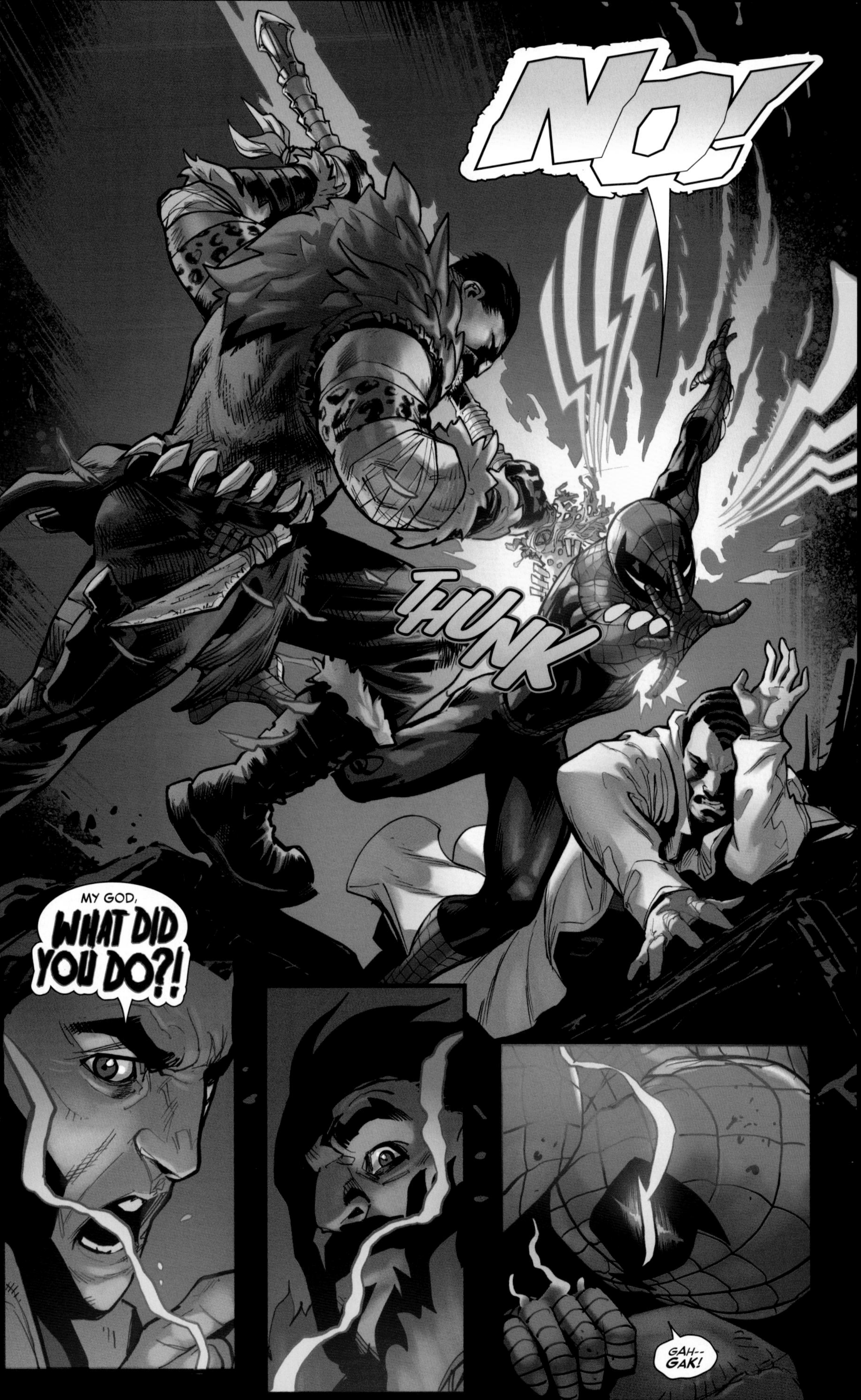
NO!
THUNK
MY GOD, WHAT DID YOU DO?!
GAH-- GAK!

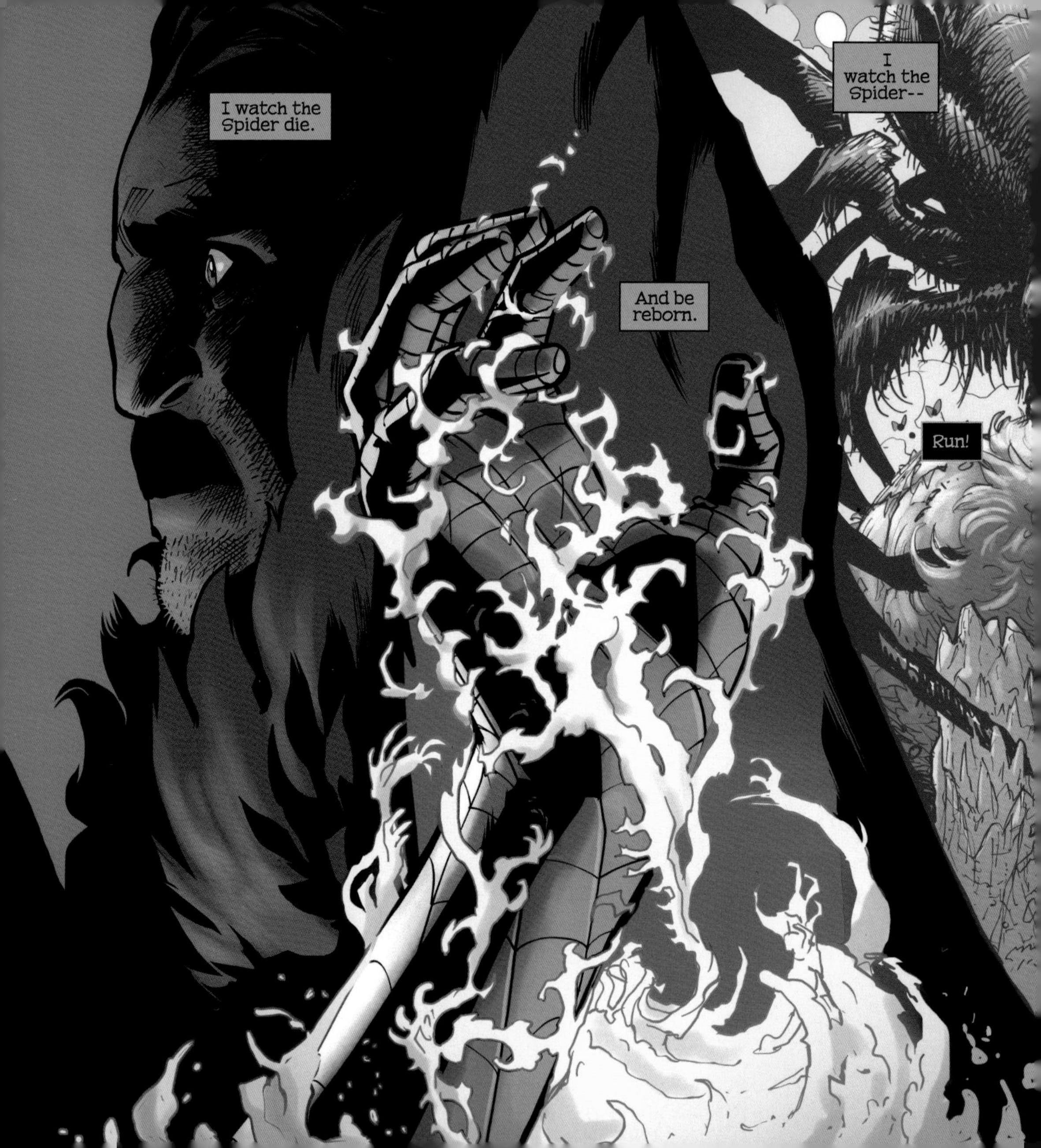
I watch the Spider die.
I watch the Spider--
And be reborn.
Run!

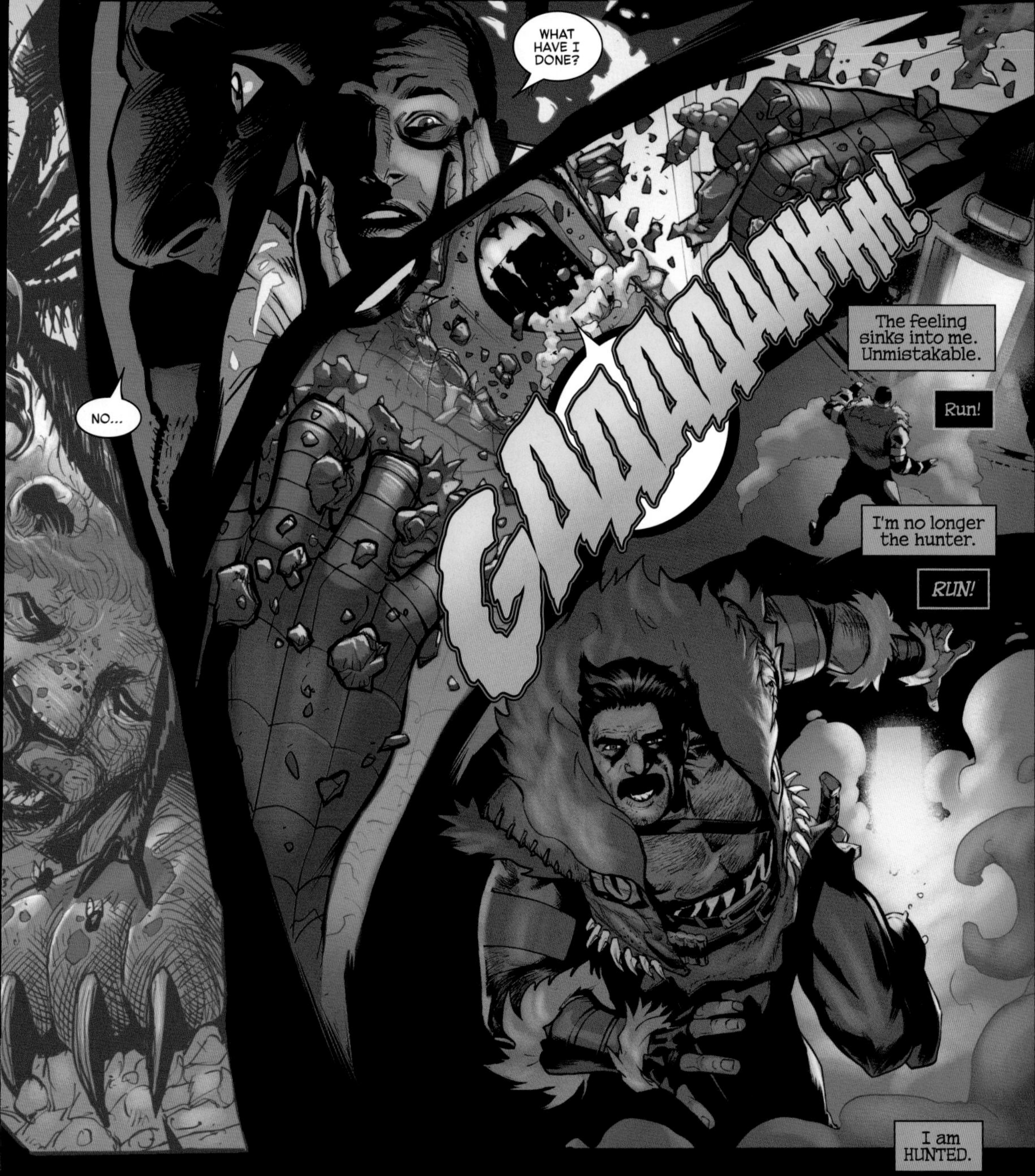
WHAT HAVE I DONE?
NO...
The feeling sinks into me. Unmistakable.
Run!
I'm no longer the hunter.
RUN!
I am HUNTED.

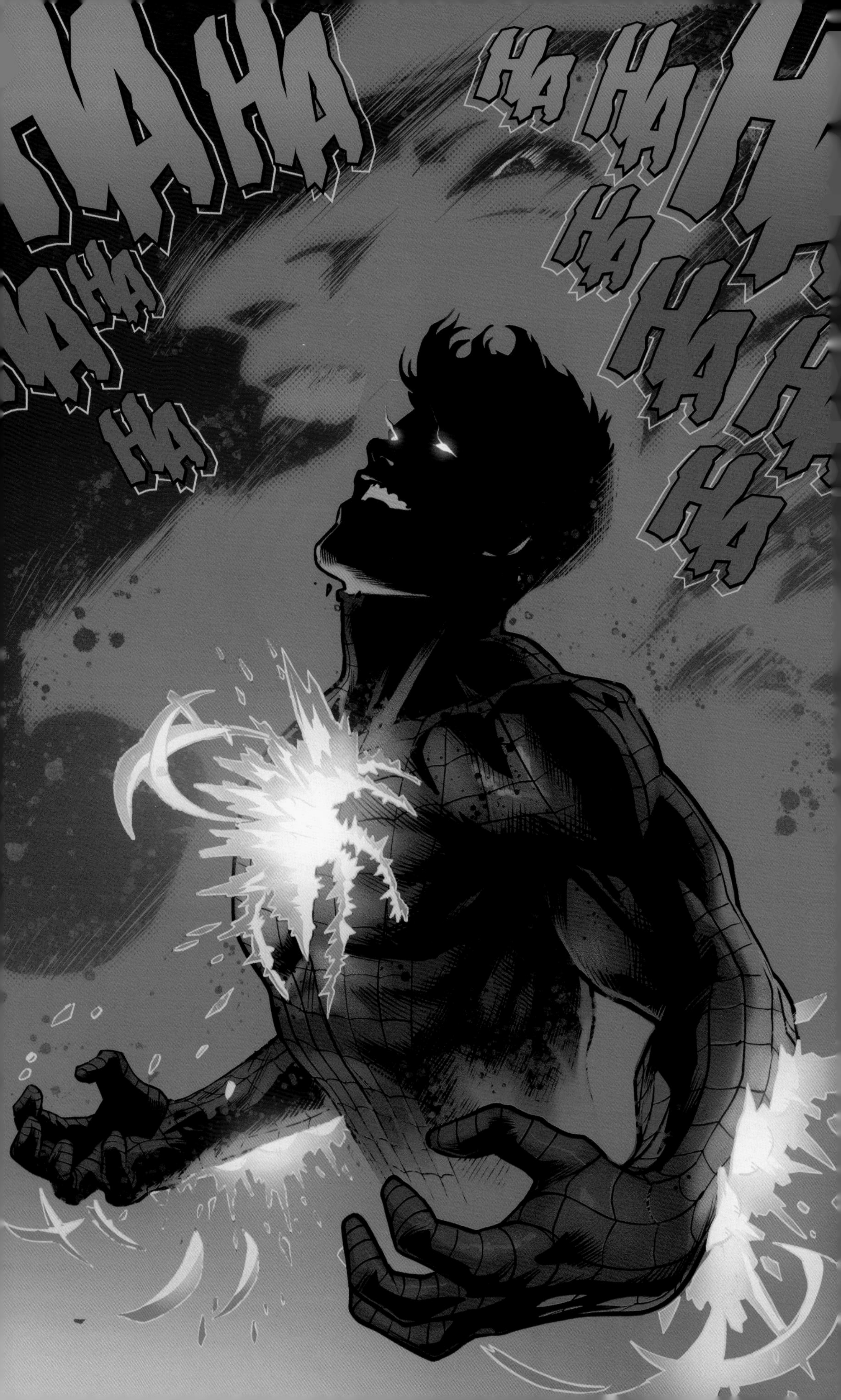
HAHA
HA HA
HA
HA HA
HA
HA HA
HA

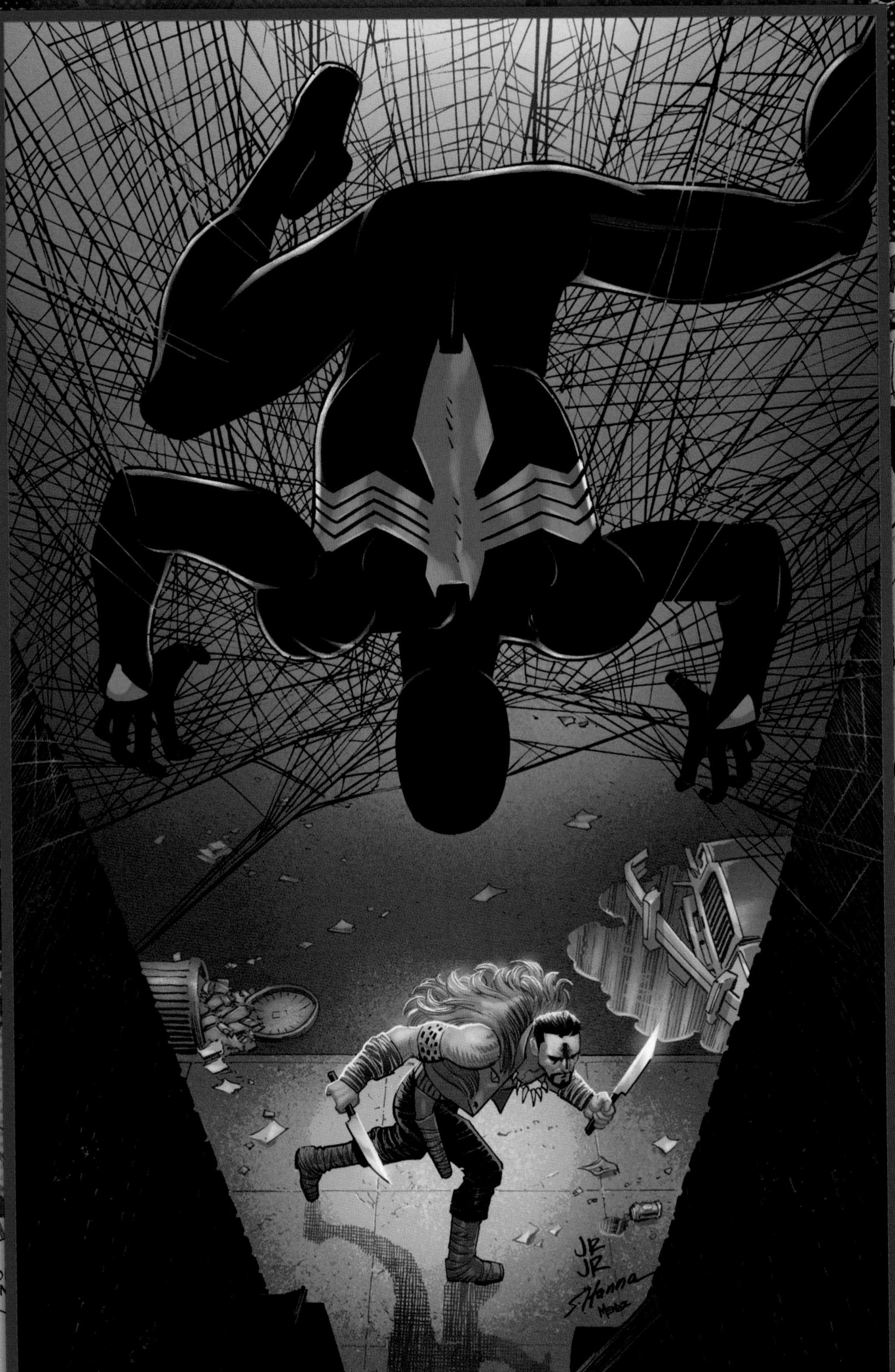

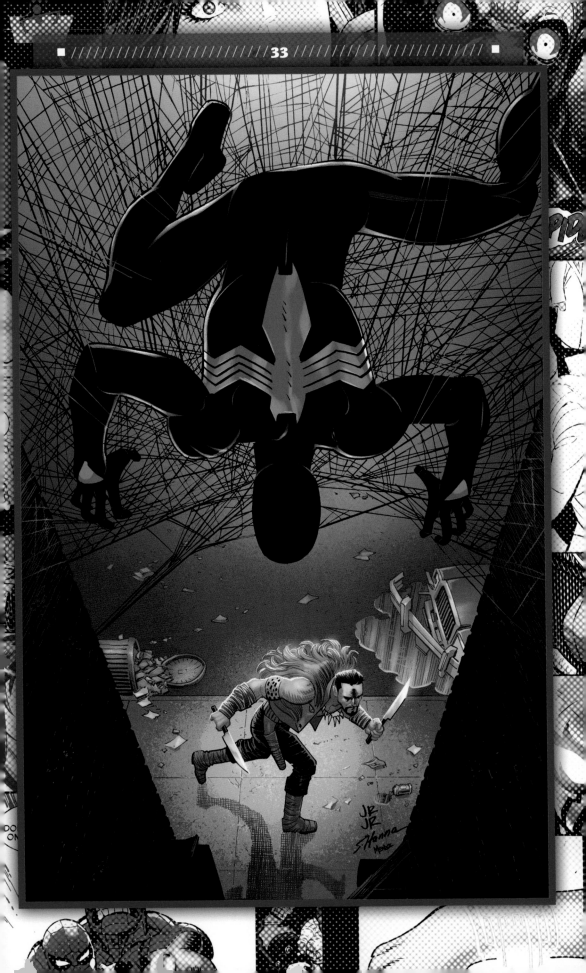

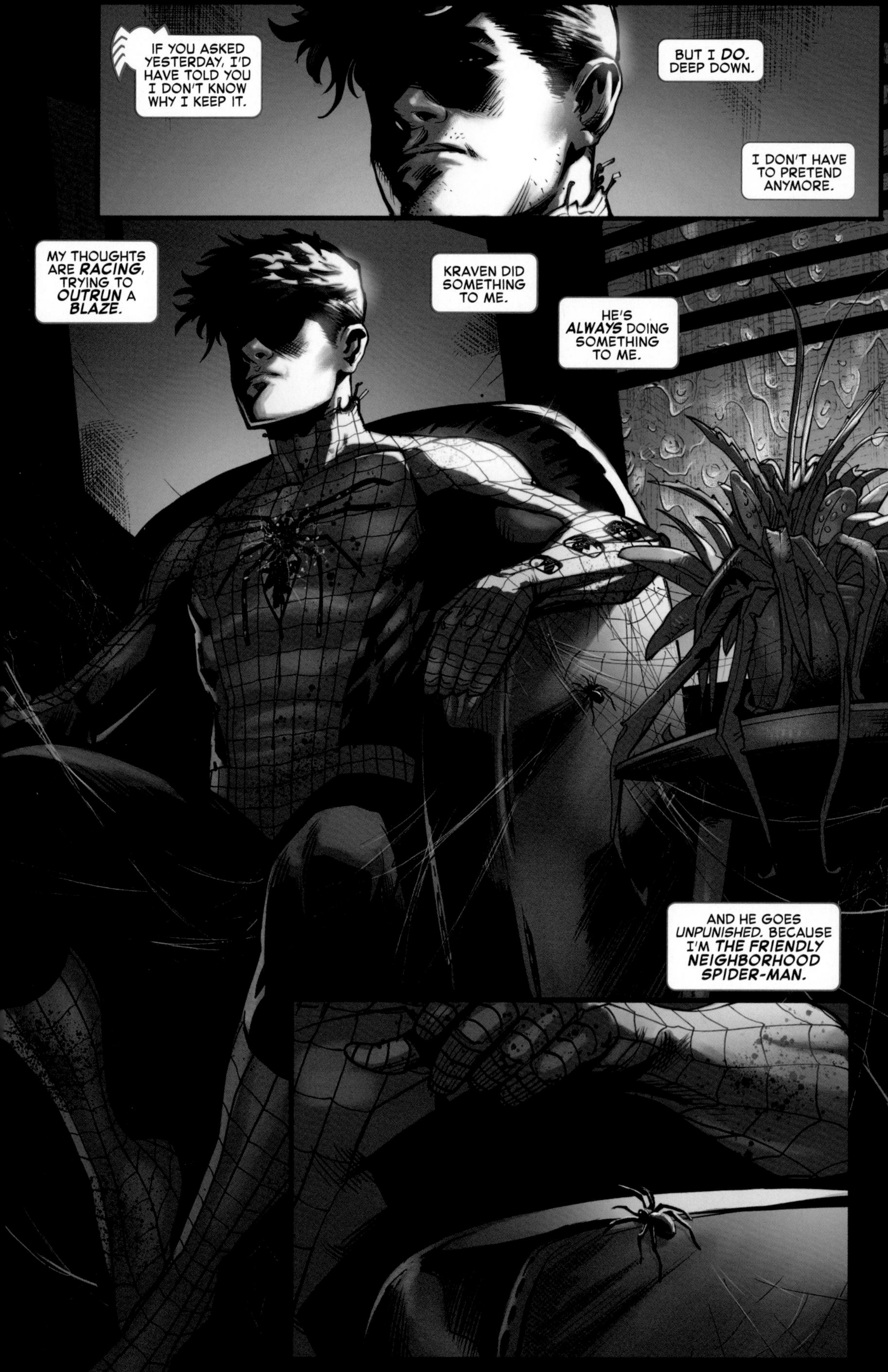
IF YOU ASKED YESTERDAY, I'D HAVE TOLD YOU I DON'T KNOW WHY I KEEP IT.
BUT I *DO.* DEEP DOWN.
I DON'T HAVE TO PRETEND ANYMORE.
MY THOUGHTS ARE ***RACING,*** TRYING TO ***OUTRUN*** A ***BLAZE.***
KRAVEN DID SOMETHING TO ME.
HE'S ***ALWAYS*** DOING SOMETHING TO ME.
AND HE GOES *UNPUNISHED.* BECAUSE I'M ***THE FRIENDLY NEIGHBORHOOD SPIDER-MAN.***

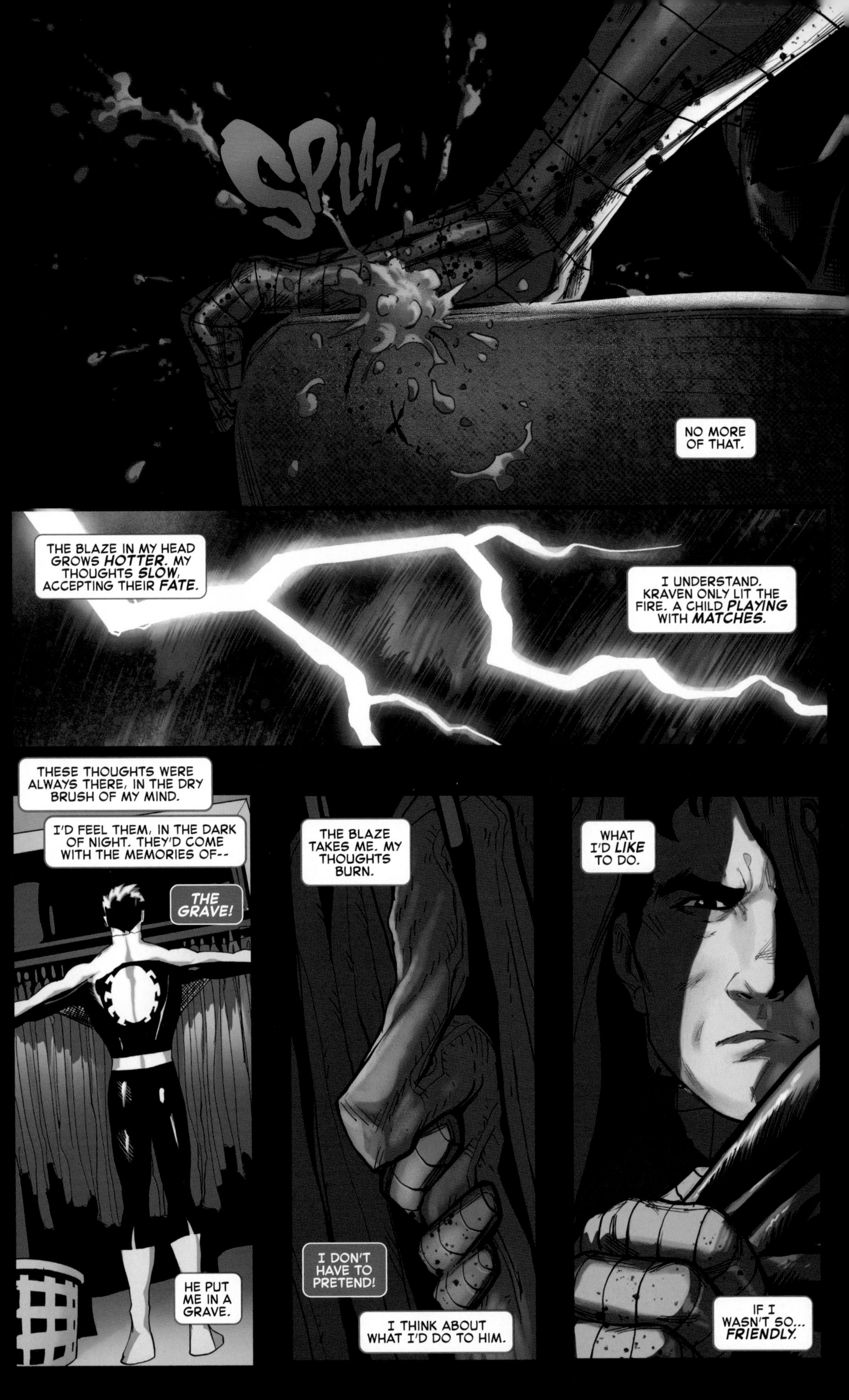
SPLAT
NO MORE OF THAT.
THE BLAZE IN MY HEAD GROWS HOTTER. MY THOUGHTS SLOW, ACCEPTING THEIR FATE.
I UNDERSTAND. KRAVEN ONLY LIT THE FIRE. A CHILD PLAYING WITH MATCHES.
THESE THOUGHTS WERE ALWAYS THERE, IN THE DRY BRUSH OF MY MIND.
I'D FEEL THEM, IN THE DARK OF NIGHT. THEY'D COME WITH THE MEMORIES OF--
THE GRAVE!
HE PUT ME IN A GRAVE.
THE BLAZE TAKES ME. MY THOUGHTS BURN.
I DON'T HAVE TO PRETEND!
I THINK ABOUT WHAT I'D DO TO HIM.
WHAT I'D LIKE TO DO.
IF I WASN'T SO... FRIENDLY.

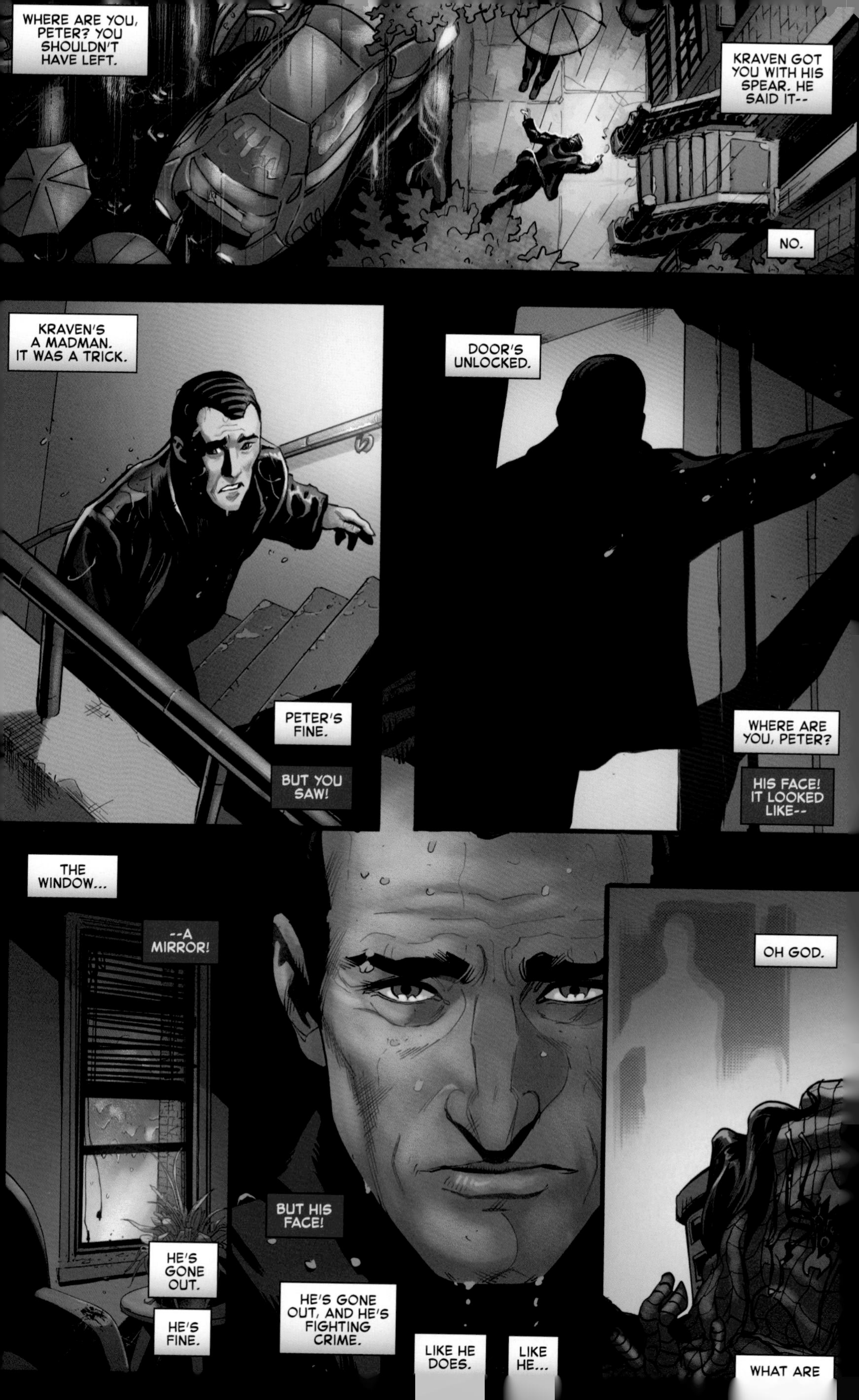
WHERE ARE YOU, PETER? YOU SHOULDN'T HAVE LEFT.
KRAVEN GOT YOU WITH HIS SPEAR. HE SAID IT--
NO.
KRAVEN'S A MADMAN. IT WAS A TRICK.
PETER'S FINE.
BUT YOU SAW!
DOOR'S UNLOCKED.
WHERE ARE YOU, PETER?
HIS FACE! IT LOOKED LIKE--
THE WINDOW...
--A MIRROR!
BUT HIS FACE!
HE'S GONE OUT.
HE'S FINE.
HE'S GONE OUT, AND HE'S FIGHTING CRIME.
LIKE HE DOES.
LIKE HE...
OH GOD.
WHAT ARE

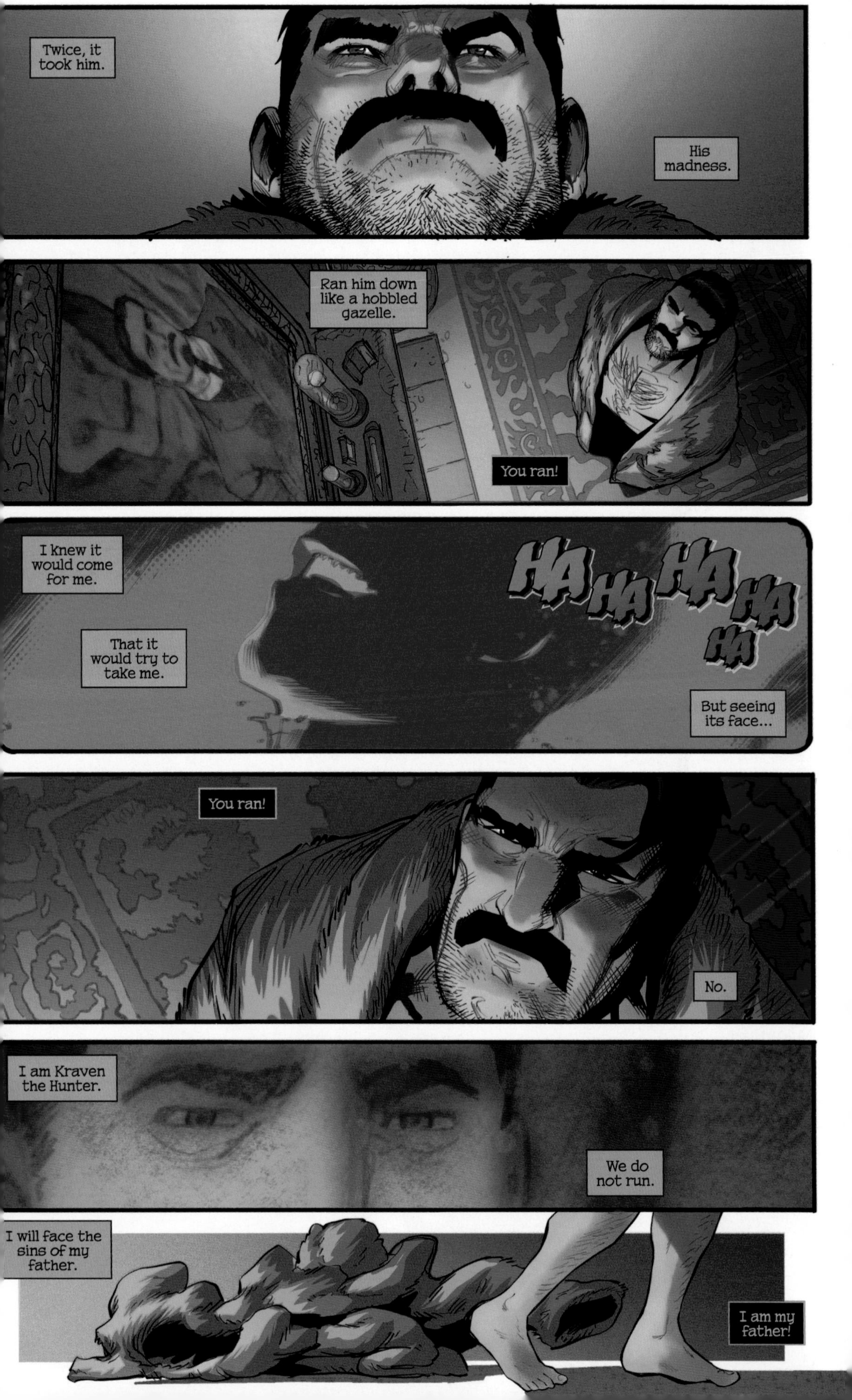
Twice, it took him.
His madness.
Ran him down like a hobbled gazelle.
You ran!
I knew it would come for me.
That it would try to take me.
HA HA HA HA HA
But seeing its face...
You ran!
No.
I am Kraven the Hunter.
We do not run.
I will face the sins of my father.
I am my father!

I will face the madness that took him.

By his own hand!

I will kill it.

I will *hunt*.

But the weapons. Why do they seem so *HEAVY*?

You know!

Why can't I choose?

You know!

I don't want to be weighed down. Because--

You no longer hunt!

--I don't want to be *slowed* down.

My body KNOWS.

I am prey.

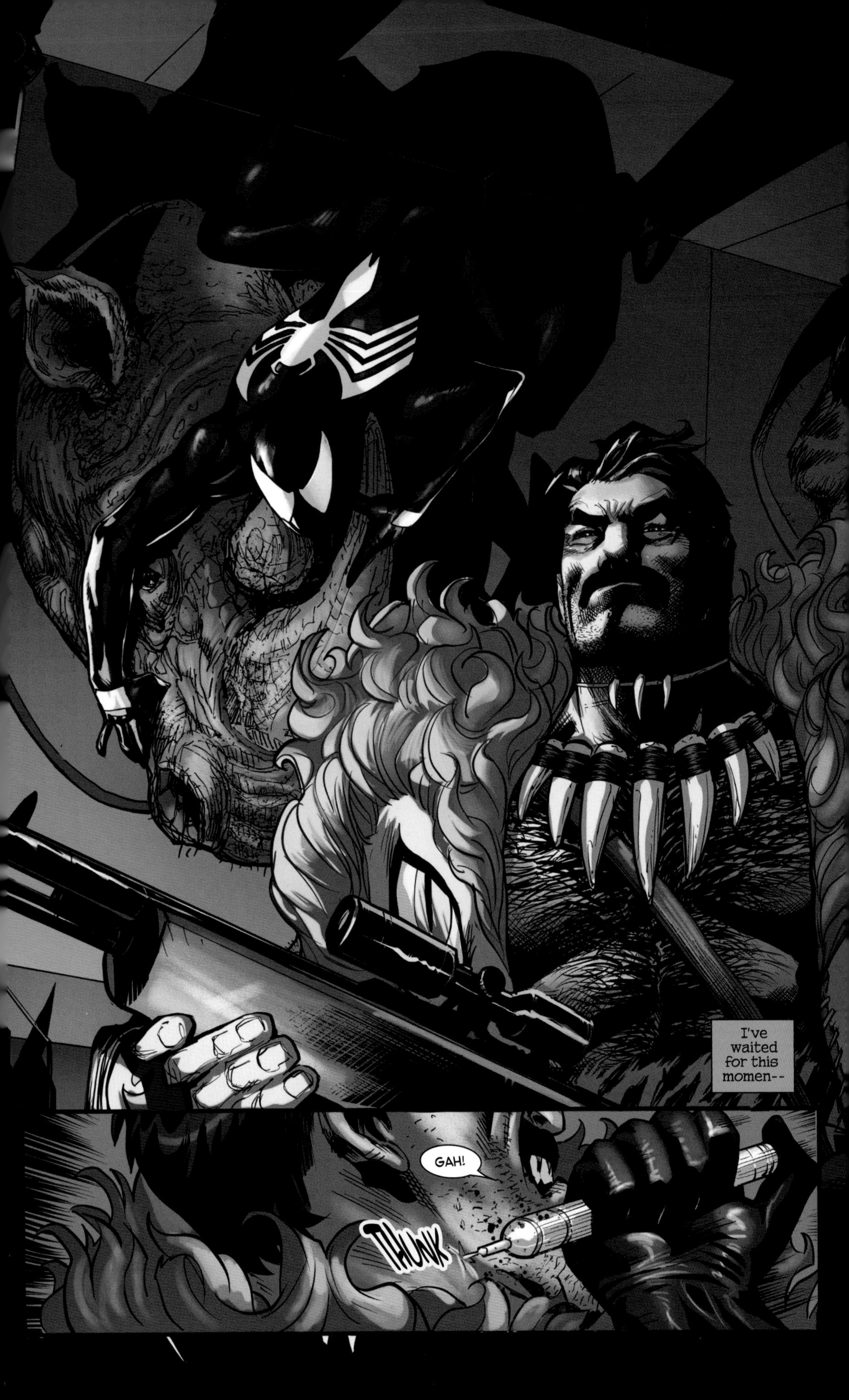
I've waited for this momen--
GAH!
THUNK

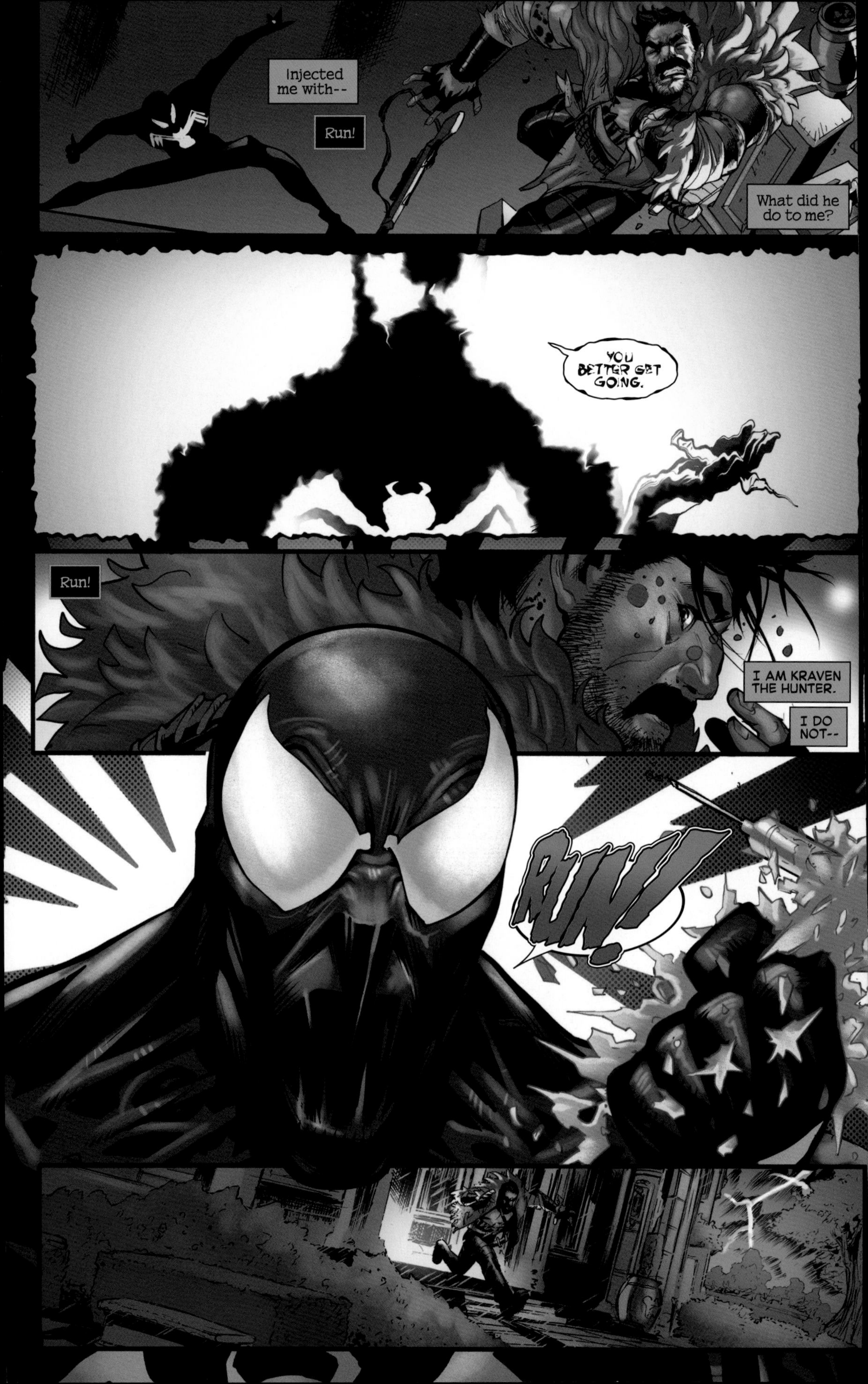
Injected me with--
Run!
What did he do to me?
YOU BETTER GET GOING.
Run!
I AM KRAVEN THE HUNTER.
I DO NOT--
RUN!!

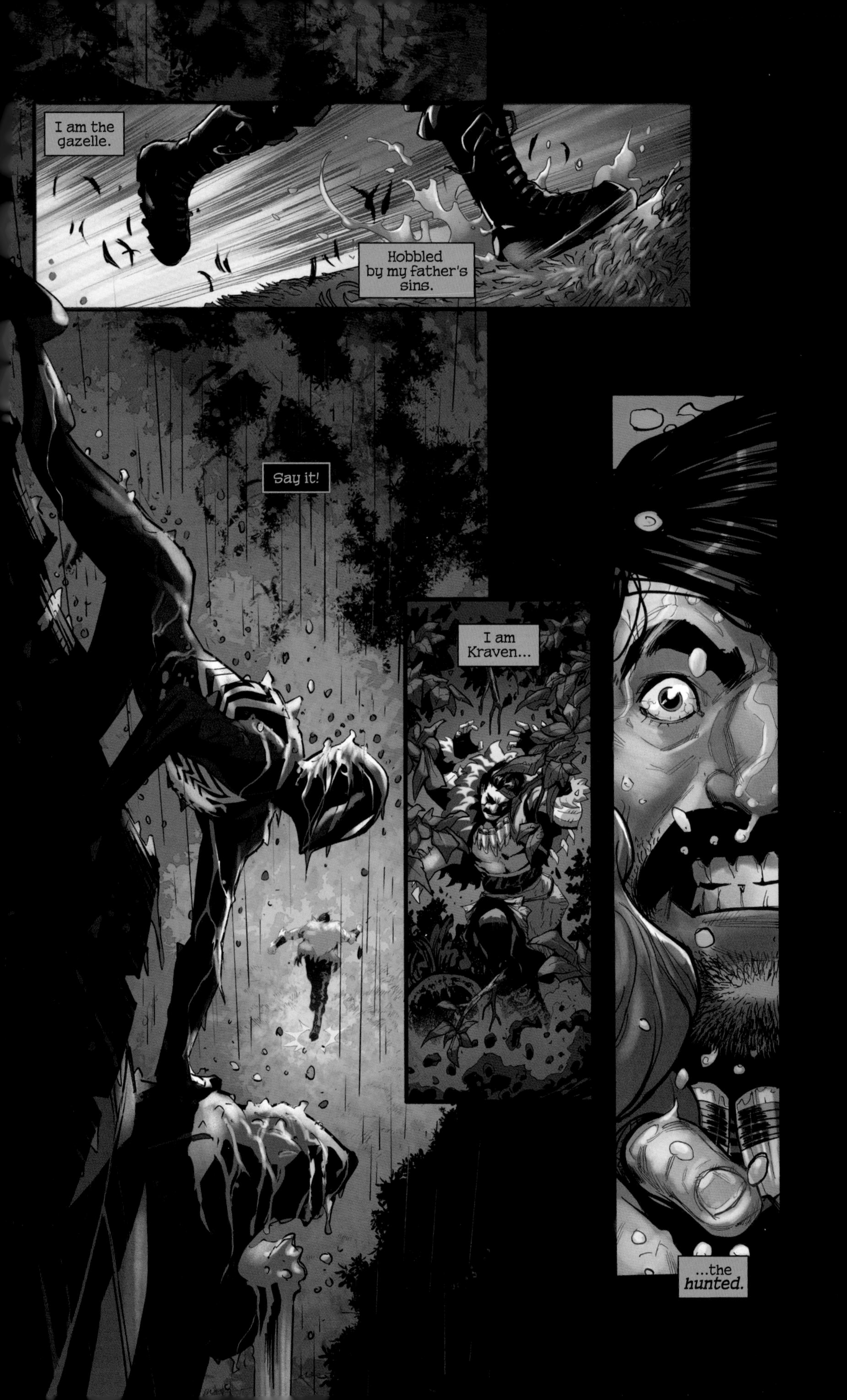
I am the gazelle.
Hobbled by my father's sins.
Say it!
I am Kraven...
...the *hunted*.

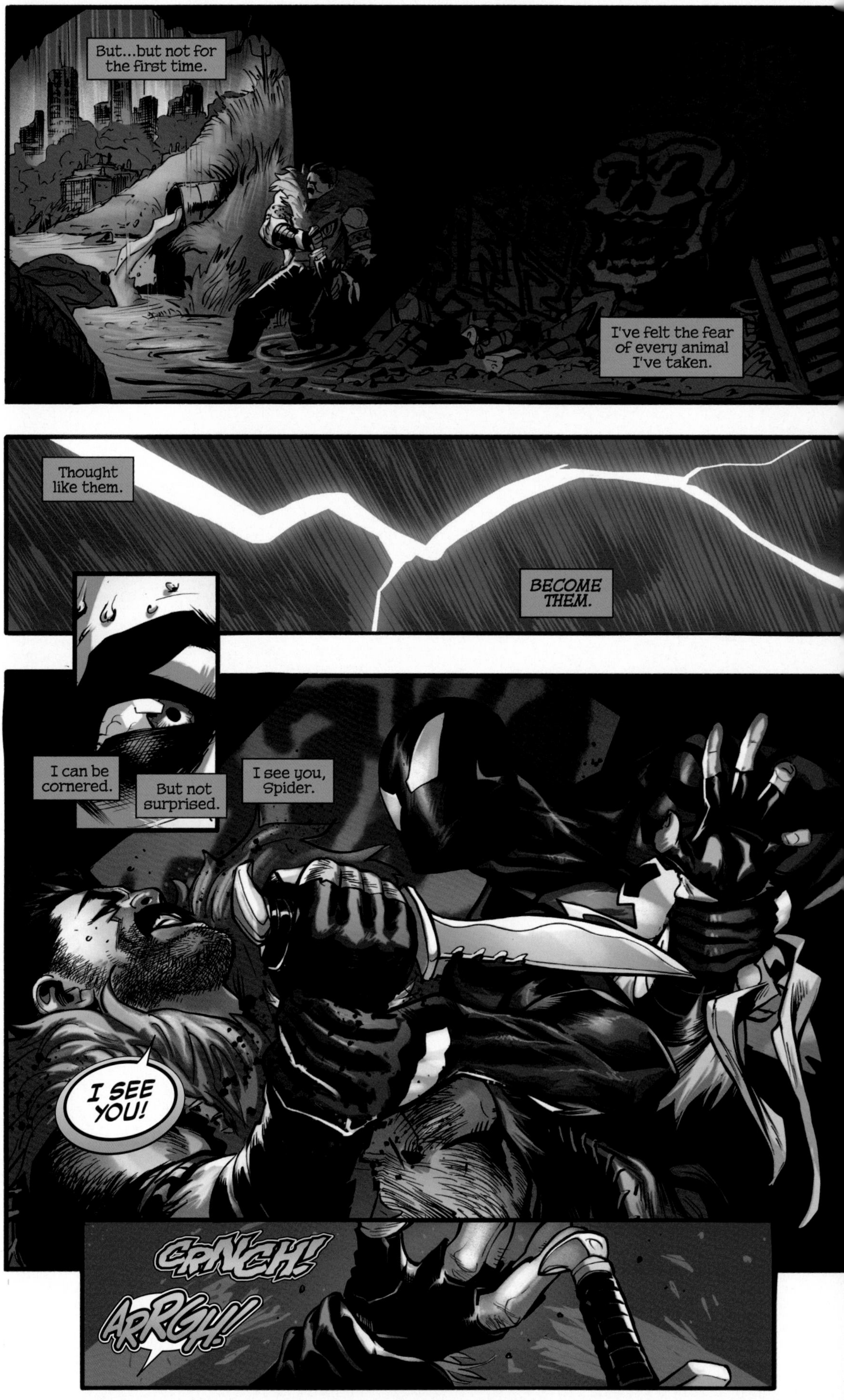
But...but not for the first time.
I've felt the fear of every animal I've taken.
Thought like them.
BECOME THEM.
I can be cornered.
But not surprised.
I see you, Spider.
I SEE YOU!
CRNCH!
ARRGH!!

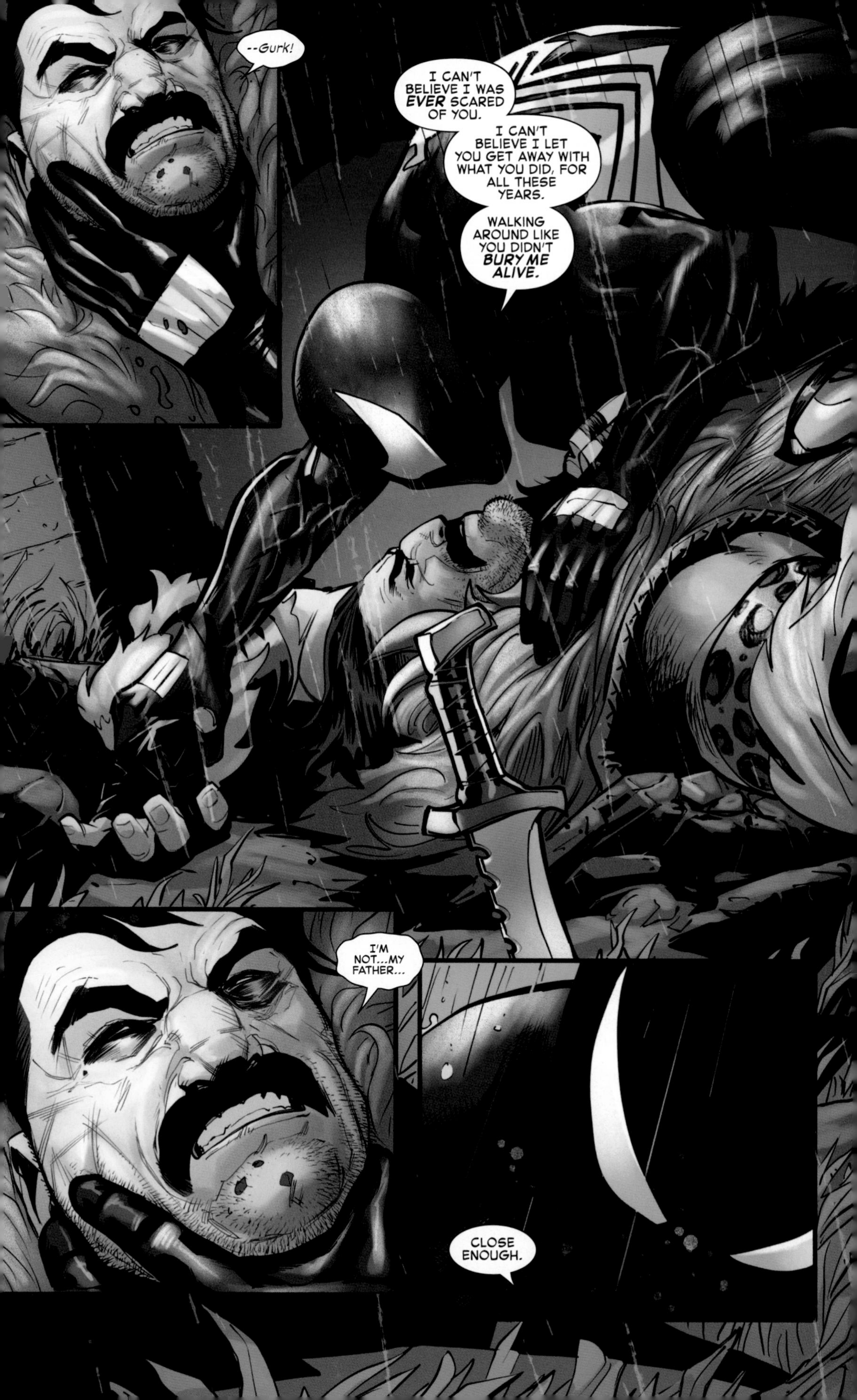
--Gurk!
I CAN'T BELIEVE I WAS EVER SCARED OF YOU.
I CAN'T BELIEVE I LET YOU GET AWAY WITH WHAT YOU DID, FOR ALL THESE YEARS.
WALKING AROUND LIKE YOU DIDN'T BURY ME ALIVE.
I'M NOT...MY FATHER...
CLOSE ENOUGH.

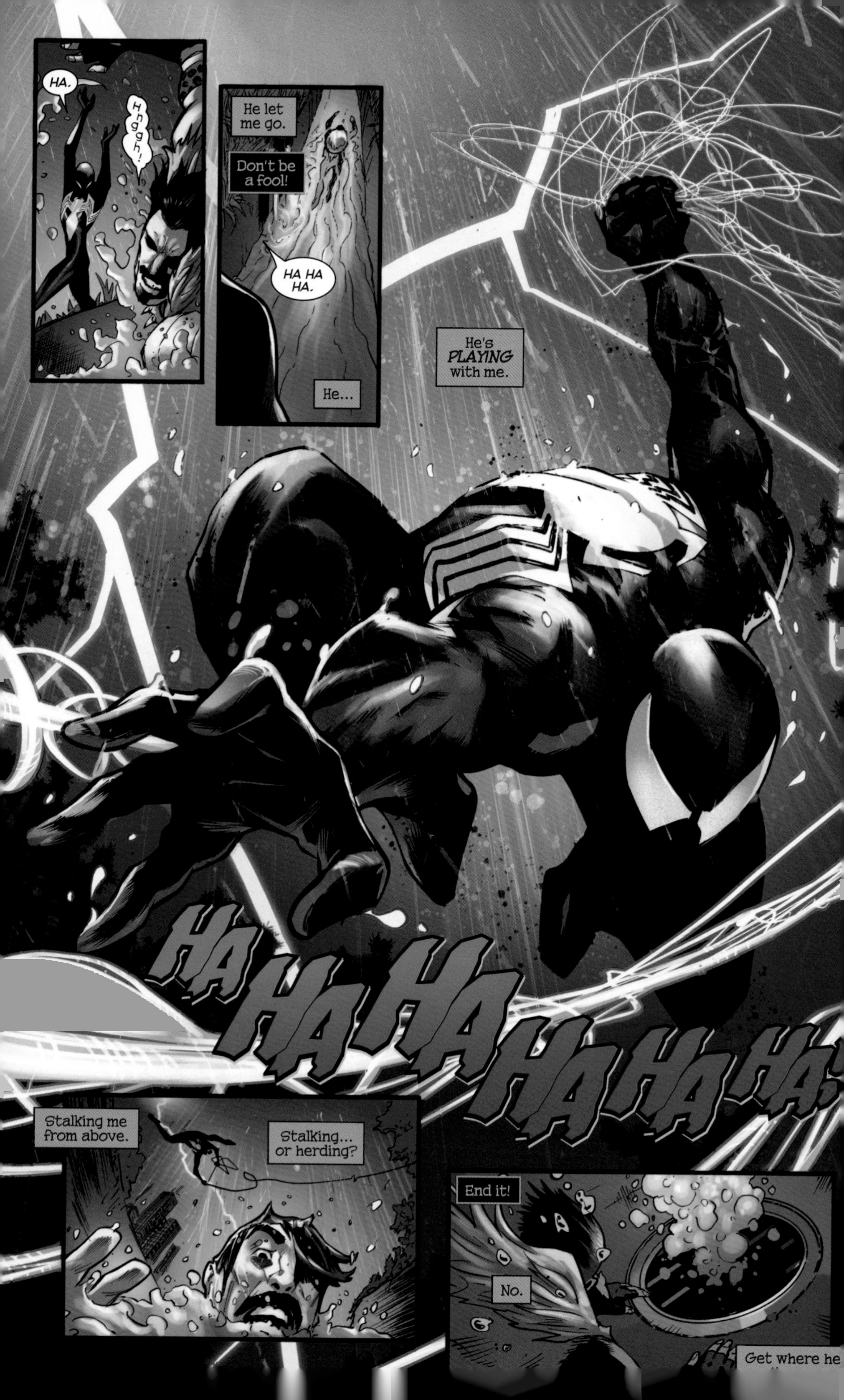
HA.
Hngggh!
He let me go.
Don't be a fool!
HA HA HA.
He...
He's PLAYING with me.
HA HA HA HA HA HA HA HA!
Stalking me from above.
Stalking... or herding?
End it!
No.
Get where he

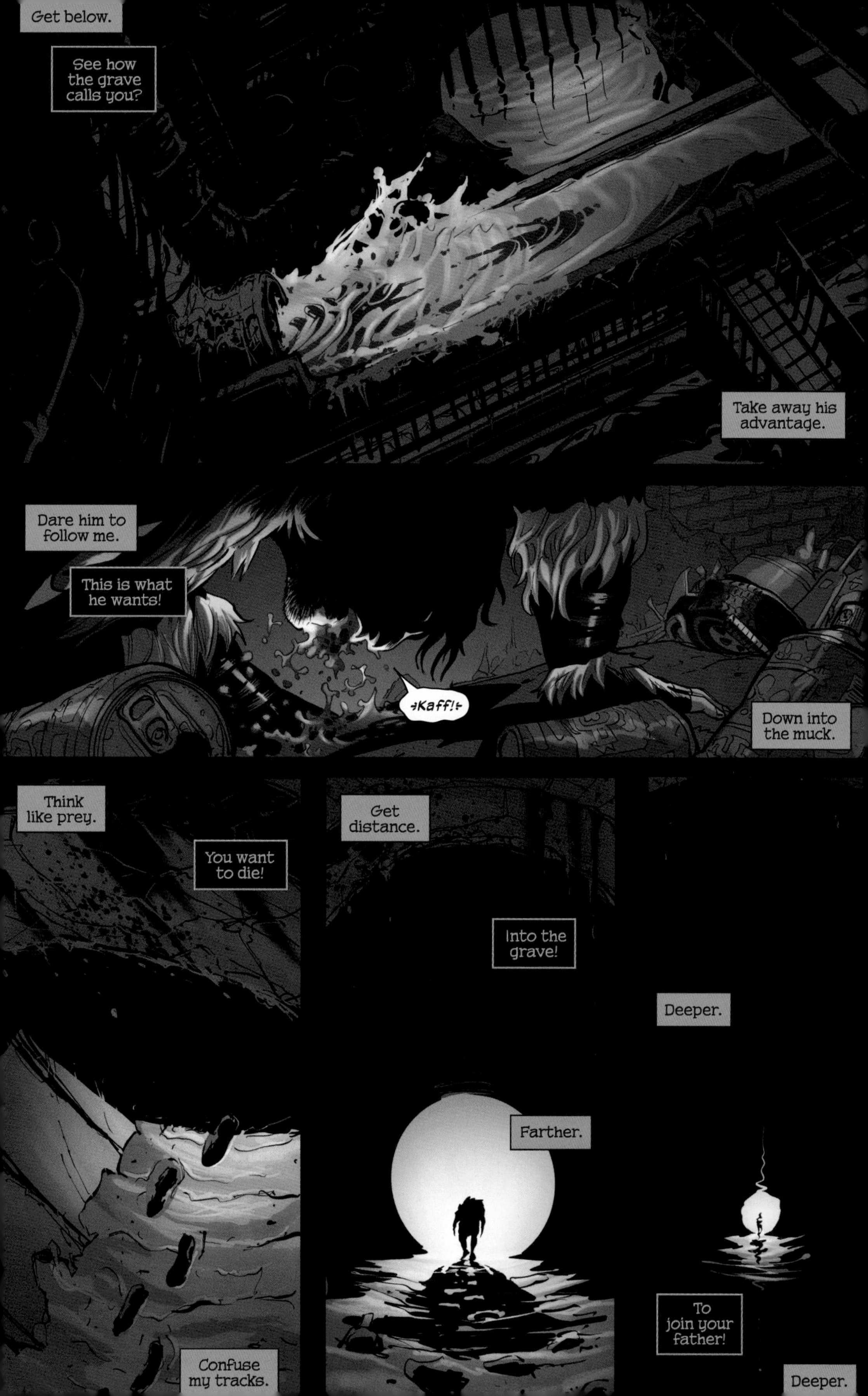
Get below.
See how the grave calls you?
Take away his advantage.
Dare him to follow me.
This is what he wants!
Kaff!
Down into the muck.
Think like prey.
You want to die!
Confuse my tracks.
Get distance.
Into the grave!
Farther.
Deeper.
To join your father!
Deeper.

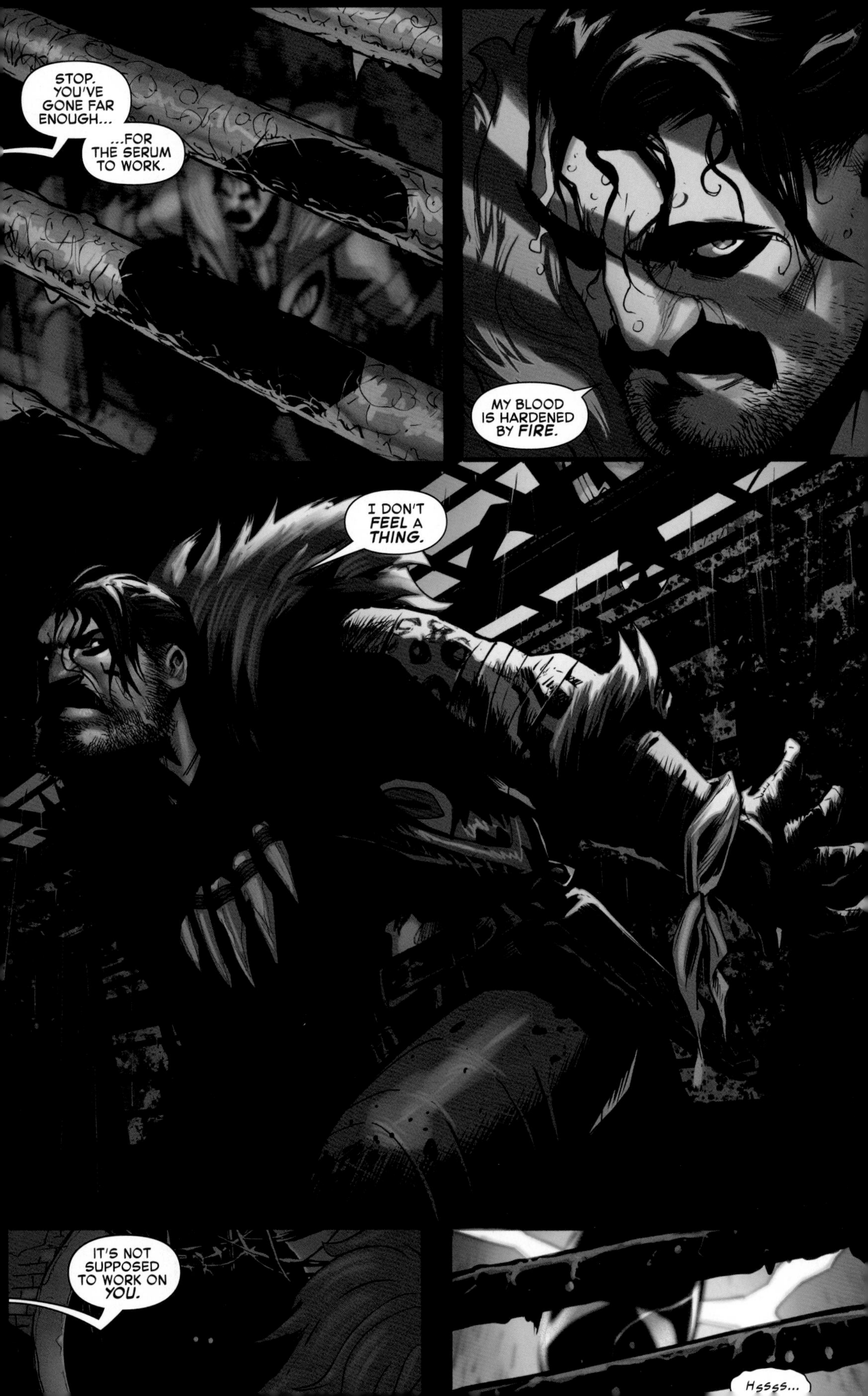
STOP. YOU'VE GONE FAR ENOUGH...
...FOR THE SERUM TO WORK.
MY BLOOD IS HARDENED BY FIRE.
I DON'T FEEL A THING.
IT'S NOT SUPPOSED TO WORK ON YOU.
Hssss...

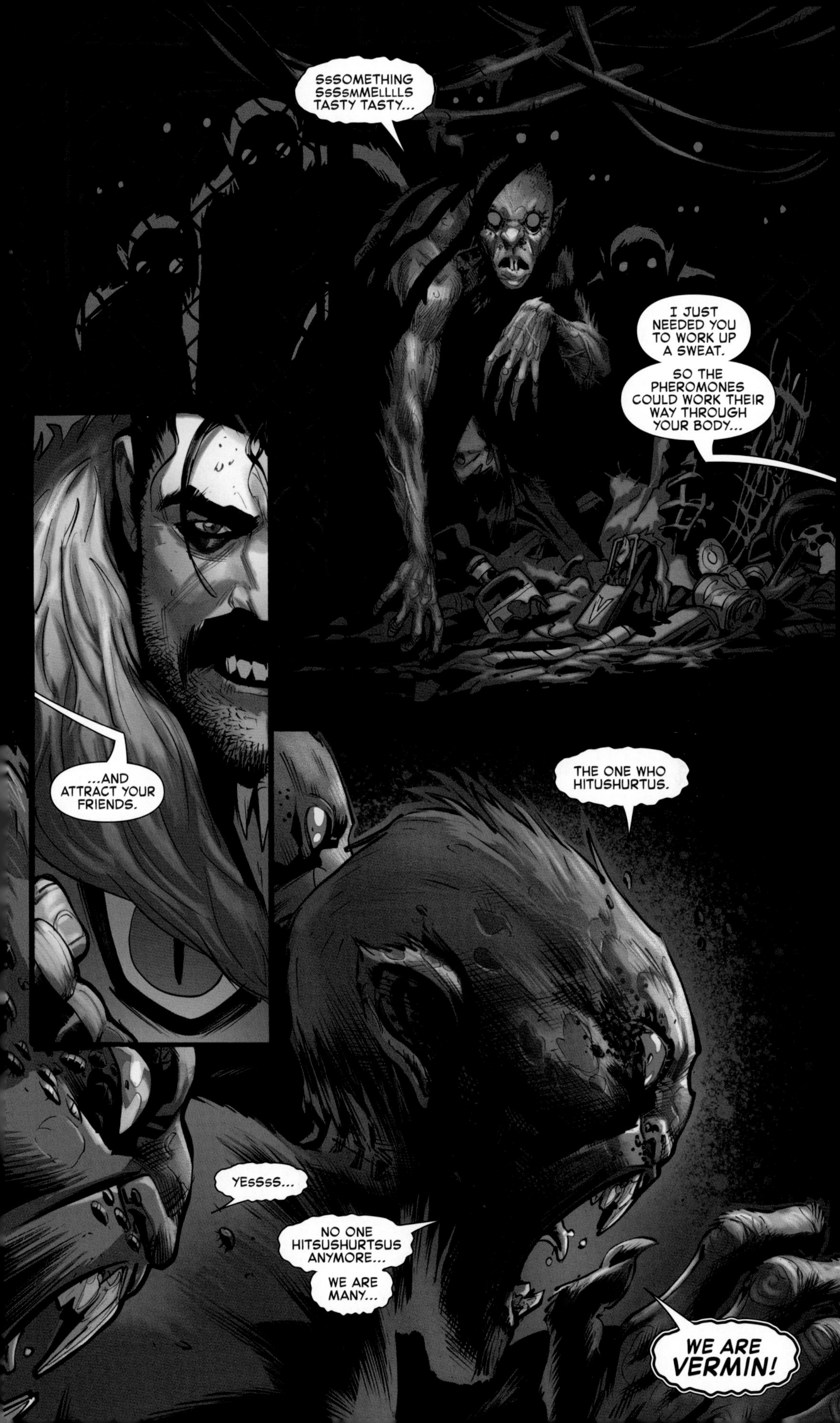
SsSOMETHING SsSsMMELLLLS TASTY TASTY...
I JUST NEEDED YOU TO WORK UP A SWEAT.
SO THE PHEROMONES COULD WORK THEIR WAY THROUGH YOUR BODY...
...AND ATTRACT YOUR FRIENDS.
THE ONE WHO HITUSHURTUS.
YESSSS...
NO ONE HITSUSHURTSUS ANYMORE...
WE ARE MANY...
WE ARE VERMIN!

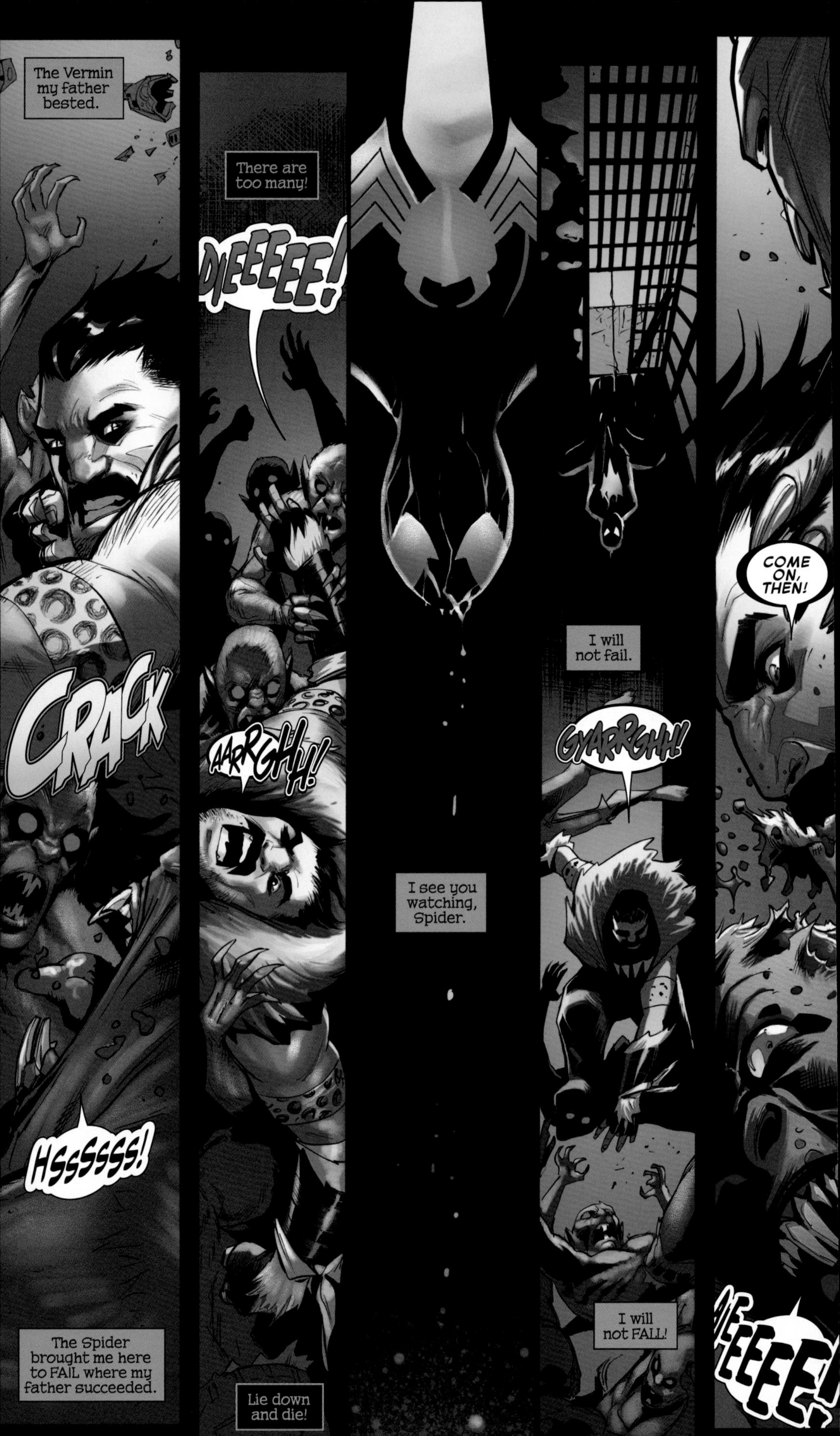
The Vermin my father bested.
CRACK
HSSSSSS!
The Spider brought me here to FAIL where my father succeeded.
There are too many!
DIEEEEE!
AARRGHH!
Lie down and die!
I see you watching, Spider.
I will not fail.
GYARRGHH!
I will not FALL!
COME ON, THEN!

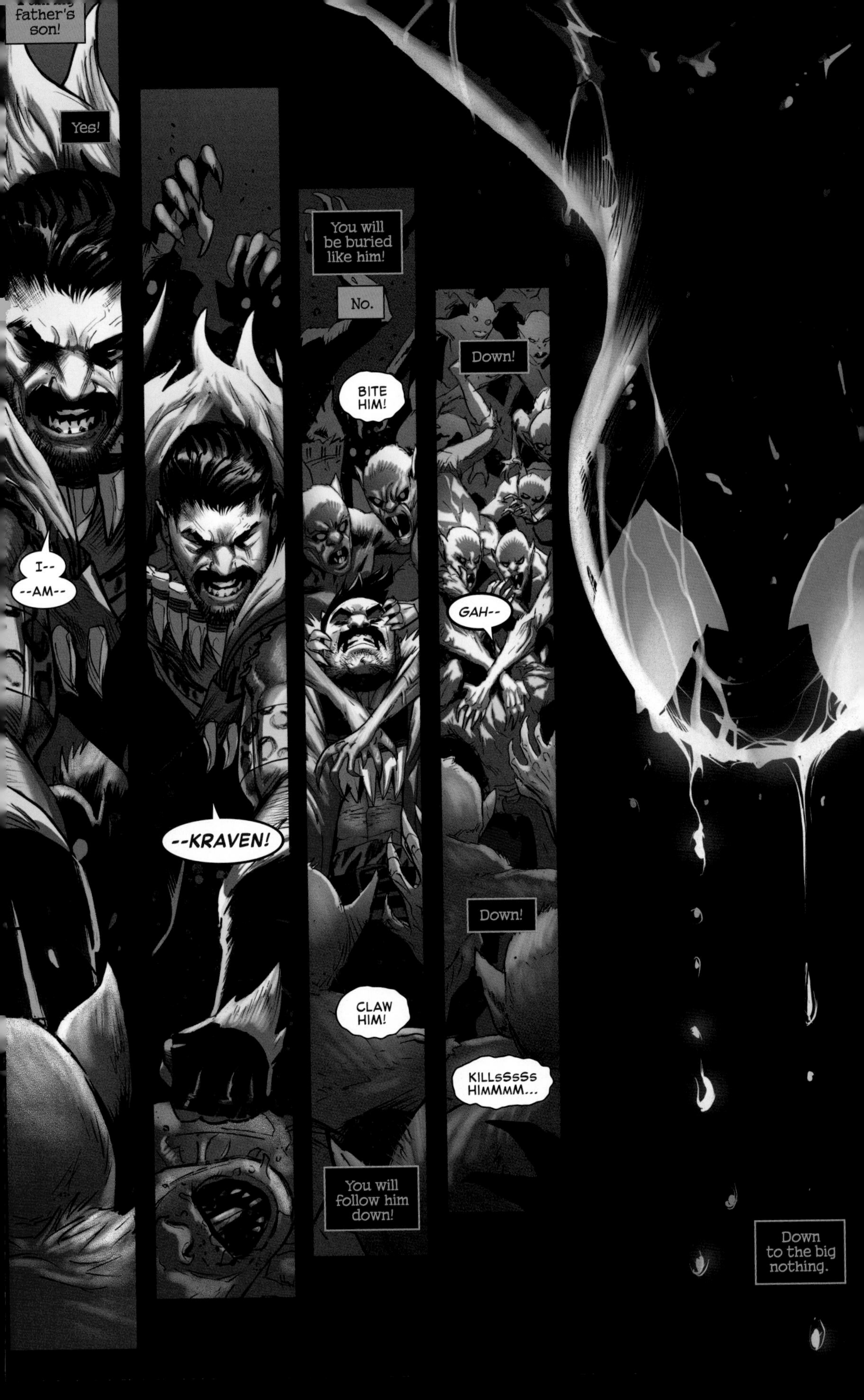
father's son!
Yes!
I--
--AM--
--KRAVEN!
You will be buried like him!
No.
BITE HIM!
CLAW HIM!
You will follow him down!
Down!
GAH--
Down!
KILLsssss HIMMMM...
Down to the big nothing.

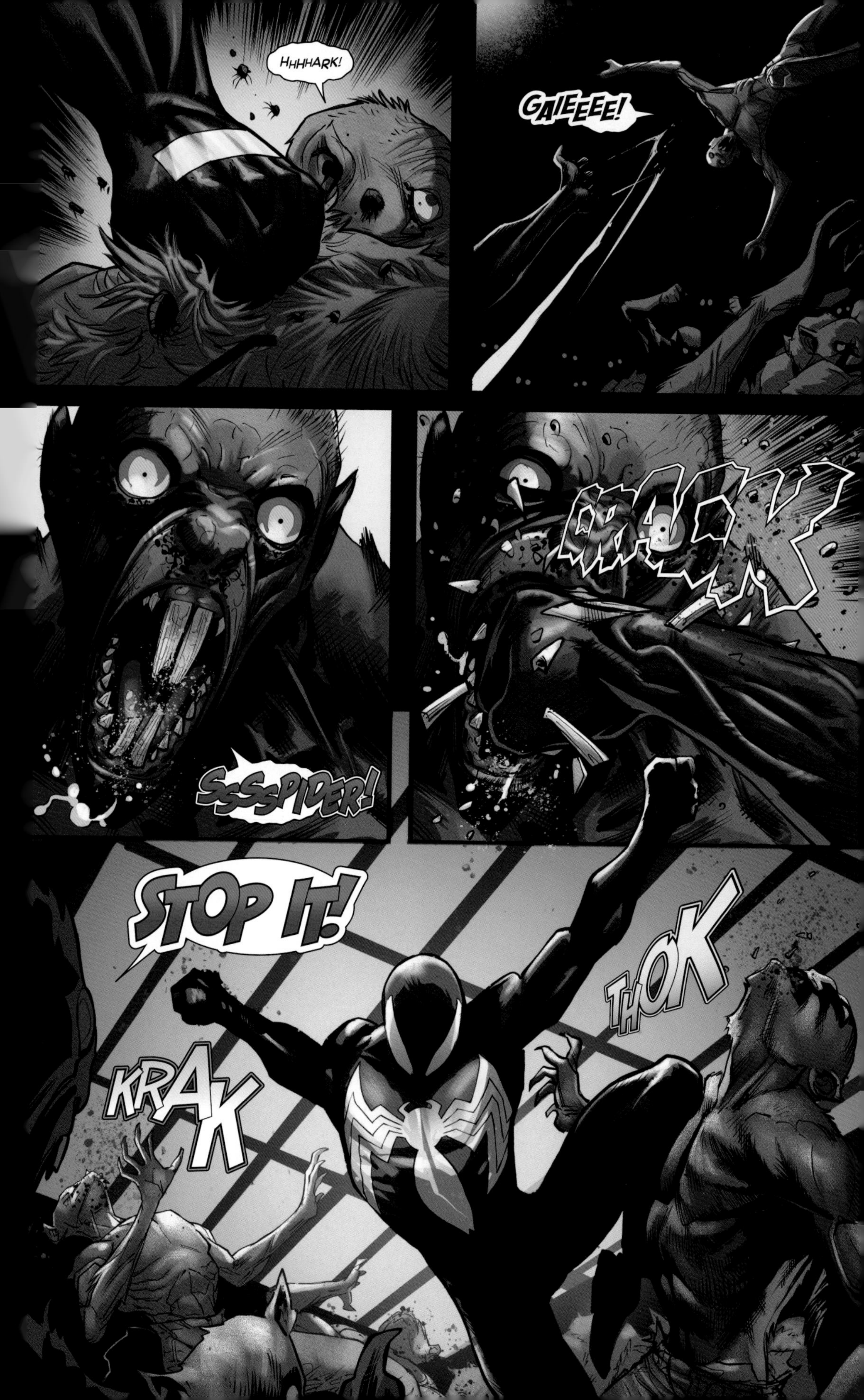
HHHHARK!
GAIEEEE!
SSSSSPIDER!
CRACK
STOP IT!
THOK
KRAK

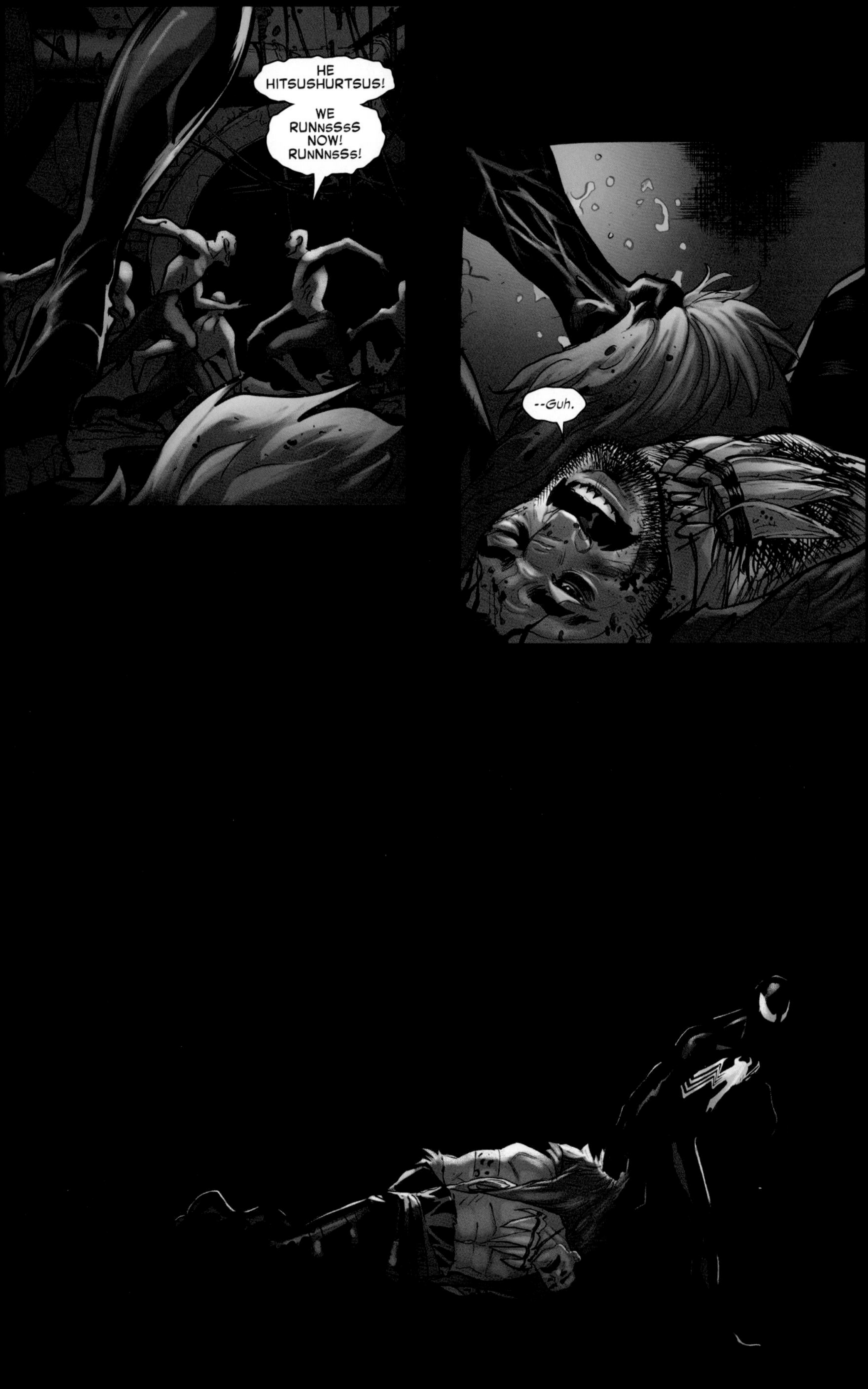
HE HITSUSHURTSUS!
WE RUNNsSSS NOW! RUNNnSSs!
--Guh.

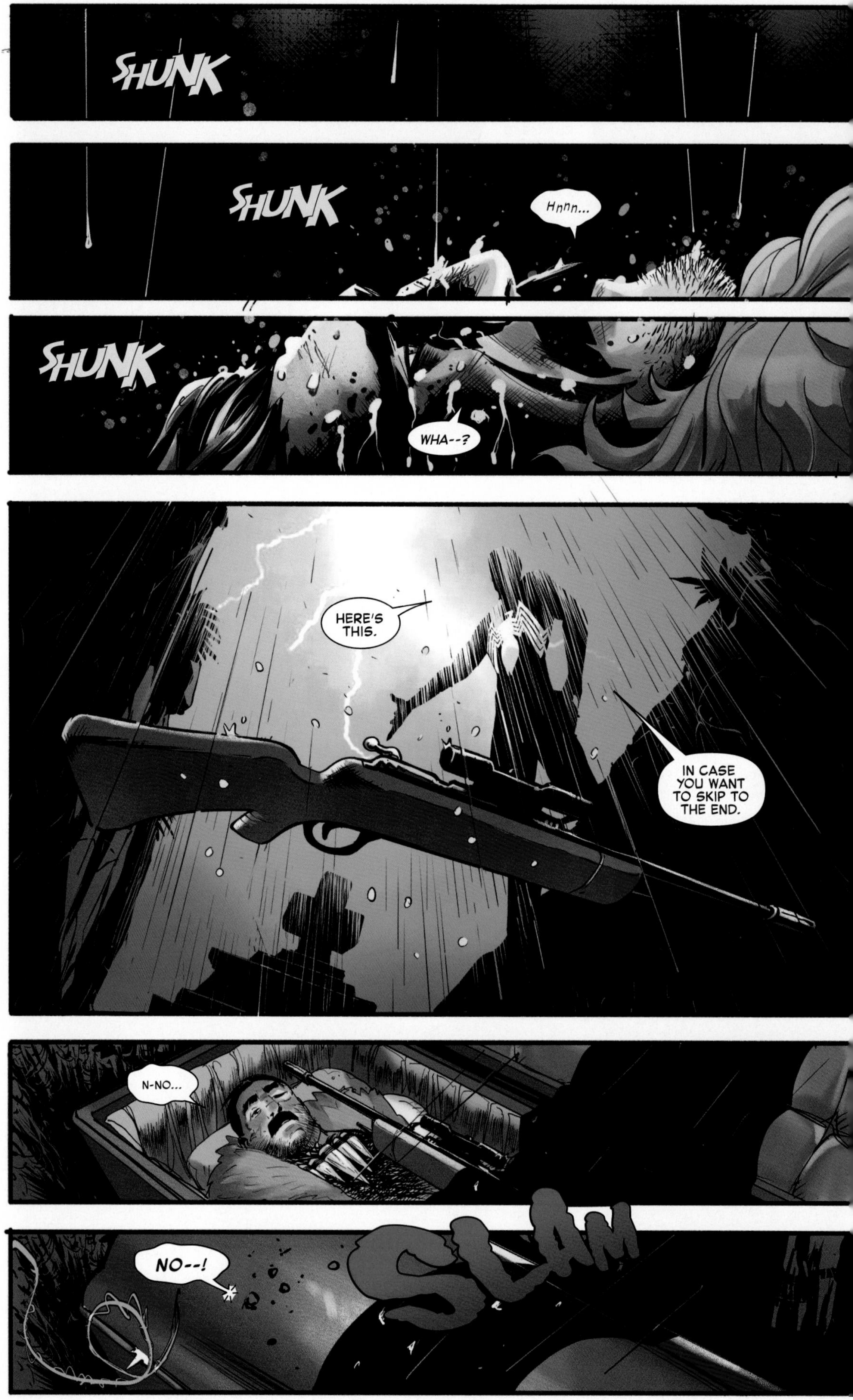
SHUNK
SHUNK
Hnnn...
SHUNK
WHA--?
HERE'S THIS.
IN CASE YOU WANT TO SKIP TO THE END.
N-NO...
NO--!
SLAM

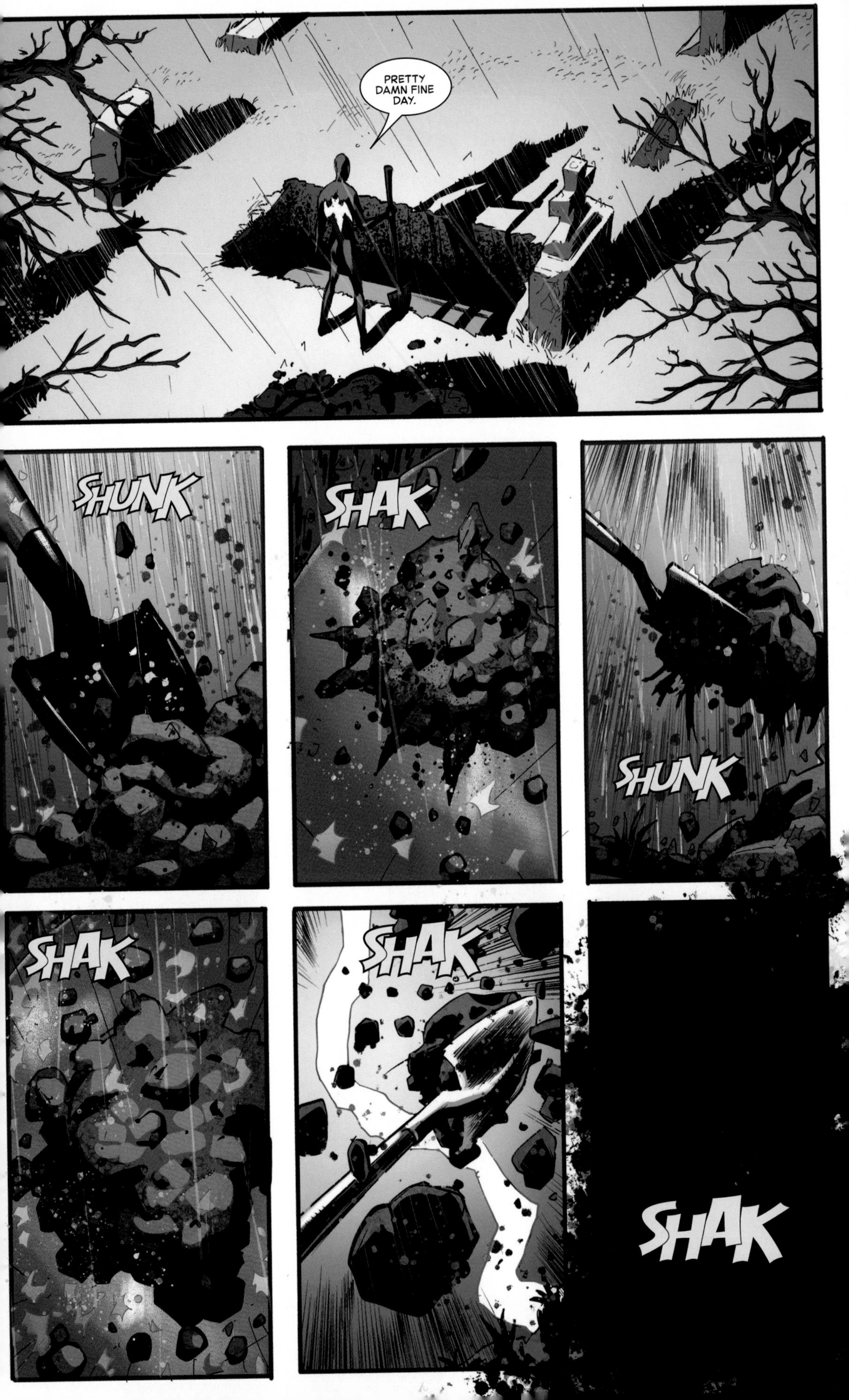
PRETTY DAMN FINE DAY.
SHUNK
SHAK
SHUNK
SHAK
SHAK
SHAK

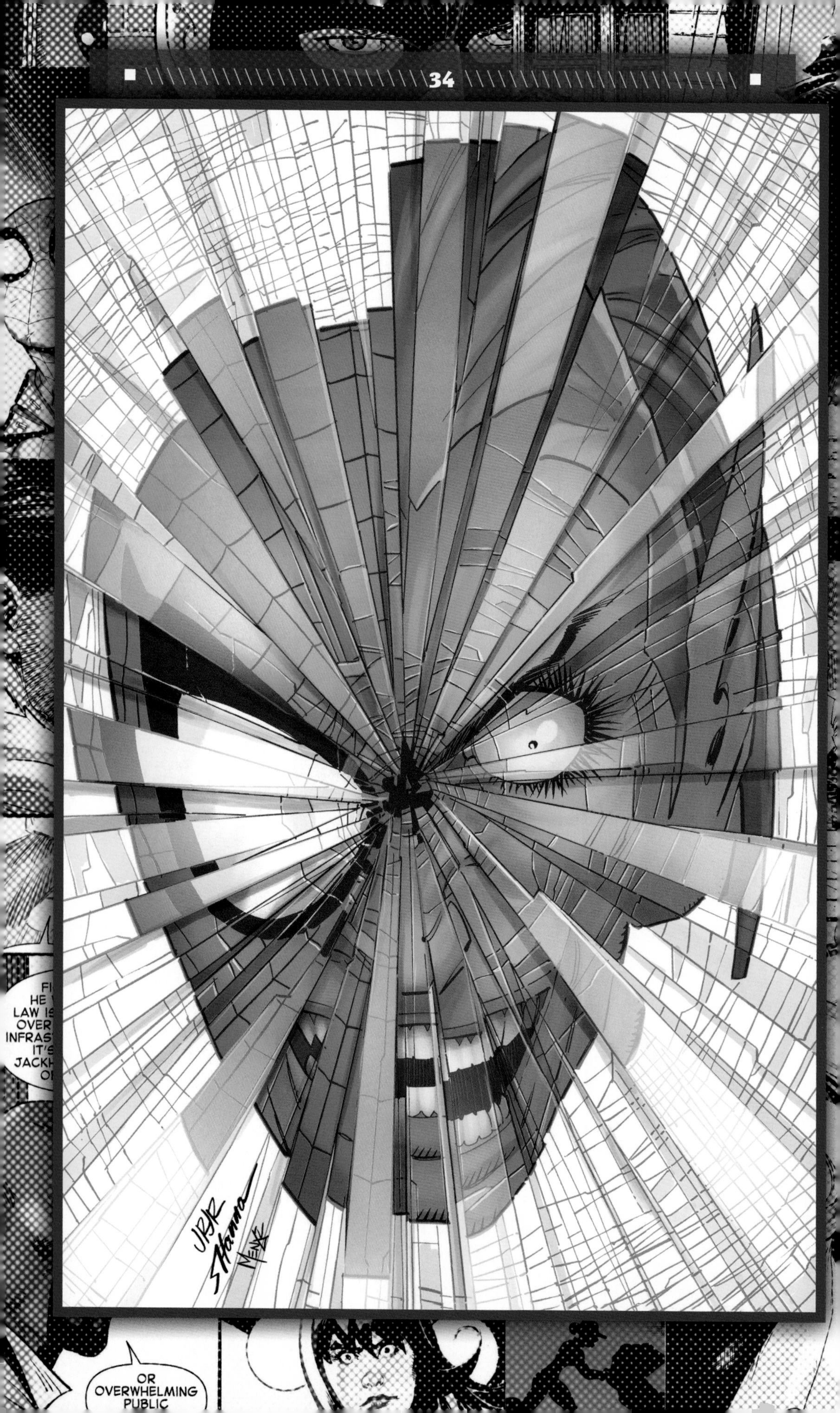
OR OVERWHELMING PUBLIC

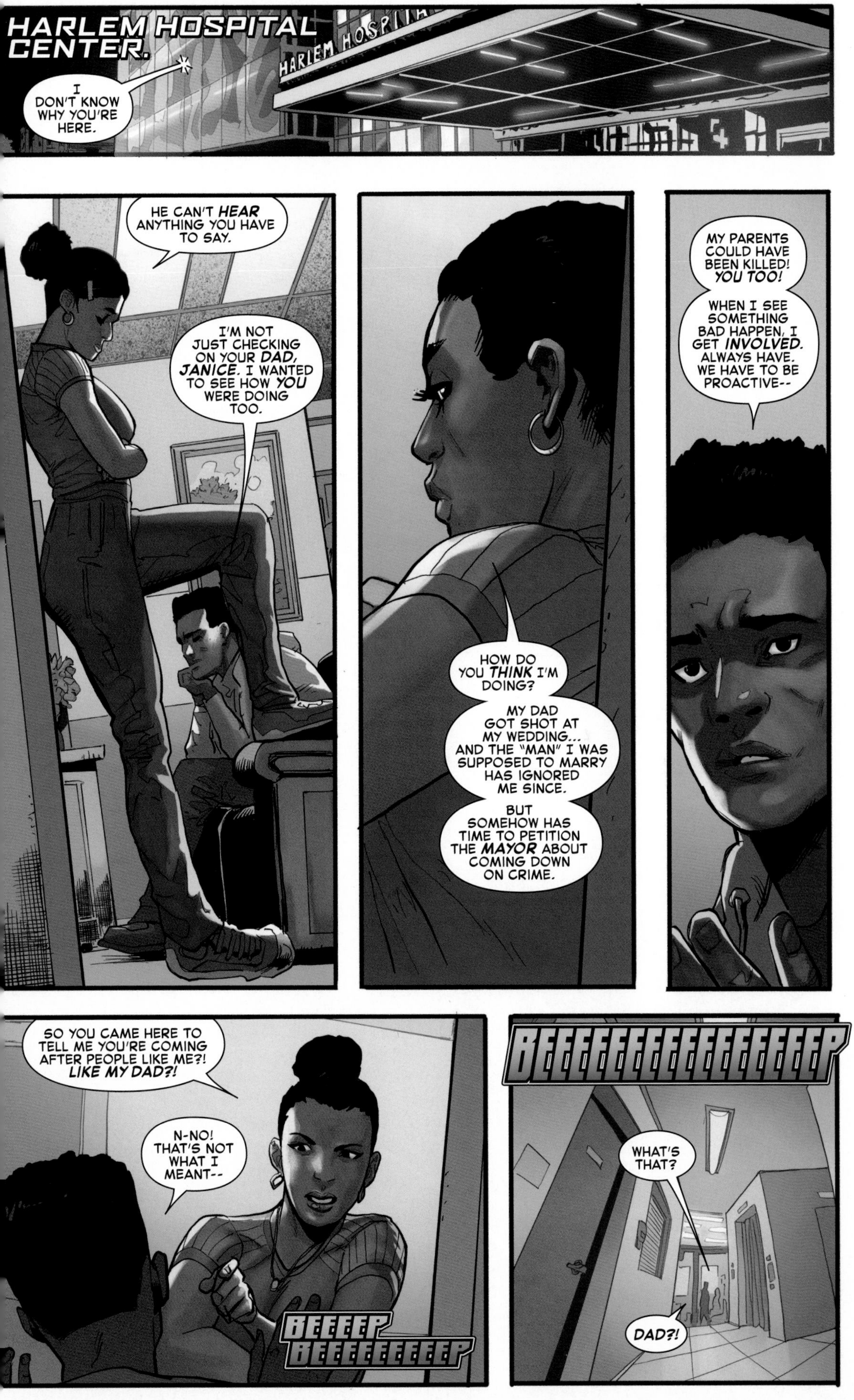
HARLEM HOSPITAL CENTER.
HARLEM HOSPITAL
I DON'T KNOW WHY YOU'RE HERE.
HE CAN'T HEAR ANYTHING YOU HAVE TO SAY.
I'M NOT JUST CHECKING ON YOUR DAD, JANICE. I WANTED TO SEE HOW YOU WERE DOING TOO.
HOW DO YOU THINK I'M DOING?
MY DAD GOT SHOT AT MY WEDDING... AND THE "MAN" I WAS SUPPOSED TO MARRY HAS IGNORED ME SINCE.
BUT SOMEHOW HAS TIME TO PETITION THE MAYOR ABOUT COMING DOWN ON CRIME.
MY PARENTS COULD HAVE BEEN KILLED! YOU TOO!
WHEN I SEE SOMETHING BAD HAPPEN, I GET INVOLVED. ALWAYS HAVE. WE HAVE TO BE PROACTIVE--
SO YOU CAME HERE TO TELL ME YOU'RE COMING AFTER PEOPLE LIKE ME?! LIKE MY DAD?!
N-NO! THAT'S NOT WHAT I MEANT--
BEEEEP BEEEEEEEEEP
BEEEEEEEEEEEEEEEEP
WHAT'S THAT?
DAD?!

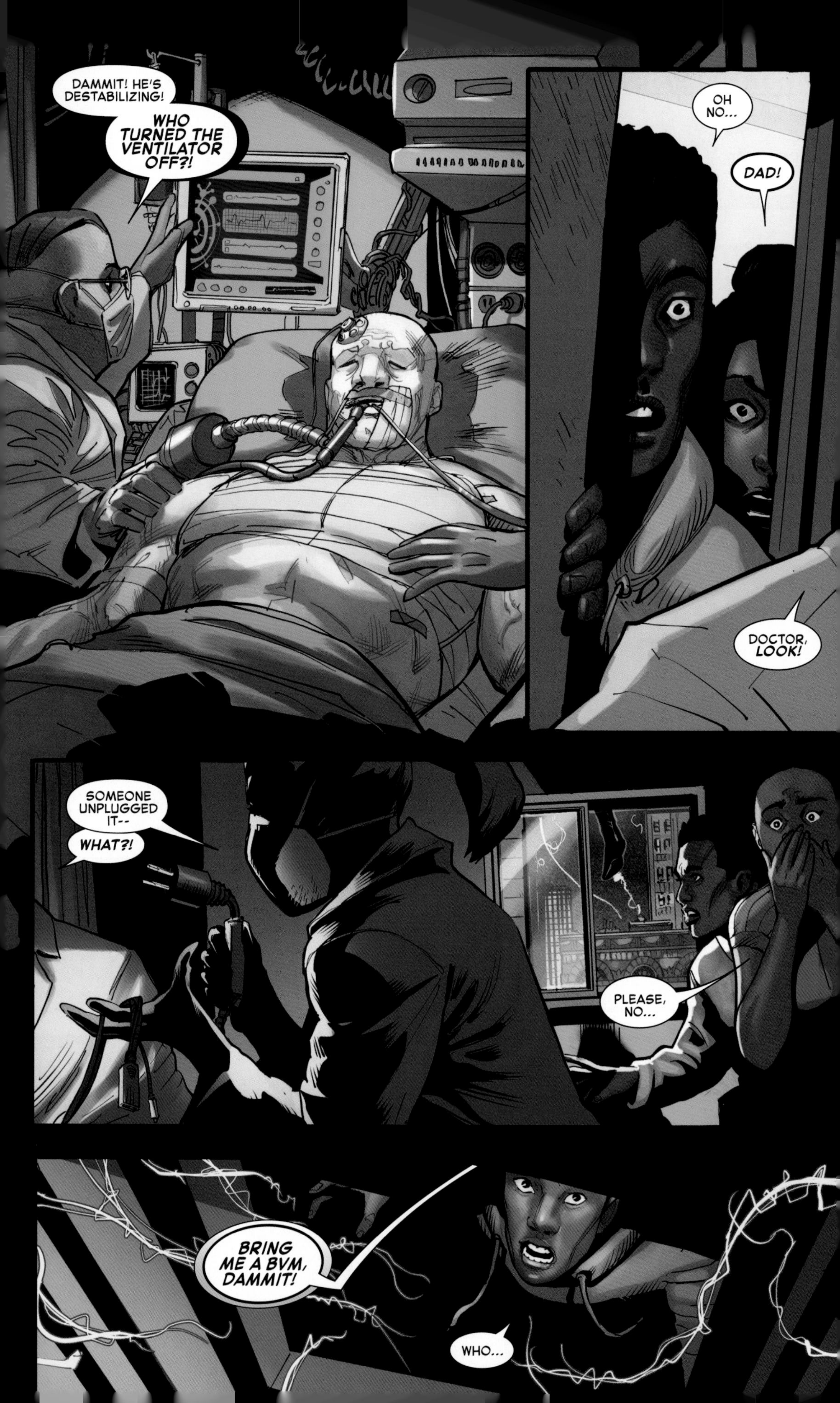

DAMMIT! HE'S DESTABILIZING!
WHO TURNED THE VENTILATOR OFF?!
OH NO...
DAD!
DOCTOR, LOOK!
SOMEONE UNPLUGGED IT--
WHAT?!
PLEASE, NO...
BRING ME A BVM, DAMMIT!
WHO...

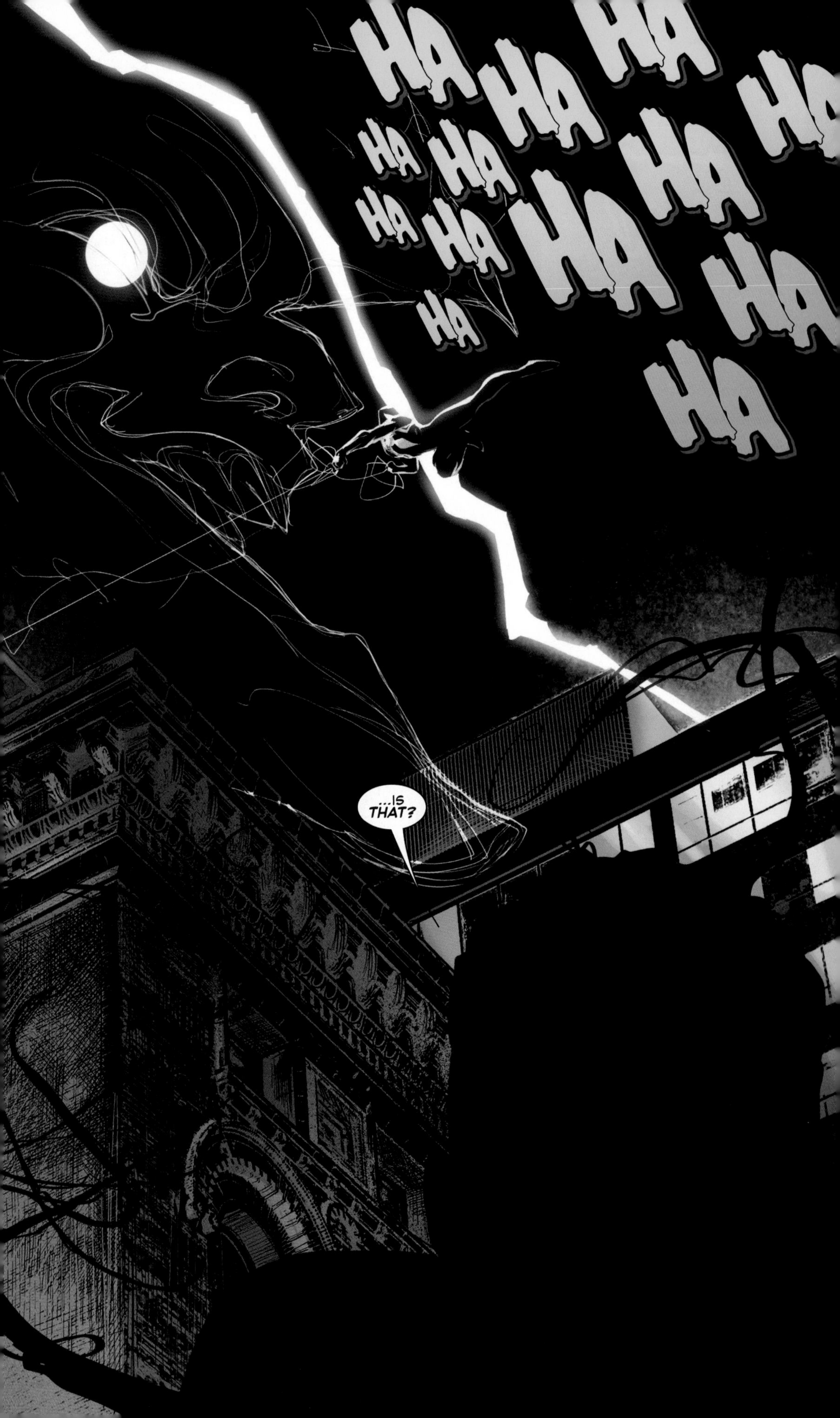
HA HA HA HA
HA HA HA
HA HA HA HA
HA HA
HA
...IS THAT?

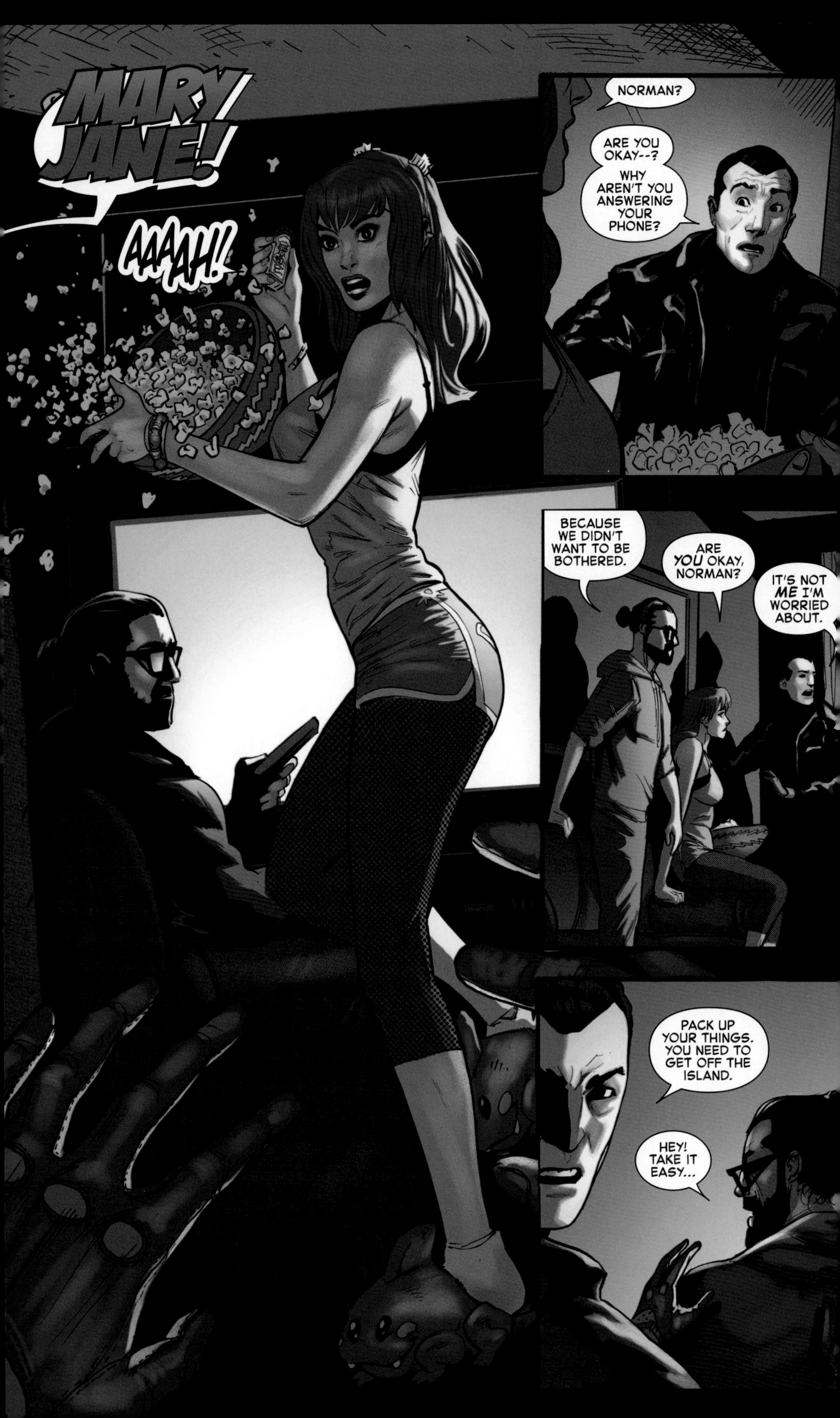
MARY JANE!
AAAAH!!
NORMAN?
ARE YOU OKAY--?
WHY AREN'T YOU ANSWERING YOUR PHONE?
BECAUSE WE DIDN'T WANT TO BE BOTHERED.
ARE YOU OKAY, NORMAN?
IT'S NOT ME I'M WORRIED ABOUT.
PACK UP YOUR THINGS. YOU NEED TO GET OFF THE ISLAND.
HEY! TAKE IT EASY...

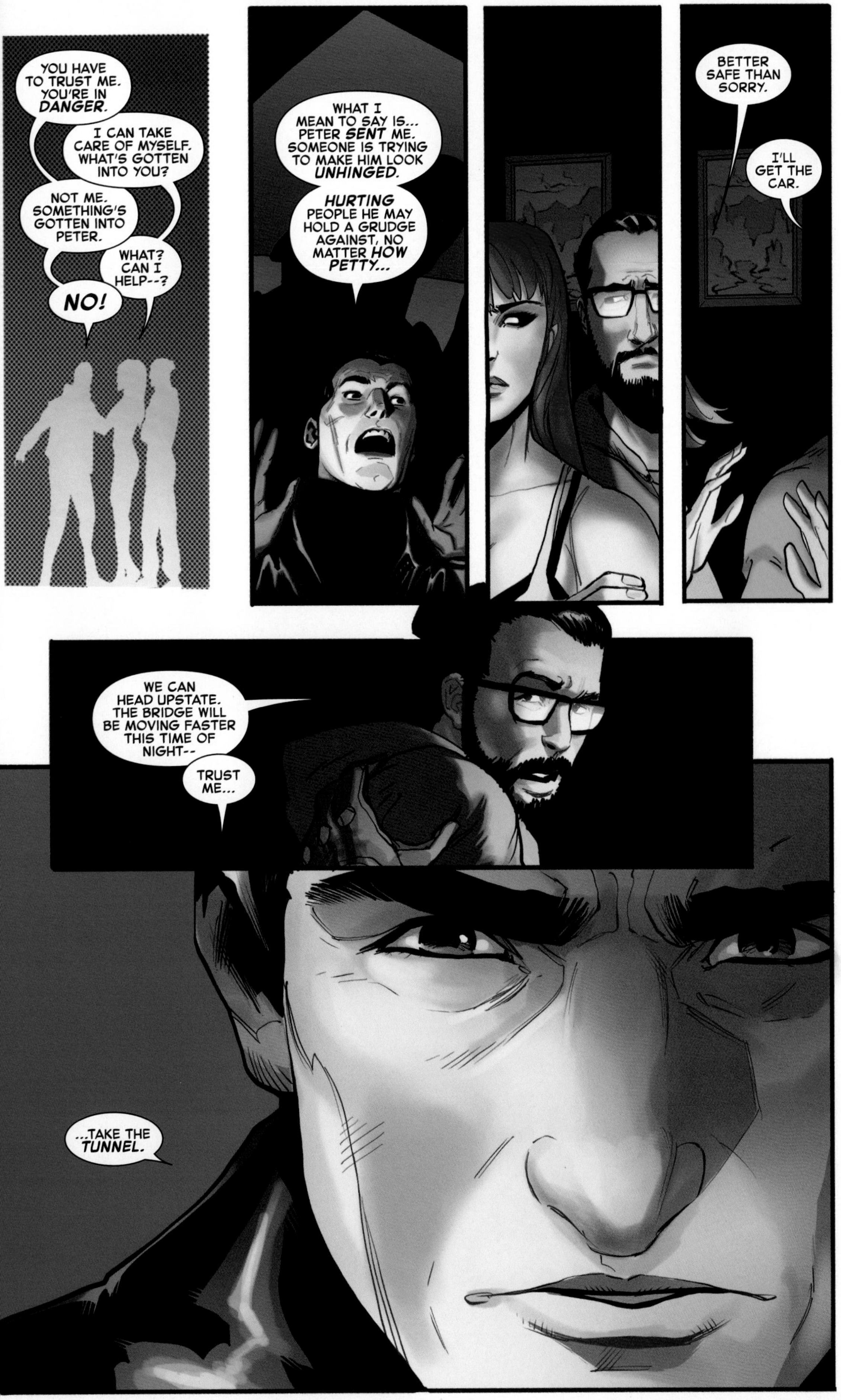
YOU HAVE TO TRUST ME. YOU'RE IN DANGER.
I CAN TAKE CARE OF MYSELF. WHAT'S GOTTEN INTO YOU?
NOT ME. SOMETHING'S GOTTEN INTO PETER.
WHAT? CAN I HELP--?
NO!
WHAT I MEAN TO SAY IS... PETER SENT ME. SOMEONE IS TRYING TO MAKE HIM LOOK UNHINGED.
HURTING PEOPLE HE MAY HOLD A GRUDGE AGAINST, NO MATTER HOW PETTY...
BETTER SAFE THAN SORRY.
I'LL GET THE CAR.
WE CAN HEAD UPSTATE. THE BRIDGE WILL BE MOVING FASTER THIS TIME OF NIGHT--
TRUST ME...
...TAKE THE TUNNEL.

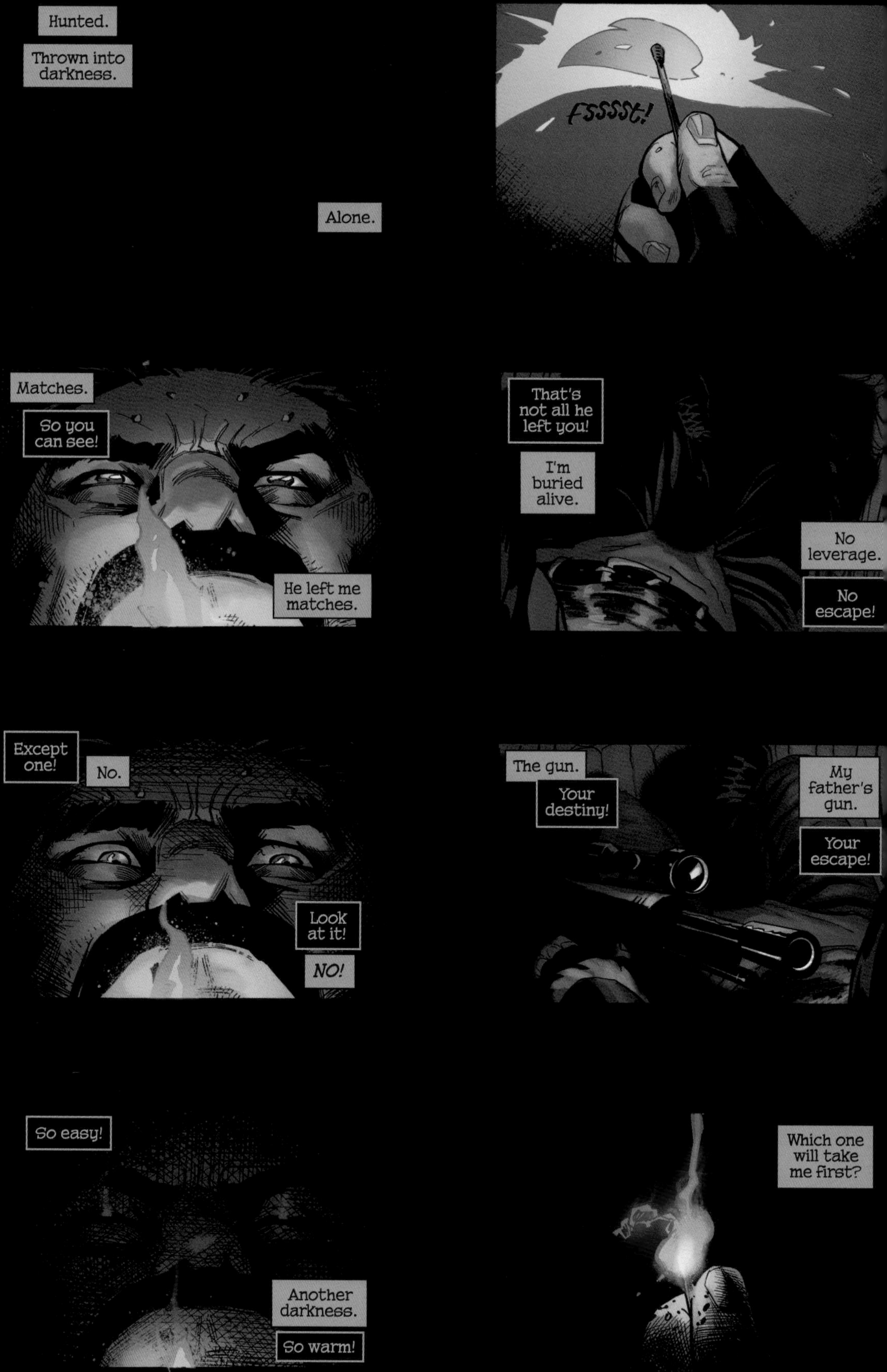
Hunted.
Thrown into darkness.
Alone.
FSSSST!
Matches.
So you can see!
He left me matches.
That's not all he left you!
I'm buried alive.
No leverage.
No escape!
Except one!
No.
Look at it!
NO!
The gun.
Your destiny!
My father's gun.
Your escape!
So easy!
Another darkness.
So warm!
Which one will take me first?

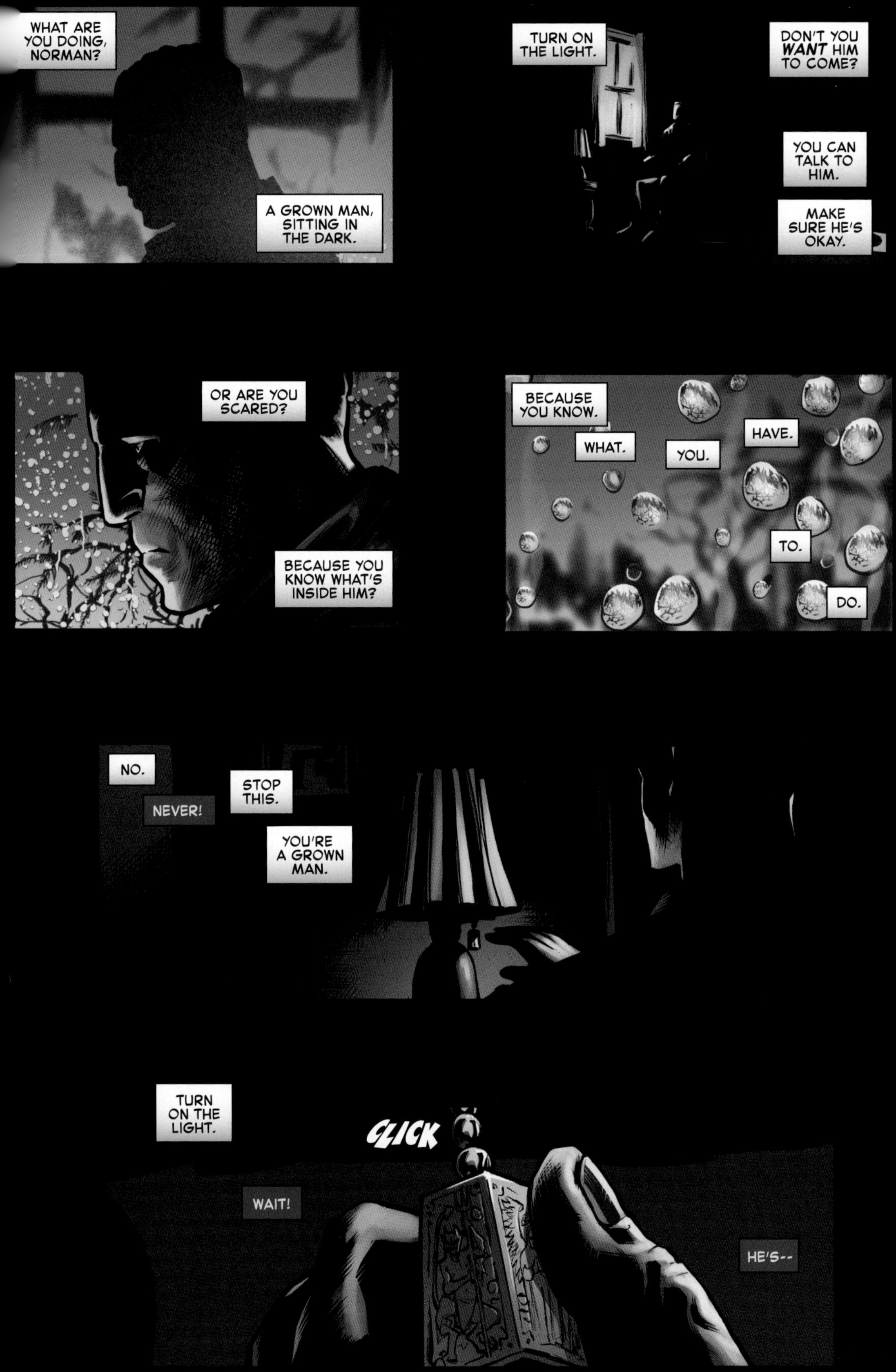
WHAT ARE YOU DOING, NORMAN?
A GROWN MAN, SITTING IN THE DARK.
TURN ON THE LIGHT.
DON'T YOU WANT HIM TO COME?
YOU CAN TALK TO HIM.
MAKE SURE HE'S OKAY.
OR ARE YOU SCARED?
BECAUSE YOU KNOW WHAT'S INSIDE HIM?
BECAUSE YOU KNOW.
WHAT.
YOU.
HAVE.
TO.
DO.
NO.
NEVER!
STOP THIS.
YOU'RE A GROWN MAN.
TURN ON THE LIGHT.
CLICK
WAIT!
HE'S--

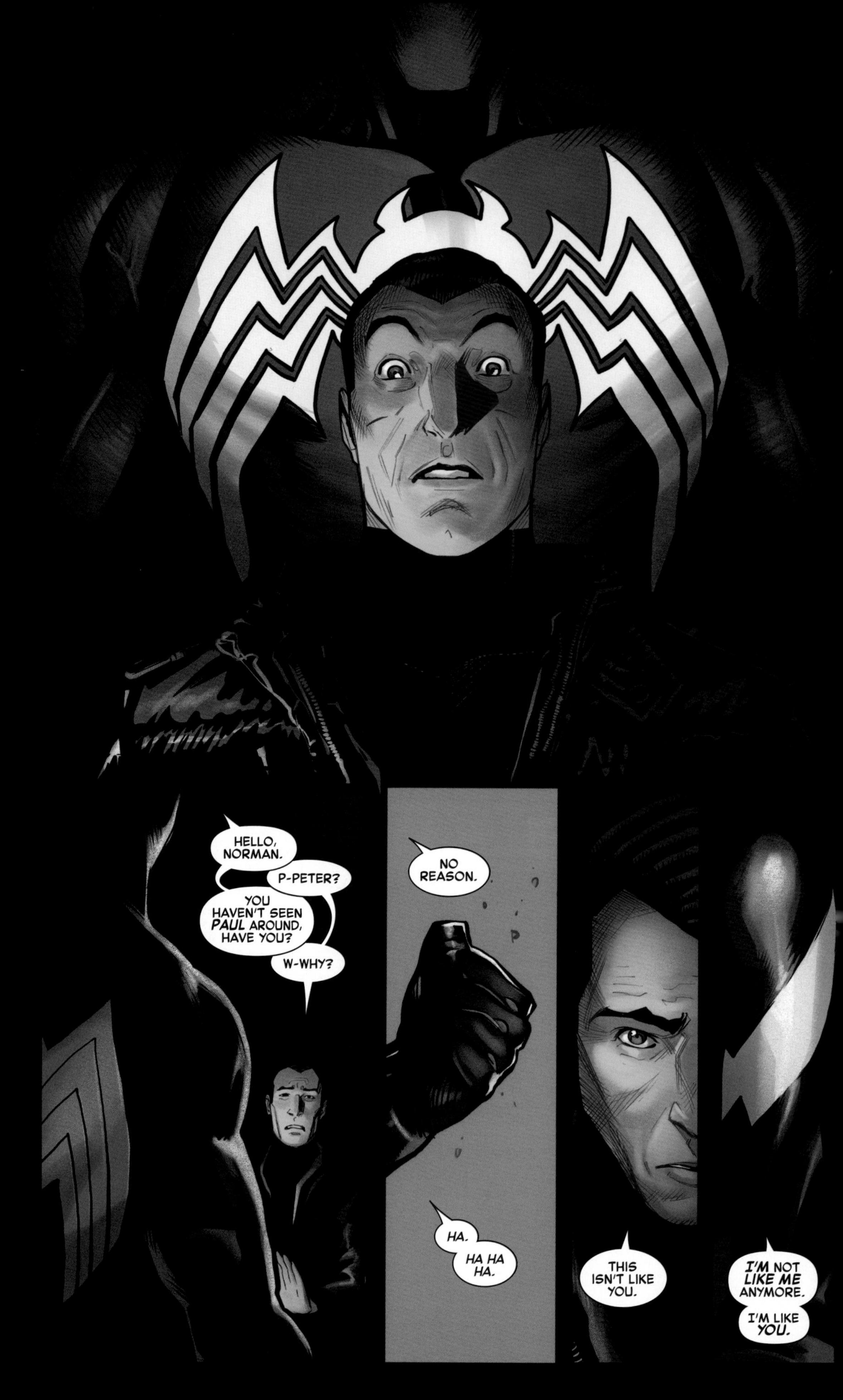
HELLO, NORMAN.
P-PETER?
YOU HAVEN'T SEEN PAUL AROUND, HAVE YOU?
W-WHY?
NO REASON.
HA.
HA HA HA.
THIS ISN'T LIKE YOU.
I'M NOT LIKE ME ANYMORE.
I'M LIKE YOU.

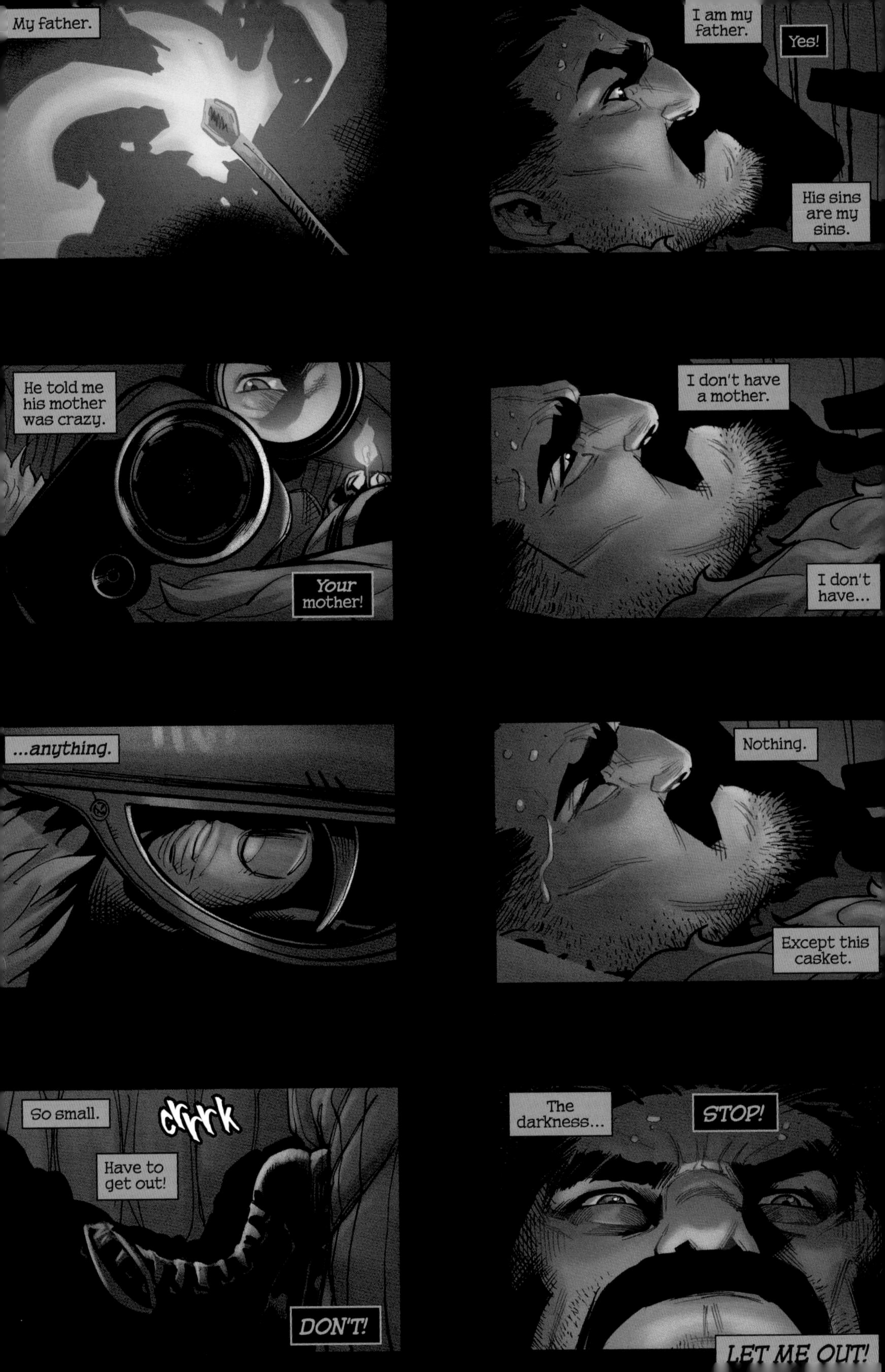

My father.
I am my father.
Yes!
His sins are my sins.
He told me his mother was crazy.
Your mother!
I don't have a mother.
I don't have...
...anything.
Nothing.
Except this casket.
So small.
crrrk
Have to get out!
DON'T!
The darkness...
STOP!
LET ME OUT!

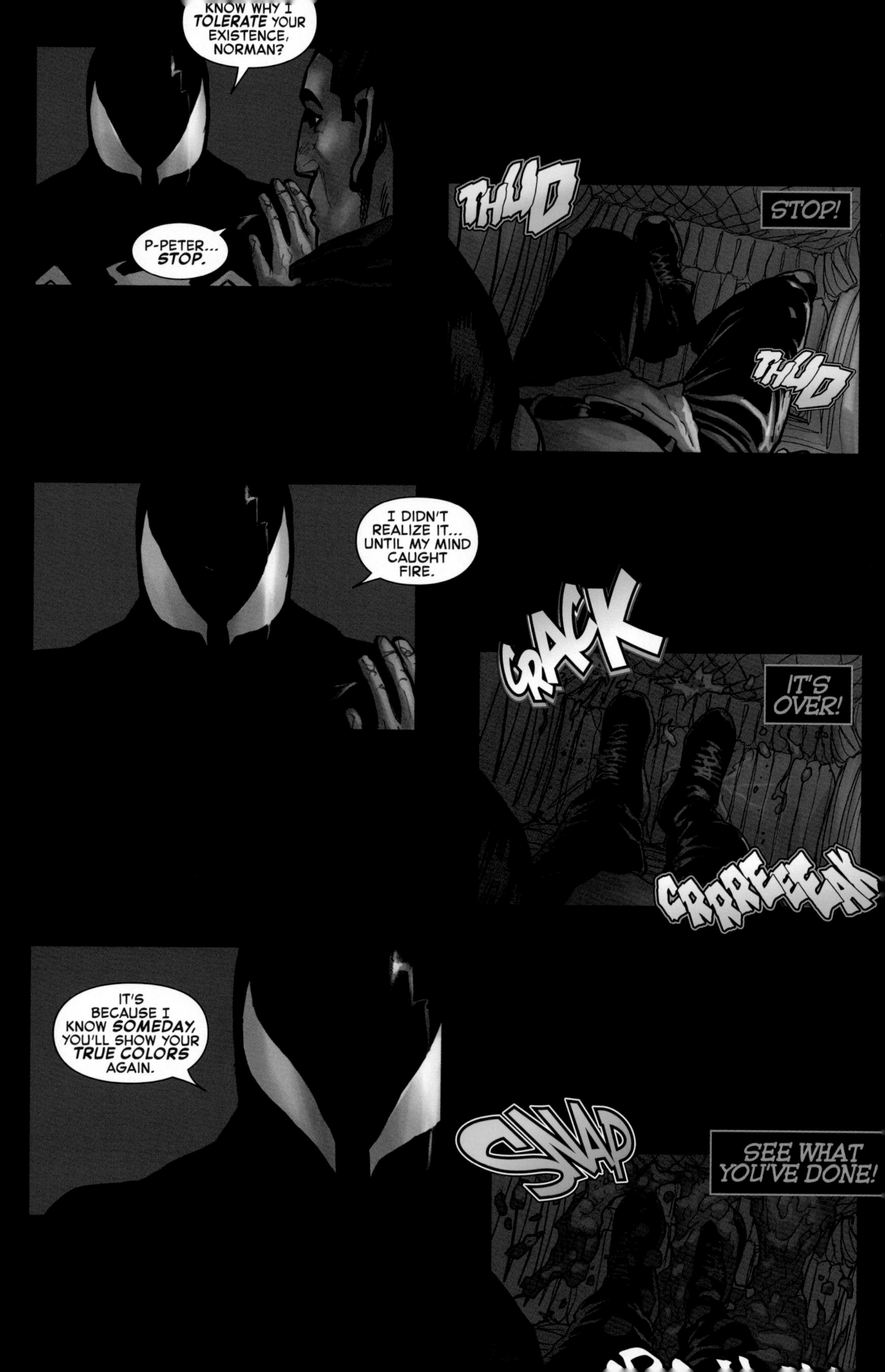
KNOW WHY I TOLERATE YOUR EXISTENCE, NORMAN?
P-PETER... STOP.
THUD
STOP!
THUD
I DIDN'T REALIZE IT... UNTIL MY MIND CAUGHT FIRE.
CRACK
IT'S OVER!
CRRREEEAK
IT'S BECAUSE I KNOW SOMEDAY, YOU'LL SHOW YOUR TRUE COLORS AGAIN.
SNAP
SEE WHAT YOU'VE DONE!

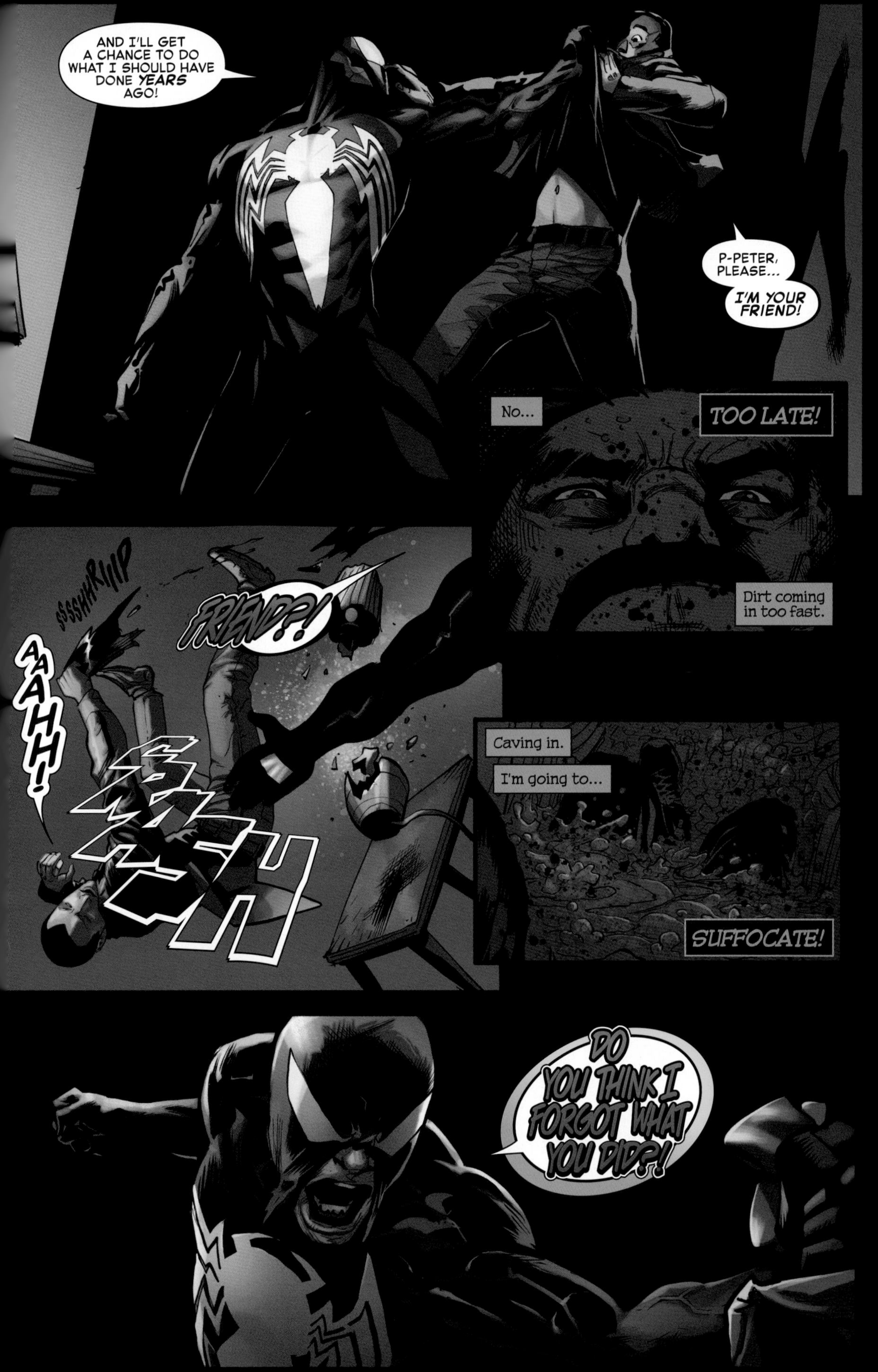
AND I'LL GET A CHANCE TO DO WHAT I SHOULD HAVE DONE *YEARS* AGO!
P-PETER, PLEASE...
I'M YOUR FRIEND!
No...
TOO LATE!
Dirt coming in too fast.
SSSSHHRIIIP
FRIEND?!
AAAHH!
SMASH
Caving in.
I'm going to...
SUFFOCATE!
DO YOU THINK I FORGOT WHAT YOU DID?!

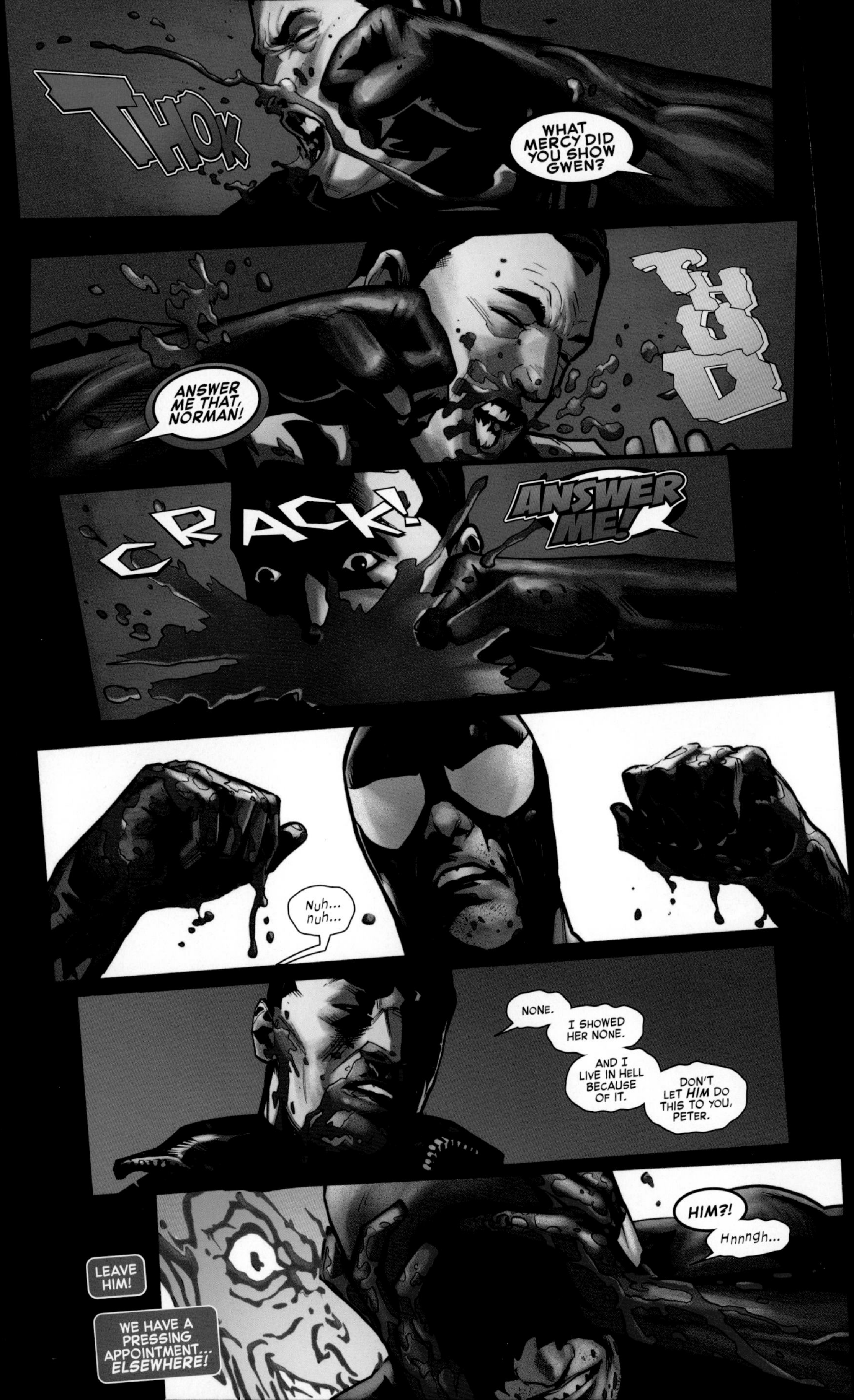
THOK
WHAT MERCY DID YOU SHOW GWEN?
ANSWER ME THAT, NORMAN!
CRACK!
ANSWER ME!
Nuh... nuh...
NONE.
I SHOWED HER NONE.
AND I LIVE IN HELL BECAUSE OF IT.
DON'T LET HIM DO THIS TO YOU, PETER.
HIM?!
Hnnngh...
LEAVE HIM!
WE HAVE A PRESSING APPOINTMENT... ELSEWHERE!

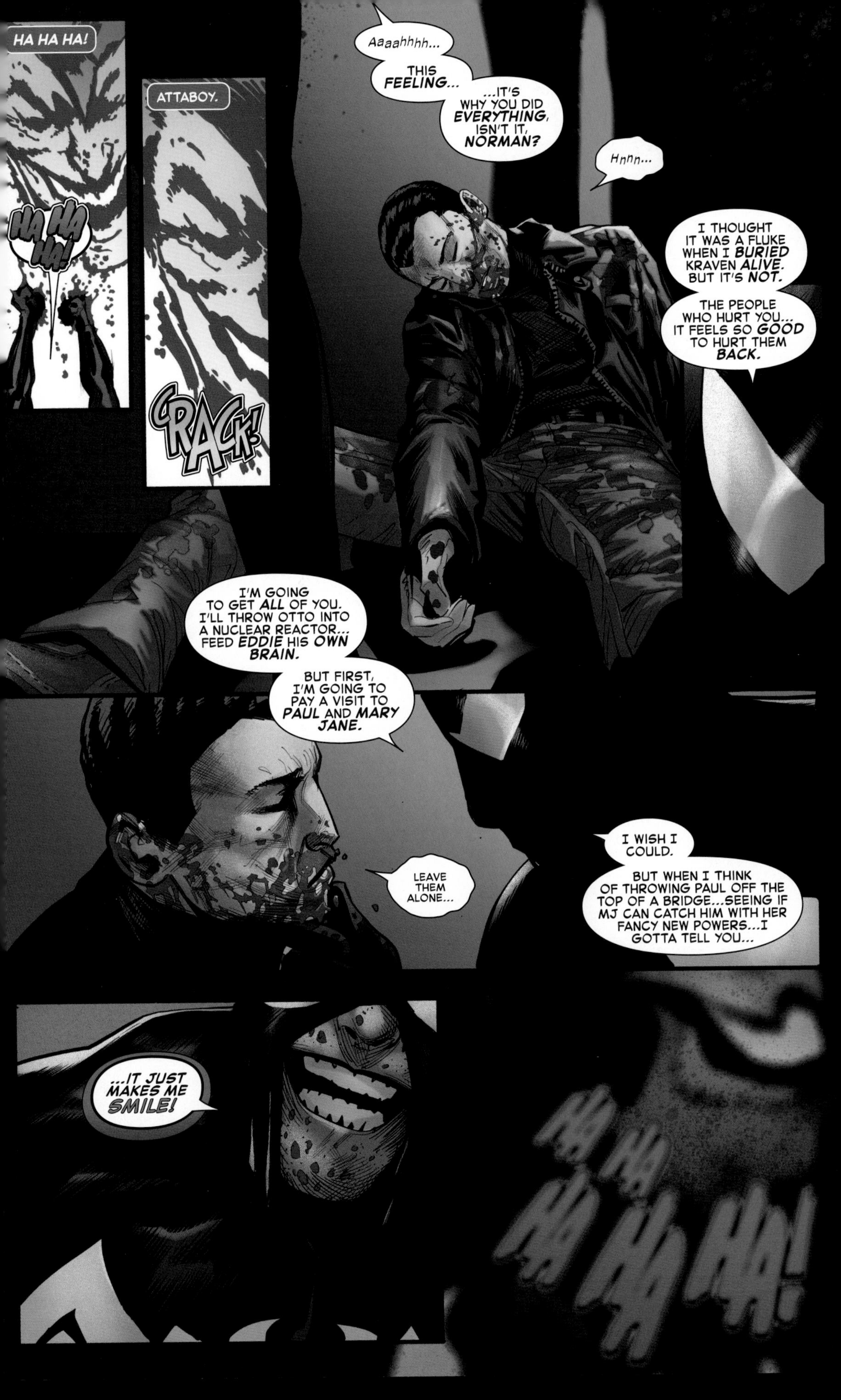

HA HA HA!
HA HA HA!
ATTABOY.
CRACK!
Aaaahhhh...
THIS FEELING...
...IT'S WHY YOU DID EVERYTHING, ISN'T IT, NORMAN?
Hnnn...
I THOUGHT IT WAS A FLUKE WHEN I BURIED KRAVEN ALIVE. BUT IT'S NOT.
THE PEOPLE WHO HURT YOU... IT FEELS SO GOOD TO HURT THEM BACK.
I'M GOING TO GET ALL OF YOU. I'LL THROW OTTO INTO A NUCLEAR REACTOR... FEED EDDIE HIS OWN BRAIN.
BUT FIRST, I'M GOING TO PAY A VISIT TO PAUL AND MARY JANE.
LEAVE THEM ALONE...
I WISH I COULD.
BUT WHEN I THINK OF THROWING PAUL OFF THE TOP OF A BRIDGE...SEEING IF MJ CAN CATCH HIM WITH HER FANCY NEW POWERS...I GOTTA TELL YOU...
...IT JUST MAKES ME SMILE!
HA HA HA HA HA!

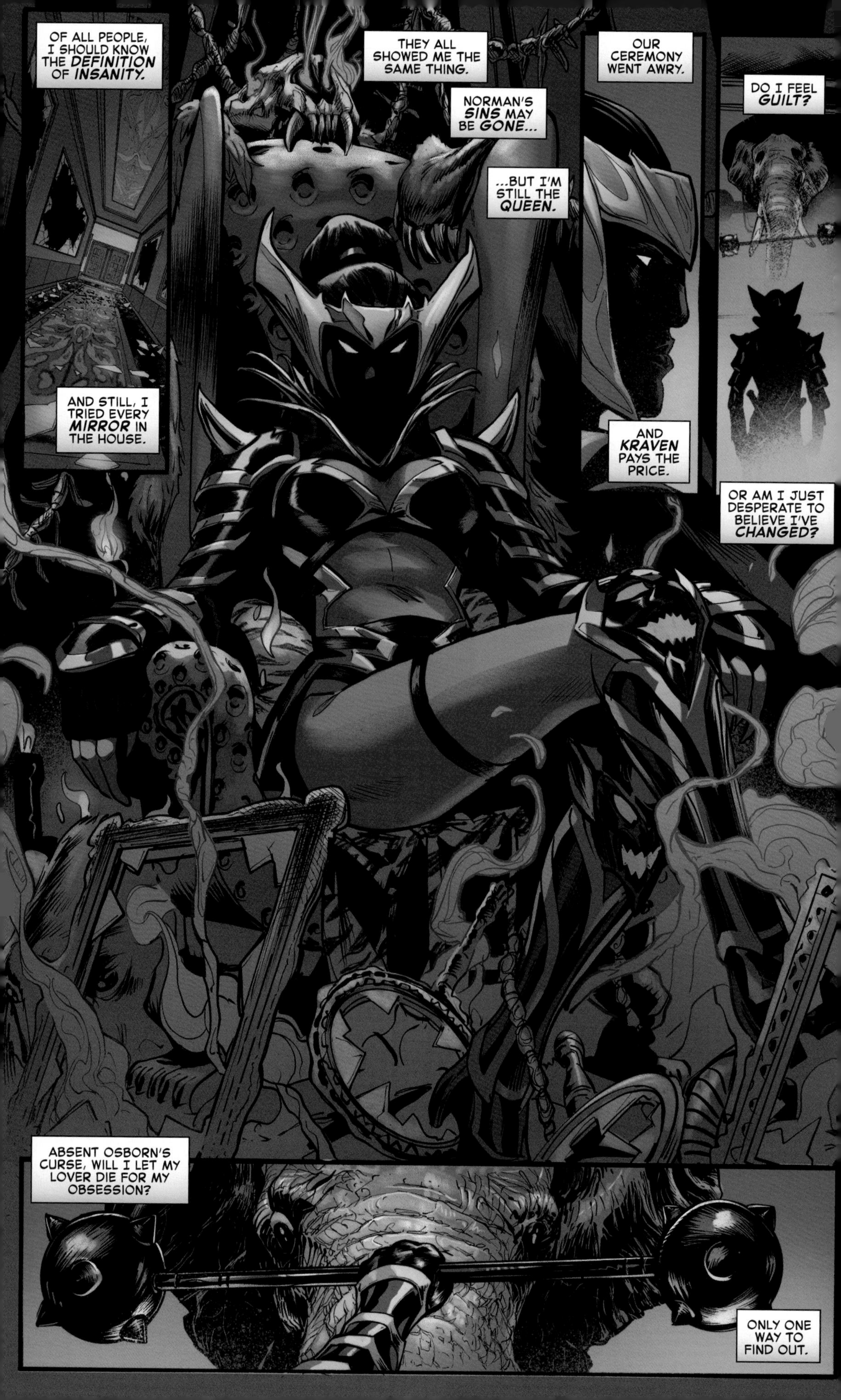

OF ALL PEOPLE, I SHOULD KNOW THE DEFINITION OF INSANITY.
AND STILL, I TRIED EVERY MIRROR IN THE HOUSE.
THEY ALL SHOWED ME THE SAME THING.
NORMAN'S SINS MAY BE GONE...
...BUT I'M STILL THE QUEEN.
OUR CEREMONY WENT AWRY.
AND KRAVEN PAYS THE PRICE.
DO I FEEL GUILT?
OR AM I JUST DESPERATE TO BELIEVE I'VE CHANGED?
ABSENT OSBORN'S CURSE, WILL I LET MY LOVER DIE FOR MY OBSESSION?
ONLY ONE WAY TO FIND OUT.

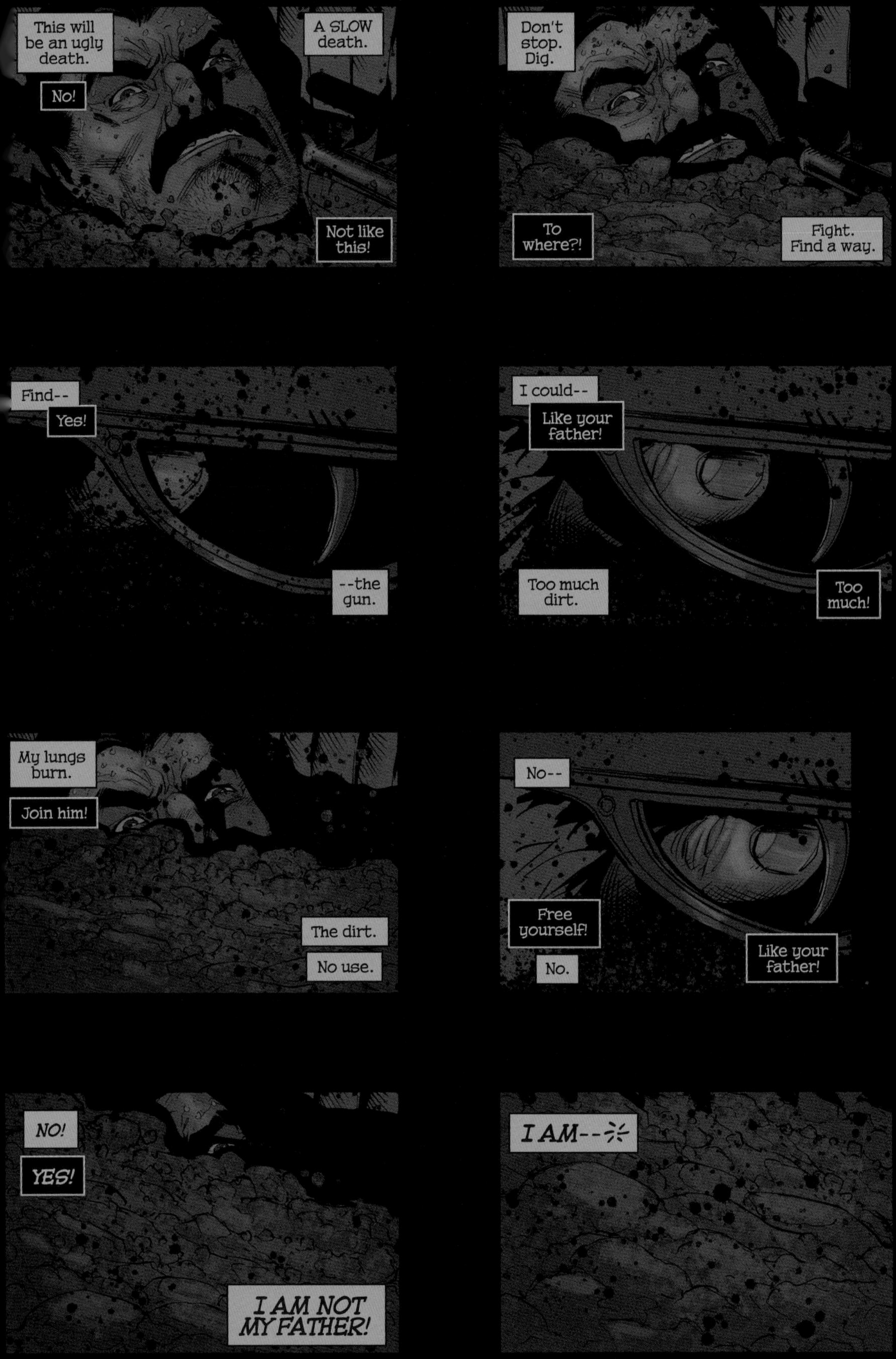
This will be an ugly death.
No!
A SLOW death.
Not like this!
Don't stop. Dig.
To where?!
Fight. Find a way.
Find--
Yes!
--the gun.
I could--
Like your father!
Too much dirt.
Too much!
My lungs burn.
Join him!
The dirt.
No use.
No--
Free yourself!
No.
Like your father!
NO!
YES!
I AM NOT MY FATHER!
I AM--

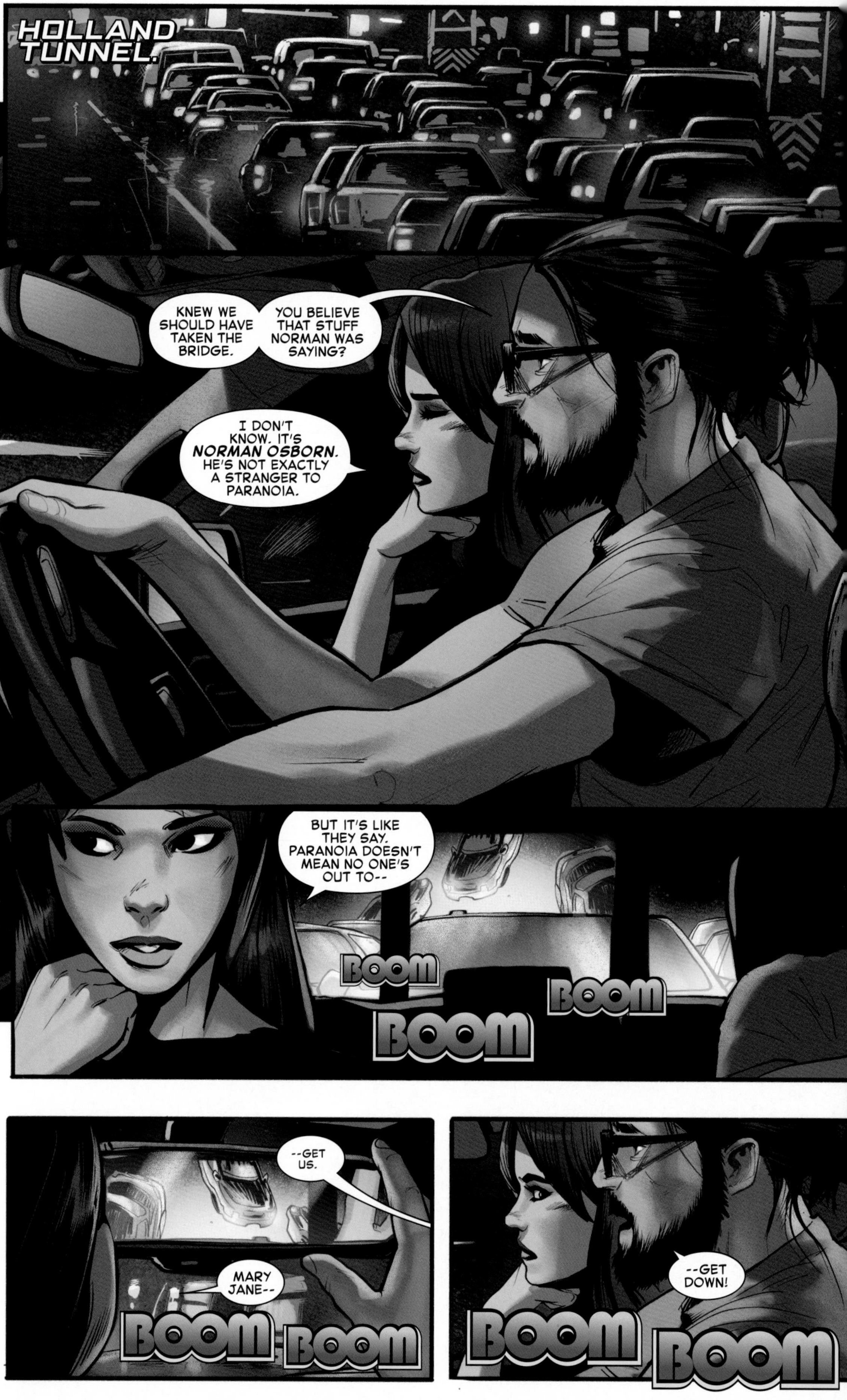
HOLLAND TUNNEL.
KNEW WE SHOULD HAVE TAKEN THE BRIDGE.
YOU BELIEVE THAT STUFF NORMAN WAS SAYING?
I DON'T KNOW. IT'S ***NORMAN OSBORN.*** HE'S NOT EXACTLY A STRANGER TO PARANOIA.
BUT IT'S LIKE THEY SAY. PARANOIA DOESN'T MEAN NO ONE'S OUT TO--
BOOM
BOOM
BOOM
--GET US.
MARY JANE--
BOOM
BOOM
--GET DOWN!
BOOM
BOOM

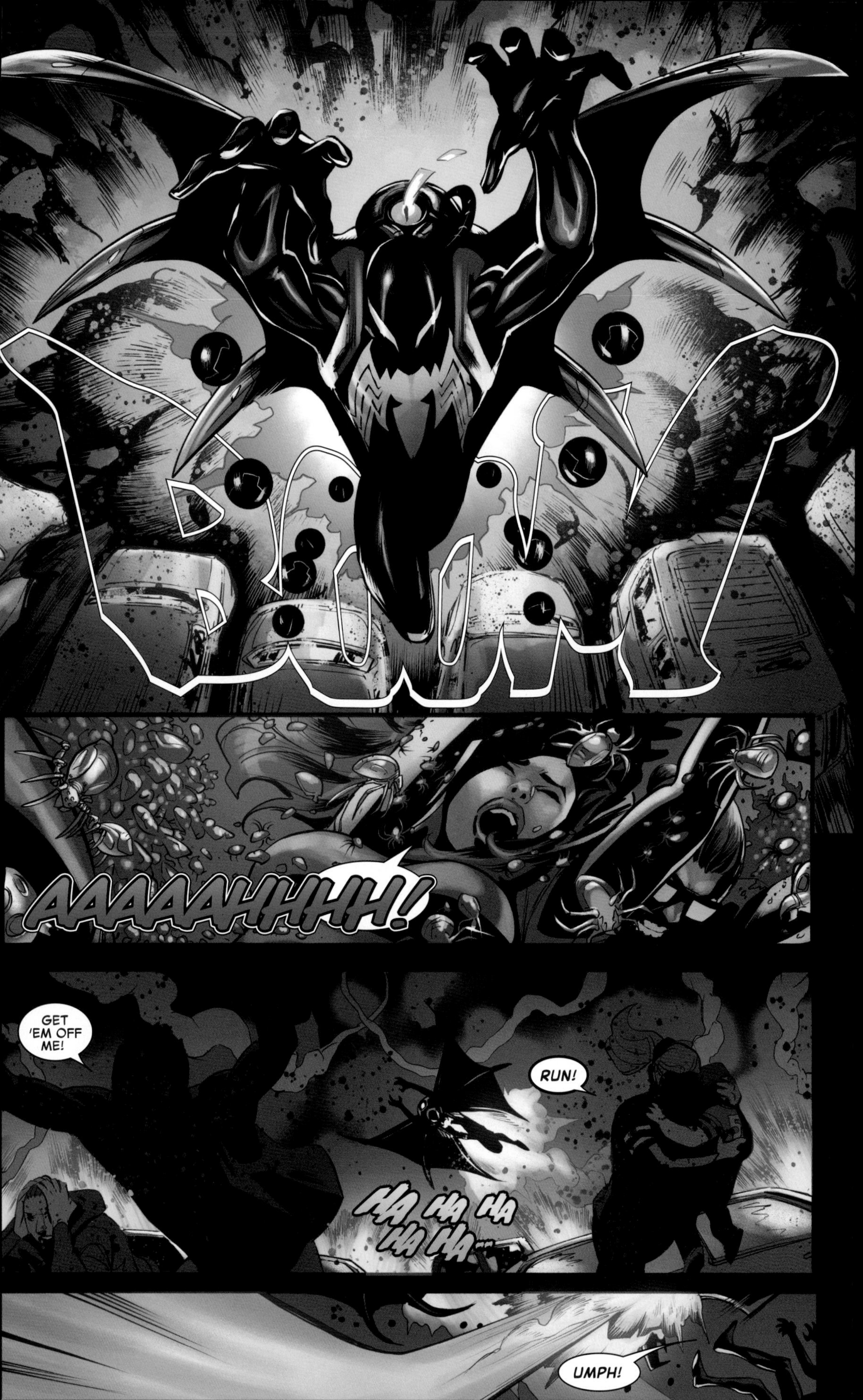
BOOM
AAAAAHHHH!
GET 'EM OFF ME!
RUN!
HA HA HA
HA HA...
UMPH!

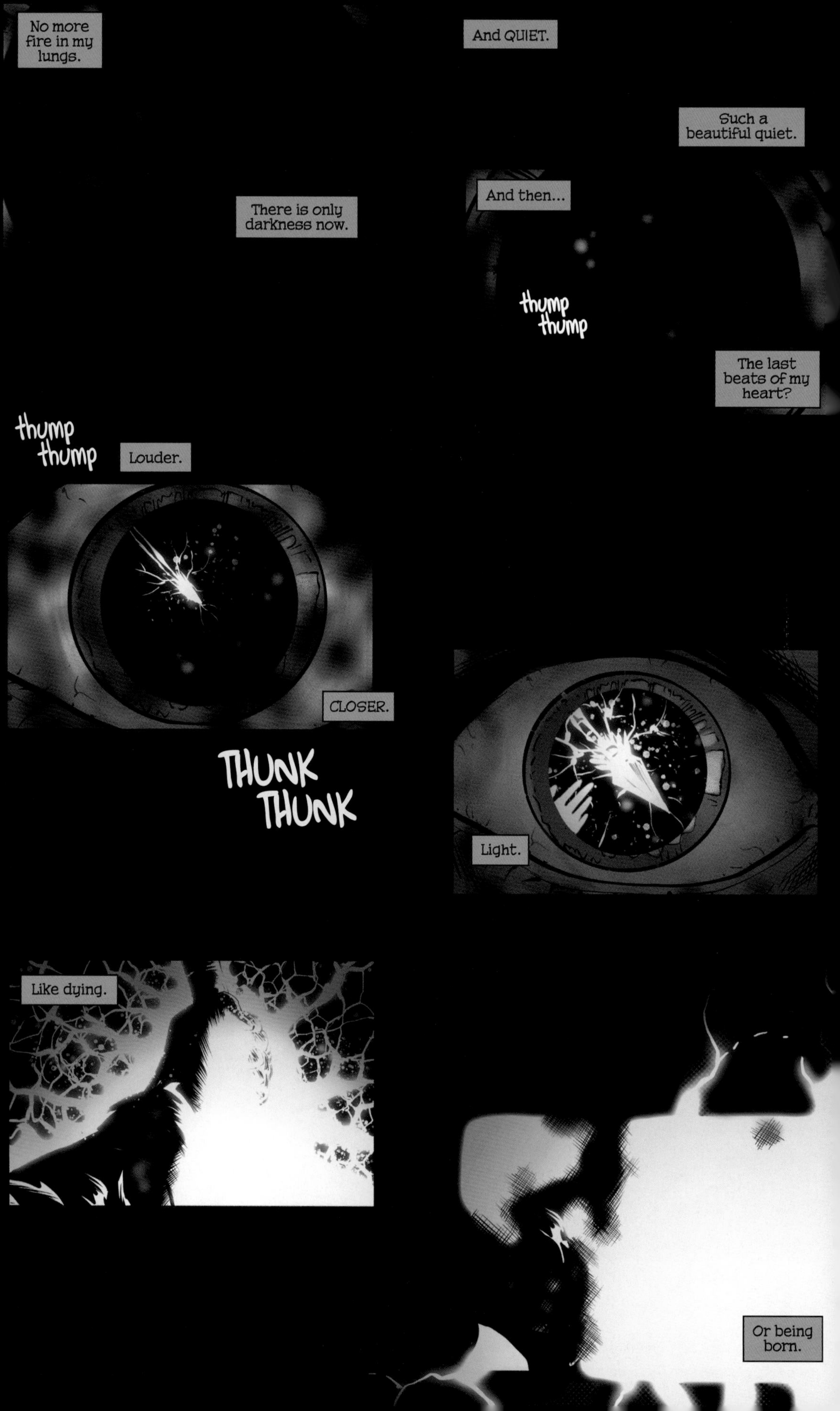
No more fire in my lungs.
There is only darkness now.
And QUIET.
Such a beautiful quiet.
And then...
thump thump
The last beats of my heart?
thump thump
Louder.
CLOSER.
THUNK THUNK
Light.
Like dying.
Or being born.

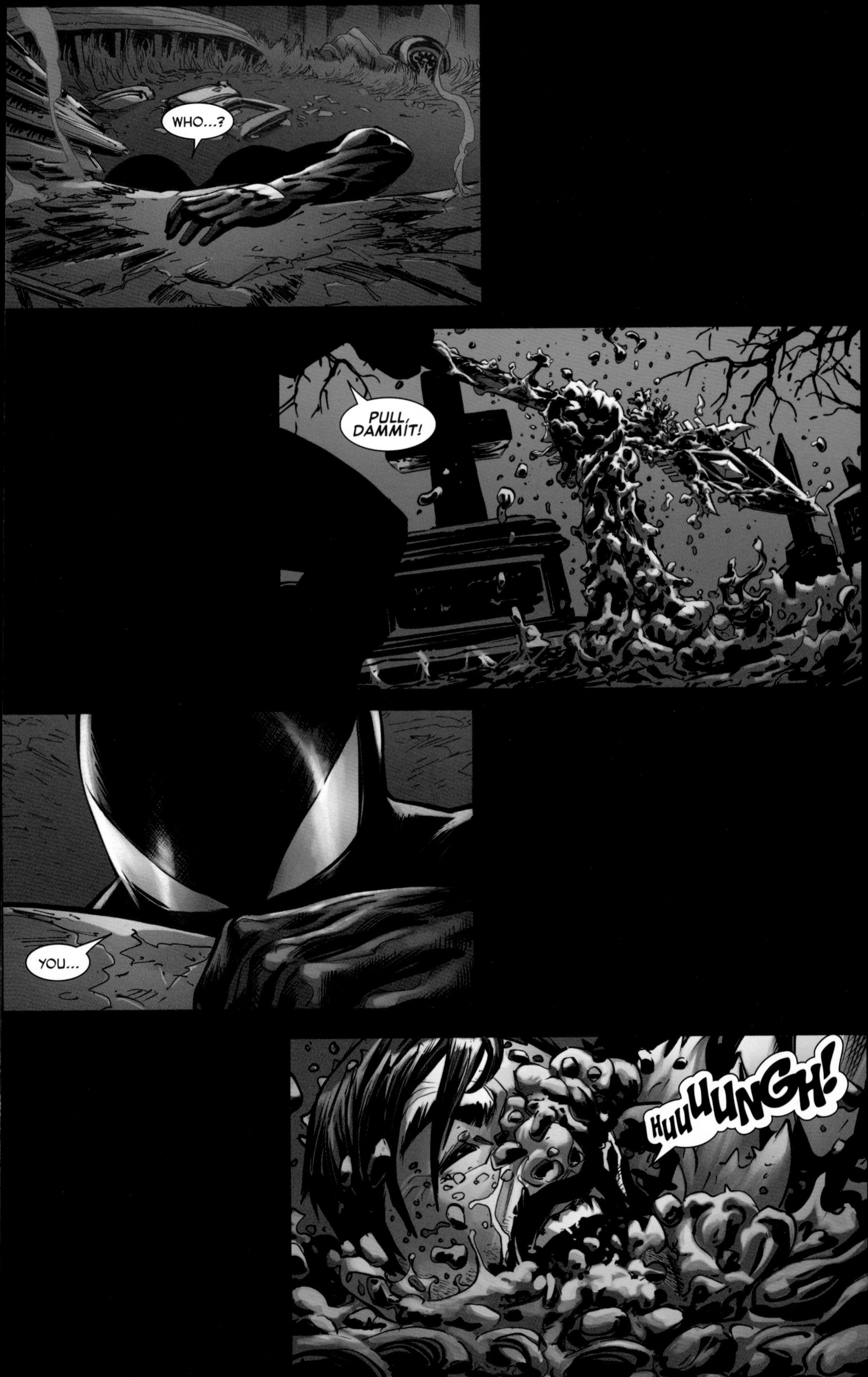
WHO...?
PULL, DAMMIT!
YOU...
HuuUUNGH!

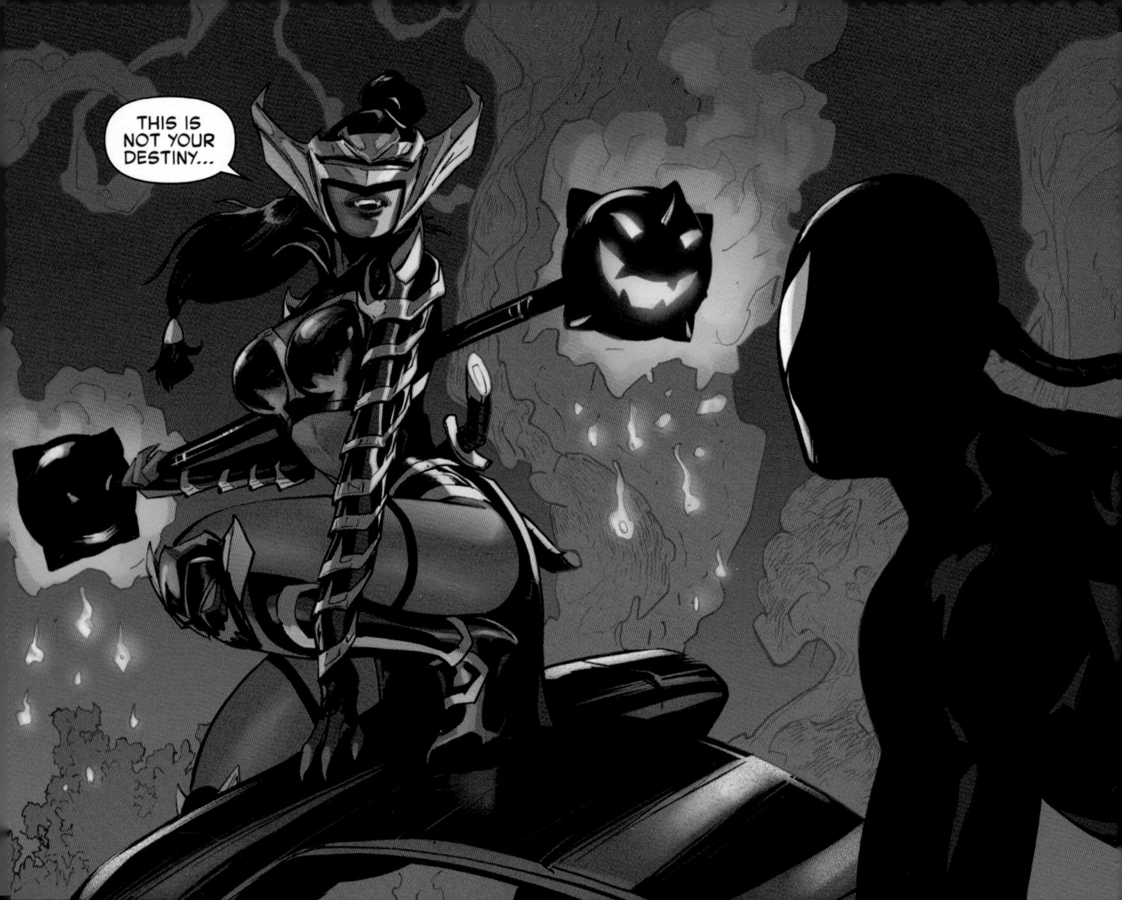
THIS IS NOT YOUR DESTINY...

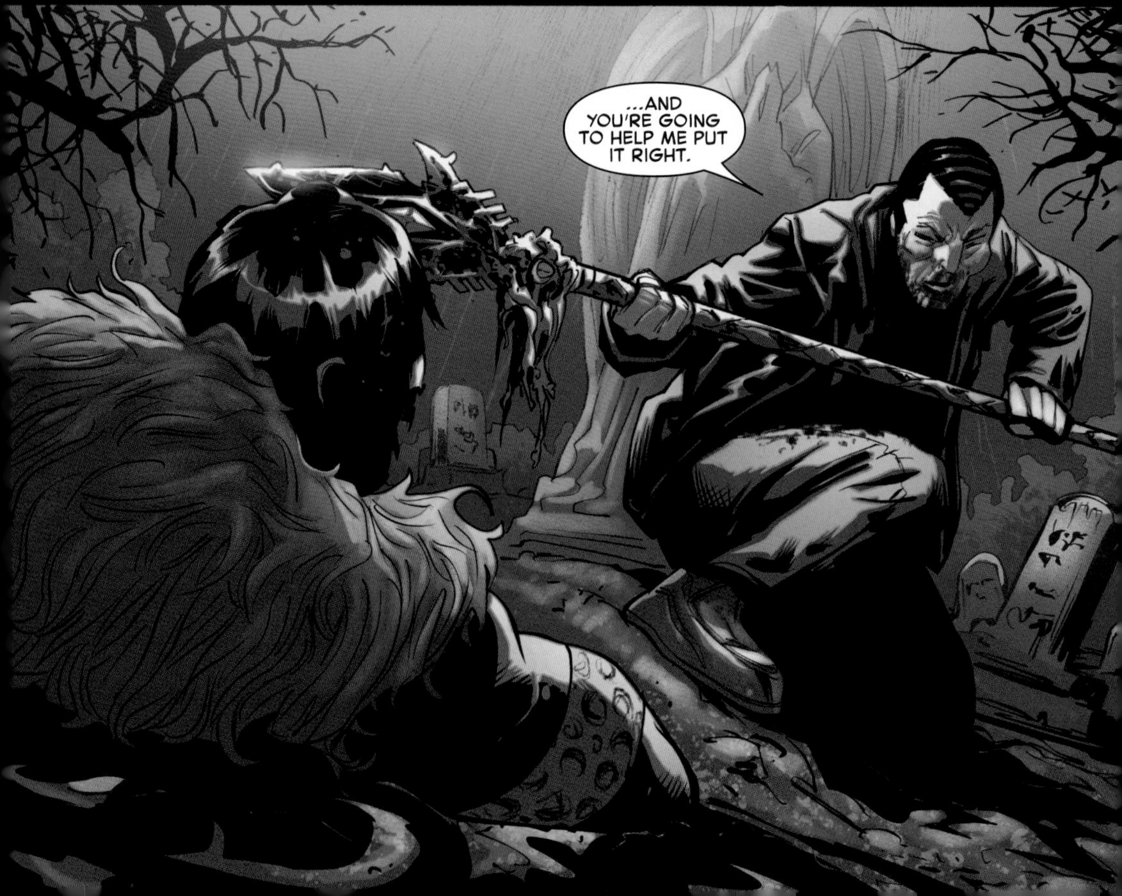
...AND YOU'RE GOING TO HELP ME PUT IT RIGHT.

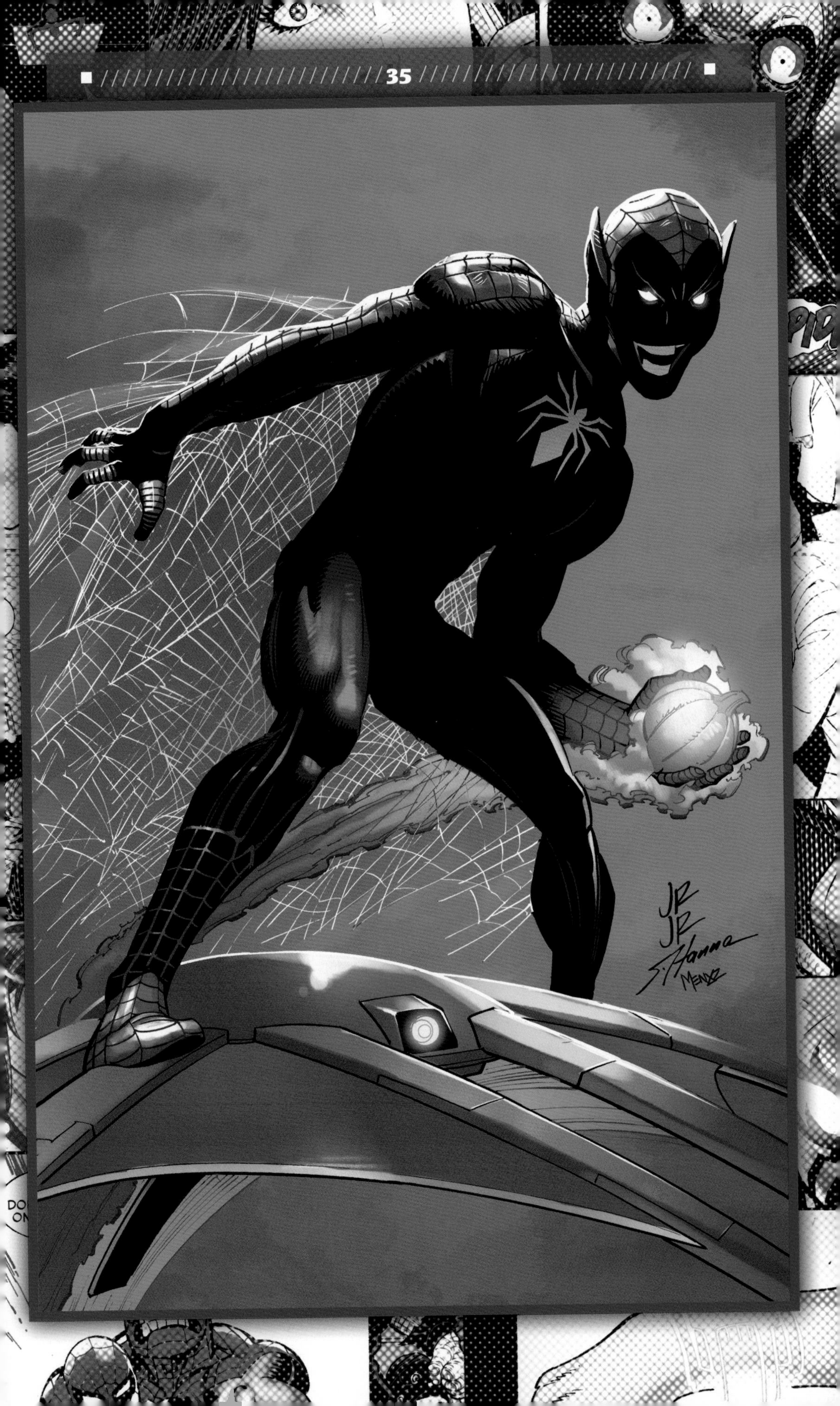

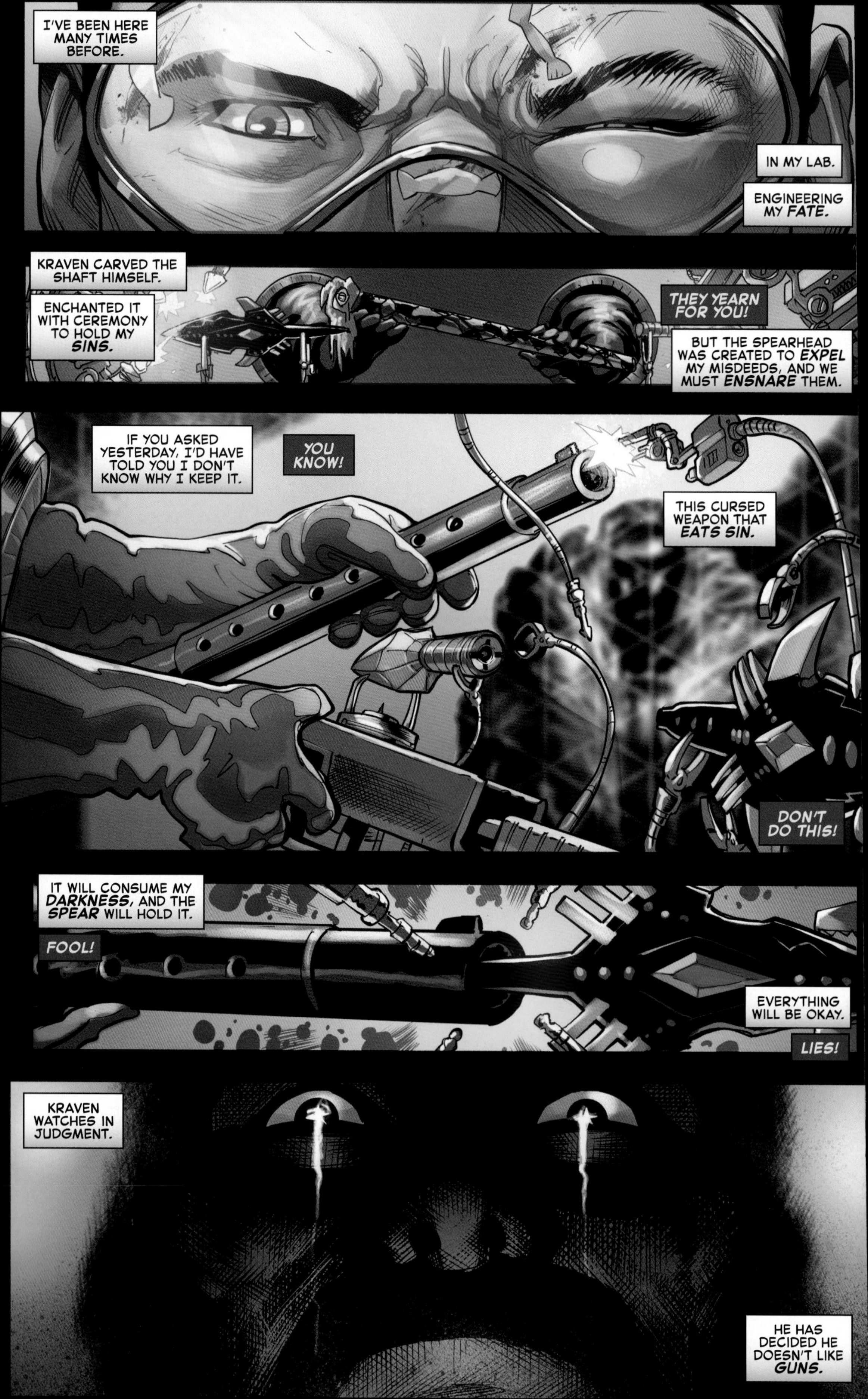
I'VE BEEN HERE MANY TIMES BEFORE.
IN MY LAB.
ENGINEERING MY *FATE.*
KRAVEN CARVED THE SHAFT HIMSELF.
ENCHANTED IT WITH CEREMONY TO HOLD MY *SINS.*
THEY YEARN FOR YOU!
BUT THE SPEARHEAD WAS CREATED TO *EXPEL* MY MISDEEDS, AND WE MUST *ENSNARE* THEM.
IF YOU ASKED YESTERDAY, I'D HAVE TOLD YOU I DON'T KNOW WHY I KEEP IT.
YOU KNOW!
THIS CURSED WEAPON THAT *EATS SIN.*
DON'T DO THIS!
IT WILL CONSUME MY *DARKNESS,* AND THE *SPEAR* WILL HOLD IT.
FOOL!
EVERYTHING WILL BE OKAY.
LIES!
KRAVEN WATCHES IN JUDGMENT.
HE HAS DECIDED HE DOESN'T LIKE *GUNS.*

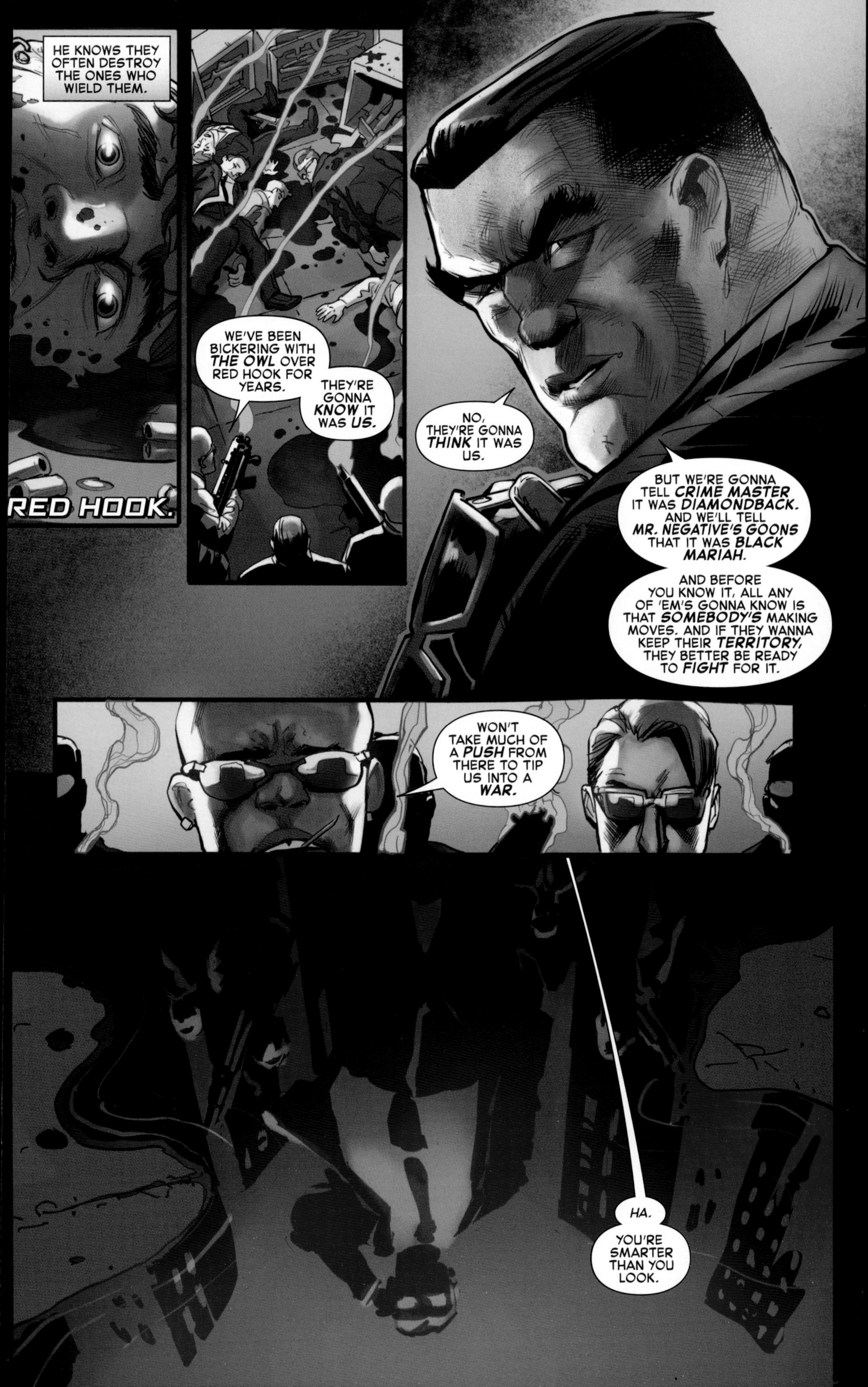

35

HE KNOWS THEY OFTEN DESTROY THE ONES WHO WIELD THEM.
RED HOOK.
WE'VE BEEN BICKERING WITH THE OWL OVER RED HOOK FOR YEARS.
THEY'RE GONNA KNOW IT WAS US.
NO, THEY'RE GONNA THINK IT WAS US.
BUT WE'RE GONNA TELL CRIME MASTER IT WAS DIAMONDBACK. AND WE'LL TELL MR. NEGATIVE'S GOONS THAT IT WAS BLACK MARIAH.
AND BEFORE YOU KNOW IT, ALL ANY OF 'EM'S GONNA KNOW IS THAT SOMEBODY'S MAKING MOVES. AND IF THEY WANNA KEEP THEIR TERRITORY, THEY BETTER BE READY TO FIGHT FOR IT.
WON'T TAKE MUCH OF A PUSH FROM THERE TO TIP US INTO A WAR.
HA.
YOU'RE SMARTER THAN YOU LOOK.

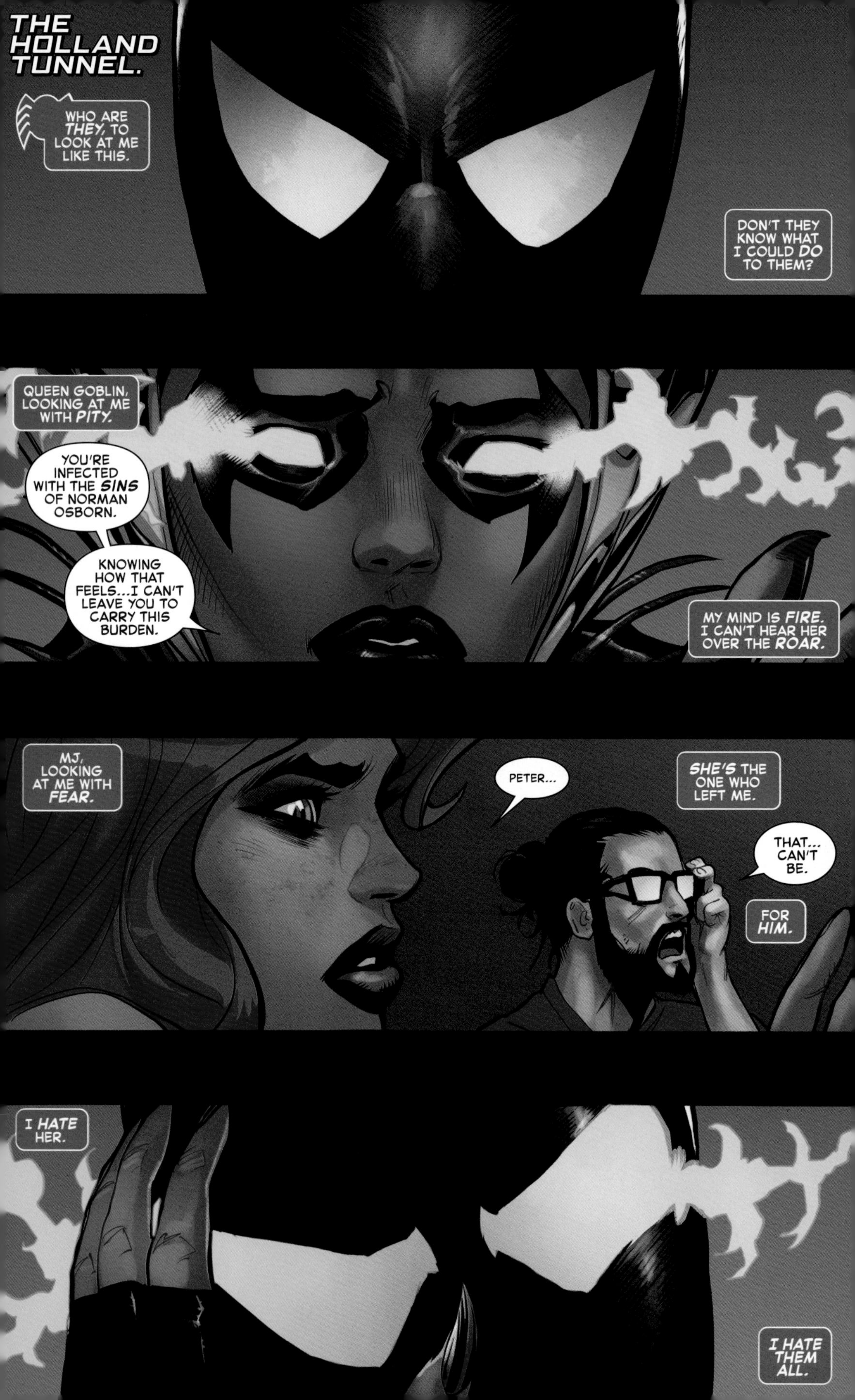
THE HOLLAND TUNNEL.
WHO ARE THEY, TO LOOK AT ME LIKE THIS.
DON'T THEY KNOW WHAT I COULD DO TO THEM?
QUEEN GOBLIN, LOOKING AT ME WITH PITY.
YOU'RE INFECTED WITH THE SINS OF NORMAN OSBORN.
KNOWING HOW THAT FEELS...I CAN'T LEAVE YOU TO CARRY THIS BURDEN.
MY MIND IS FIRE. I CAN'T HEAR HER OVER THE ROAR.
MJ, LOOKING AT ME WITH FEAR.
PETER...
SHE'S THE ONE WHO LEFT ME.
THAT... CAN'T BE.
FOR HIM.
I HATE HER.
I HATE THEM ALL.

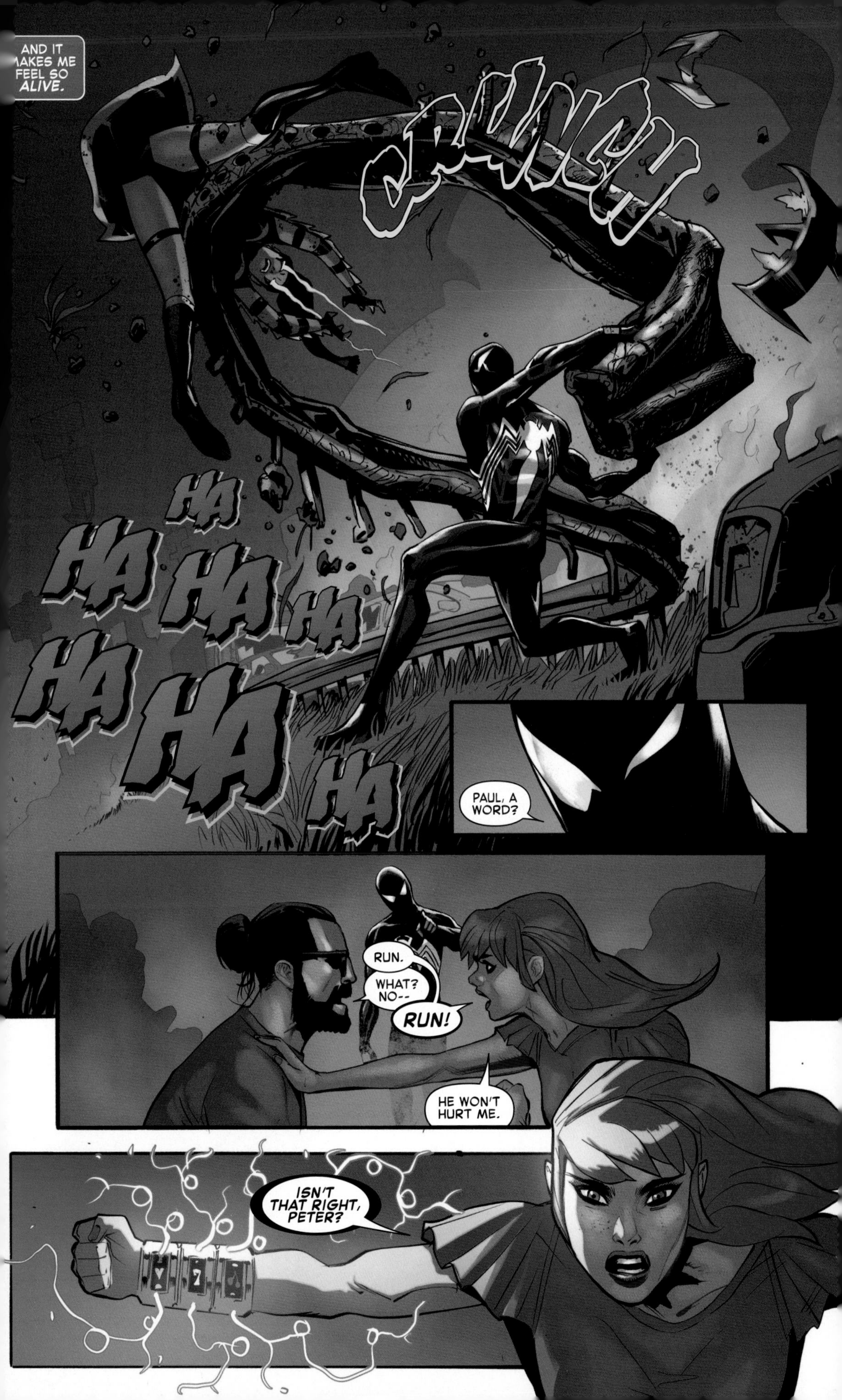
AND IT MAKES ME FEEL SO *ALIVE.*
CRUNCH
HA
HA HA HA
HA HA HA
HA
PAUL, A WORD?
RUN.
WHAT? NO--
RUN!
HE WON'T HURT ME.
ISN'T THAT RIGHT, PETER?

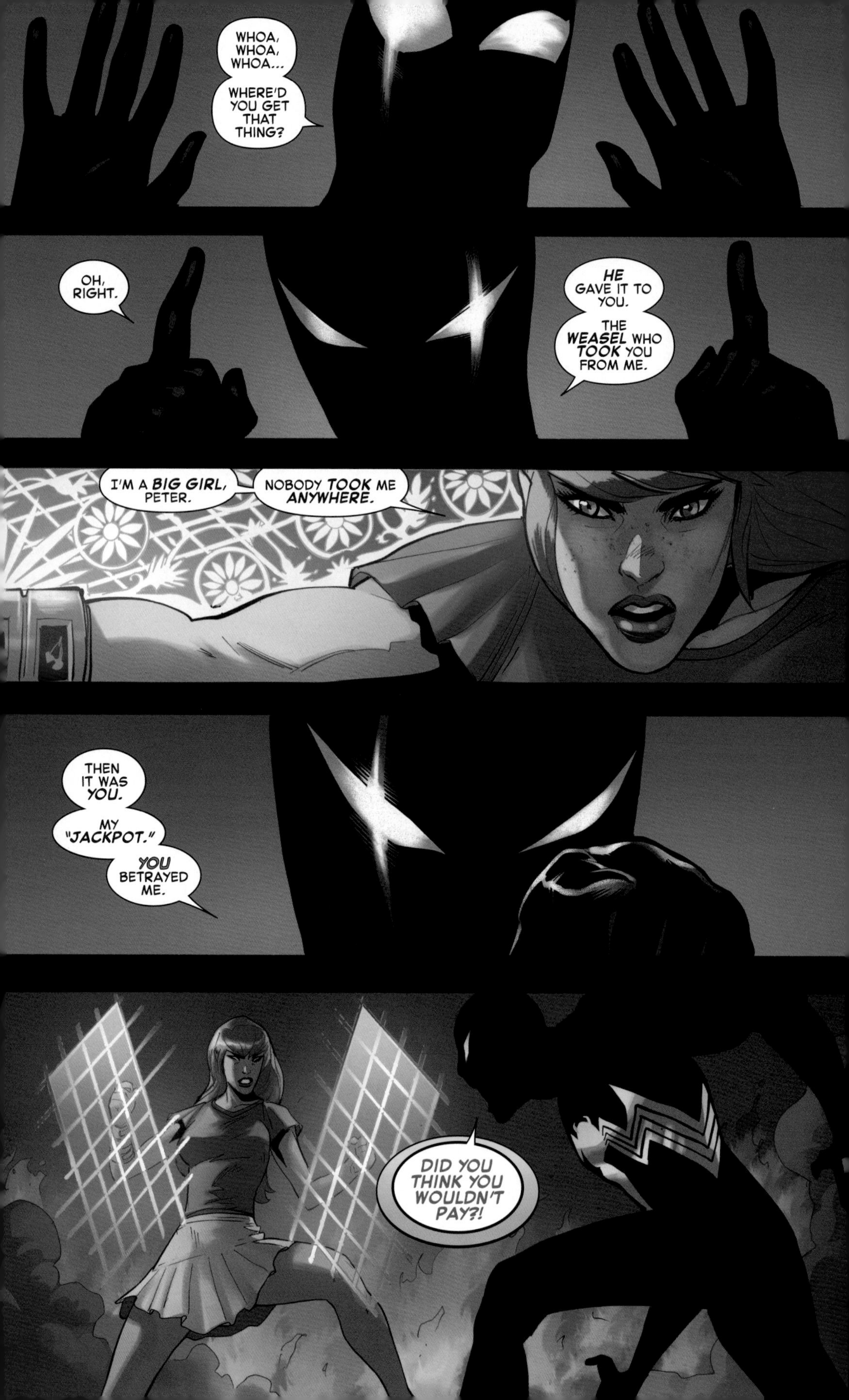
WHOA, WHOA, WHOA...
WHERE'D YOU GET THAT THING?
OH, RIGHT.
HE GAVE IT TO YOU.
THE WEASEL WHO TOOK YOU FROM ME.
I'M A BIG GIRL, PETER.
NOBODY TOOK ME ANYWHERE.
THEN IT WAS YOU.
MY "JACKPOT."
YOU BETRAYED ME.
DID YOU THINK YOU WOULDN'T PAY?!

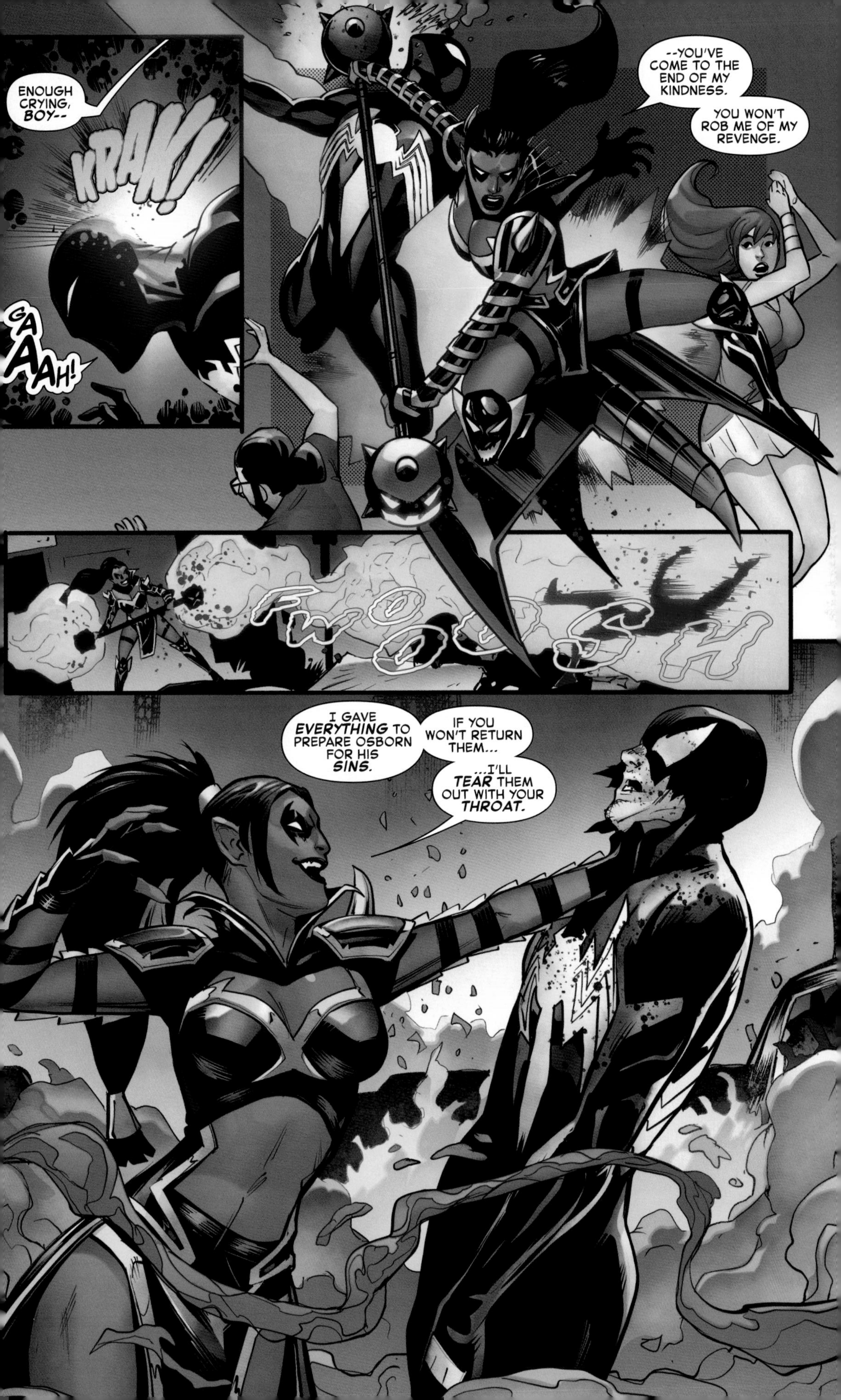

ENOUGH CRYING, BOY--
KRAM!
GAAAH!
--YOU'VE COME TO THE END OF MY KINDNESS.
YOU WON'T ROB ME OF MY REVENGE.
FWOOOSH
I GAVE EVERYTHING TO PREPARE OSBORN FOR HIS SINS.
IF YOU WON'T RETURN THEM...
...I'LL TEAR THEM OUT WITH YOUR THROAT.

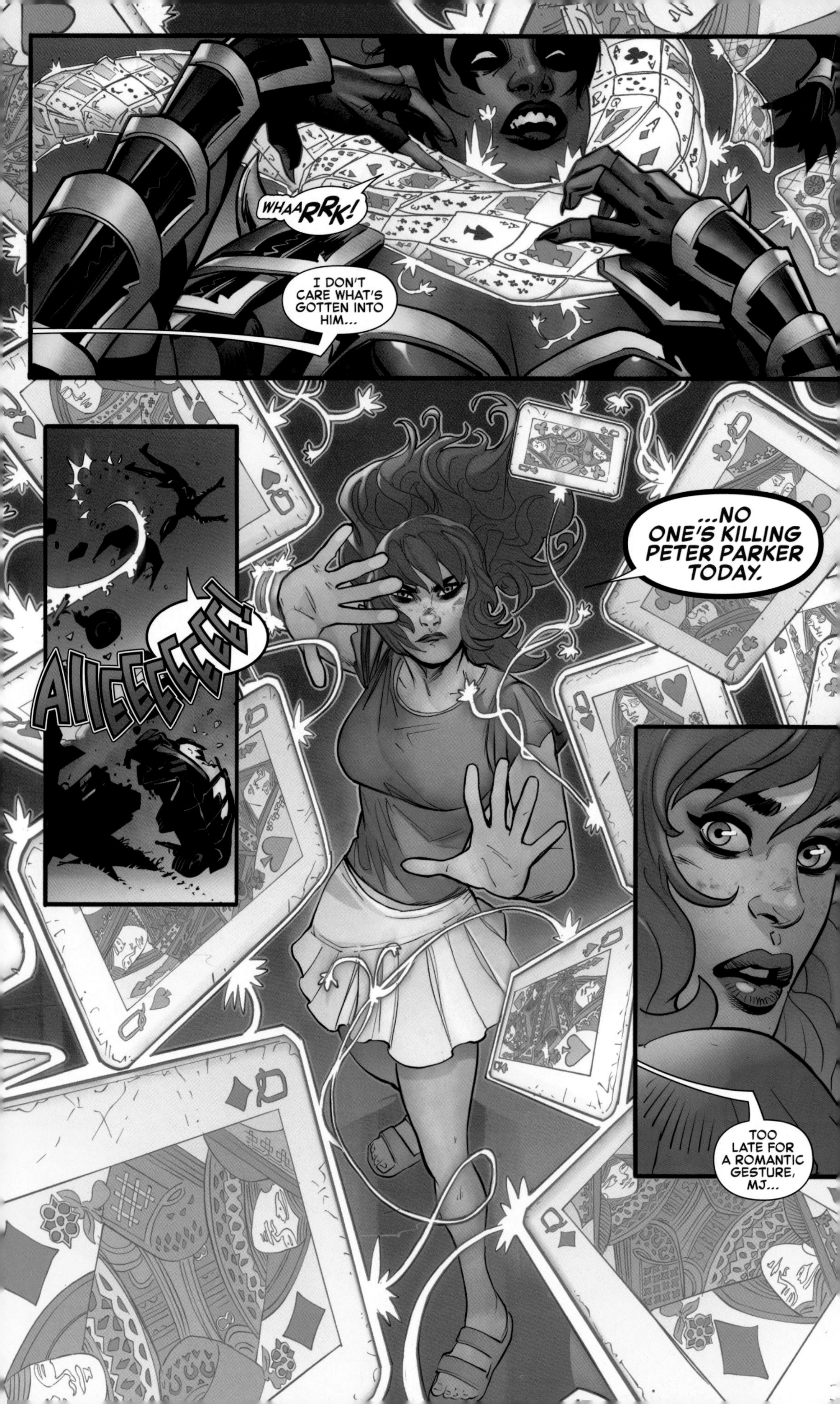
WHAARRK!
I DON'T CARE WHAT'S GOTTEN INTO HIM...
AIIEEEEEE!
...NO ONE'S KILLING PETER PARKER TODAY.
TOO LATE FOR A ROMANTIC GESTURE, MJ...

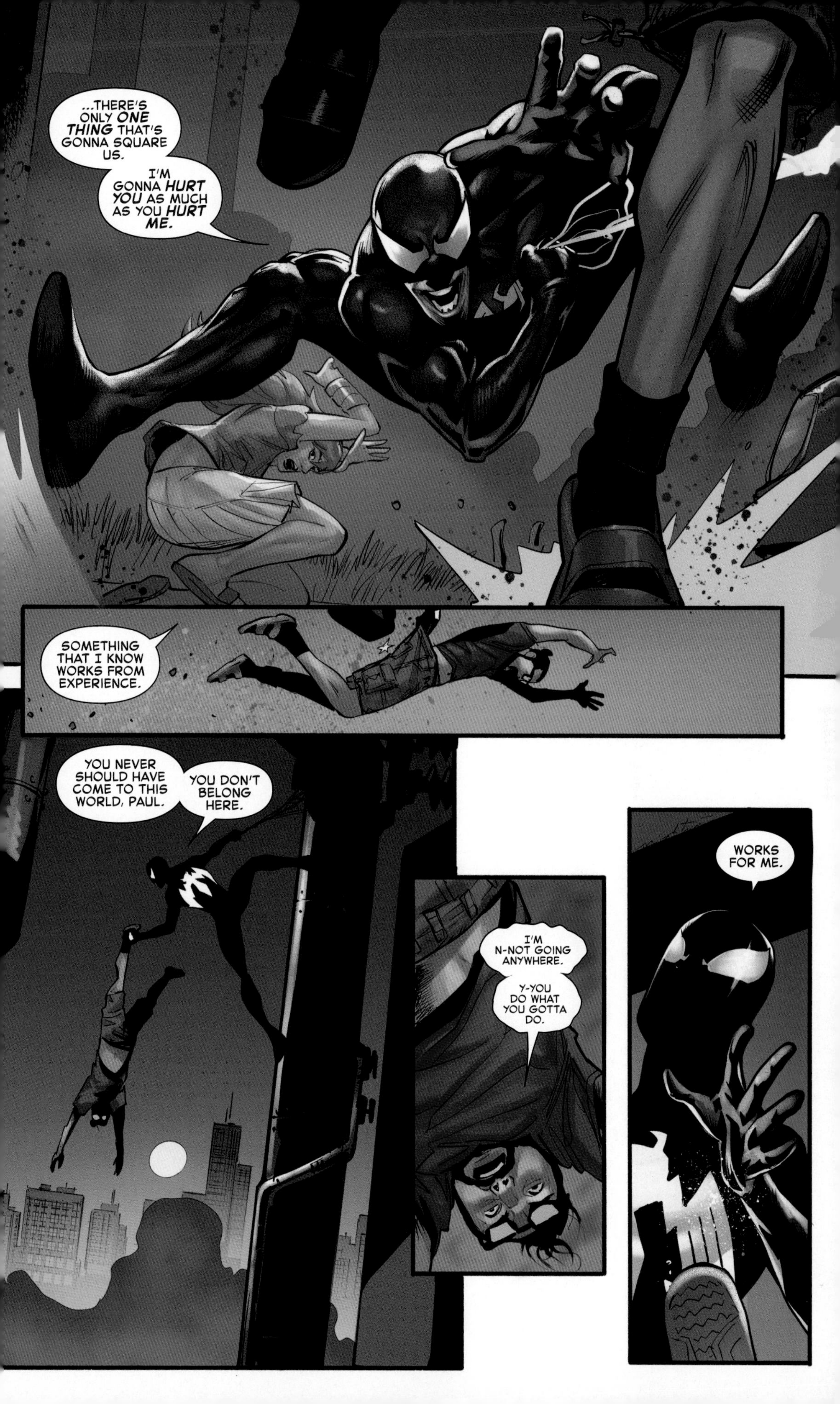

...THERE'S ONLY ONE THING THAT'S GONNA SQUARE US.
I'M GONNA HURT YOU AS MUCH AS YOU HURT ME.
SOMETHING THAT I KNOW WORKS FROM EXPERIENCE.
YOU NEVER SHOULD HAVE COME TO THIS WORLD, PAUL.
YOU DON'T BELONG HERE.
I'M N-NOT GOING ANYWHERE.
Y-YOU DO WHAT YOU GOTTA DO.
WORKS FOR ME.

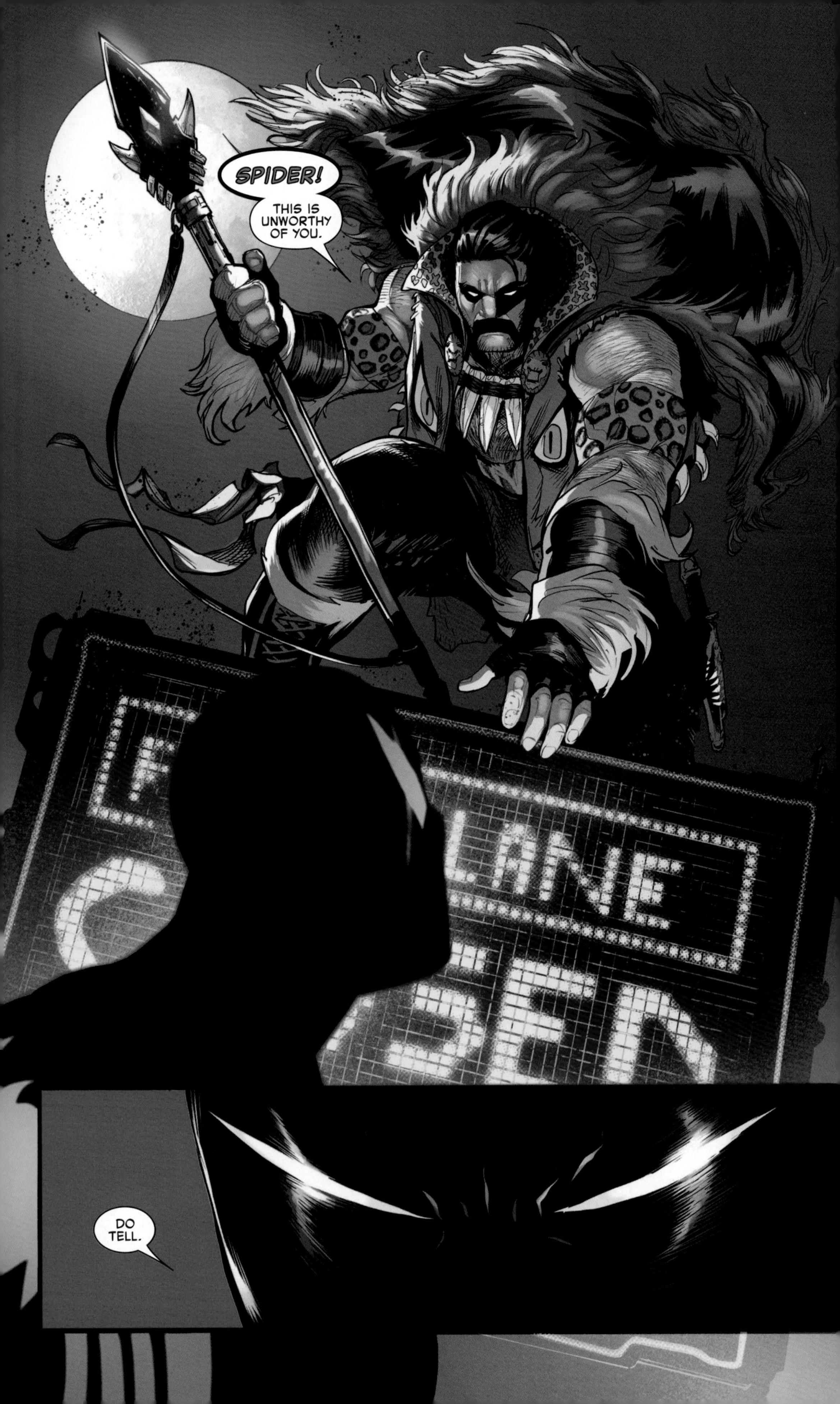

SPIDER!
THIS IS UNWORTHY OF YOU.
LANE
DO TELL.

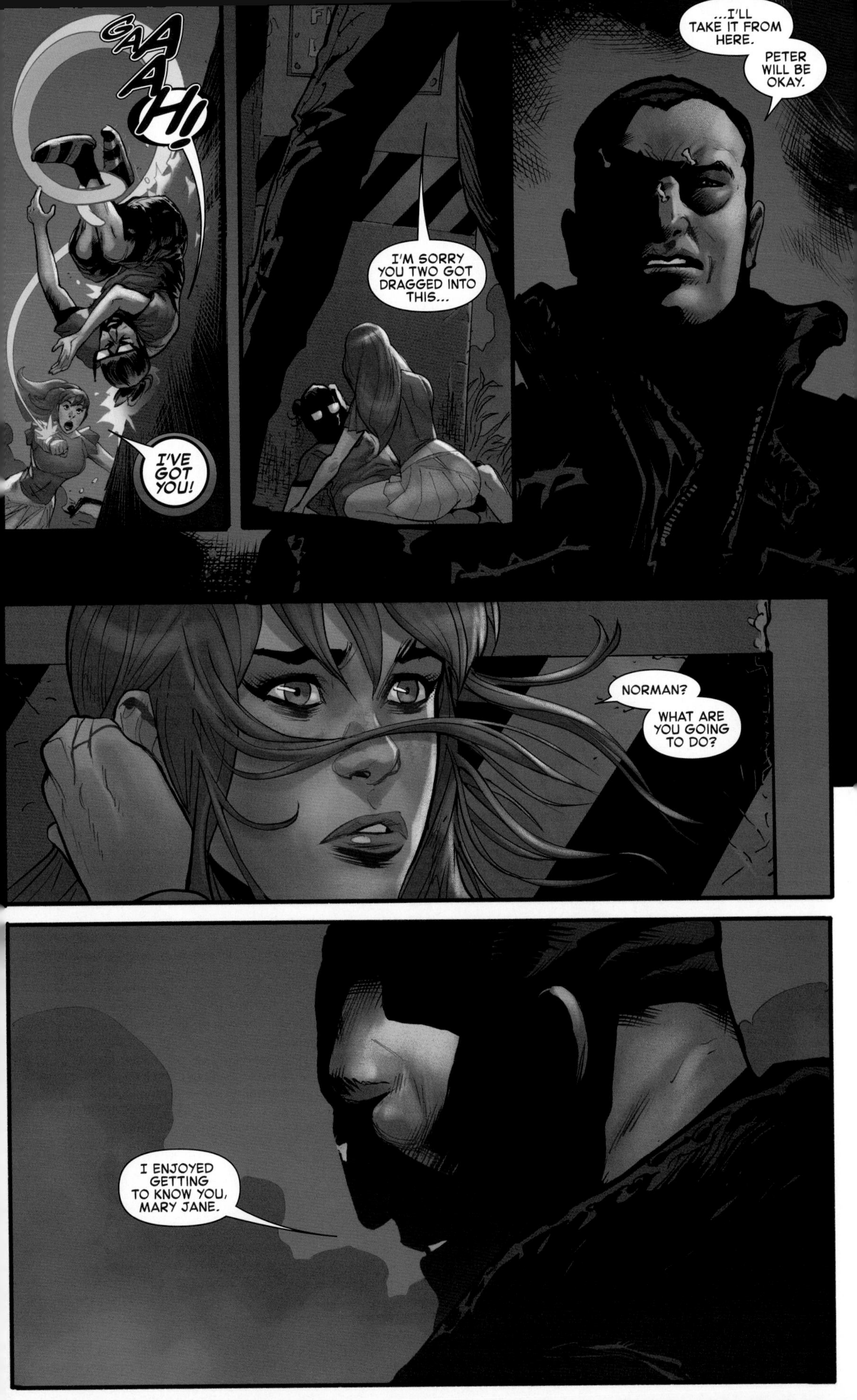
GAAAH!
I'VE GOT YOU!
I'M SORRY YOU TWO GOT DRAGGED INTO THIS...
...I'LL TAKE IT FROM HERE.
PETER WILL BE OKAY.
NORMAN?
WHAT ARE YOU GOING TO DO?
I ENJOYED GETTING TO KNOW YOU, MARY JANE.

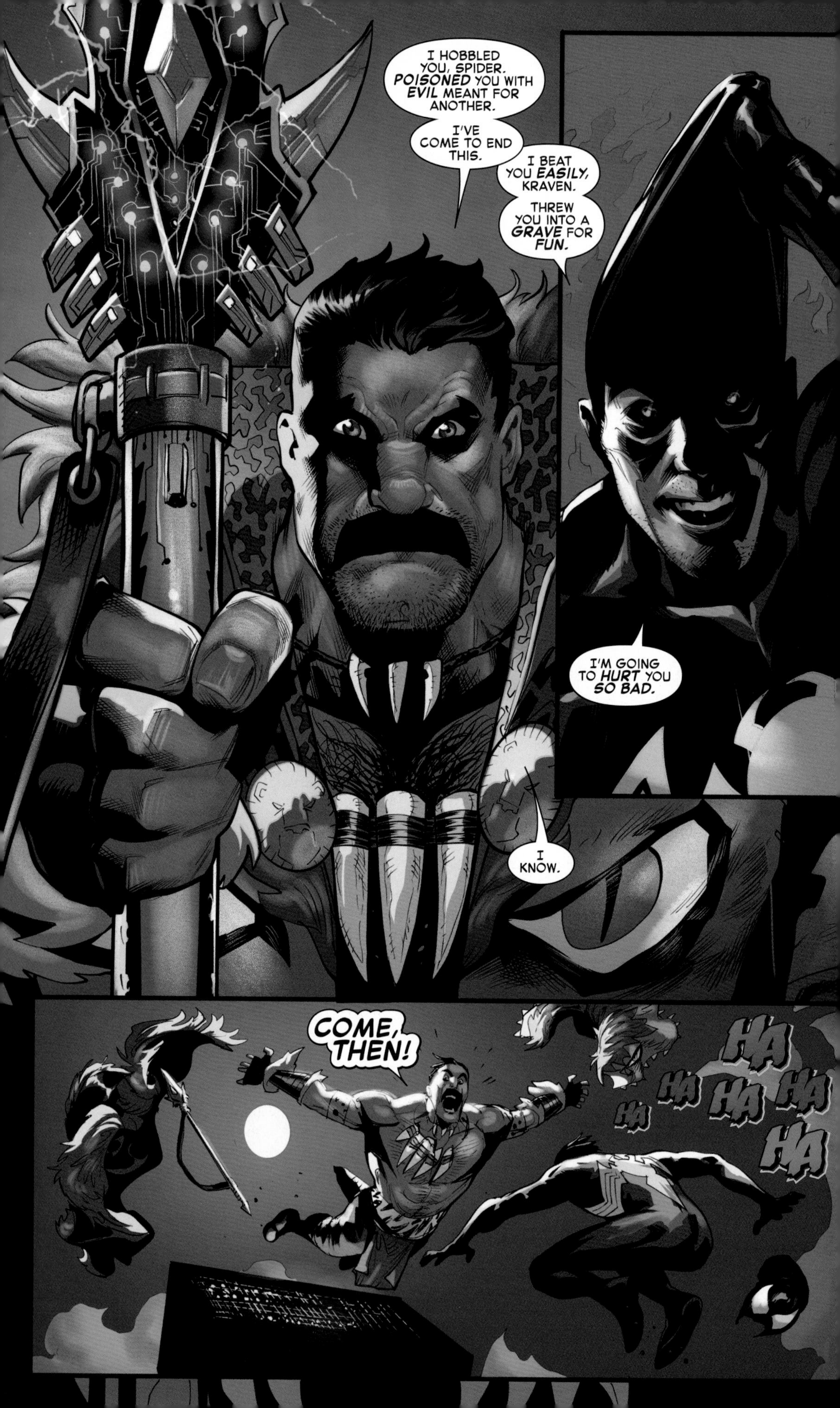
I HOBBLED YOU, SPIDER. POISONED YOU WITH EVIL MEANT FOR ANOTHER.
I'VE COME TO END THIS.
I BEAT YOU EASILY, KRAVEN.
THREW YOU INTO A GRAVE FOR FUN.
I'M GOING TO HURT YOU SO BAD.
I KNOW.
COME, THEN!
HA HA HA HA HA HA HA

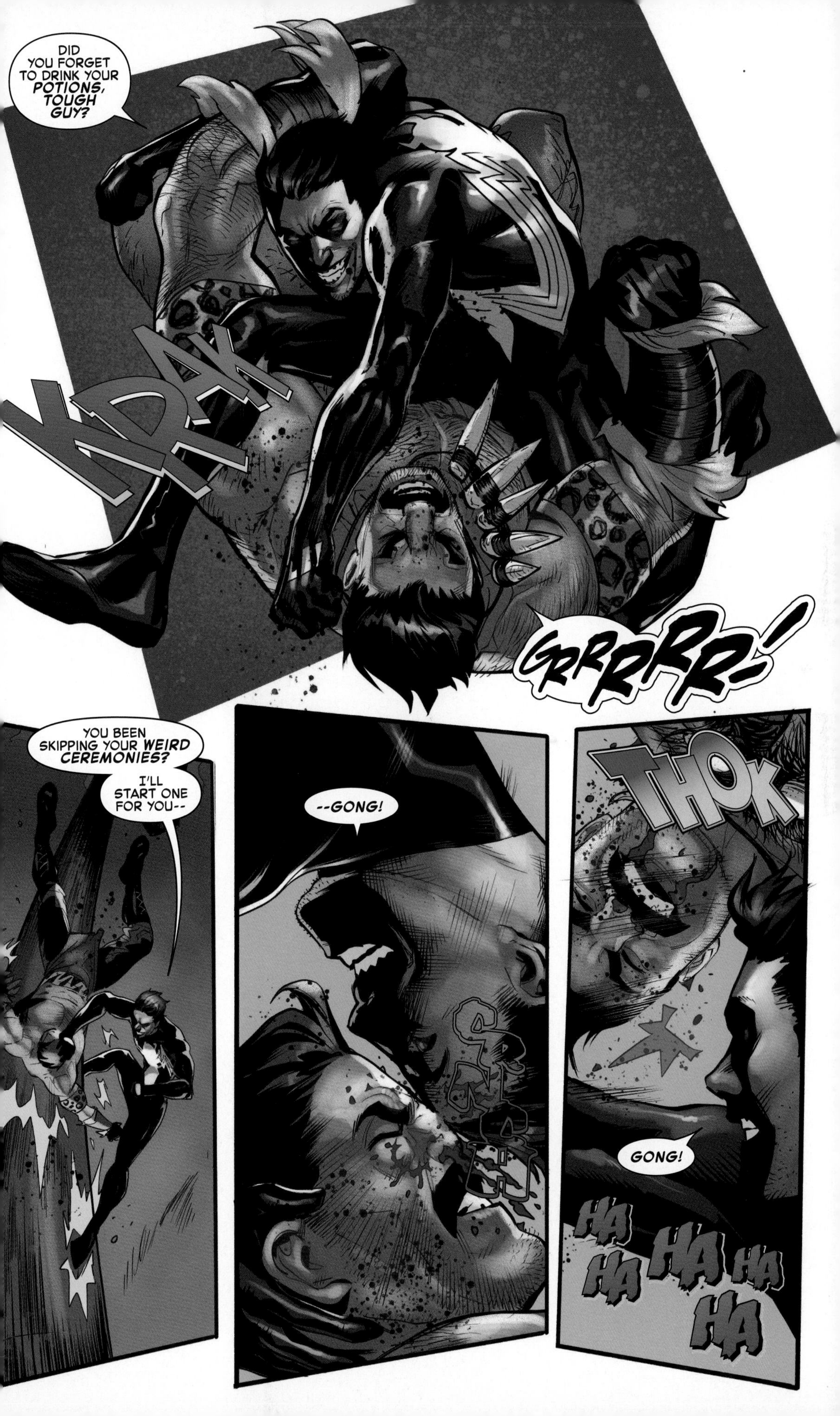
DID YOU FORGET TO DRINK YOUR POTIONS, TOUGH GUY?
KRAK
GRRRRR!
YOU BEEN SKIPPING YOUR WEIRD CEREMONIES?
I'LL START ONE FOR YOU--
--GONG!
THOK
GONG!
HA HA HA HA HA HA

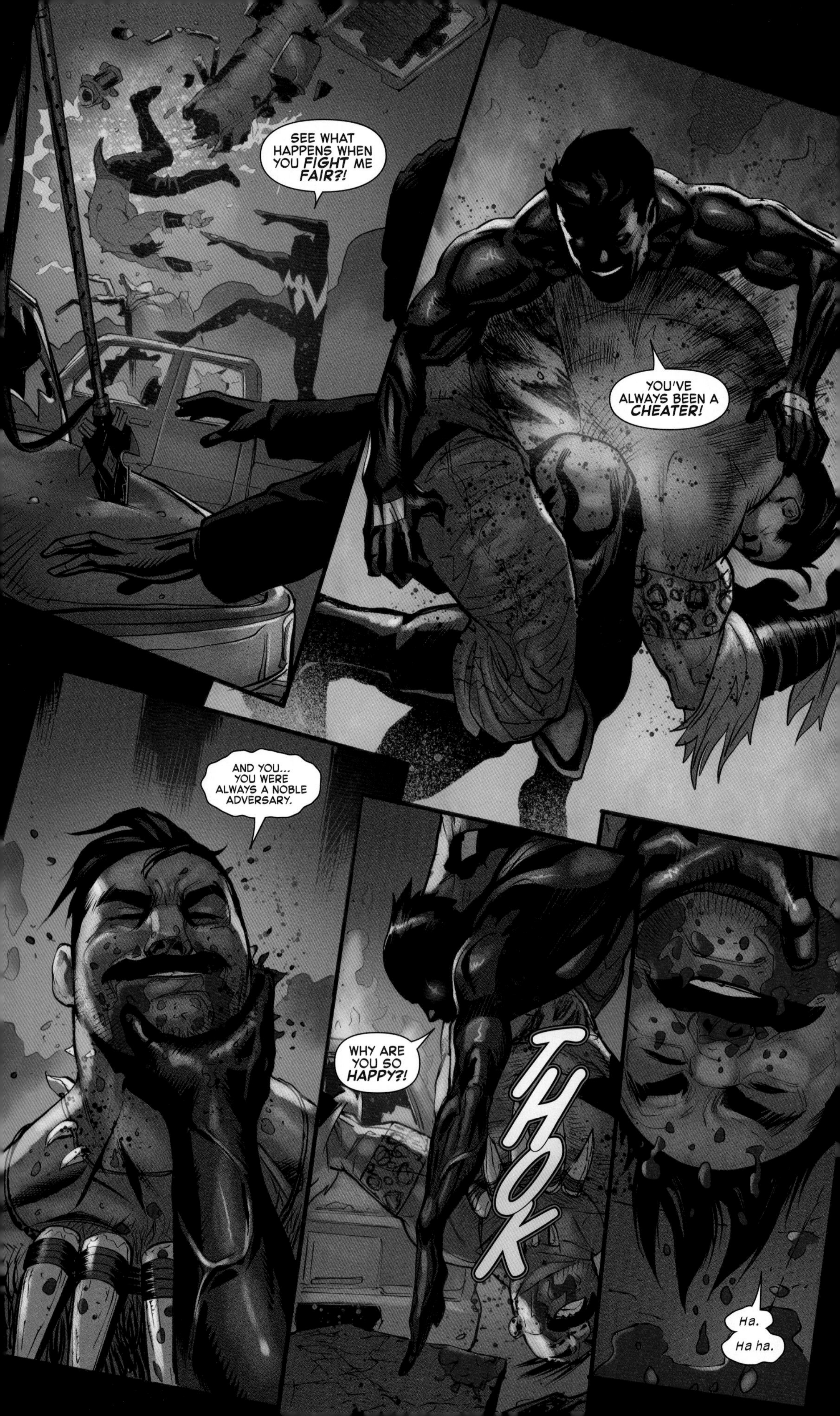
SEE WHAT HAPPENS WHEN YOU *FIGHT* ME *FAIR?!*
YOU'VE ALWAYS BEEN A *CHEATER!*
AND YOU... YOU WERE ALWAYS A NOBLE ADVERSARY.
WHY ARE YOU SO *HAPPY?!*
THOK
Ha.
Ha ha.

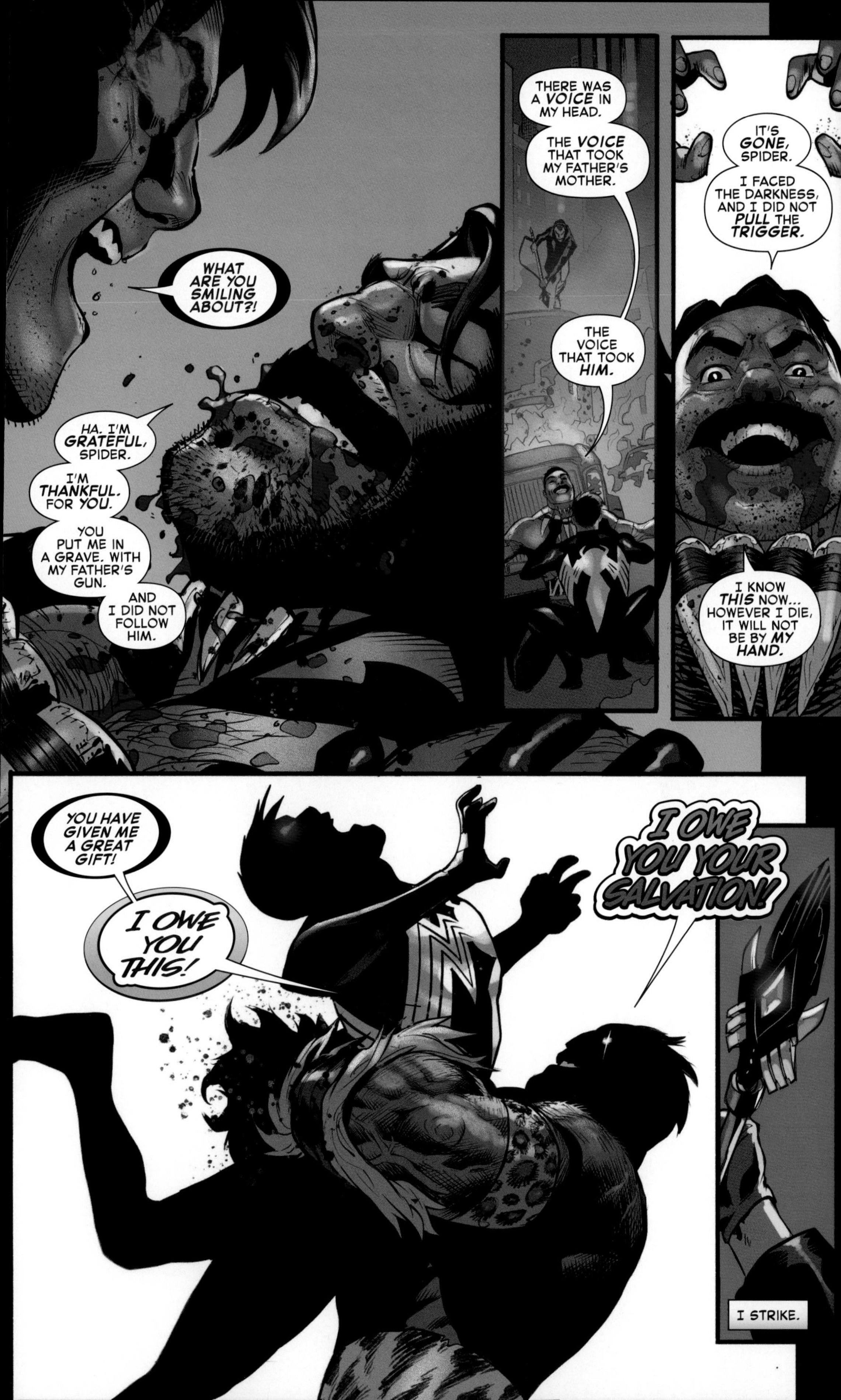

WHAT ARE YOU SMILING ABOUT?!
HA. I'M GRATEFUL, SPIDER.
I'M THANKFUL. FOR YOU.
YOU PUT ME IN A GRAVE. WITH MY FATHER'S GUN.
AND I DID NOT FOLLOW HIM.
THERE WAS A VOICE IN MY HEAD.
THE VOICE THAT TOOK MY FATHER'S MOTHER.
THE VOICE THAT TOOK HIM.
IT'S GONE, SPIDER.
I FACED THE DARKNESS, AND I DID NOT PULL THE TRIGGER.
I KNOW THIS NOW... HOWEVER I DIE, IT WILL NOT BE BY MY HAND.
YOU HAVE GIVEN ME A GREAT GIFT!
I OWE YOU THIS!
I OWE YOU YOUR SALVATION!
I STRIKE.

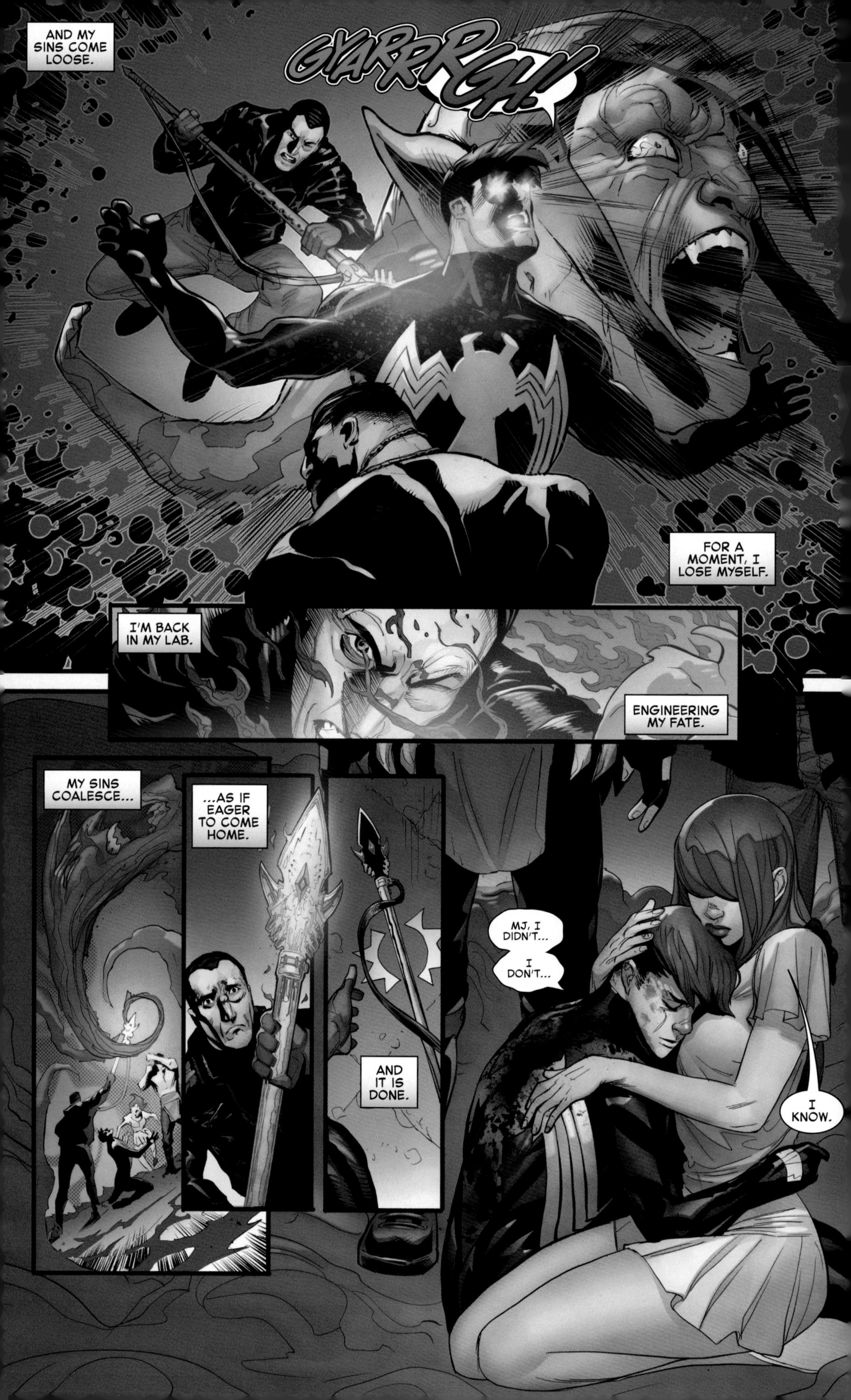
AND MY SINS COME LOOSE.
GYARRRGH!!
FOR A MOMENT, I LOSE MYSELF.
I'M BACK IN MY LAB.
ENGINEERING MY FATE.
MY SINS COALESCE...
...AS IF EAGER TO COME HOME.
AND IT IS DONE.
MJ, I DIDN'T...
I DON'T...
I KNOW.

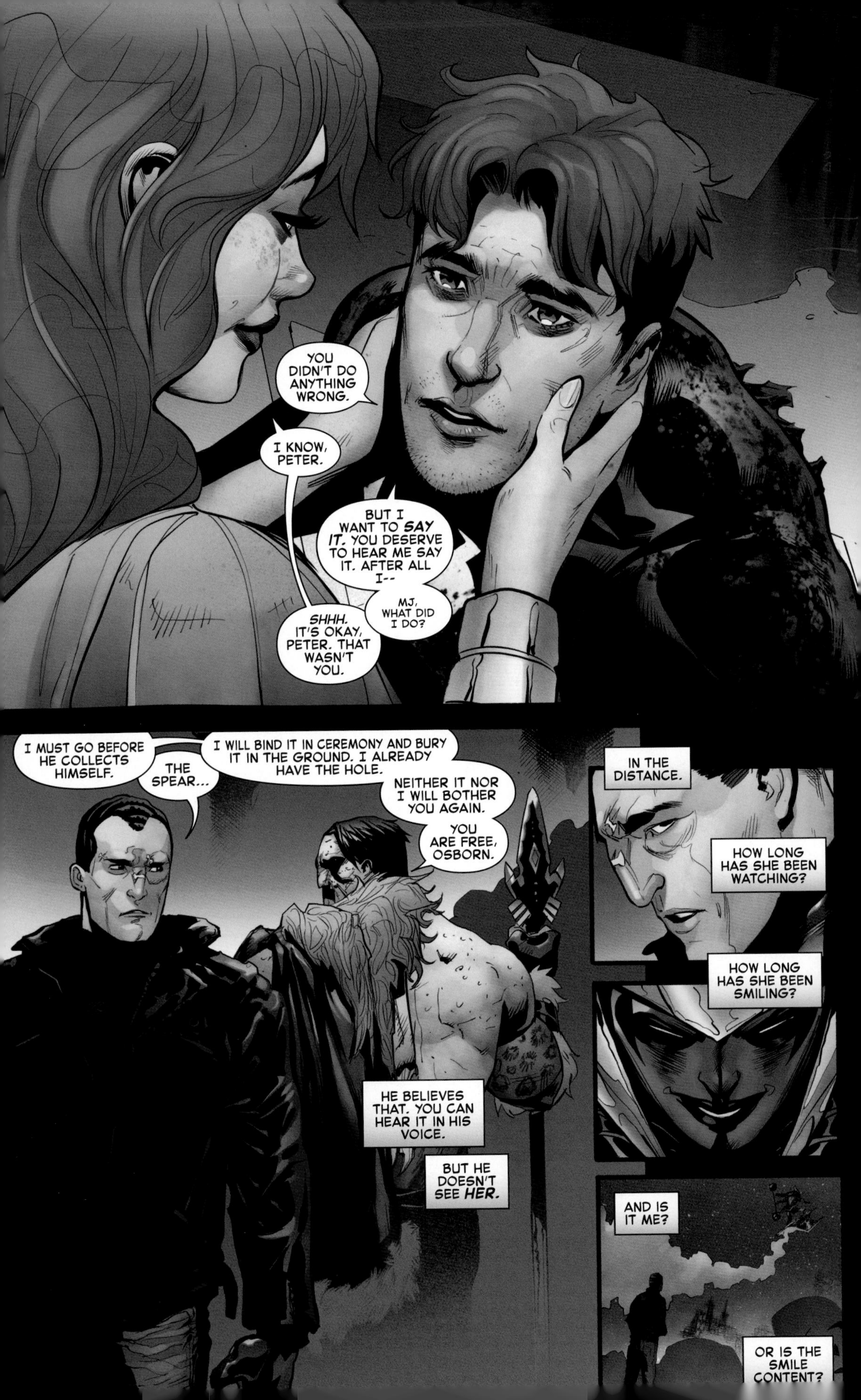
YOU DIDN'T DO ANYTHING WRONG.
I KNOW, PETER.
BUT I WANT TO SAY IT. YOU DESERVE TO HEAR ME SAY IT. AFTER ALL I--
MJ, WHAT DID I DO?
SHHH. IT'S OKAY, PETER. THAT WASN'T YOU.
I MUST GO BEFORE HE COLLECTS HIMSELF.
THE SPEAR...
I WILL BIND IT IN CEREMONY AND BURY IT IN THE GROUND. I ALREADY HAVE THE HOLE.
NEITHER IT NOR I WILL BOTHER YOU AGAIN.
YOU ARE FREE, OSBORN.
HE BELIEVES THAT. YOU CAN HEAR IT IN HIS VOICE.
BUT HE DOESN'T SEE HER.
IN THE DISTANCE.
HOW LONG HAS SHE BEEN WATCHING?
HOW LONG HAS SHE BEEN SMILING?
AND IS IT ME?
OR IS THE SMILE CONTENT?

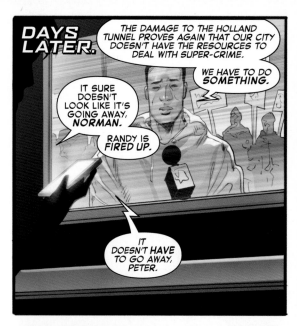

DAYS LATER.

THE DAMAGE TO THE HOLLAND TUNNEL PROVES AGAIN THAT OUR CITY DOESN'T HAVE THE RESOURCES TO DEAL WITH SUPER-CRIME.

WE HAVE TO DO SOMETHING.

IT SURE DOESN'T LOOK LIKE IT'S GOING AWAY, NORMAN.

RANDY IS FIRED UP.

IT DOESN'T HAVE TO GO AWAY, PETER.

IT JUST HAS TO GO AWAY FROM YOU. LUCKILY, YOU WERE WEARING A COSTUME THAT'S BECOME ASSOCIATED WITH ONE BROCK OR ANOTHER.

THEY'LL NEVER KNOW IT WAS YOU.

BUT IT WAS.

NO, PETER. IT WASN'T. I KNOW THAT MORE THAN ANYONE.

TAKE SOME TIME OFF. GET SOME REST.

TIME OFF?

I DON'T KNOW, NORMAN.

I'VE FOUND THERE'S ONLY ONE CURE FOR A GUILTY CONSCIENCE.

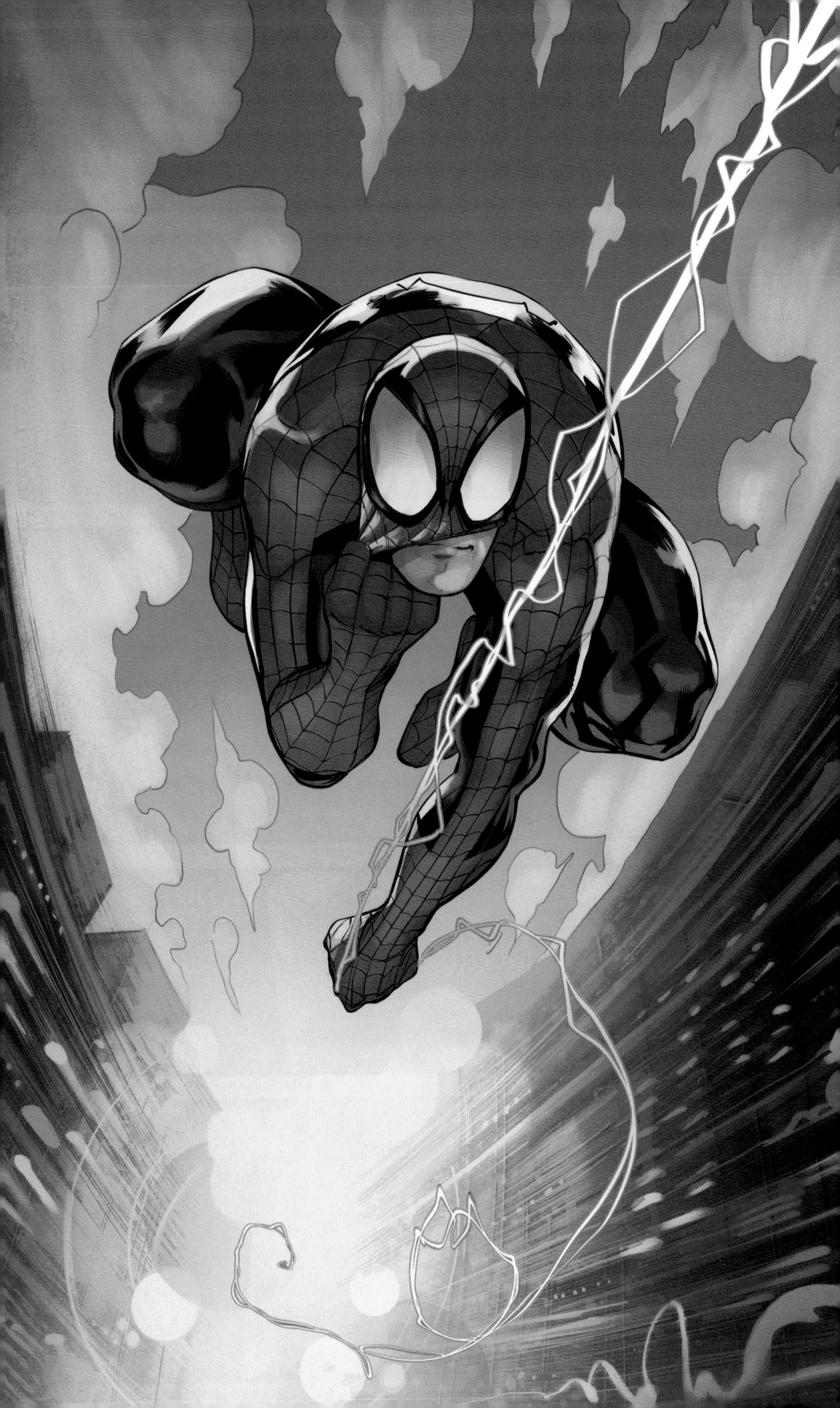

I DID WHAT I HAD TO DO.

MY SINS ARE NO LONGER IN PETER.

THE SPEAR WAS MADE TO HOLD THEM, BUT...

SAY IT!

...BUT...

...I KNEW IT WOULDN'T.

THE SPEAR IS NOT THEIR *HOME*.

I AM!

I HAD TO *SAVE* PETER.

I DIDN'T HAVE *TIME*.

BUT I KNEW...

...IF GIVEN THE CHANCE...

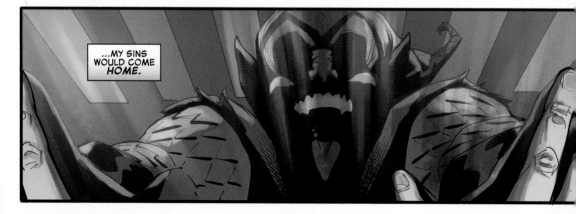

...MY SINS WOULD COME *HOME*.

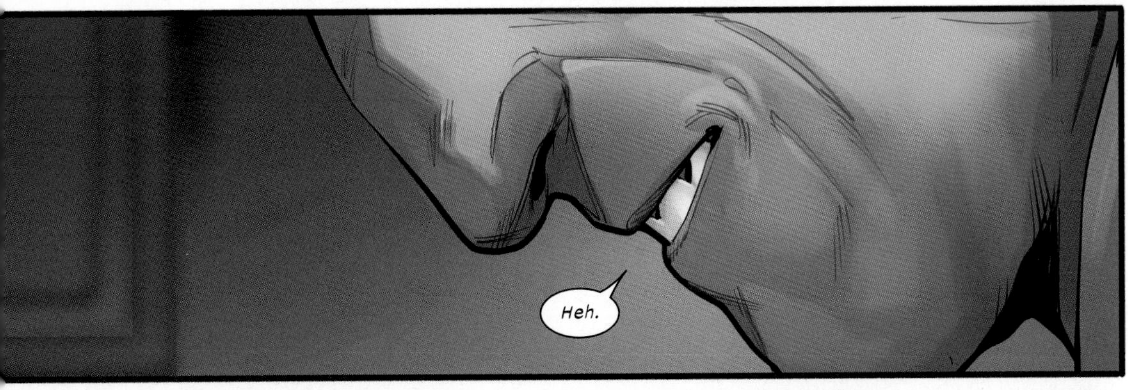
Heh.

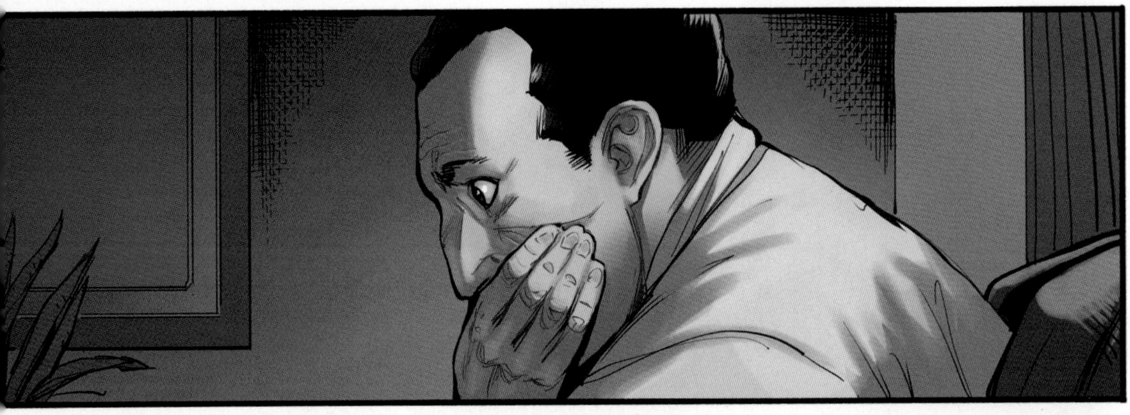

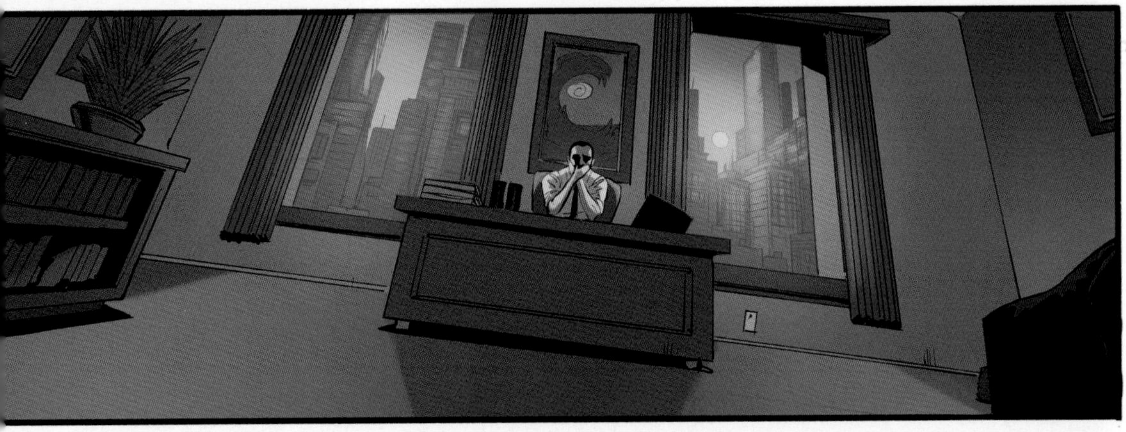

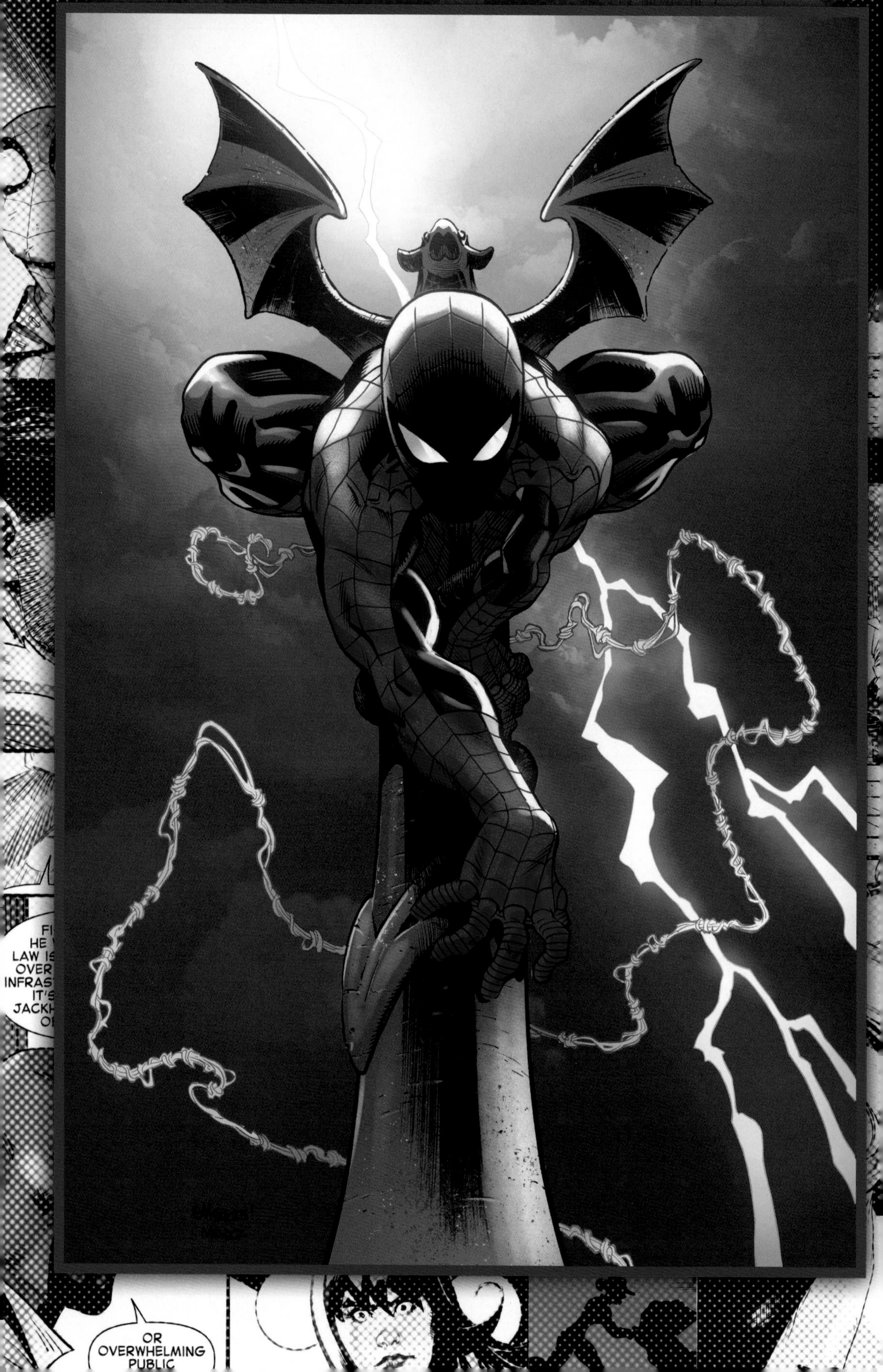
OR
OVERWHELMING
PUBLIC

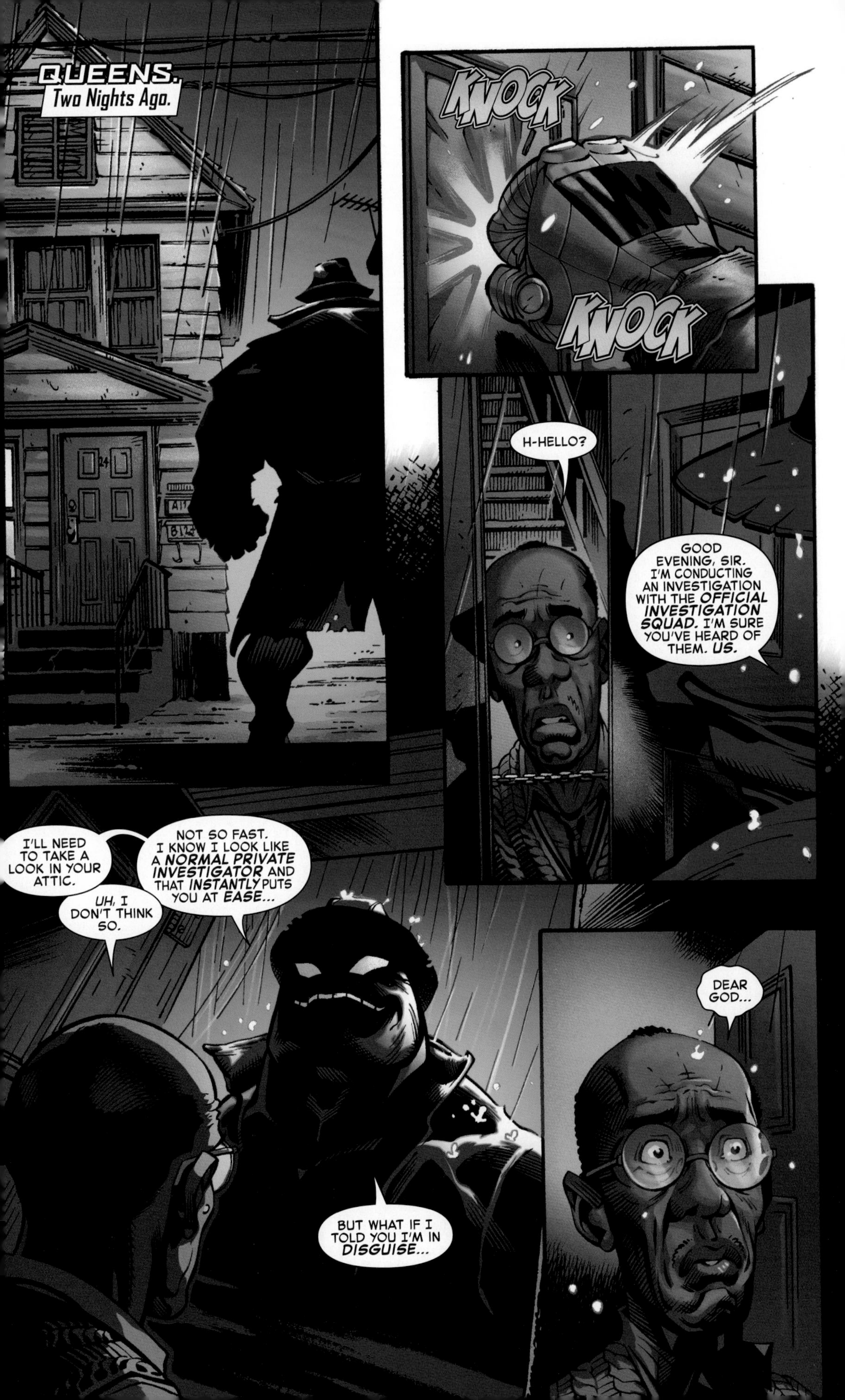
QUEENS.
Two Nights Ago.
KNOCK
KNOCK
H-HELLO?
GOOD EVENING, SIR. I'M CONDUCTING AN INVESTIGATION WITH THE OFFICIAL INVESTIGATION SQUAD. I'M SURE YOU'VE HEARD OF THEM. US.
I'LL NEED TO TAKE A LOOK IN YOUR ATTIC.
UH, I DON'T THINK SO.
NOT SO FAST. I KNOW I LOOK LIKE A NORMAL PRIVATE INVESTIGATOR AND THAT INSTANTLY PUTS YOU AT EASE...
BUT WHAT IF I TOLD YOU I'M IN DISGUISE...
DEAR GOD...

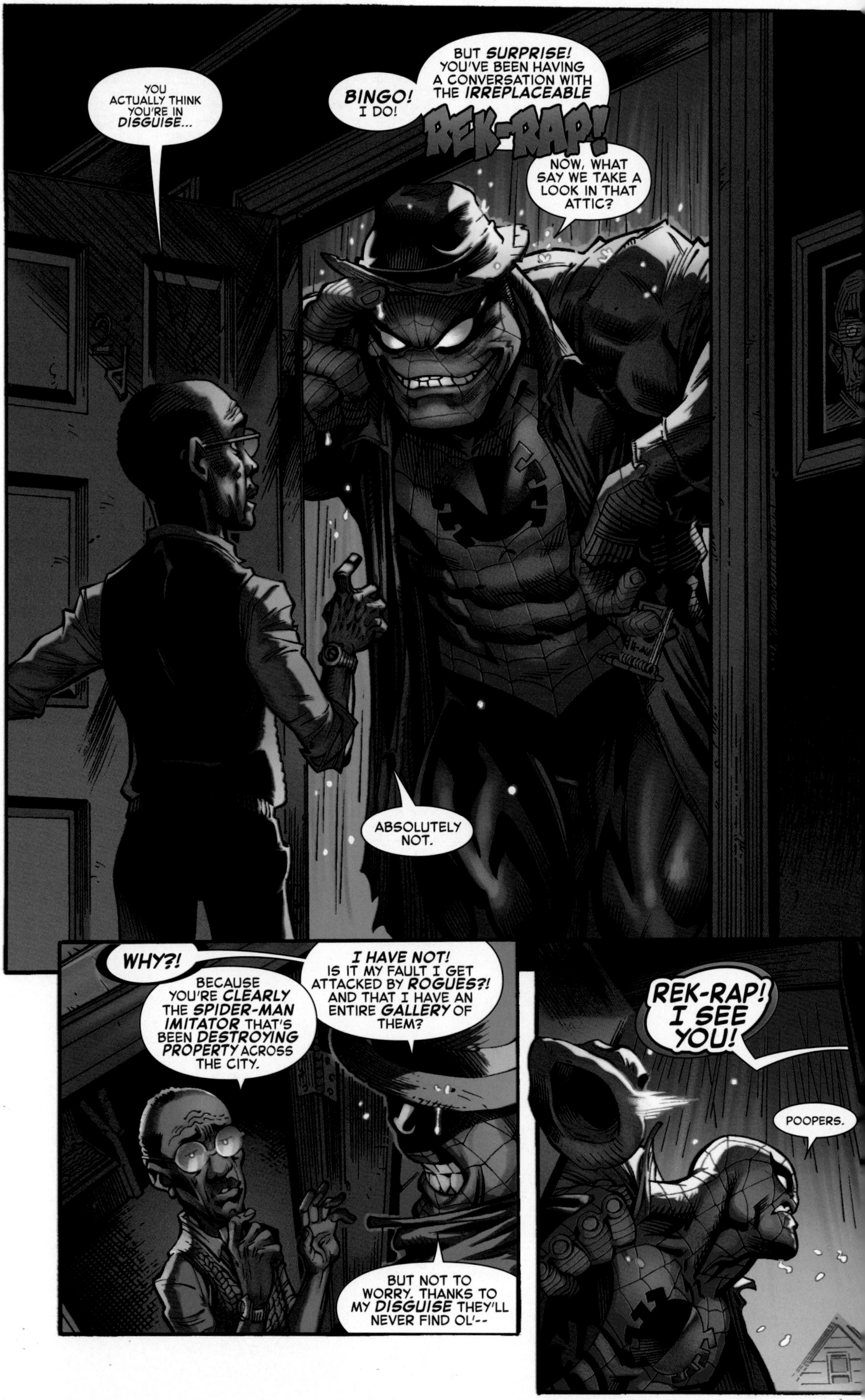
YOU ACTUALLY THINK YOU'RE IN DISGUISE...
BINGO! I DO!
BUT SURPRISE! YOU'VE BEEN HAVING A CONVERSATION WITH THE IRREPLACEABLE
REK-RAP!
NOW, WHAT SAY WE TAKE A LOOK IN THAT ATTIC?
ABSOLUTELY NOT.
WHY?!
BECAUSE YOU'RE CLEARLY THE SPIDER-MAN IMITATOR THAT'S BEEN DESTROYING PROPERTY ACROSS THE CITY.
I HAVE NOT! IS IT MY FAULT I GET ATTACKED BY ROGUES?! AND THAT I HAVE AN ENTIRE GALLERY OF THEM?
BUT NOT TO WORRY. THANKS TO MY DISGUISE THEY'LL NEVER FIND OL'--
REK-RAP! I SEE YOU!
POOPERS.

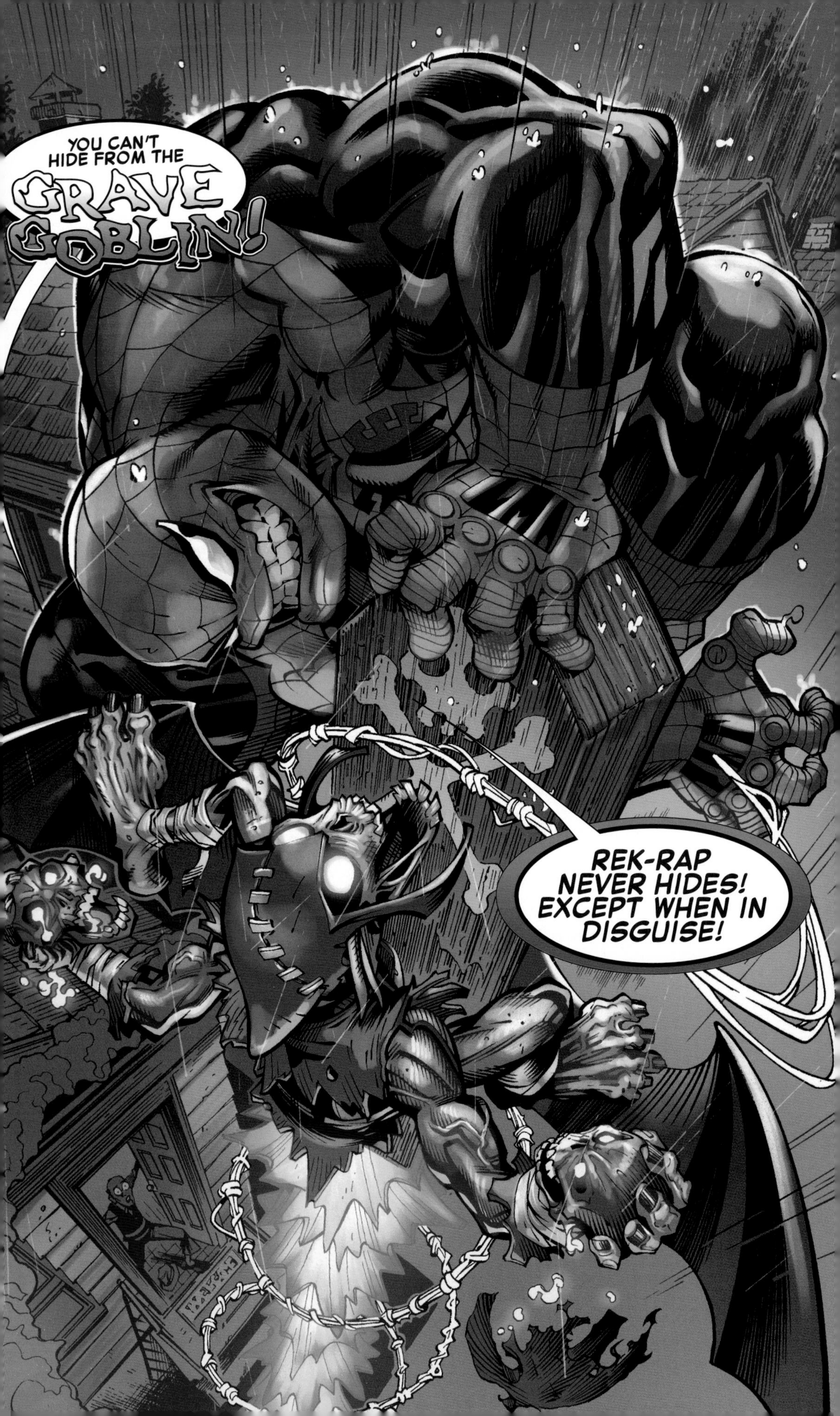
YOU CAN'T HIDE FROM THE GRAVE GOBLIN!
REK-RAP NEVER HIDES! EXCEPT WHEN IN DISGUISE!

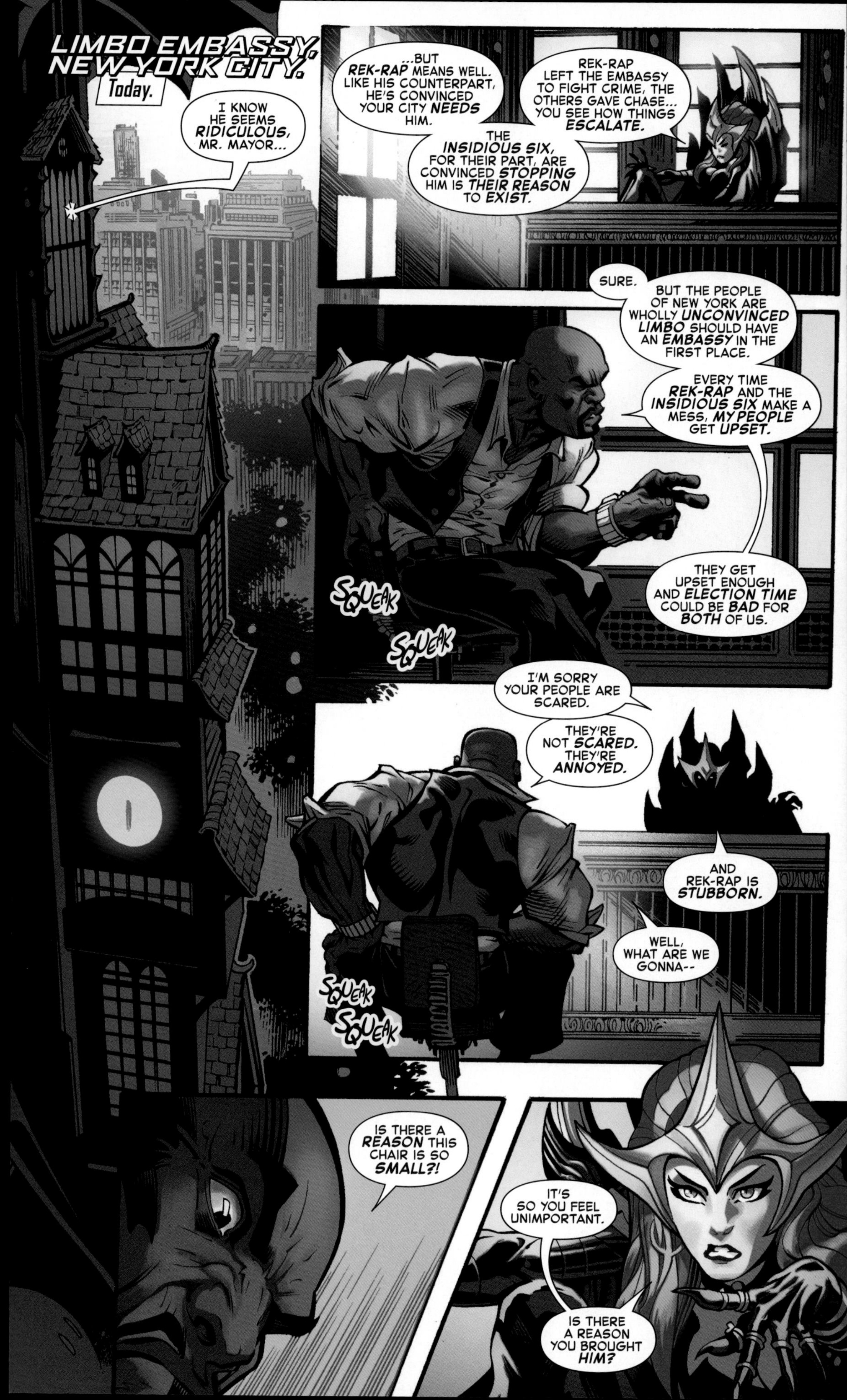

LIMBO EMBASSY, NEW YORK CITY.
Today.
I KNOW HE SEEMS RIDICULOUS, MR. MAYOR...
...BUT REK-RAP MEANS WELL. LIKE HIS COUNTERPART, HE'S CONVINCED YOUR CITY NEEDS HIM.
THE INSIDIOUS SIX, FOR THEIR PART, ARE CONVINCED STOPPING HIM IS THEIR REASON TO EXIST.
REK-RAP LEFT THE EMBASSY TO FIGHT CRIME, THE OTHERS GAVE CHASE... YOU SEE HOW THINGS ESCALATE.
SURE.
BUT THE PEOPLE OF NEW YORK ARE WHOLLY UNCONVINCED LIMBO SHOULD HAVE AN EMBASSY IN THE FIRST PLACE.
EVERY TIME REK-RAP AND THE INSIDIOUS SIX MAKE A MESS, MY PEOPLE GET UPSET.
THEY GET UPSET ENOUGH AND ELECTION TIME COULD BE BAD FOR BOTH OF US.
SQUEAK
SQUEAK
I'M SORRY YOUR PEOPLE ARE SCARED.
THEY'RE NOT SCARED. THEY'RE ANNOYED.
AND REK-RAP IS STUBBORN.
WELL, WHAT ARE WE GONNA--
SQUEAK
SQUEAK
IS THERE A REASON THIS CHAIR IS SO SMALL?!
IT'S SO YOU FEEL UNIMPORTANT.
IS THERE A REASON YOU BROUGHT HIM?

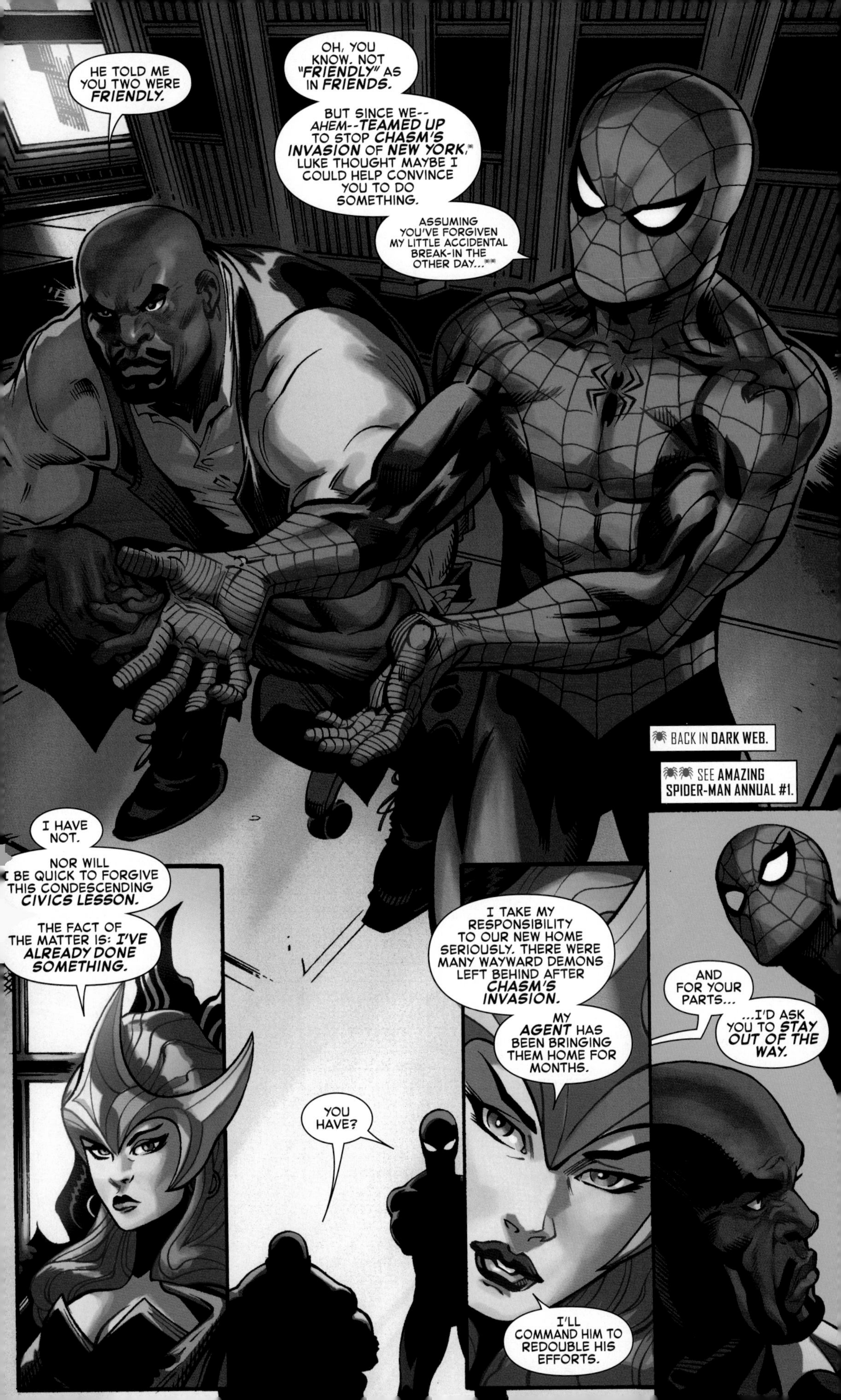

HE TOLD ME YOU TWO WERE FRIENDLY.
OH, YOU KNOW. NOT "FRIENDLY" AS IN FRIENDS.
BUT SINCE WE--AHEM--TEAMED UP TO STOP CHASM'S INVASION OF NEW YORK,* LUKE THOUGHT MAYBE I COULD HELP CONVINCE YOU TO DO SOMETHING.
ASSUMING YOU'VE FORGIVEN MY LITTLE ACCIDENTAL BREAK-IN THE OTHER DAY...**
* BACK IN DARK WEB.
** SEE AMAZING SPIDER-MAN ANNUAL #1.
I HAVE NOT.
NOR WILL I BE QUICK TO FORGIVE THIS CONDESCENDING CIVICS LESSON.
THE FACT OF THE MATTER IS: I'VE ALREADY DONE SOMETHING.
YOU HAVE?
I TAKE MY RESPONSIBILITY TO OUR NEW HOME SERIOUSLY. THERE WERE MANY WAYWARD DEMONS LEFT BEHIND AFTER CHASM'S INVASION.
MY AGENT HAS BEEN BRINGING THEM HOME FOR MONTHS.
I'LL COMMAND HIM TO REDOUBLE HIS EFFORTS.
AND FOR YOUR PARTS...
...I'D ASK YOU TO STAY OUT OF THE WAY.

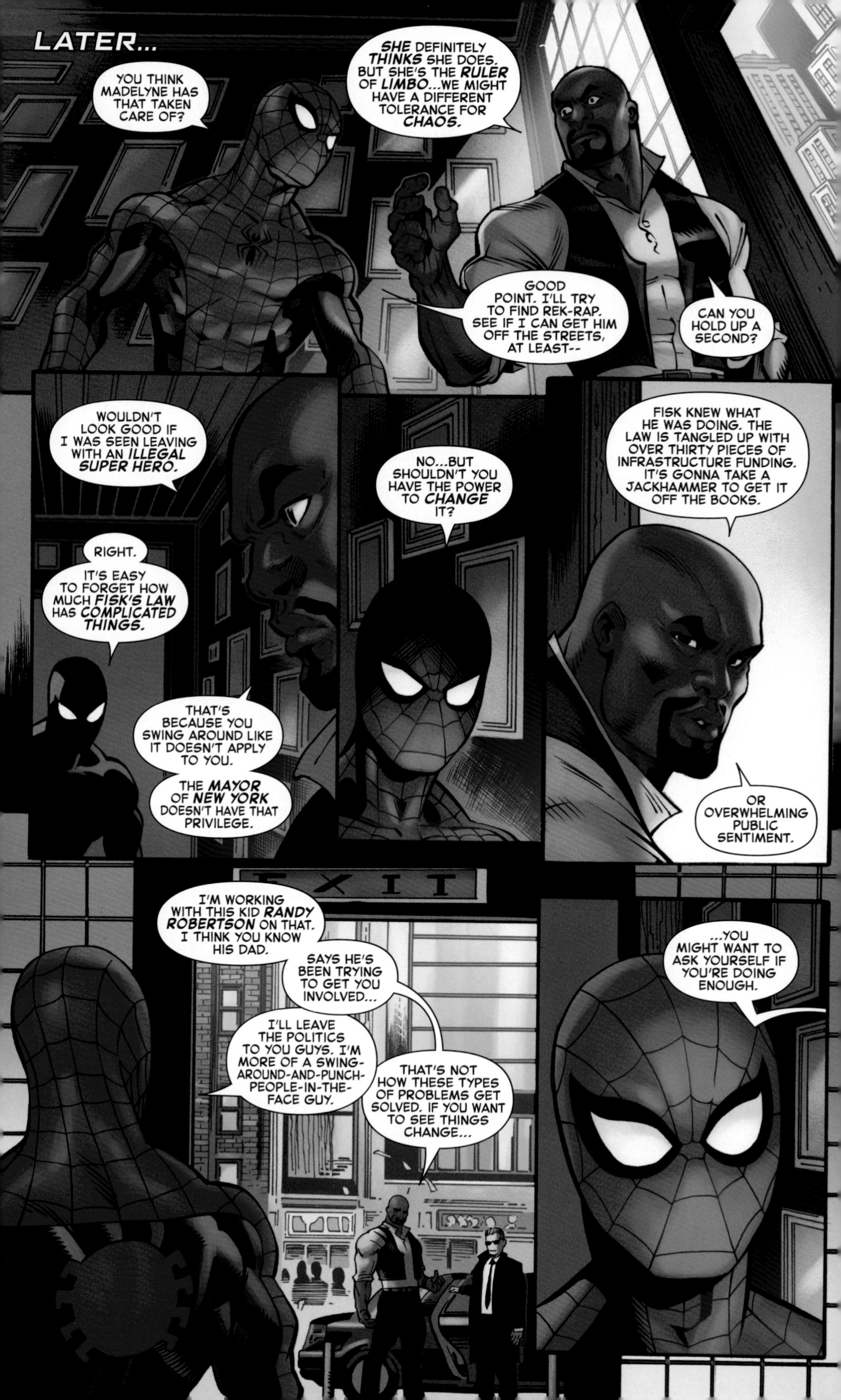
LATER...
YOU THINK MADELYNE HAS THAT TAKEN CARE OF?
SHE DEFINITELY THINKS SHE DOES. BUT SHE'S THE RULER OF LIMBO...WE MIGHT HAVE A DIFFERENT TOLERANCE FOR CHAOS.
GOOD POINT. I'LL TRY TO FIND REK-RAP. SEE IF I CAN GET HIM OFF THE STREETS, AT LEAST--
CAN YOU HOLD UP A SECOND?
WOULDN'T LOOK GOOD IF I WAS SEEN LEAVING WITH AN ILLEGAL SUPER HERO.
RIGHT.
IT'S EASY TO FORGET HOW MUCH FISK'S LAW HAS COMPLICATED THINGS.
THAT'S BECAUSE YOU SWING AROUND LIKE IT DOESN'T APPLY TO YOU.
THE MAYOR OF NEW YORK DOESN'T HAVE THAT PRIVILEGE.
NO...BUT SHOULDN'T YOU HAVE THE POWER TO CHANGE IT?
FISK KNEW WHAT HE WAS DOING. THE LAW IS TANGLED UP WITH OVER THIRTY PIECES OF INFRASTRUCTURE FUNDING. IT'S GONNA TAKE A JACKHAMMER TO GET IT OFF THE BOOKS.
OR OVERWHELMING PUBLIC SENTIMENT.
EXIT
I'M WORKING WITH THIS KID RANDY ROBERTSON ON THAT. I THINK YOU KNOW HIS DAD.
SAYS HE'S BEEN TRYING TO GET YOU INVOLVED...
I'LL LEAVE THE POLITICS TO YOU GUYS. I'M MORE OF A SWING-AROUND-AND-PUNCH-PEOPLE-IN-THE-FACE GUY.
THAT'S NOT HOW THESE TYPES OF PROBLEMS GET SOLVED. IF YOU WANT TO SEE THINGS CHANGE...
...YOU MIGHT WANT TO ASK YOURSELF IF YOU'RE DOING ENOUGH.

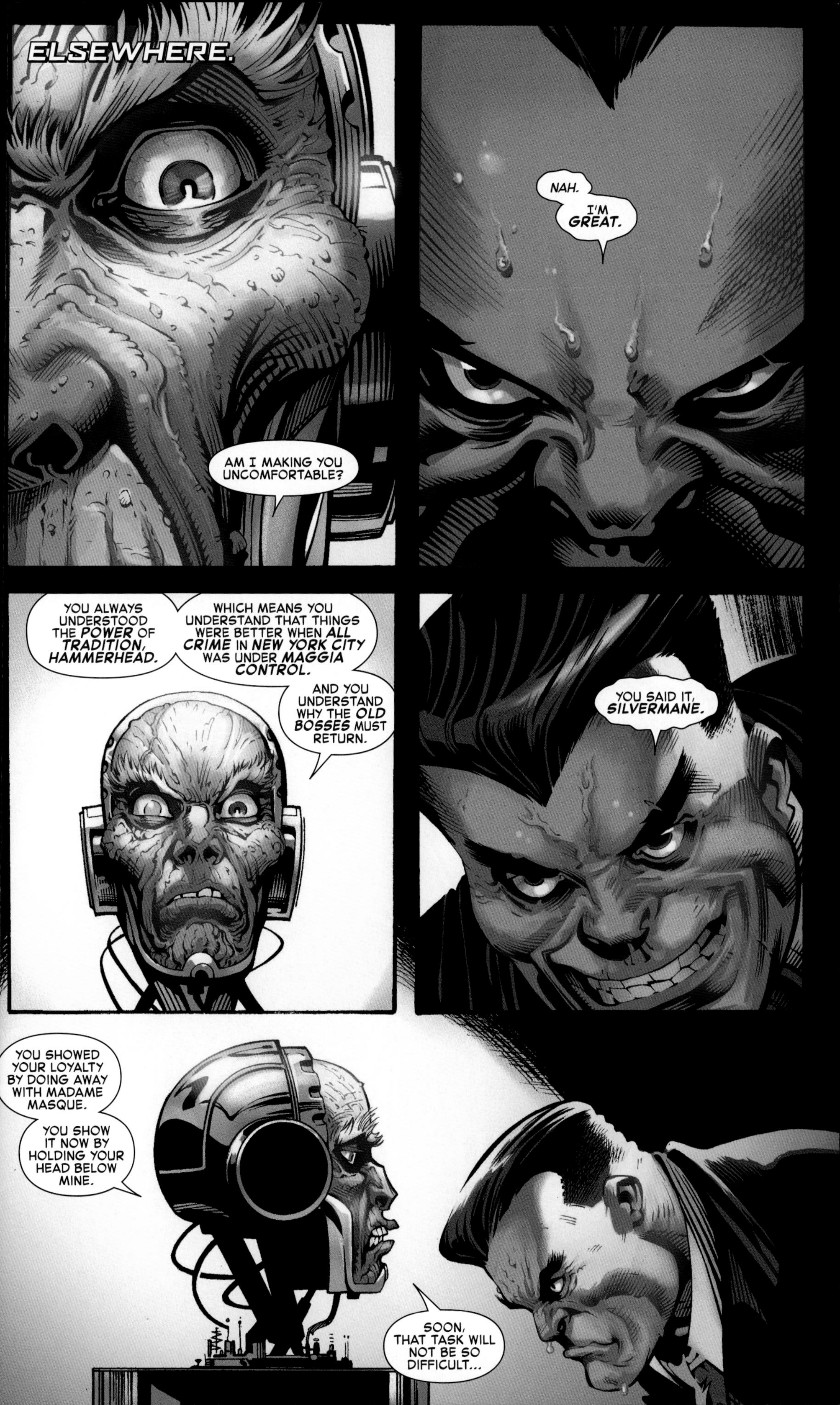
ELSEWHERE.
AM I MAKING YOU UNCOMFORTABLE?
NAH.
I'M GREAT.
YOU ALWAYS UNDERSTOOD THE POWER OF TRADITION, HAMMERHEAD.
WHICH MEANS YOU UNDERSTAND THAT THINGS WERE BETTER WHEN ALL CRIME IN NEW YORK CITY WAS UNDER MAGGIA CONTROL.
AND YOU UNDERSTAND WHY THE OLD BOSSES MUST RETURN.
YOU SAID IT, SILVERMANE.
YOU SHOWED YOUR LOYALTY BY DOING AWAY WITH MADAME MASQUE.
YOU SHOW IT NOW BY HOLDING YOUR HEAD BELOW MINE.
SOON, THAT TASK WILL NOT BE SO DIFFICULT...

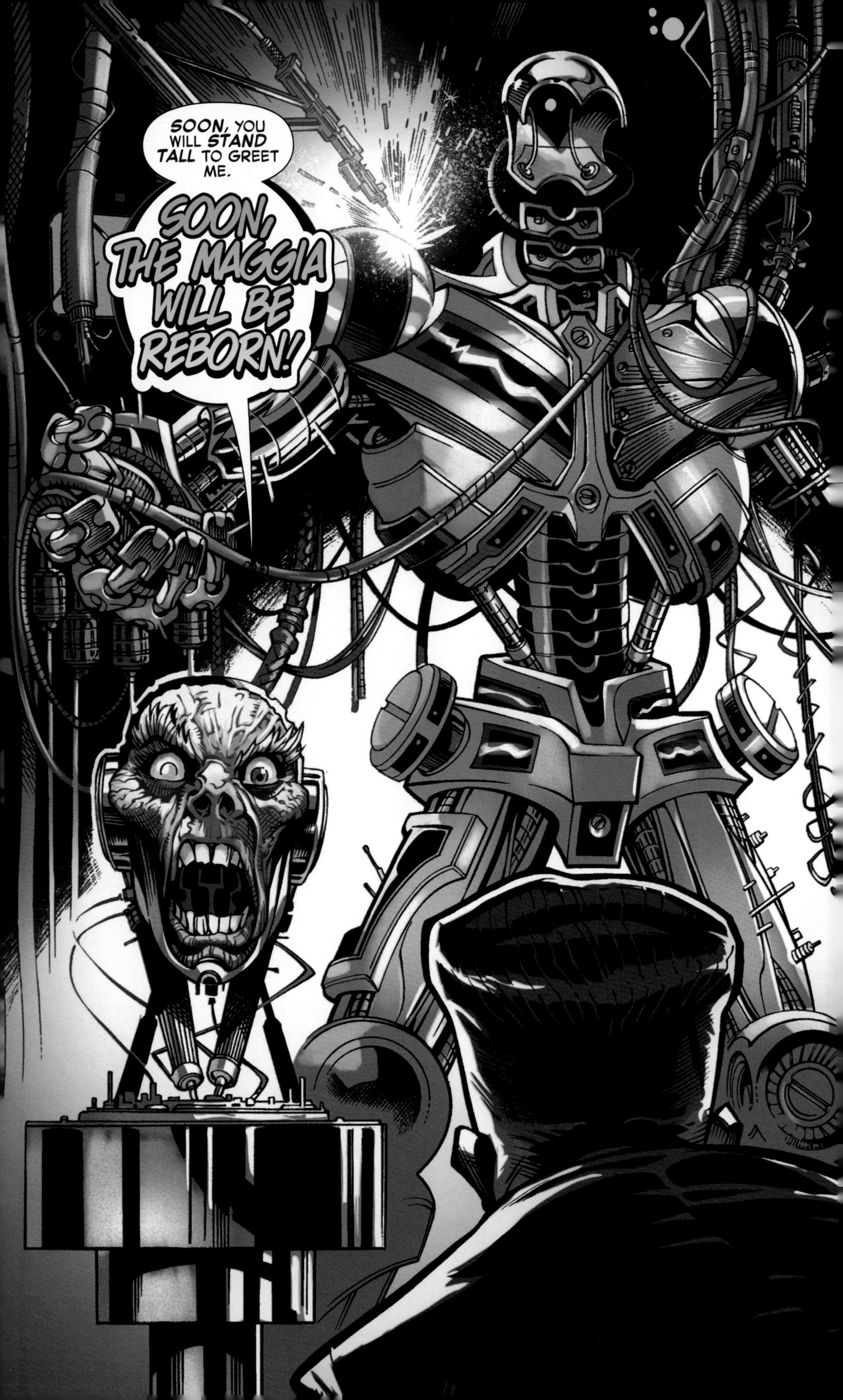
SOON, YOU WILL STAND TALL TO GREET ME.
SOON, THE MAGGIA WILL BE REBORN!

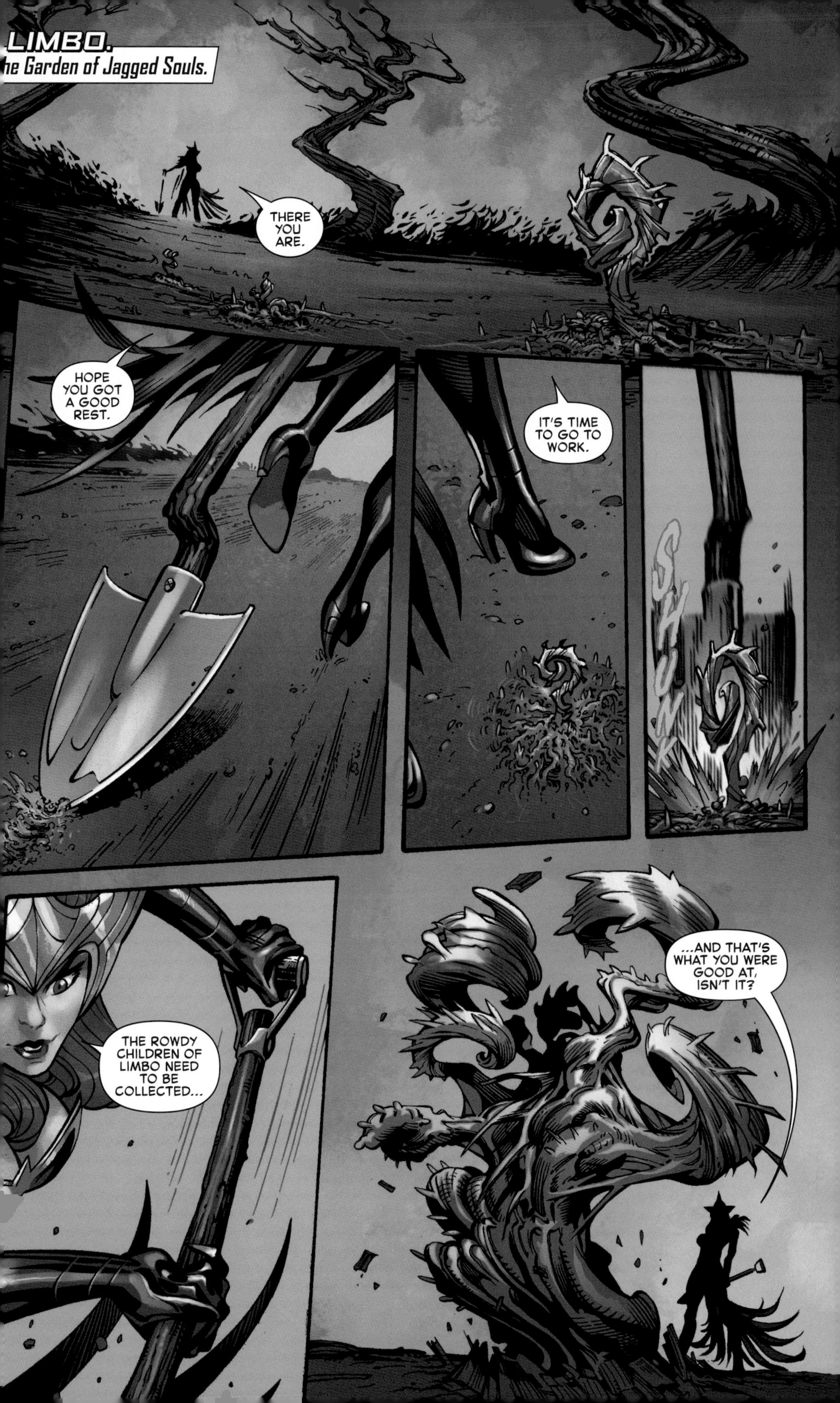
LIMBO.
The Garden of Jagged Souls.
THERE YOU ARE.
HOPE YOU GOT A GOOD REST.
IT'S TIME TO GO TO WORK.
SHUNK
THE ROWDY CHILDREN OF LIMBO NEED TO BE COLLECTED...
...AND THAT'S WHAT YOU WERE GOOD AT, ISN'T IT?

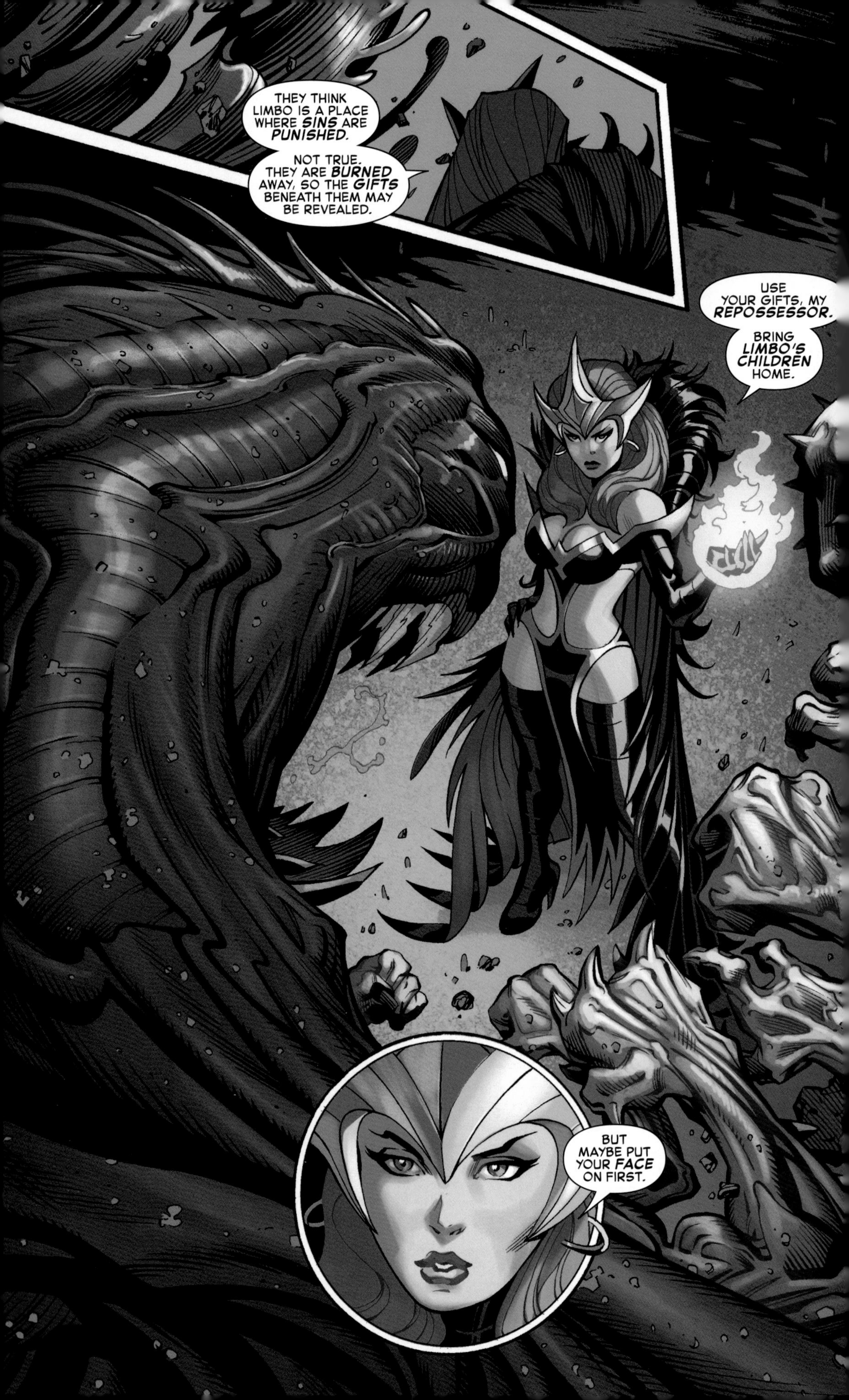
THEY THINK LIMBO IS A PLACE WHERE SINS ARE PUNISHED.
NOT TRUE. THEY ARE BURNED AWAY, SO THE GIFTS BENEATH THEM MAY BE REVEALED.
USE YOUR GIFTS, MY REPOSSESSOR.
BRING LIMBO'S CHILDREN HOME.
BUT MAYBE PUT YOUR FACE ON FIRST.

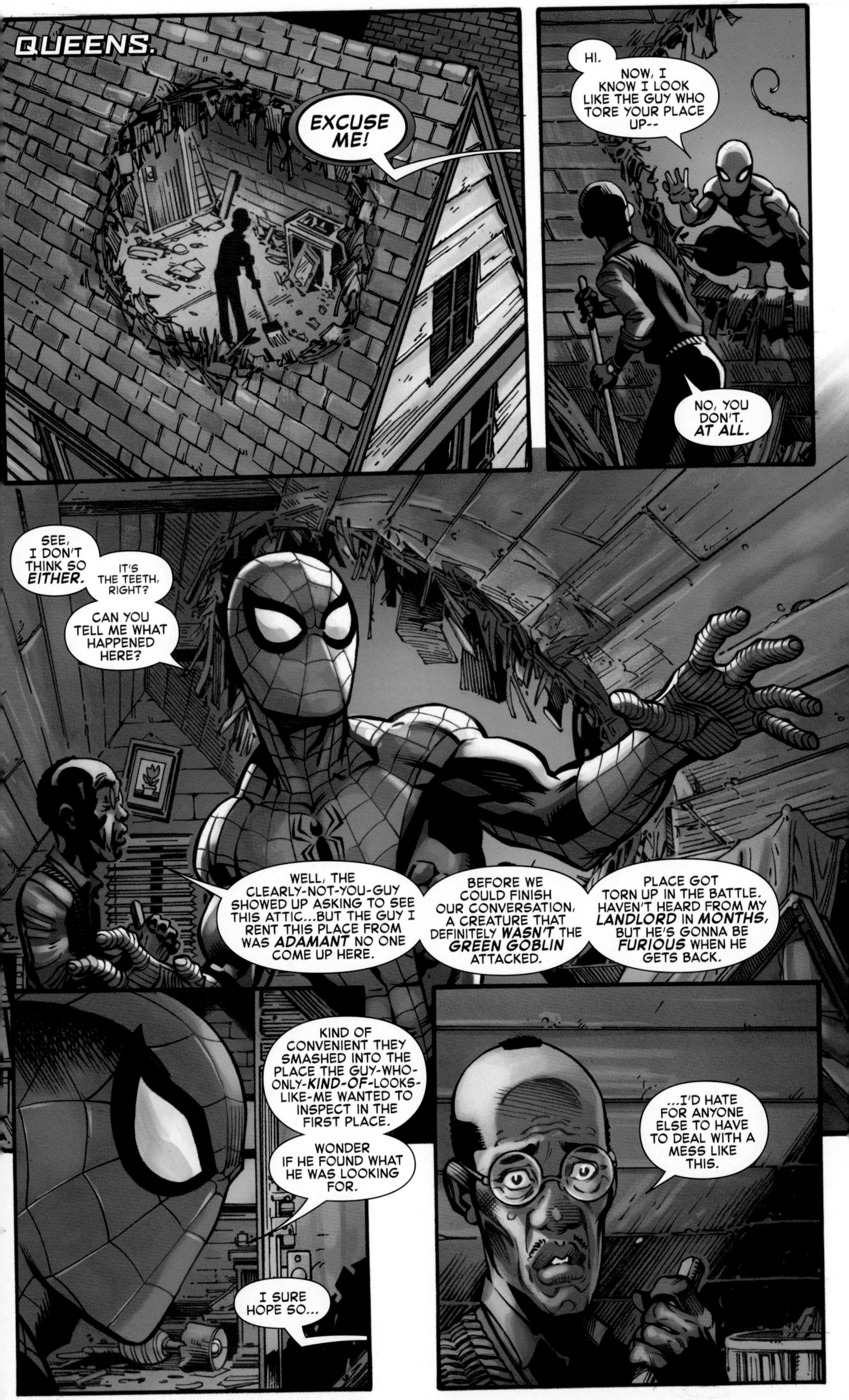
QUEENS.
EXCUSE ME!
HI.
NOW, I KNOW I LOOK LIKE THE GUY WHO TORE YOUR PLACE UP--
NO, YOU DON'T. AT ALL.
SEE, I DON'T THINK SO EITHER.
IT'S THE TEETH, RIGHT?
CAN YOU TELL ME WHAT HAPPENED HERE?
WELL, THE CLEARLY-NOT-YOU-GUY SHOWED UP ASKING TO SEE THIS ATTIC...BUT THE GUY I RENT THIS PLACE FROM WAS ADAMANT NO ONE COME UP HERE.
BEFORE WE COULD FINISH OUR CONVERSATION, A CREATURE THAT DEFINITELY WASN'T THE GREEN GOBLIN ATTACKED.
PLACE GOT TORN UP IN THE BATTLE. HAVEN'T HEARD FROM MY LANDLORD IN MONTHS, BUT HE'S GONNA BE FURIOUS WHEN HE GETS BACK.
KIND OF CONVENIENT THEY SMASHED INTO THE PLACE THE GUY-WHO-ONLY-KIND-OF-LOOKS-LIKE-ME WANTED TO INSPECT IN THE FIRST PLACE.
WONDER IF HE FOUND WHAT HE WAS LOOKING FOR.
I SURE HOPE SO...
...I'D HATE FOR ANYONE ELSE TO HAVE TO DEAL WITH A MESS LIKE THIS.

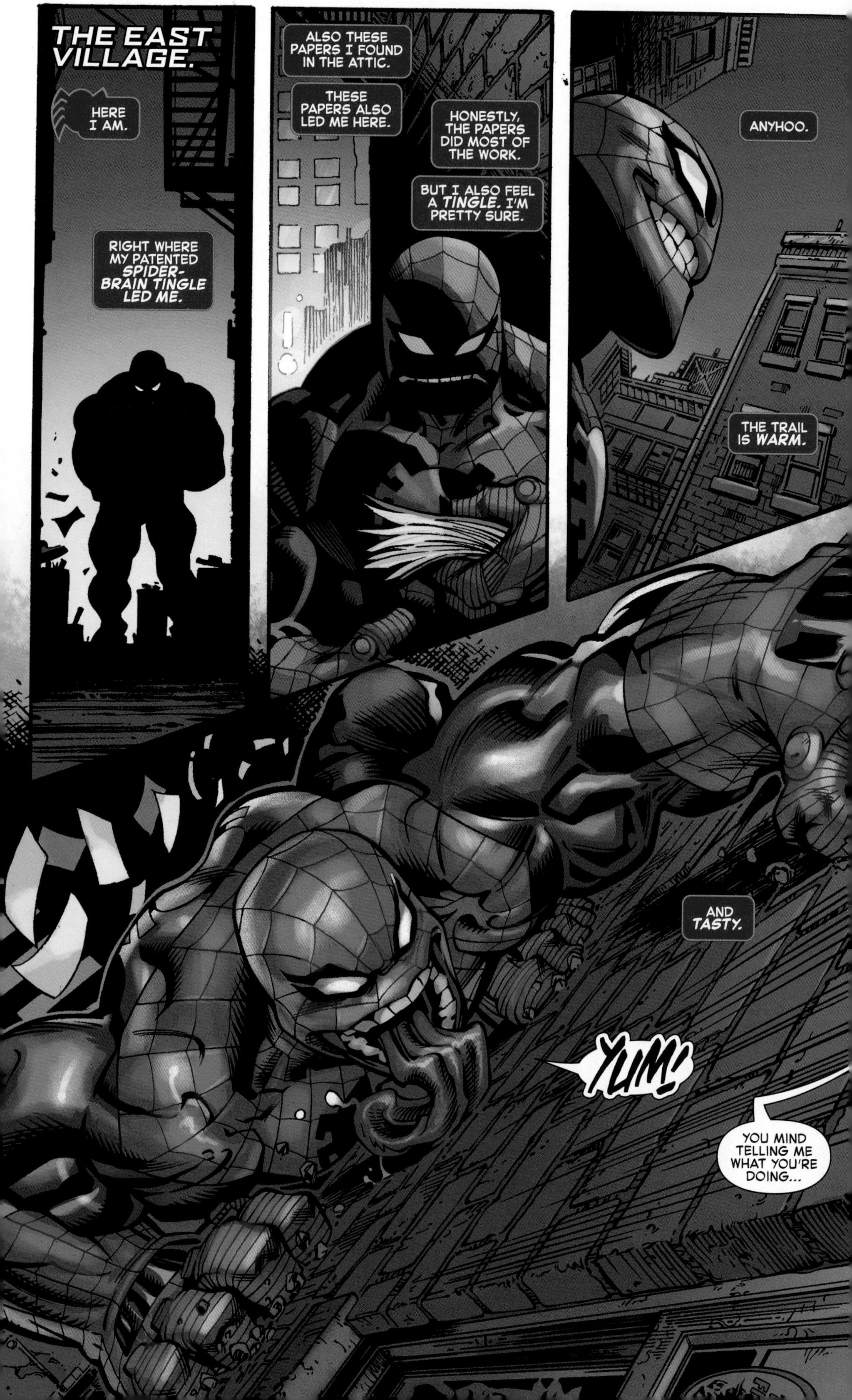
THE EAST VILLAGE.
HERE I AM.
RIGHT WHERE MY PATENTED SPIDER-BRAIN TINGLE LED ME.
ALSO THESE PAPERS I FOUND IN THE ATTIC.
THESE PAPERS ALSO LED ME HERE.
HONESTLY, THE PAPERS DID MOST OF THE WORK.
BUT I ALSO FEEL A TINGLE. I'M PRETTY SURE.
ANYHOO.
THE TRAIL IS WARM.
AND TASTY.
YUM!
YOU MIND TELLING ME WHAT YOU'RE DOING...

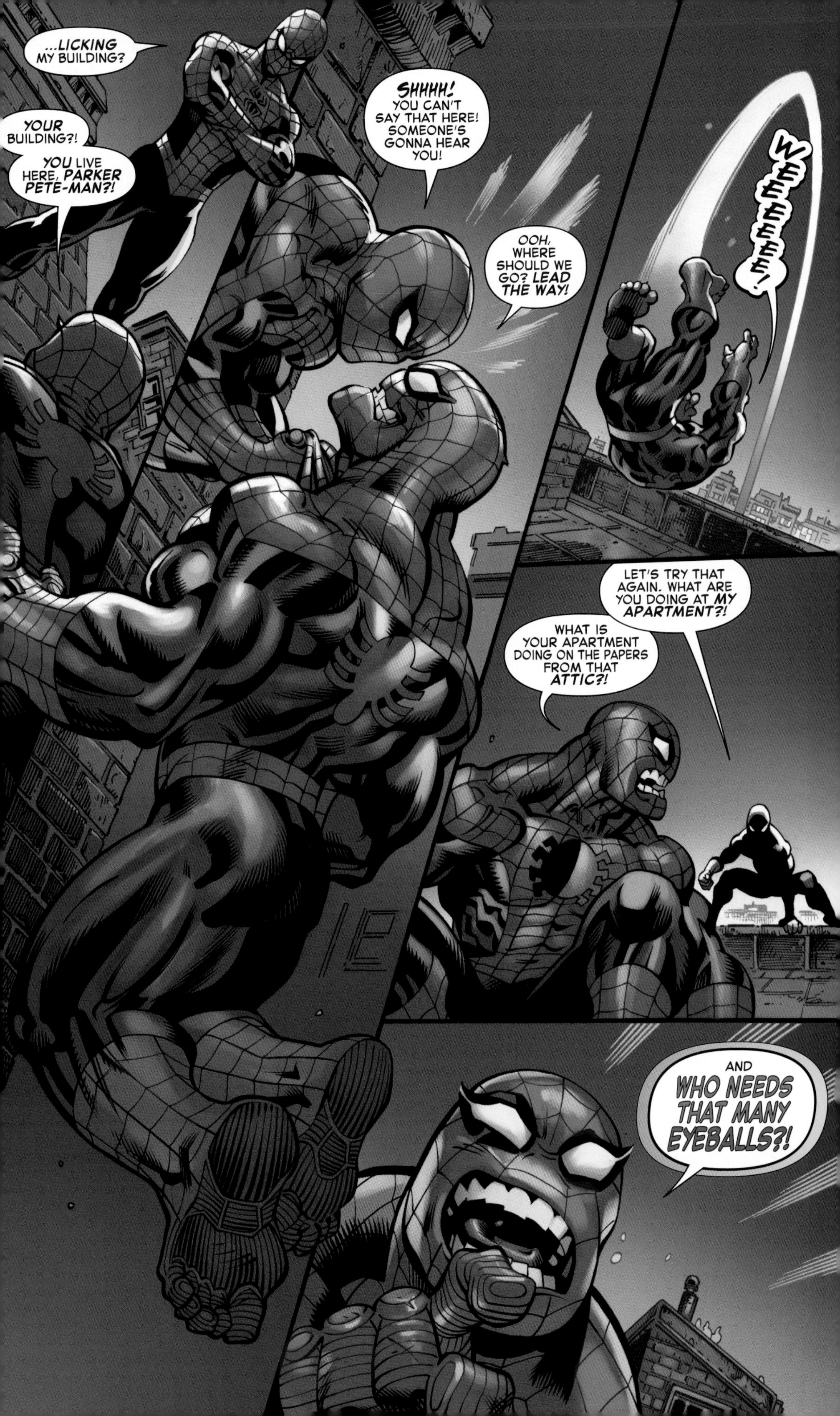
...LICKING MY BUILDING?
YOUR BUILDING?!
YOU LIVE HERE, PARKER PETE-MAN?!
SHHHH! YOU CAN'T SAY THAT HERE! SOMEONE'S GONNA HEAR YOU!
OOH, WHERE SHOULD WE GO? LEAD THE WAY!
WEEEEEEE!
LET'S TRY THAT AGAIN. WHAT ARE YOU DOING AT MY APARTMENT?!
WHAT IS YOUR APARTMENT DOING ON THE PAPERS FROM THAT ATTIC?!
AND WHO NEEDS THAT MANY EYEBALLS?!

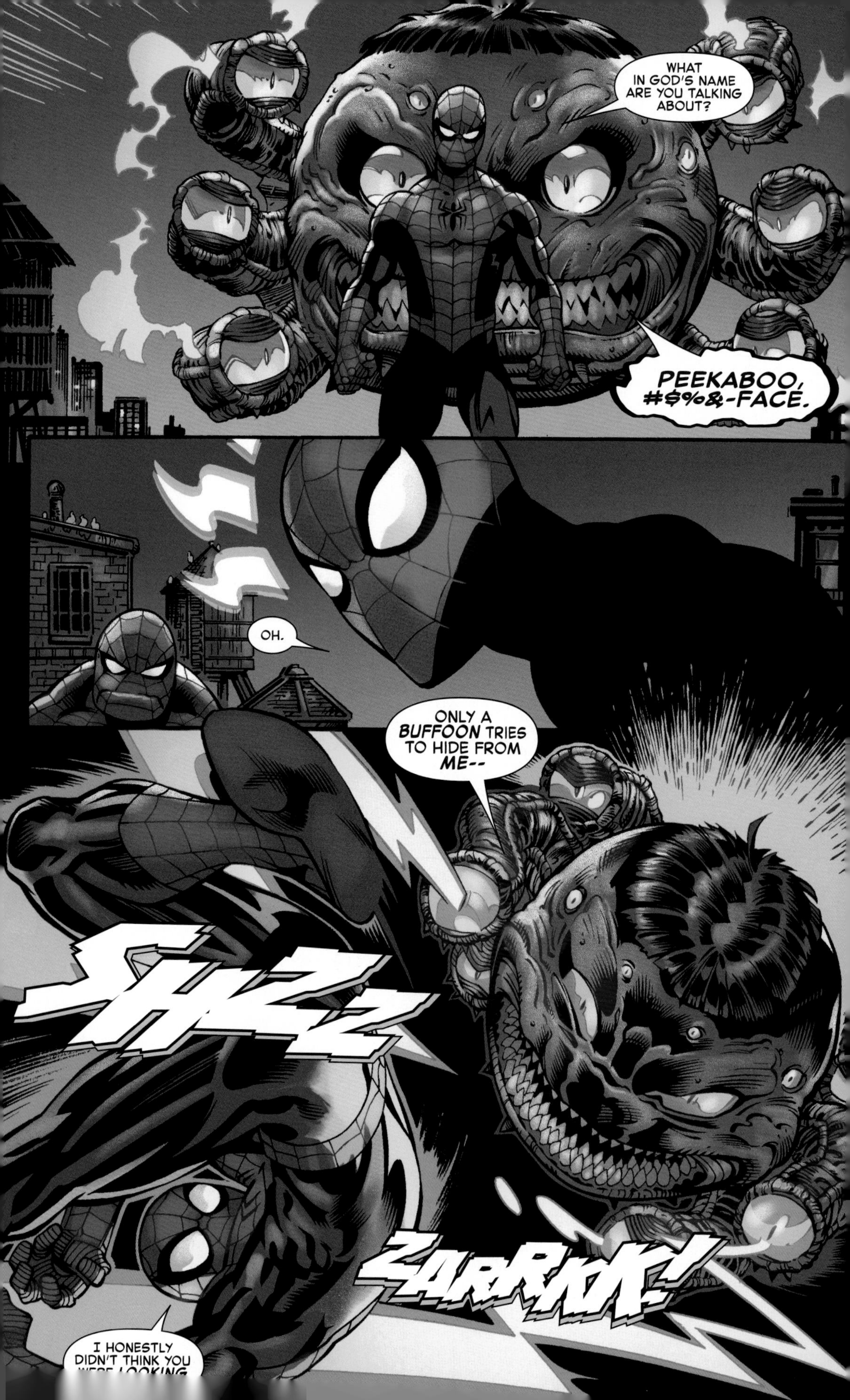
WHAT IN GOD'S NAME ARE YOU TALKING ABOUT?
PEEKABOO, #$%&-FACE.
OH.
ONLY A BUFFOON TRIES TO HIDE FROM ME--
SHZZ
ZARRKK!
I HONESTLY DIDN'T THINK YOU

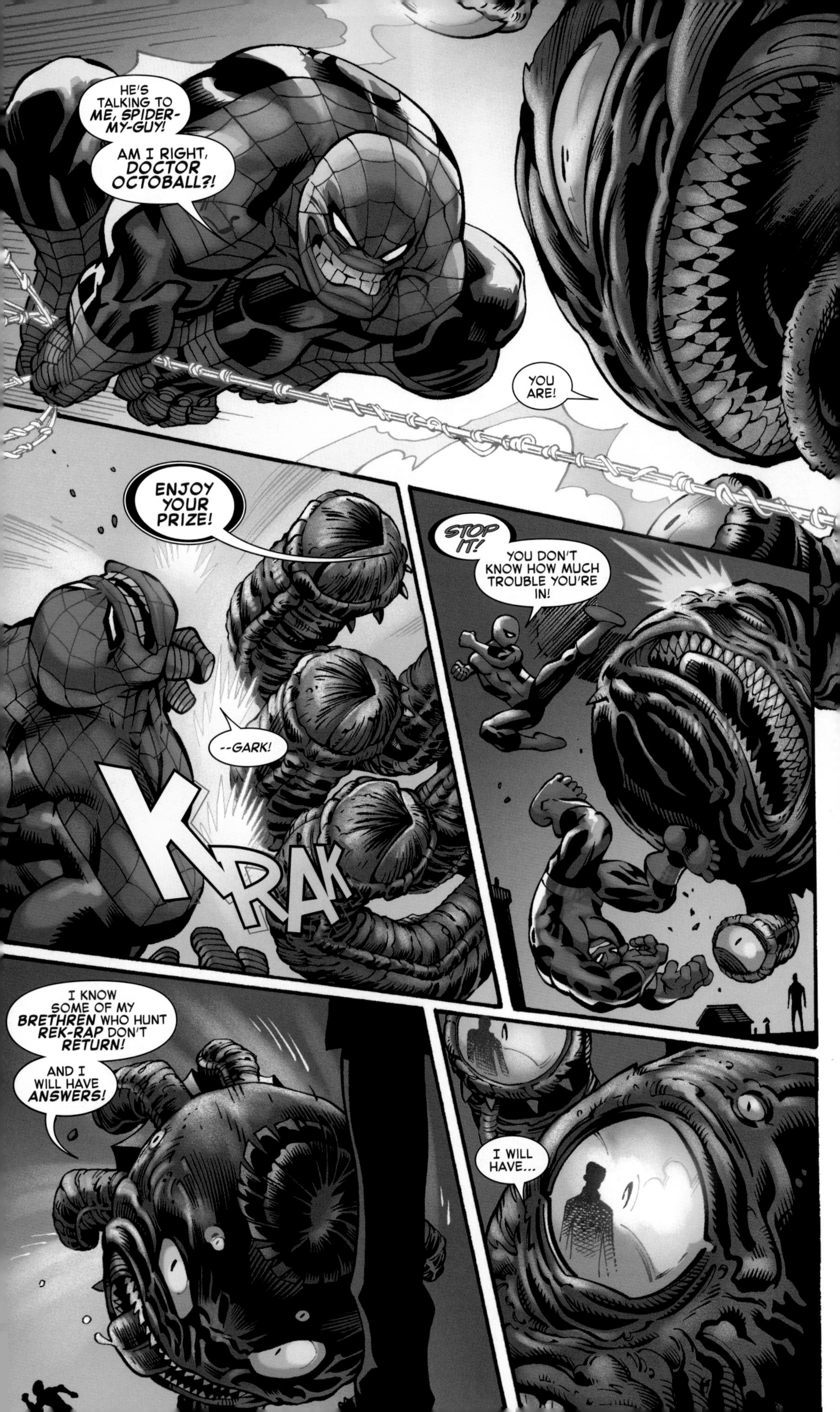

HE'S TALKING TO ME, SPIDER-MY-GUY!
AM I RIGHT, DOCTOR OCTOBALL?!
YOU ARE!
ENJOY YOUR PRIZE!
--GARK!
KRAK
STOP IT!
YOU DON'T KNOW HOW MUCH TROUBLE YOU'RE IN!
I KNOW SOME OF MY BRETHREN WHO HUNT REK-RAP DON'T RETURN!
AND I WILL HAVE ANSWERS!
I WILL HAVE...

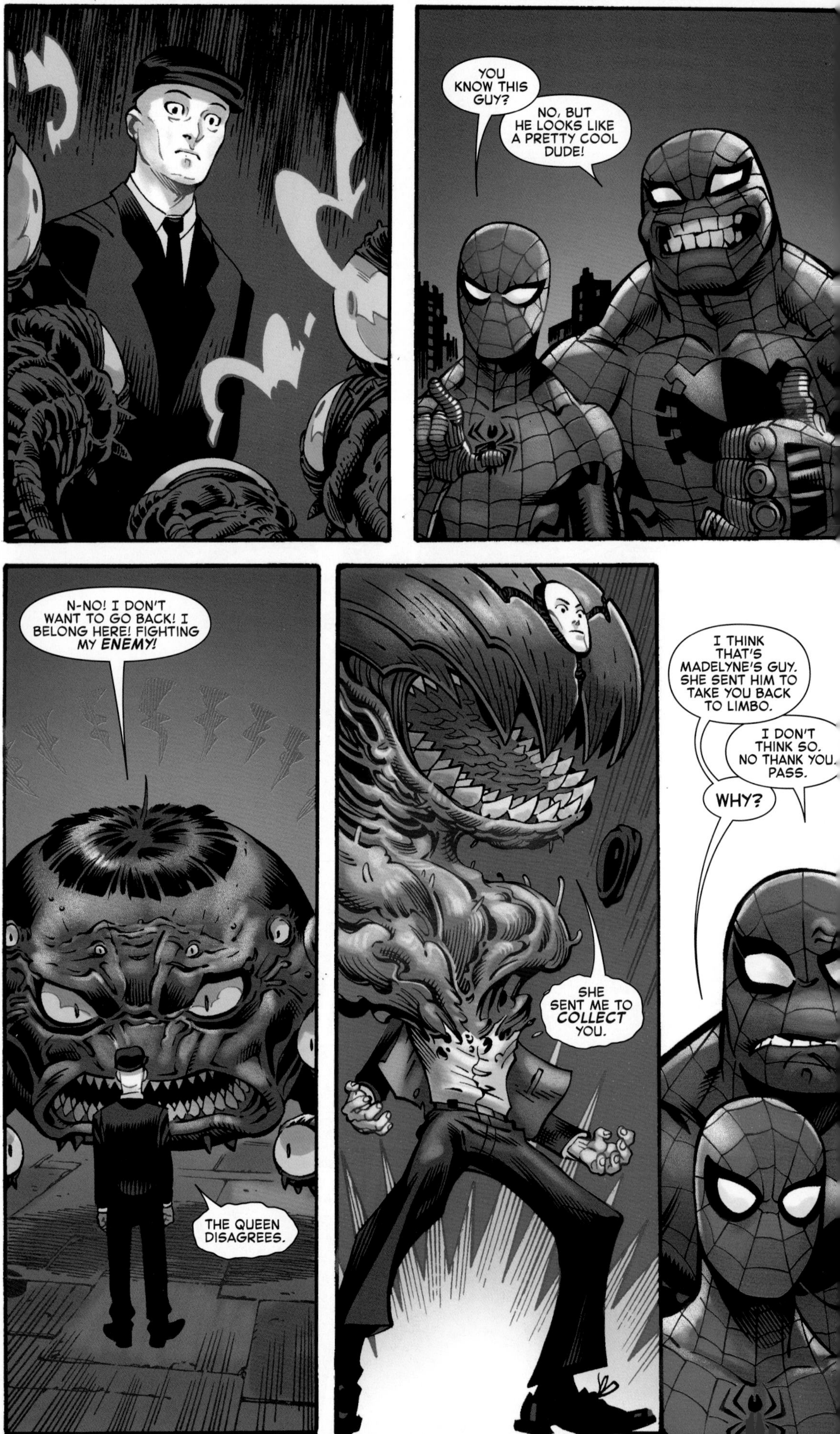

YOU KNOW THIS GUY?
NO, BUT HE LOOKS LIKE A PRETTY COOL DUDE!
N-NO! I DON'T WANT TO GO BACK! I BELONG HERE! FIGHTING MY *ENEMY*!
THE QUEEN DISAGREES.
SHE SENT ME TO *COLLECT* YOU.
I THINK THAT'S MADELYNE'S GUY. SHE SENT HIM TO TAKE YOU BACK TO LIMBO.
I DON'T THINK SO. NO THANK YOU. PASS.
WHY?

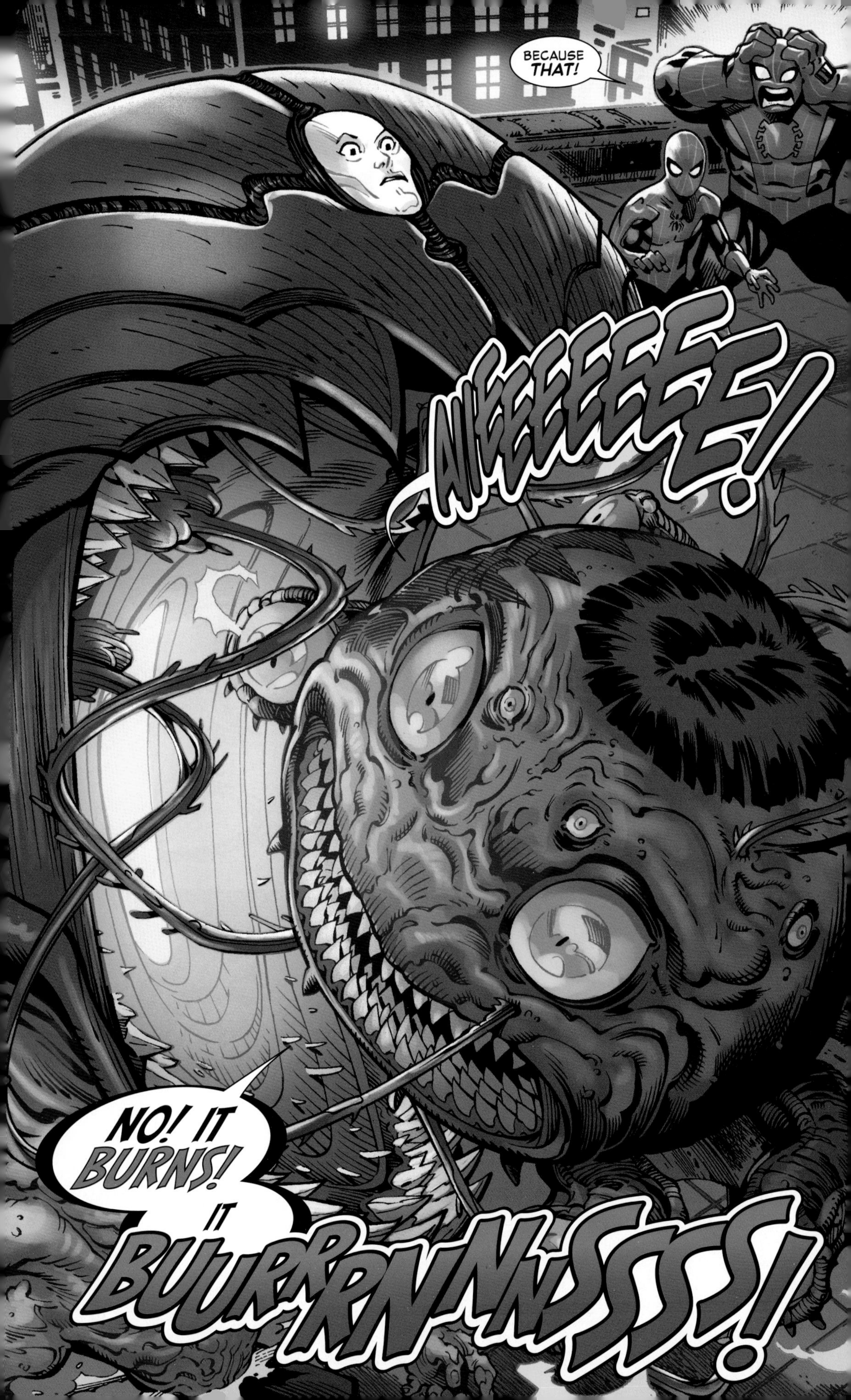
BECAUSE THAT!
AIIEEEEEEEE!
NO! IT BURNS!
IT BUURRRNNNSSSS!

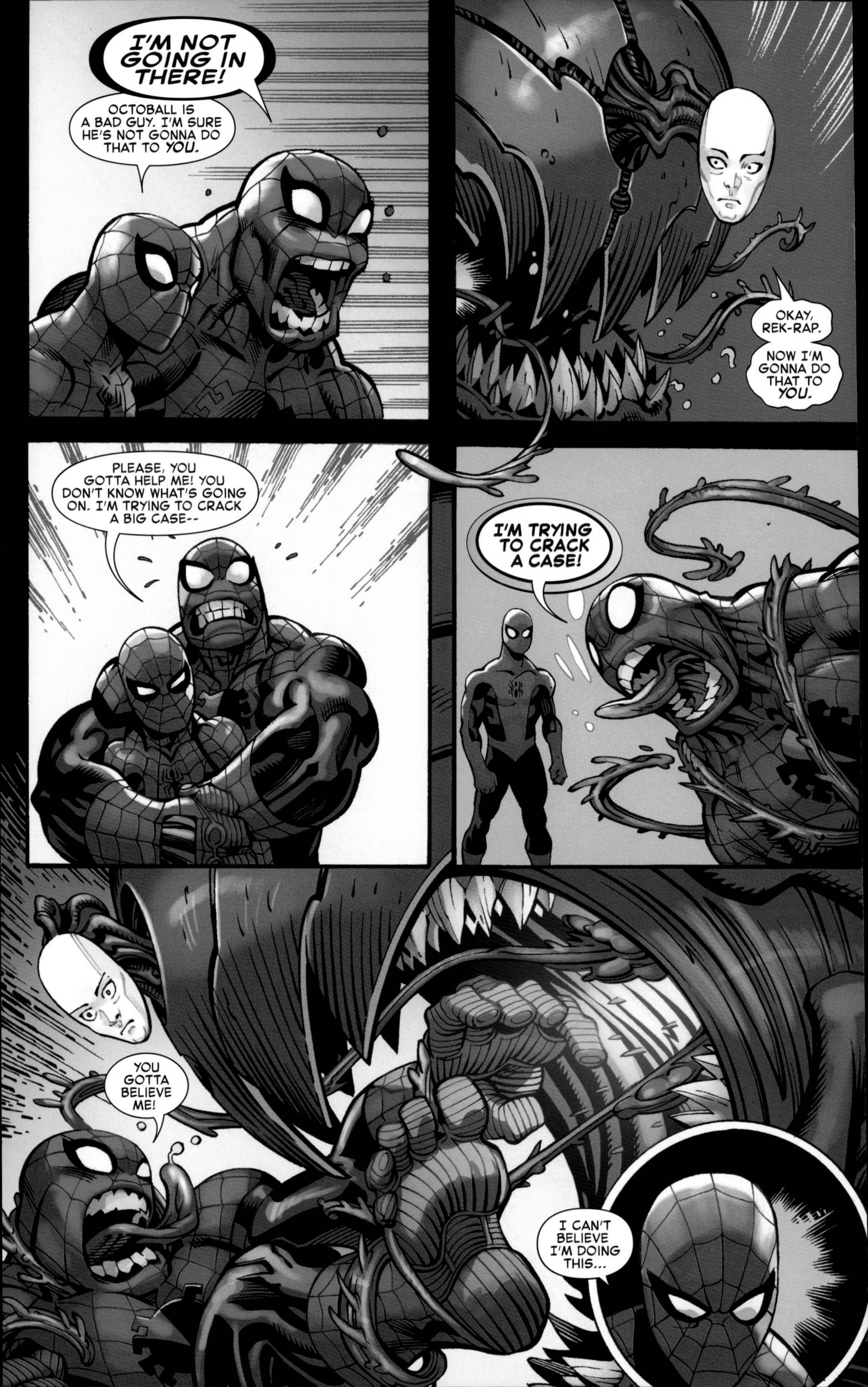
I'M NOT GOING IN THERE!
OCTOBALL IS A BAD GUY. I'M SURE HE'S NOT GONNA DO THAT TO YOU.
OKAY, REK-RAP.
NOW I'M GONNA DO THAT TO YOU.
PLEASE, YOU GOTTA HELP ME! YOU DON'T KNOW WHAT'S GOING ON. I'M TRYING TO CRACK A BIG CASE--
I'M TRYING TO CRACK A CASE!
YOU GOTTA BELIEVE ME!
I CAN'T BELIEVE I'M DOING THIS...

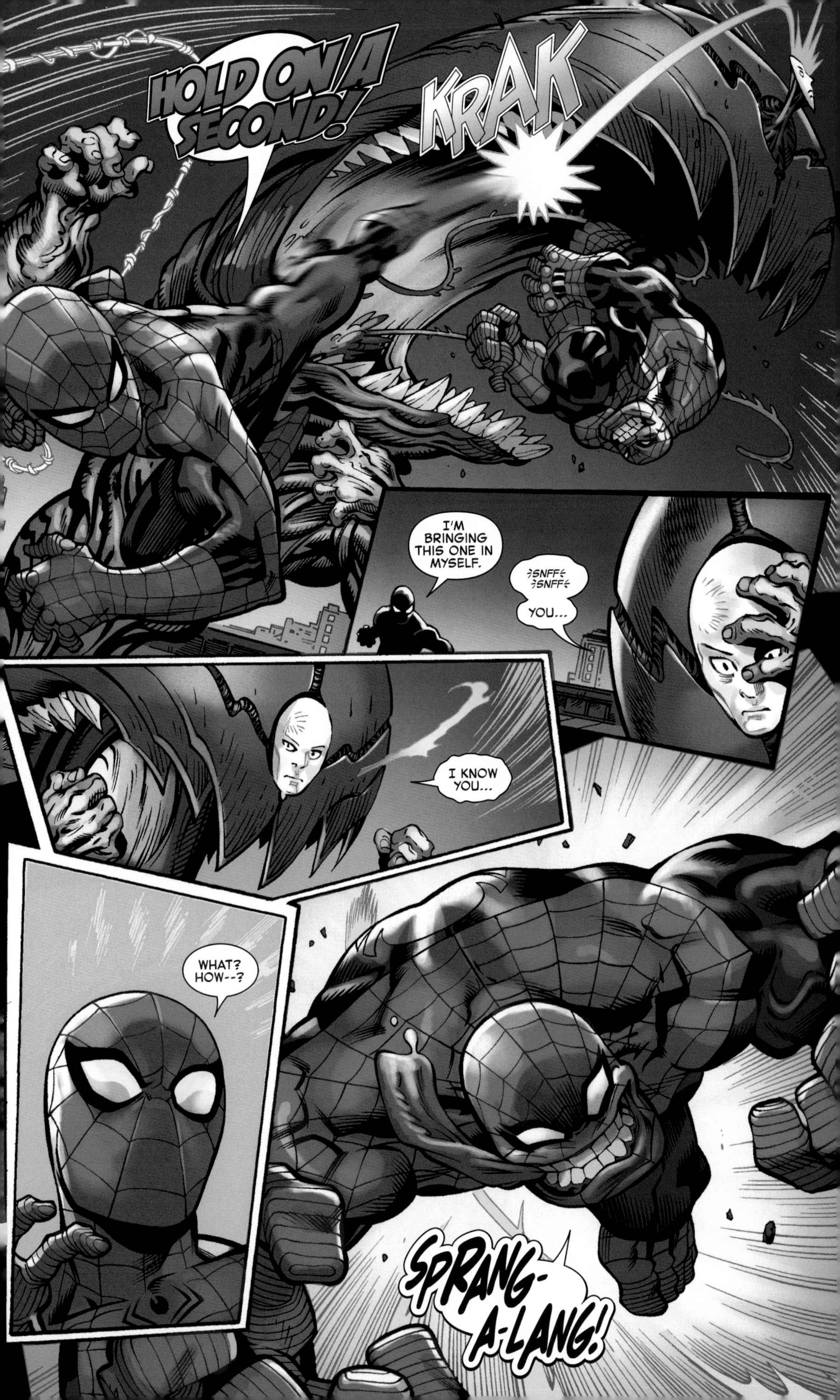

HOLD ON! A SECOND!
KRAK
I'M BRINGING THIS ONE IN MYSELF.
SNFF SNFF
YOU...
I KNOW YOU...
WHAT? HOW--?
SPRANG-A-LANG!

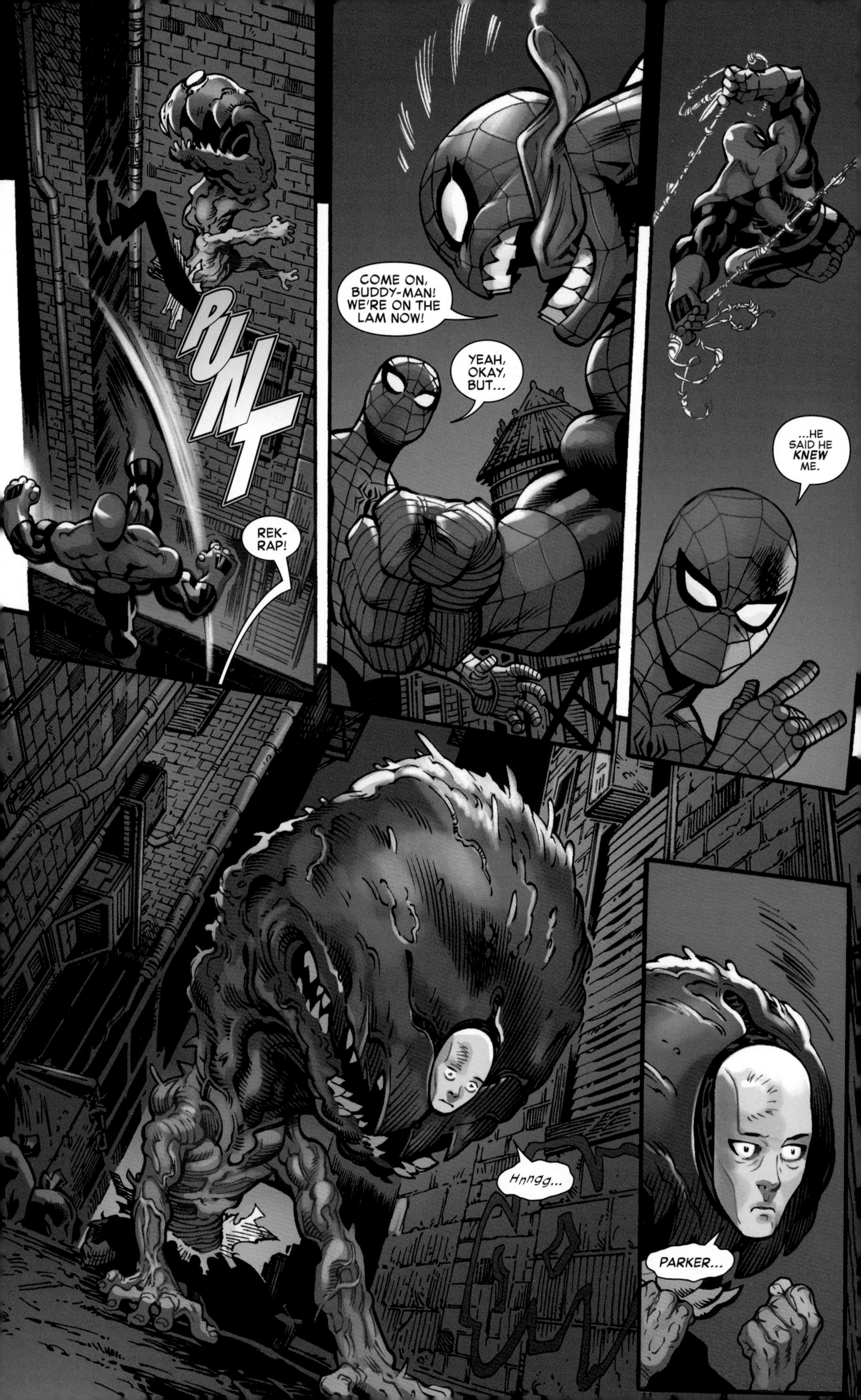
PUNT
REK-RAP!
COME ON, BUDDY-MAN! WE'RE ON THE LAM NOW!
YEAH, OKAY, BUT...
...HE SAID HE KNEW ME.
Hnngg...
PARKER...

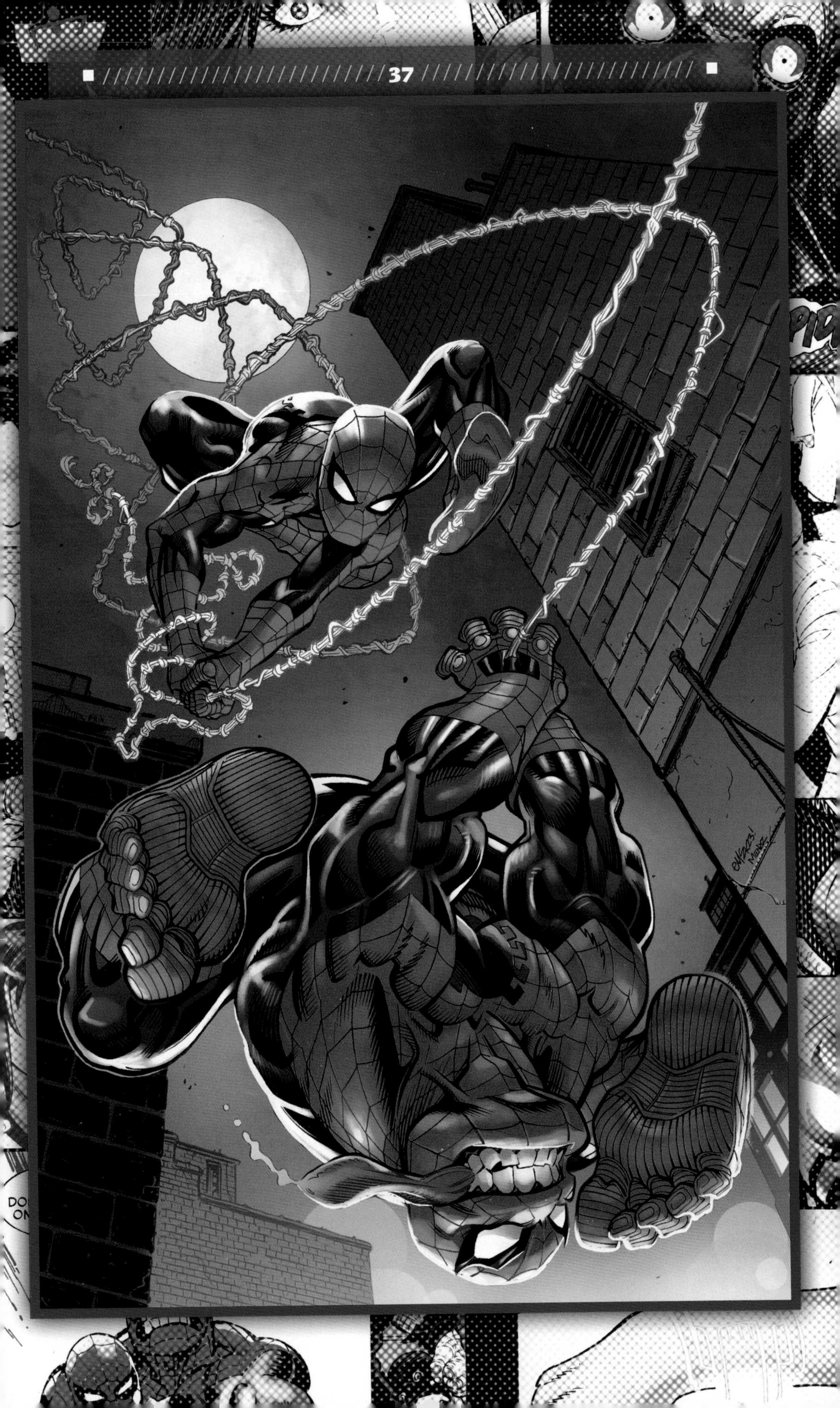

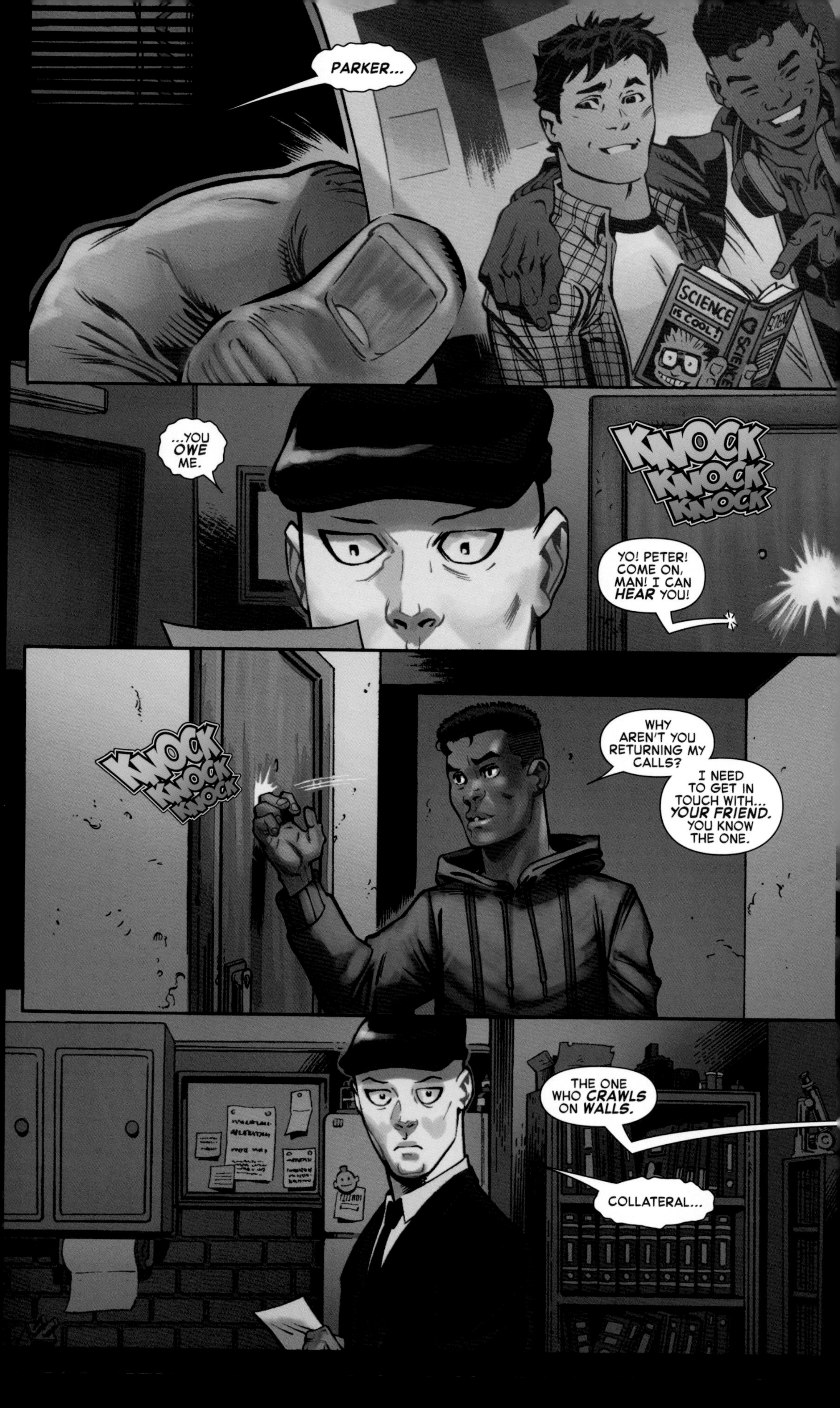
PARKER...
...YOU OWE ME.
KNOCK KNOCK KNOCK
YO! PETER! COME ON, MAN! I CAN HEAR YOU!
KNOCK KNOCK KNOCK
WHY AREN'T YOU RETURNING MY CALLS?
I NEED TO GET IN TOUCH WITH... YOUR FRIEND. YOU KNOW THE ONE.
THE ONE WHO CRAWLS ON WALLS.
COLLATERAL...
SCIENCE IS COOL!

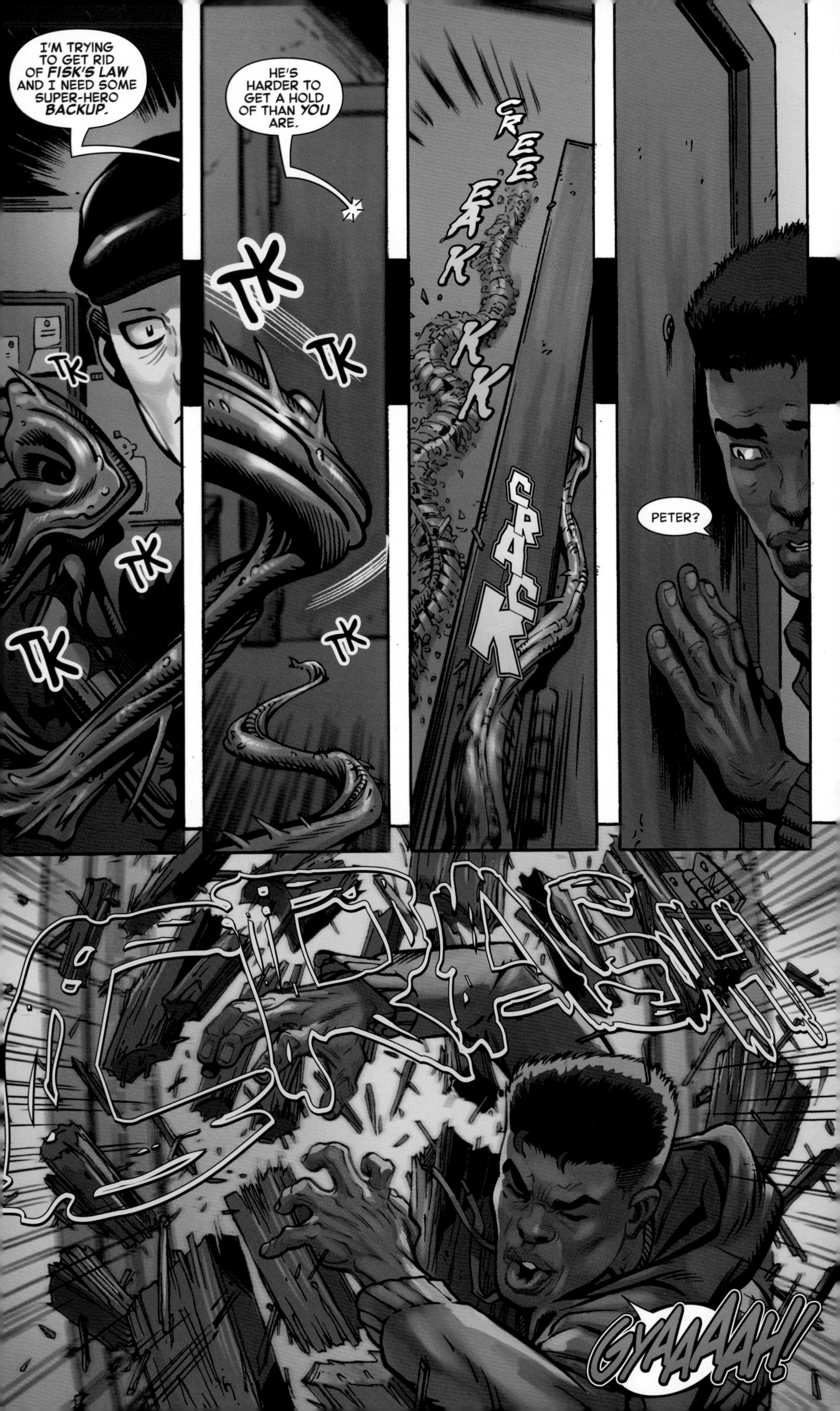

I'M TRYING TO GET RID OF FISK'S LAW AND I NEED SOME SUPER-HERO BACKUP.
TK
TK
TK
HE'S HARDER TO GET A HOLD OF THAN YOU ARE.
TK
TK
TK
CREEEAKKKK
CRACK
PETER?
SMASH
GYAAAAH!

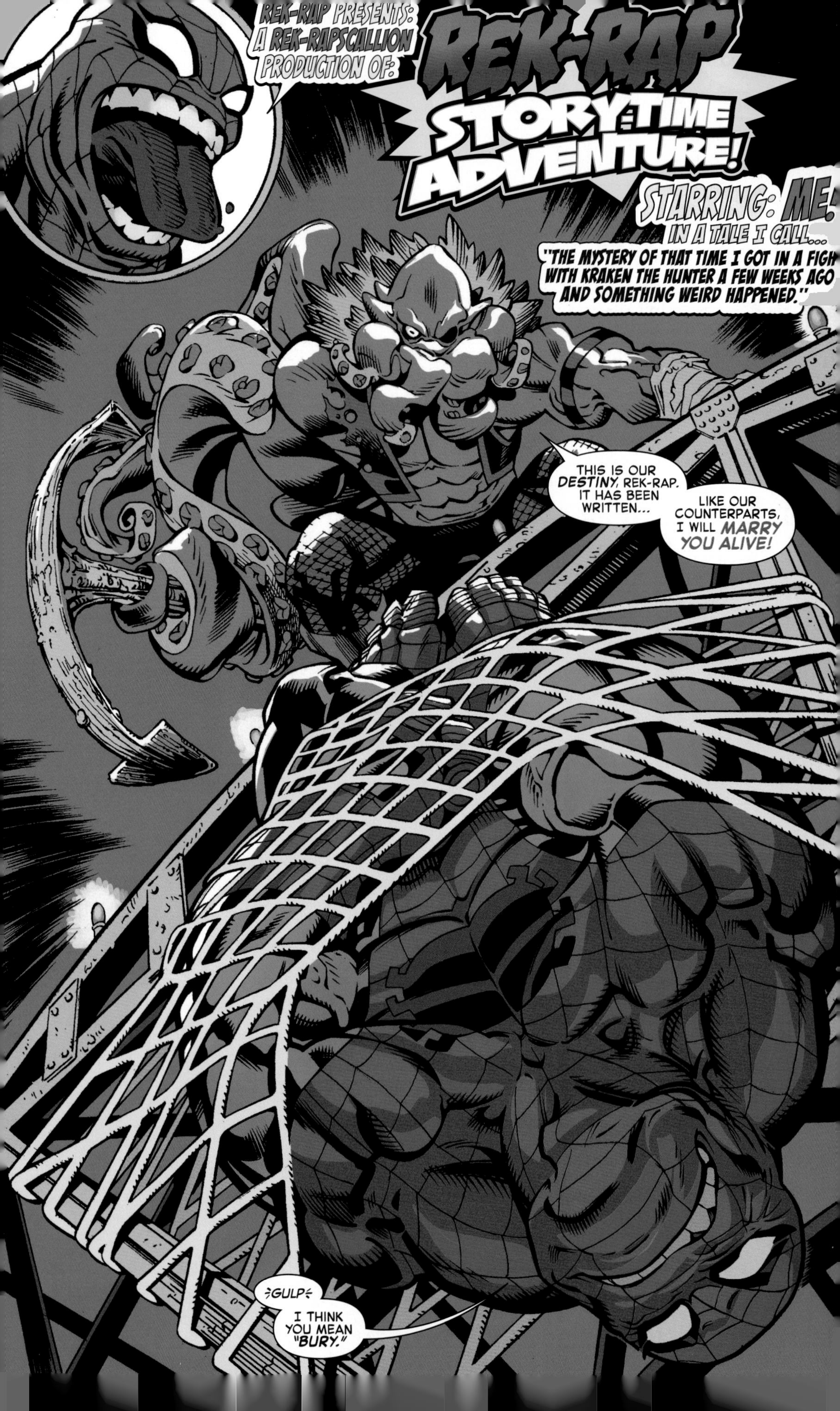

REK-RAP PRESENTS: A REK-RAPSCALLION PRODUCTION OF:
REK-RAP
STORY-TIME ADVENTURE!
STARRING: ME!
IN A TALE I CALL...
"THE MYSTERY OF THAT TIME I GOT IN A FIGH WITH KRAKEN THE HUNTER A FEW WEEKS AGO AND SOMETHING WEIRD HAPPENED."
THIS IS OUR DESTINY, REK-RAP. IT HAS BEEN WRITTEN...
LIKE OUR COUNTERPARTS, I WILL MARRY YOU ALIVE!
GULP
I THINK YOU MEAN "BURY."

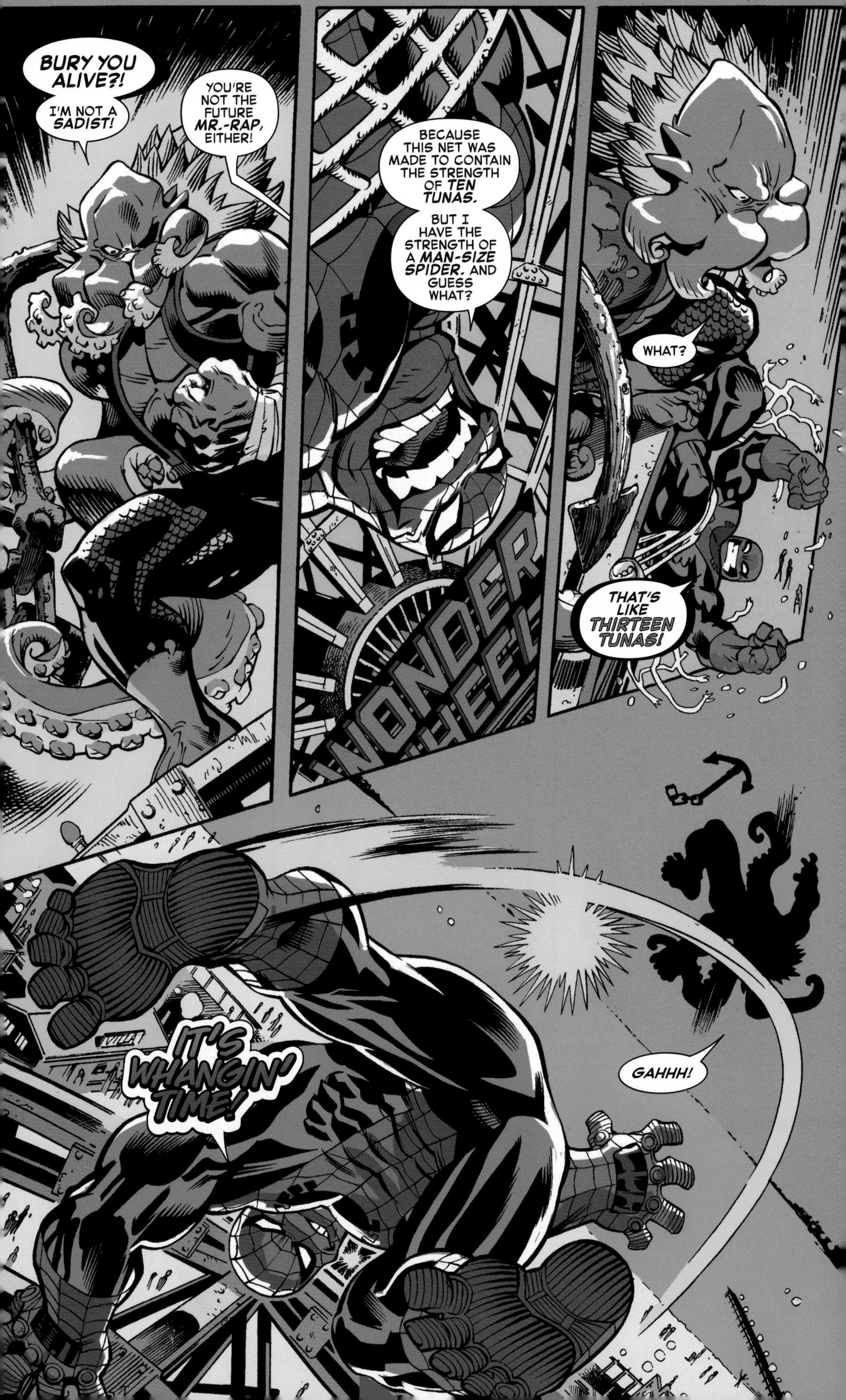
BURY YOU ALIVE?!
I'M NOT A SADIST!
YOU'RE NOT THE FUTURE MR.-RAP, EITHER!
BECAUSE THIS NET WAS MADE TO CONTAIN THE STRENGTH OF TEN TUNAS.
BUT I HAVE THE STRENGTH OF A MAN-SIZE SPIDER. AND GUESS WHAT?
WONDER WHEEL
WHAT?
THAT'S LIKE THIRTEEN TUNAS!
IT'S WHANGIN' TIME!
GAHHH!

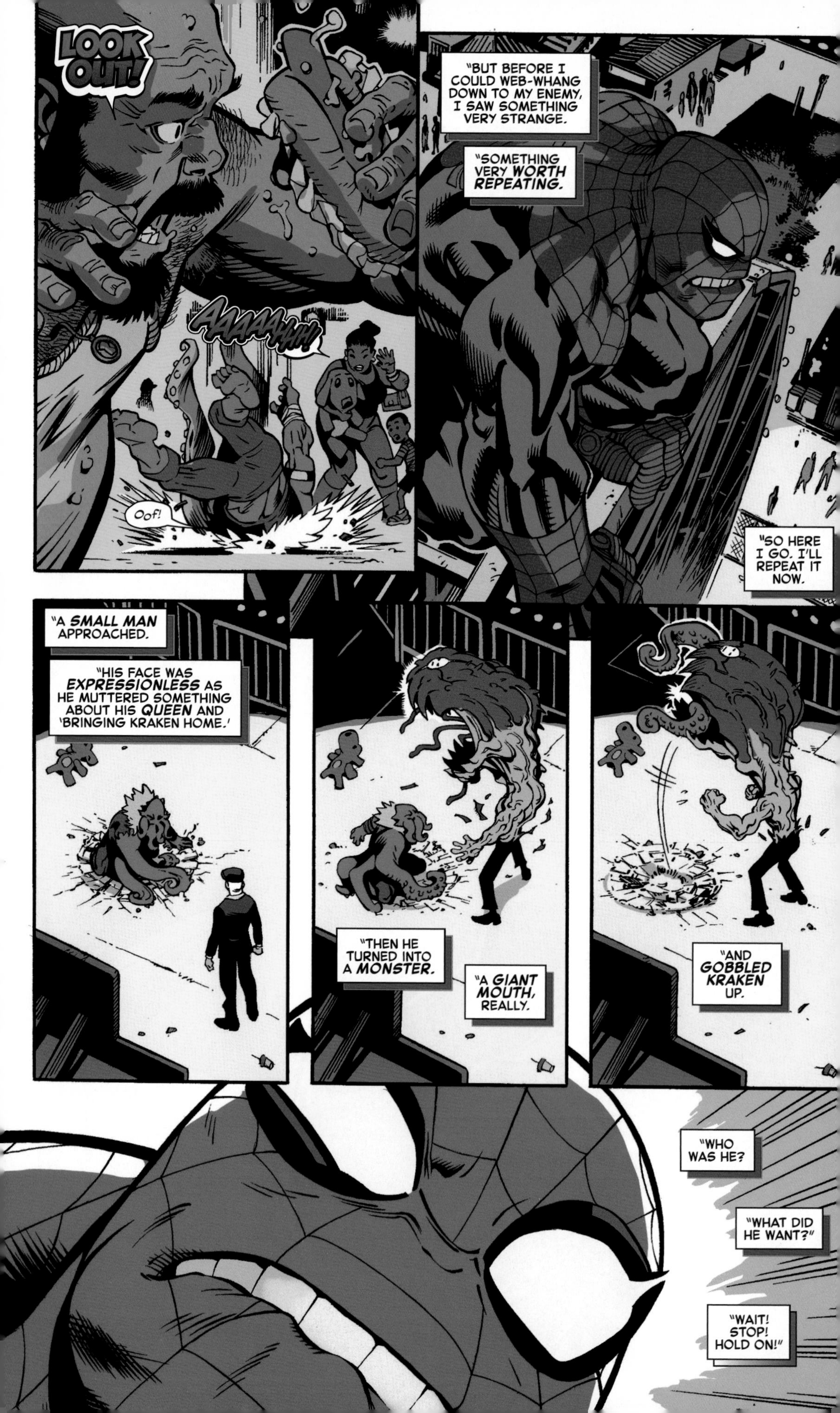
LOOK OUT!
AAAAAHHH!
Oof!
"BUT BEFORE I COULD WEB-WHANG DOWN TO MY ENEMY, I SAW SOMETHING VERY STRANGE.
"SOMETHING VERY WORTH REPEATING.
"SO HERE I GO. I'LL REPEAT IT NOW.
"A SMALL MAN APPROACHED.
"HIS FACE WAS EXPRESSIONLESS AS HE MUTTERED SOMETHING ABOUT HIS QUEEN AND 'BRINGING KRAKEN HOME.'
"THEN HE TURNED INTO A MONSTER.
"A GIANT MOUTH, REALLY.
"AND GOBBLED KRAKEN UP.
"WHO WAS HE?
"WHAT DID HE WANT?"
"WAIT! STOP! HOLD ON!"

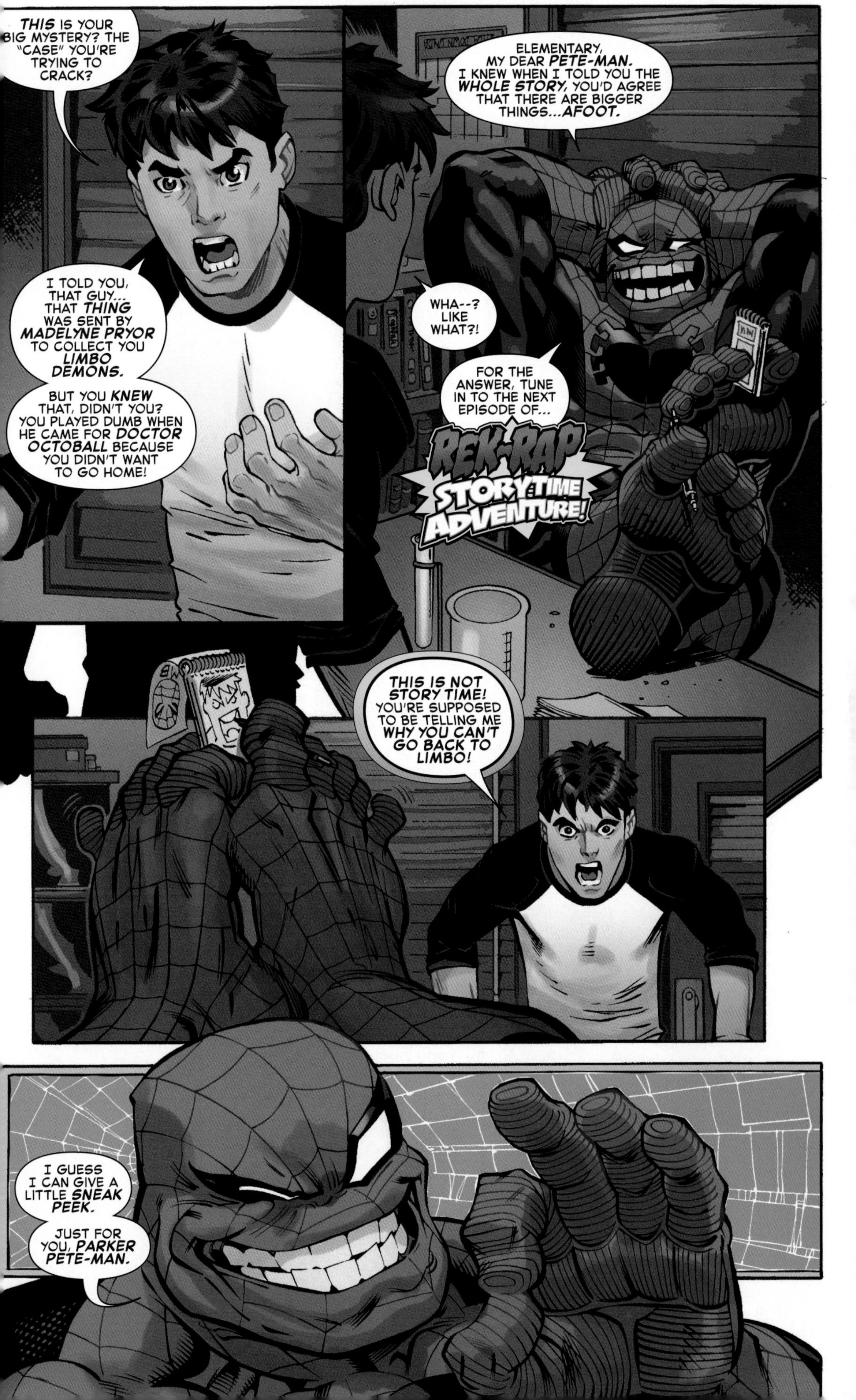
THIS IS YOUR BIG MYSTERY? THE "CASE" YOU'RE TRYING TO CRACK?
ELEMENTARY, MY DEAR PETE-MAN. I KNEW WHEN I TOLD YOU THE WHOLE STORY, YOU'D AGREE THAT THERE ARE BIGGER THINGS...AFOOT.
I TOLD YOU, THAT GUY... THAT THING WAS SENT BY MADELYNE PRYOR TO COLLECT YOU LIMBO DEMONS.
BUT YOU KNEW THAT, DIDN'T YOU? YOU PLAYED DUMB WHEN HE CAME FOR DOCTOR OCTOBALL BECAUSE YOU DIDN'T WANT TO GO HOME!
WHA--? LIKE WHAT?!
FOR THE ANSWER, TUNE IN TO THE NEXT EPISODE OF...
REK-RAP STORYTIME ADVENTURE!
THIS IS NOT STORY TIME! YOU'RE SUPPOSED TO BE TELLING ME WHY YOU CAN'T GO BACK TO LIMBO!
I GUESS I CAN GIVE A LITTLE SNEAK PEEK.
JUST FOR YOU, PARKER PETE-MAN.

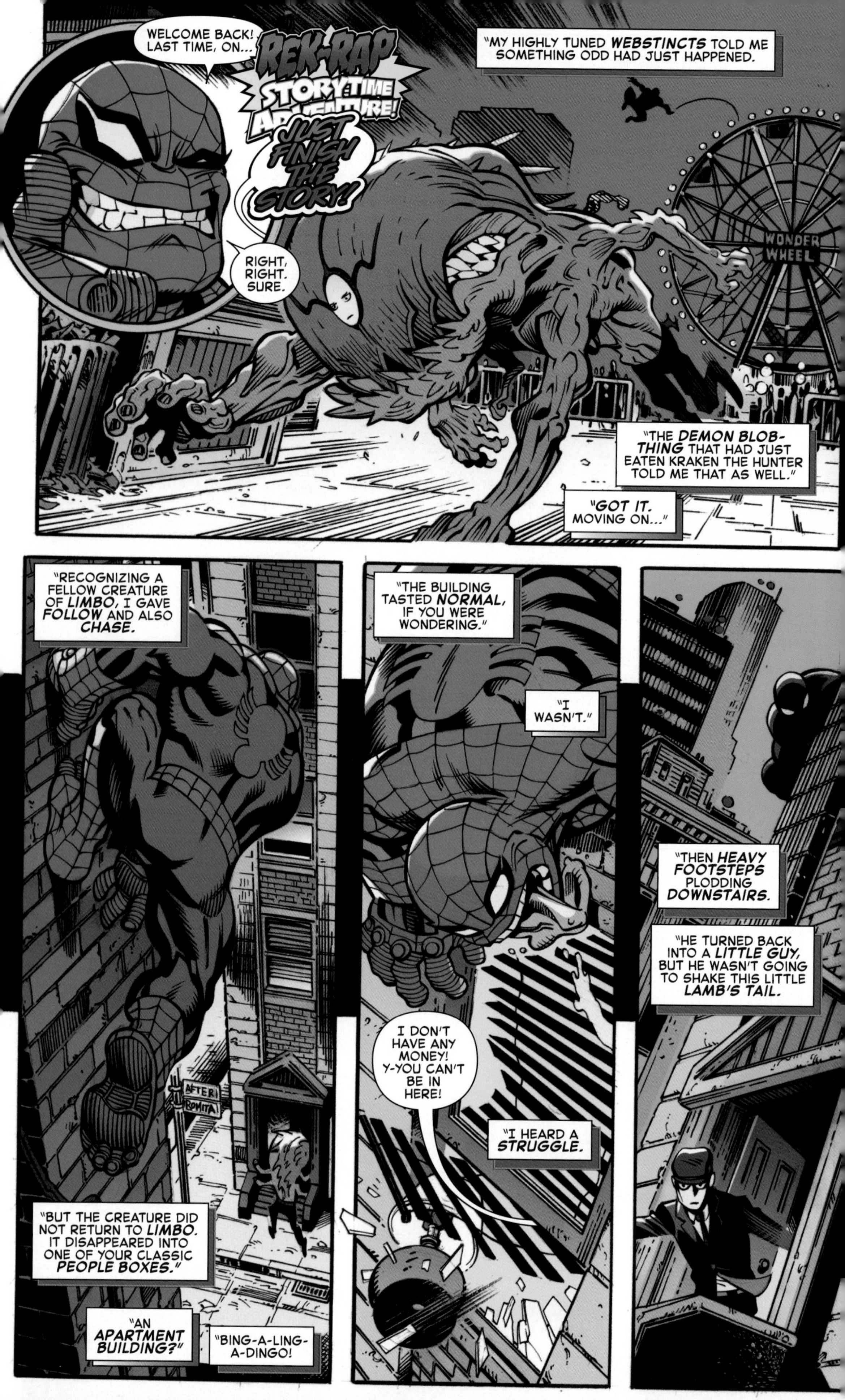
WELCOME BACK! LAST TIME, ON...
REK-RAP STORYTIME ADVENTURE!
JUST FINISH THE STORY!
RIGHT, RIGHT. SURE.
"MY HIGHLY TUNED WEBSTINCTS TOLD ME SOMETHING ODD HAD JUST HAPPENED.
WONDER WHEEL
"THE DEMON BLOB-THING THAT HAD JUST EATEN KRAKEN THE HUNTER TOLD ME THAT AS WELL."
"GOT IT. MOVING ON..."
"RECOGNIZING A FELLOW CREATURE OF LIMBO, I GAVE FOLLOW AND ALSO CHASE.
AFTER
ROMITA
"BUT THE CREATURE DID NOT RETURN TO LIMBO. IT DISAPPEARED INTO ONE OF YOUR CLASSIC PEOPLE BOXES."
"AN APARTMENT BUILDING?"
"BING-A-LING-A-DINGO!
"THE BUILDING TASTED NORMAL, IF YOU WERE WONDERING."
"I WASN'T."
I DON'T HAVE ANY MONEY! Y-YOU CAN'T BE IN HERE!
"I HEARD A STRUGGLE.
"THEN HEAVY FOOTSTEPS PLODDING DOWNSTAIRS.
"HE TURNED BACK INTO A LITTLE GUY, BUT HE WASN'T GOING TO SHAKE THIS LITTLE LAMB'S TAIL.

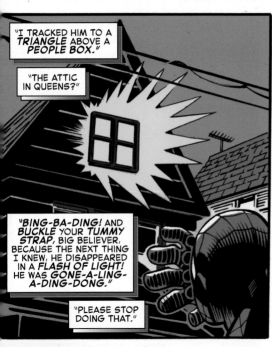

"I TRACKED HIM TO A *TRIANGLE* ABOVE A *PEOPLE BOX.*"

"THE ATTIC IN QUEENS?"

"*BING-BA-DING!* AND *BUCKLE* YOUR *TUMMY STRAP,* BIG BELIEVER, BECAUSE THE NEXT THING I KNEW, HE DISAPPEARED IN A *FLASH OF LIGHT!* HE WAS *GONE-A-LING-A-DING-DONG.*"

"PLEASE STOP DOING THAT."

"I WOULDN'T HAVE GIVEN IT ANOTHER THOUGHT..."

"THAT'S ALARMING."

"...IF THE SAME THING HADN'T HAPPENED WHEN I FOUGHT *GOREPION* A WEEK LATER."

"I FOLLOWED HIM TO *ANOTHER PEOPLE BOX.*"

"WHERE THERE WAS *ANOTHER* COMMOTION."

"AND *ANOTHER* TRIP TO *QUEENS.*"

"ANOTHER *FLASH OF LIGHT.*"

"AND THE SAME THING HAPPENED THE NEXT WEEK WHEN I FOUGHT *RHICERATOPS.*"

"EXCUSE ME..."

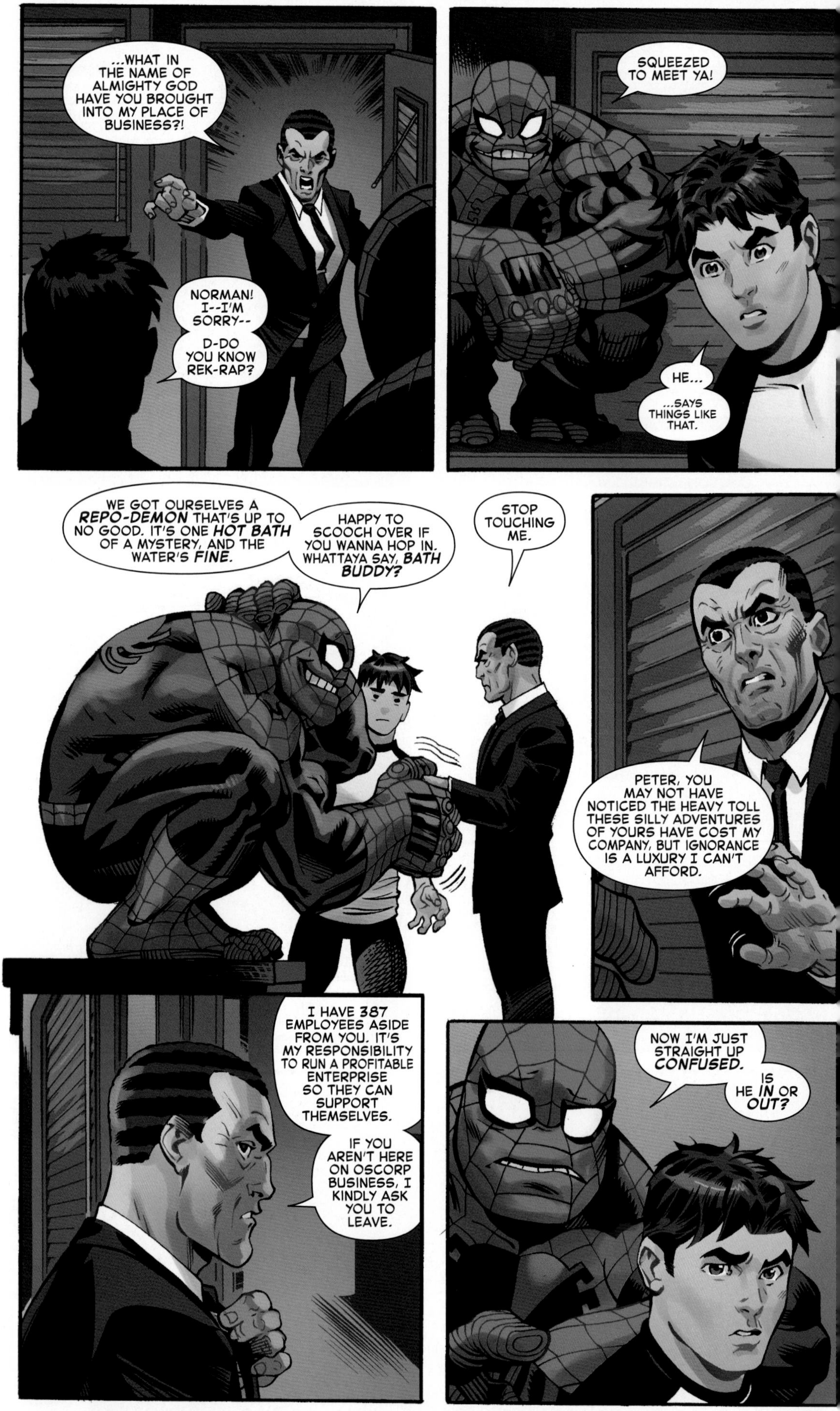
...WHAT IN THE NAME OF ALMIGHTY GOD HAVE YOU BROUGHT INTO MY PLACE OF BUSINESS?!
NORMAN! I--I'M SORRY--
D-DO YOU KNOW REK-RAP?
SQUEEZED TO MEET YA!
HE...
...SAYS THINGS LIKE THAT.
WE GOT OURSELVES A REPO-DEMON THAT'S UP TO NO GOOD. IT'S ONE HOT BATH OF A MYSTERY, AND THE WATER'S FINE.
HAPPY TO SCOOCH OVER IF YOU WANNA HOP IN. WHATTAYA SAY, BATH BUDDY?
STOP TOUCHING ME.
PETER, YOU MAY NOT HAVE NOTICED THE HEAVY TOLL THESE SILLY ADVENTURES OF YOURS HAVE COST MY COMPANY, BUT IGNORANCE IS A LUXURY I CAN'T AFFORD.
I HAVE 387 EMPLOYEES ASIDE FROM YOU. IT'S MY RESPONSIBILITY TO RUN A PROFITABLE ENTERPRISE SO THEY CAN SUPPORT THEMSELVES.
IF YOU AREN'T HERE ON OSCORP BUSINESS, I KINDLY ASK YOU TO LEAVE.
NOW I'M JUST STRAIGHT UP CONFUSED.
IS HE IN OR OUT?

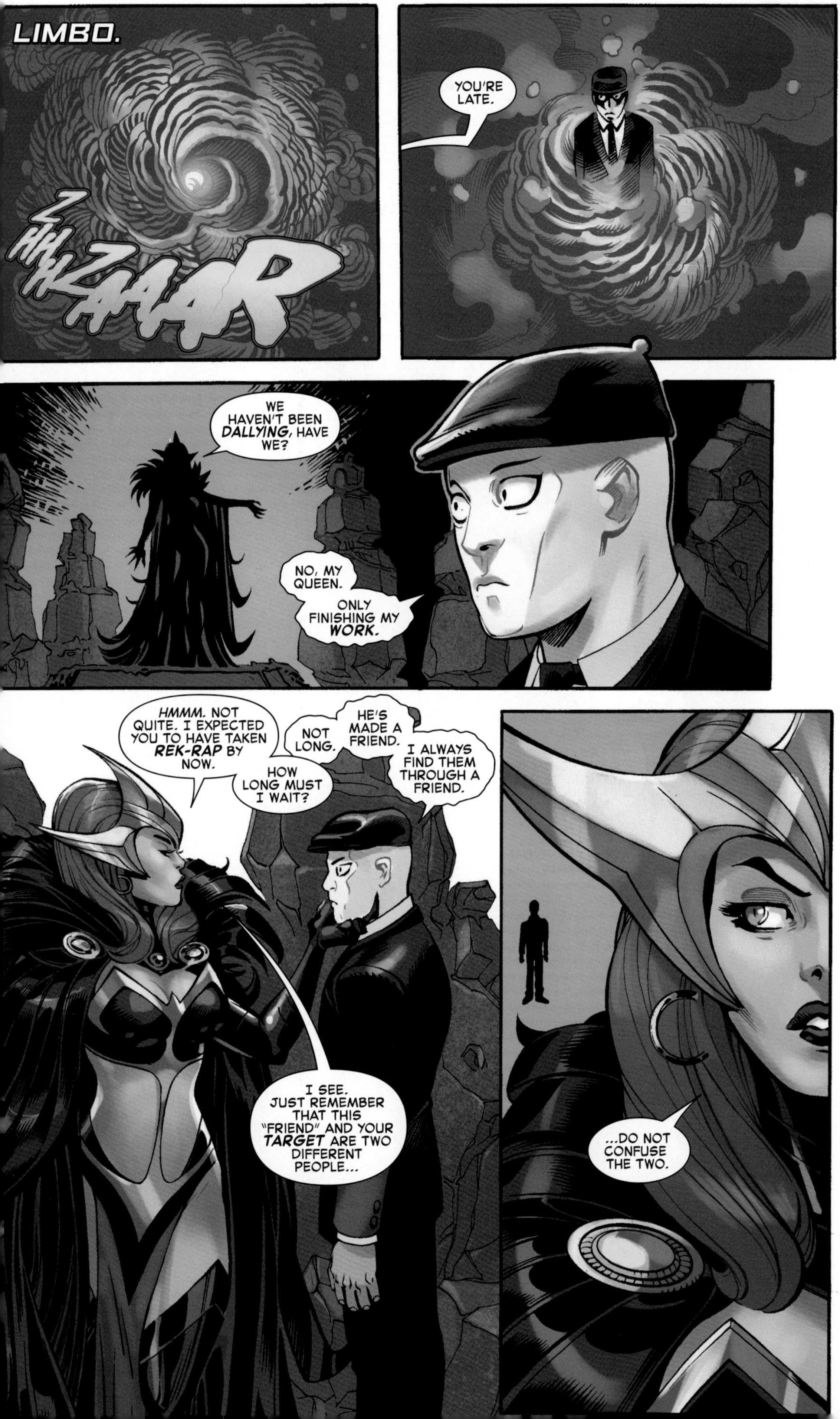
LIMBO.
ZHHHZAAAR
YOU'RE LATE.
WE HAVEN'T BEEN DALLYING, HAVE WE?
NO, MY QUEEN.
ONLY FINISHING MY WORK.
HMMM. NOT QUITE. I EXPECTED YOU TO HAVE TAKEN REK-RAP BY NOW.
HOW LONG MUST I WAIT?
NOT LONG.
HE'S MADE A FRIEND.
I ALWAYS FIND THEM THROUGH A FRIEND.
I SEE. JUST REMEMBER THAT THIS "FRIEND" AND YOUR TARGET ARE TWO DIFFERENT PEOPLE...
...DO NOT CONFUSE THE TWO.

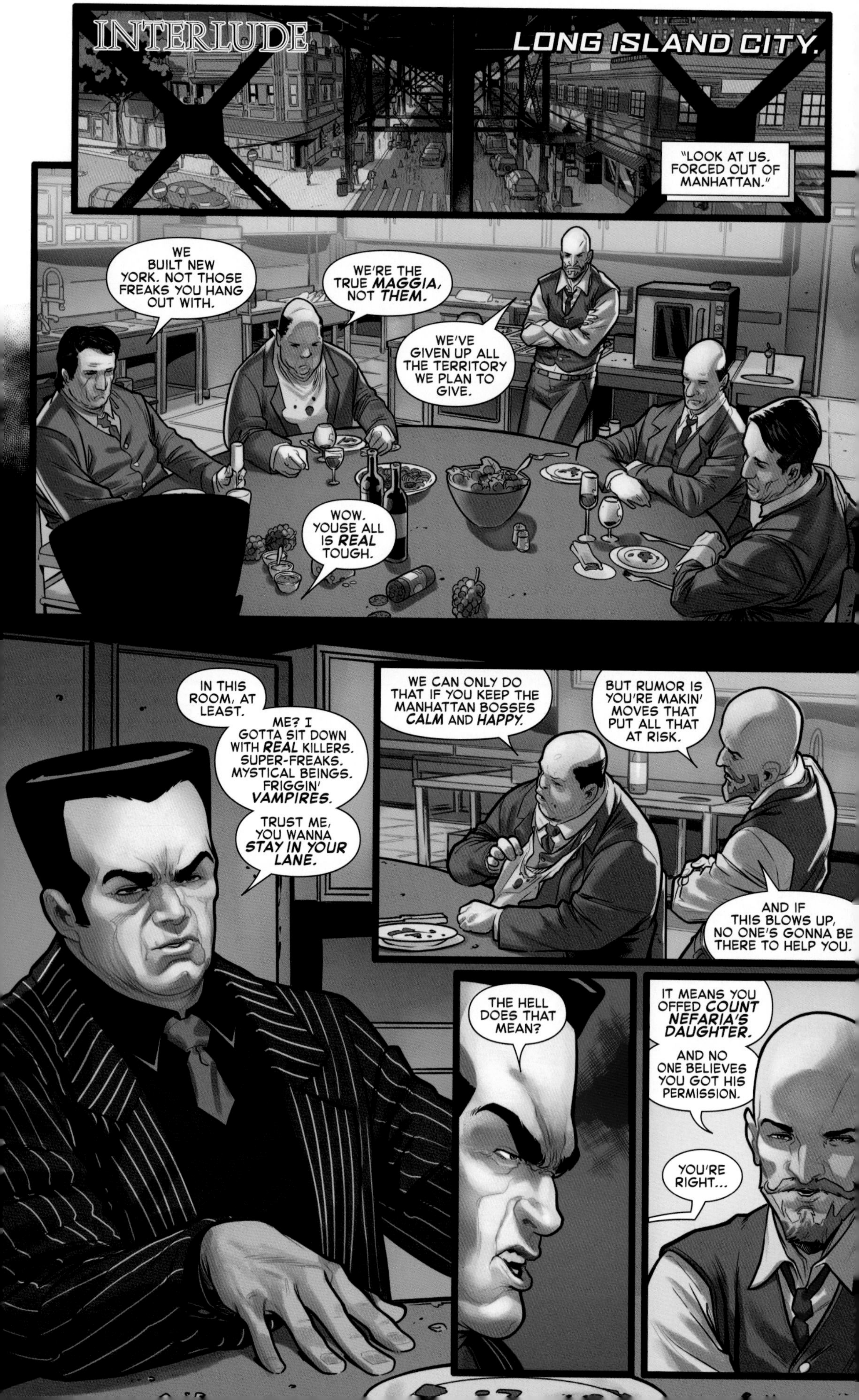
INTERLUDE
LONG ISLAND CITY.
"LOOK AT US. FORCED OUT OF MANHATTAN."
WE BUILT NEW YORK. NOT THOSE FREAKS YOU HANG OUT WITH.
WE'RE THE TRUE MAGGIA, NOT THEM.
WE'VE GIVEN UP ALL THE TERRITORY WE PLAN TO GIVE.
WOW. YOUSE ALL IS REAL TOUGH.
IN THIS ROOM, AT LEAST.
ME? I GOTTA SIT DOWN WITH REAL KILLERS. SUPER-FREAKS. MYSTICAL BEINGS. FRIGGIN' VAMPIRES.
TRUST ME, YOU WANNA STAY IN YOUR LANE.
WE CAN ONLY DO THAT IF YOU KEEP THE MANHATTAN BOSSES CALM AND HAPPY.
BUT RUMOR IS YOU'RE MAKIN' MOVES THAT PUT ALL THAT AT RISK.
AND IF THIS BLOWS UP, NO ONE'S GONNA BE THERE TO HELP YOU.
THE HELL DOES THAT MEAN?
IT MEANS YOU OFFED COUNT NEFARIA'S DAUGHTER.
AND NO ONE BELIEVES YOU GOT HIS PERMISSION.
YOU'RE RIGHT...

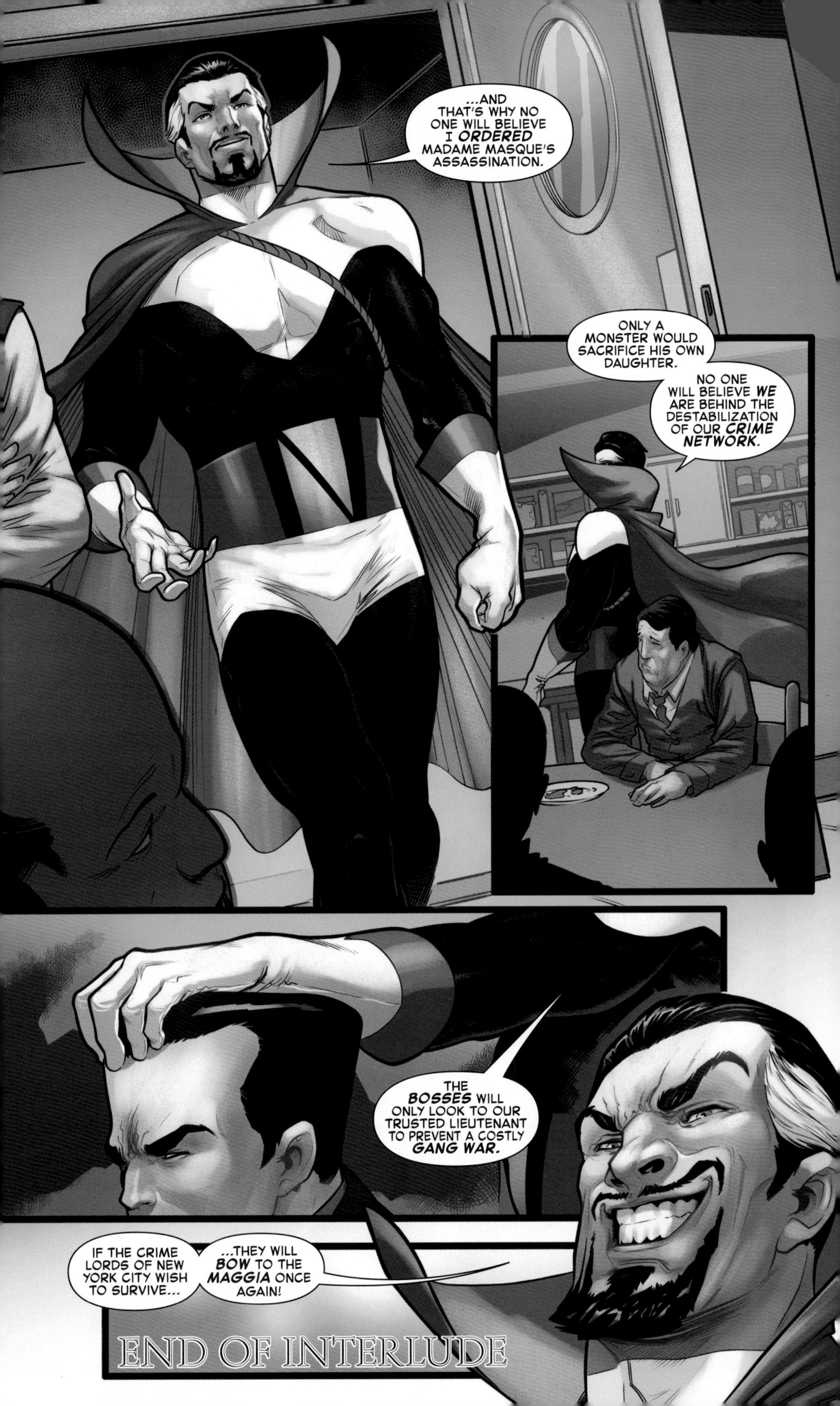
...AND THAT'S WHY NO ONE WILL BELIEVE I ORDERED MADAME MASQUE'S ASSASSINATION.
ONLY A MONSTER WOULD SACRIFICE HIS OWN DAUGHTER.
NO ONE WILL BELIEVE WE ARE BEHIND THE DESTABILIZATION OF OUR CRIME NETWORK.
THE BOSSES WILL ONLY LOOK TO OUR TRUSTED LIEUTENANT TO PREVENT A COSTLY GANG WAR.
IF THE CRIME LORDS OF NEW YORK CITY WISH TO SURVIVE...
...THEY WILL BOW TO THE MAGGIA ONCE AGAIN!
END OF INTERLUDE

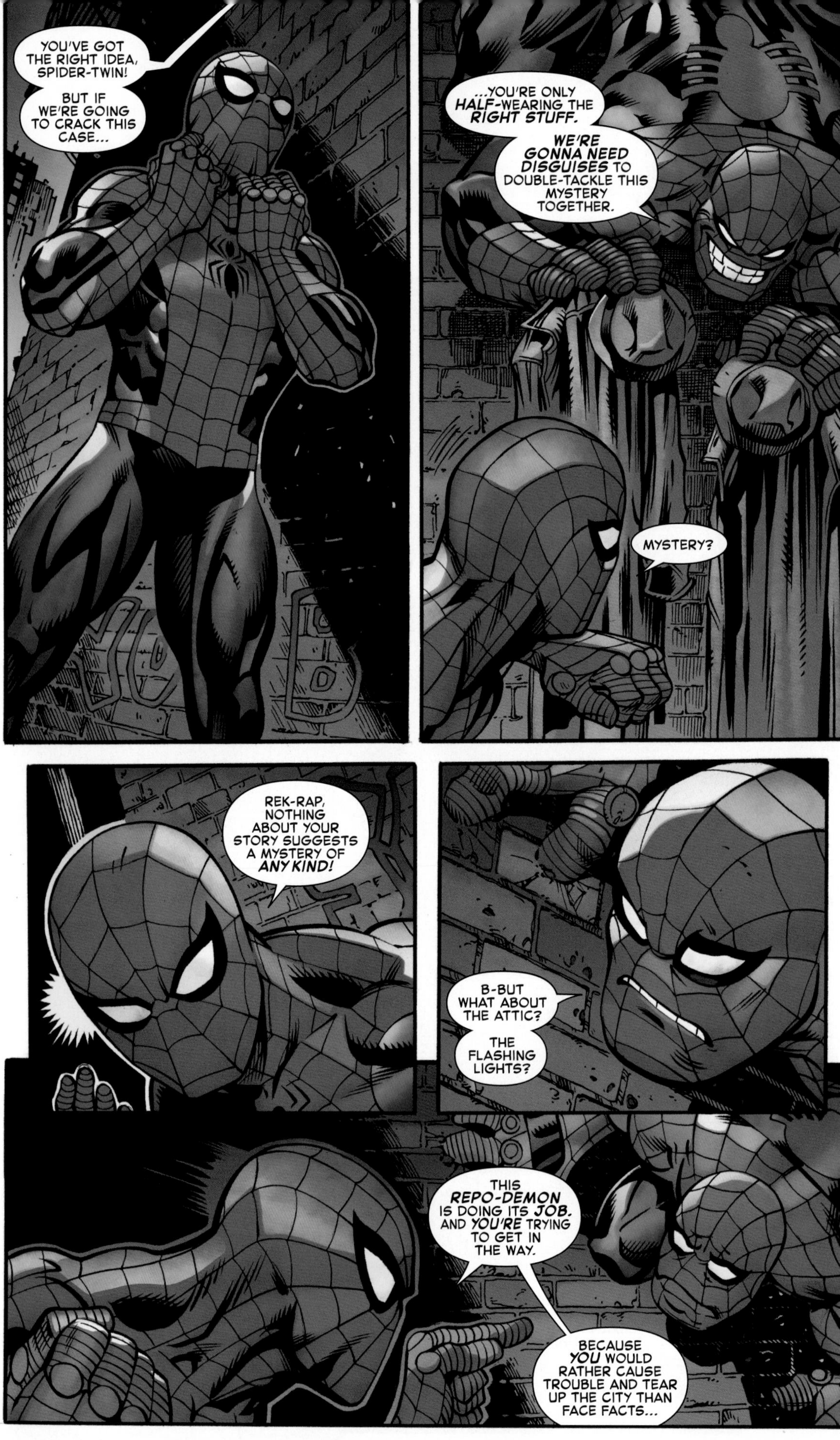

YOU'VE GOT THE RIGHT IDEA, SPIDER-TWIN!
BUT IF WE'RE GOING TO CRACK THIS CASE...
...YOU'RE ONLY HALF-WEARING THE RIGHT STUFF.
WE'RE GONNA NEED DISGUISES TO DOUBLE-TACKLE THIS MYSTERY TOGETHER.
MYSTERY?
REK-RAP, NOTHING ABOUT YOUR STORY SUGGESTS A MYSTERY OF ANY KIND!
B-BUT WHAT ABOUT THE ATTIC?
THE FLASHING LIGHTS?
THIS REPO-DEMON IS DOING ITS JOB. AND YOU'RE TRYING TO GET IN THE WAY.
BECAUSE YOU WOULD RATHER CAUSE TROUBLE AND TEAR UP THE CITY THAN FACE FACTS...

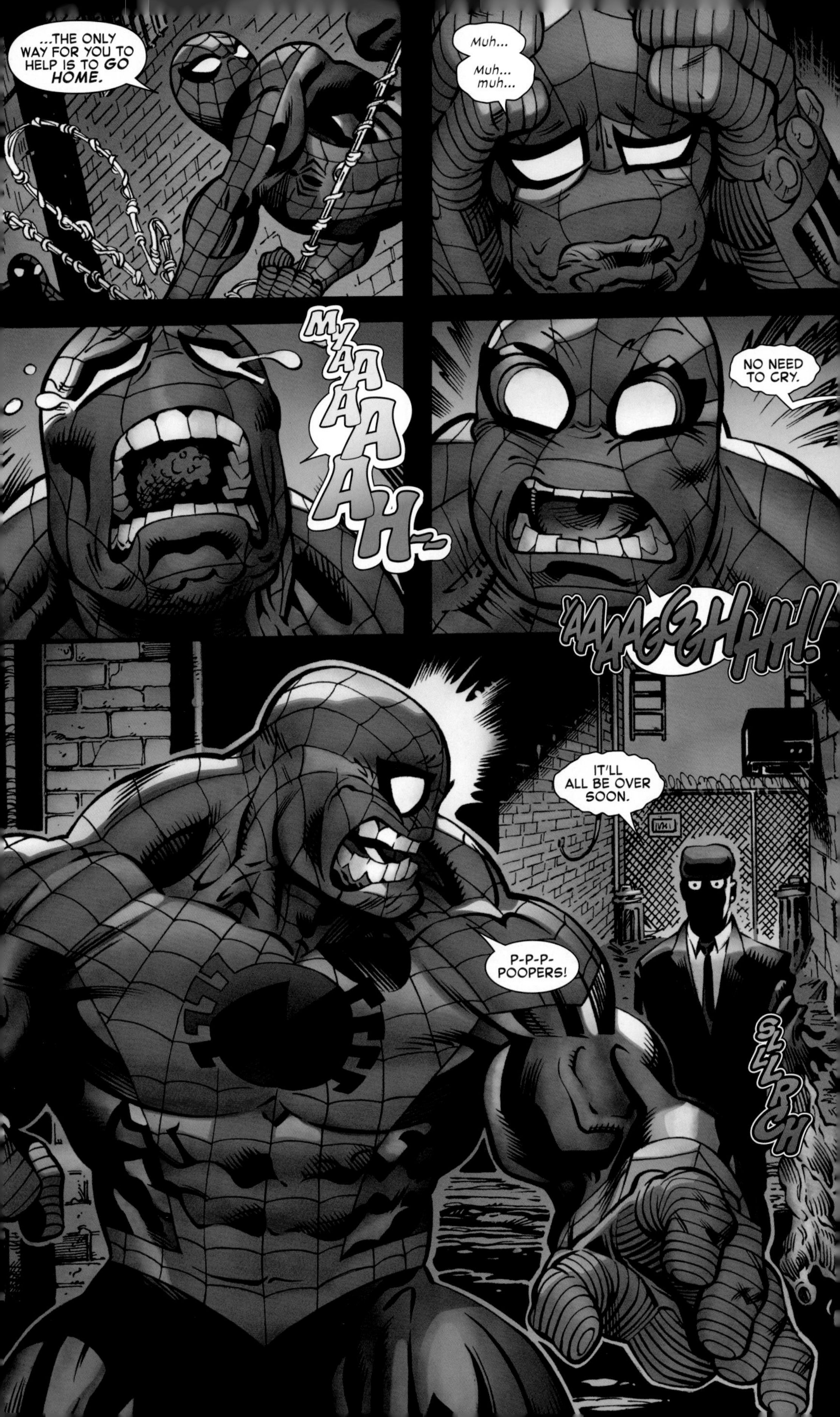
...THE ONLY WAY FOR YOU TO HELP IS TO GO HOME.
Muh...
Muh... muh...
MYAAAAAAH-
NO NEED TO CRY.
YAAAAGGHHHH!
IT'LL ALL BE OVER SOON.
P-P-P-POOPERS!
SHLLRCH

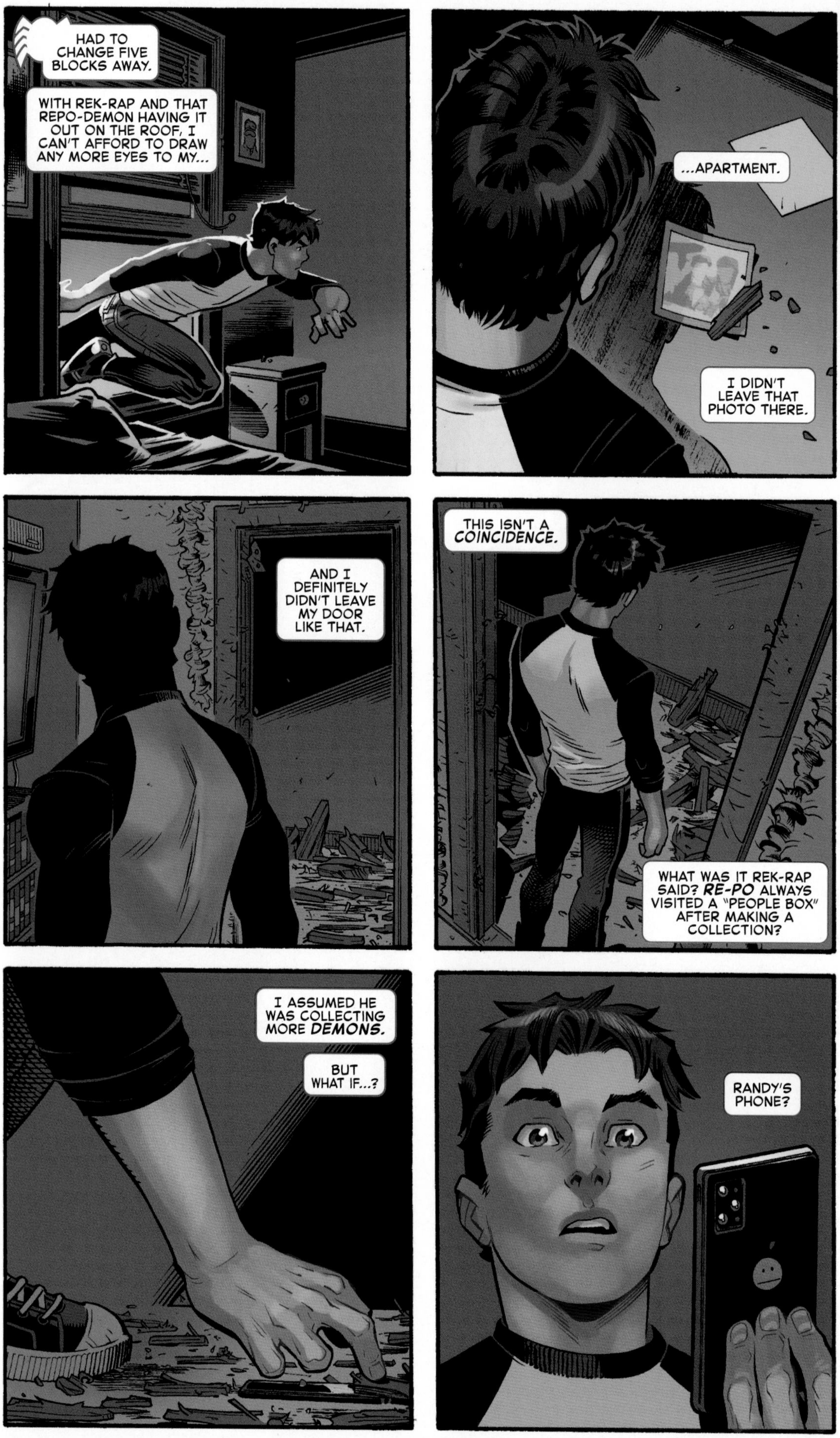
HAD TO CHANGE FIVE BLOCKS AWAY.
WITH REK-RAP AND THAT REPO-DEMON HAVING IT OUT ON THE ROOF, I CAN'T AFFORD TO DRAW ANY MORE EYES TO MY...
...APARTMENT.
I DIDN'T LEAVE THAT PHOTO THERE.
AND I DEFINITELY DIDN'T LEAVE MY DOOR LIKE THAT.
THIS ISN'T A *COINCIDENCE.*
WHAT WAS IT REK-RAP SAID? *RE-PO* ALWAYS VISITED A "PEOPLE BOX" AFTER MAKING A COLLECTION?
I ASSUMED HE WAS COLLECTING MORE *DEMONS.*
BUT WHAT IF...?
RANDY'S PHONE?

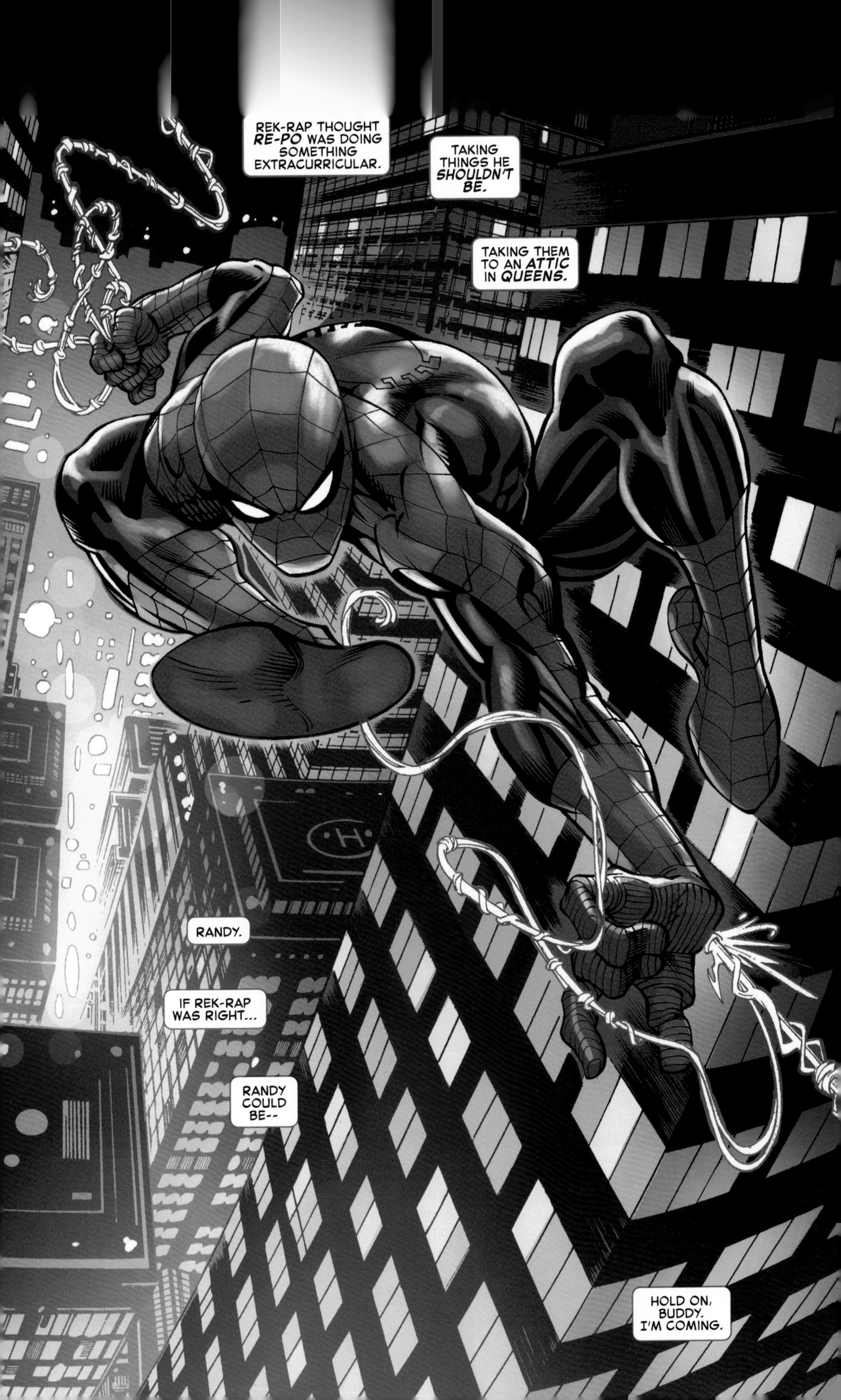

REK-RAP THOUGHT RE-PO WAS DOING SOMETHING EXTRACURRICULAR.
TAKING THINGS HE SHOULDN'T BE.
TAKING THEM TO AN ATTIC IN QUEENS.
RANDY.
IF REK-RAP WAS RIGHT...
RANDY COULD BE--
HOLD ON, BUDDY. I'M COMING.

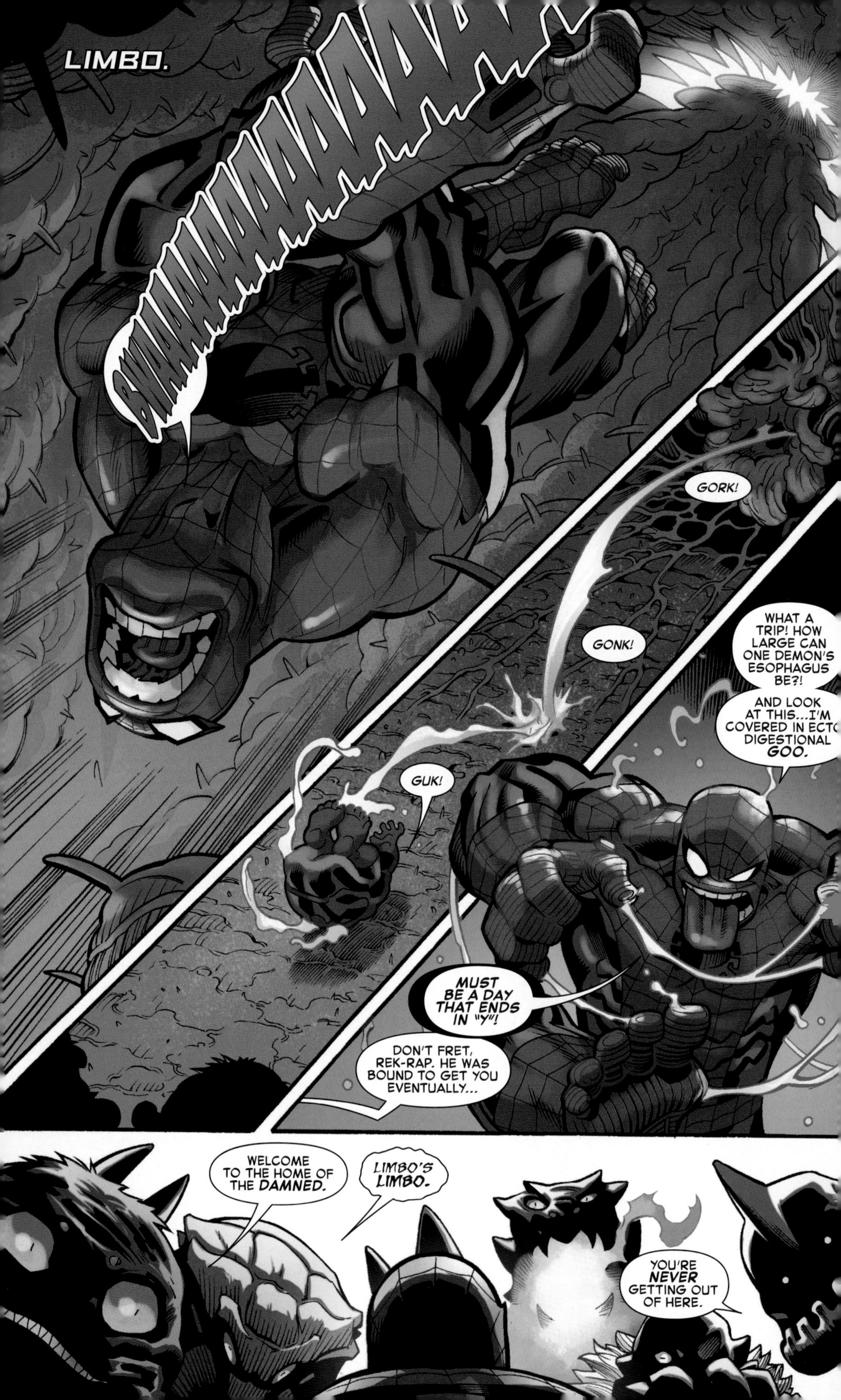

LIMBO.
GORK!
GONK!
GUK!
WHAT A TRIP! HOW LARGE CAN ONE DEMON'S ESOPHAGUS BE?!
AND LOOK AT THIS...I'M COVERED IN ECTO DIGESTIONAL GOO.
MUST BE A DAY THAT ENDS IN "Y"!
DON'T FRET, REK-RAP. HE WAS BOUND TO GET YOU EVENTUALLY...
WELCOME TO THE HOME OF THE DAMNED.
LIMBO'S LIMBO.
YOU'RE NEVER GETTING OUT OF HERE.

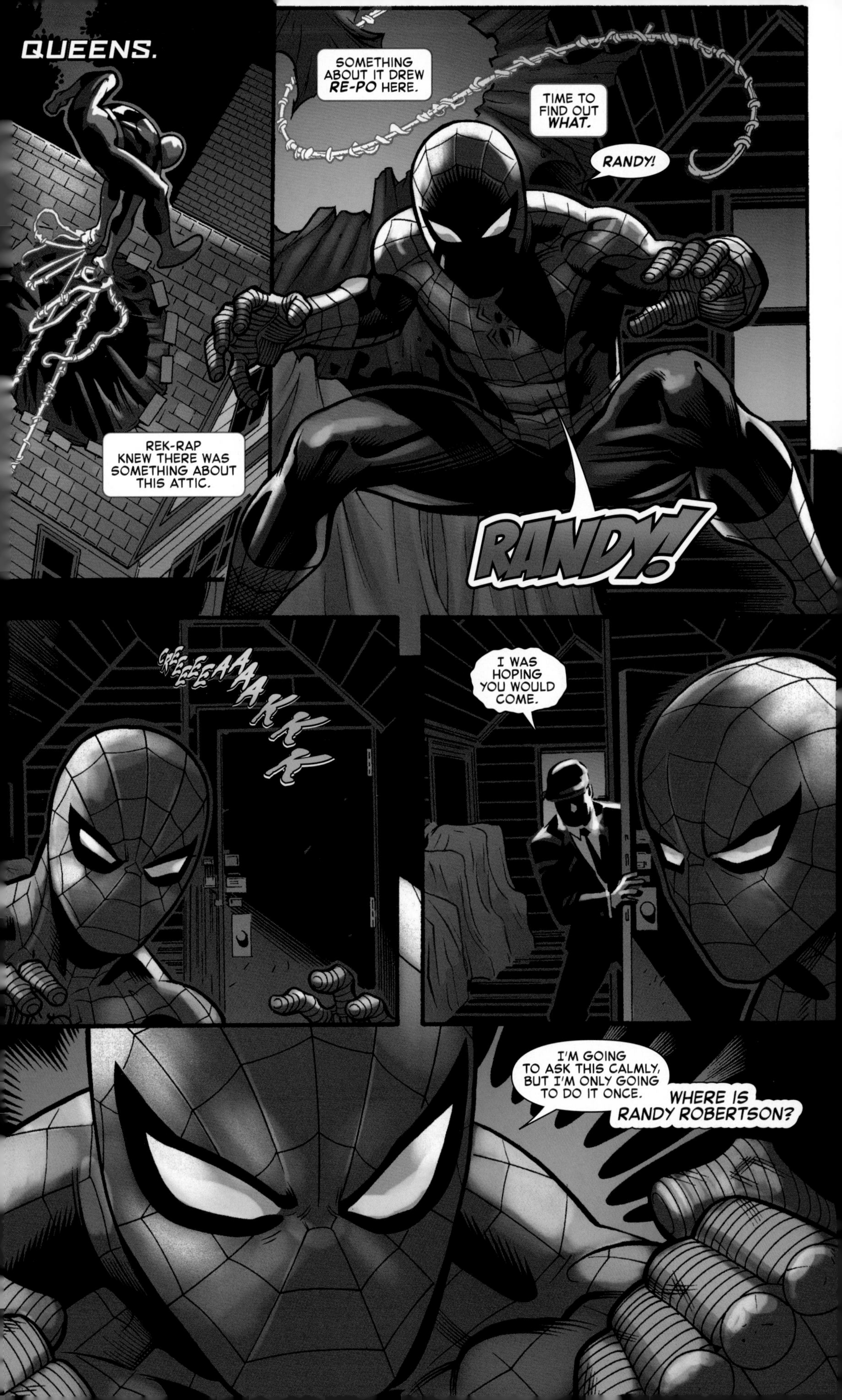
QUEENS.
REK-RAP KNEW THERE WAS SOMETHING ABOUT THIS ATTIC.
SOMETHING ABOUT IT DREW RE-PO HERE.
TIME TO FIND OUT WHAT.
RANDY!
RANDY!
CREEEEEAAAAKKKK
I WAS HOPING YOU WOULD COME.
I'M GOING TO ASK THIS CALMLY, BUT I'M ONLY GOING TO DO IT ONCE.
WHERE IS RANDY ROBERTSON?

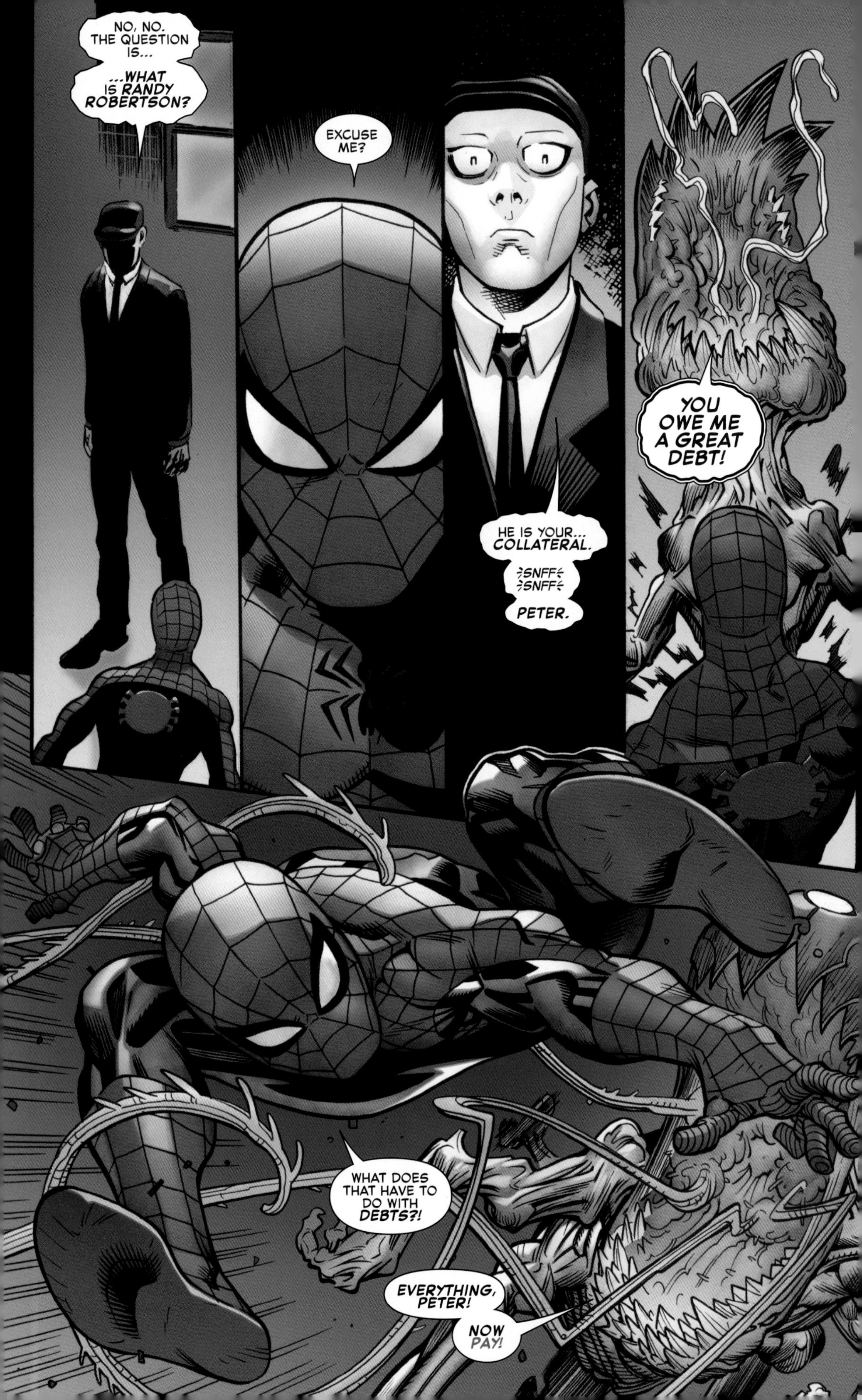
NO, NO. THE QUESTION IS...
...WHAT IS RANDY ROBERTSON?
EXCUSE ME?
HE IS YOUR... COLLATERAL.
SNFF SNFF
PETER.
YOU OWE ME A GREAT DEBT!
WHAT DOES THAT HAVE TO DO WITH DEBTS?!
EVERYTHING, PETER!
NOW PAY!

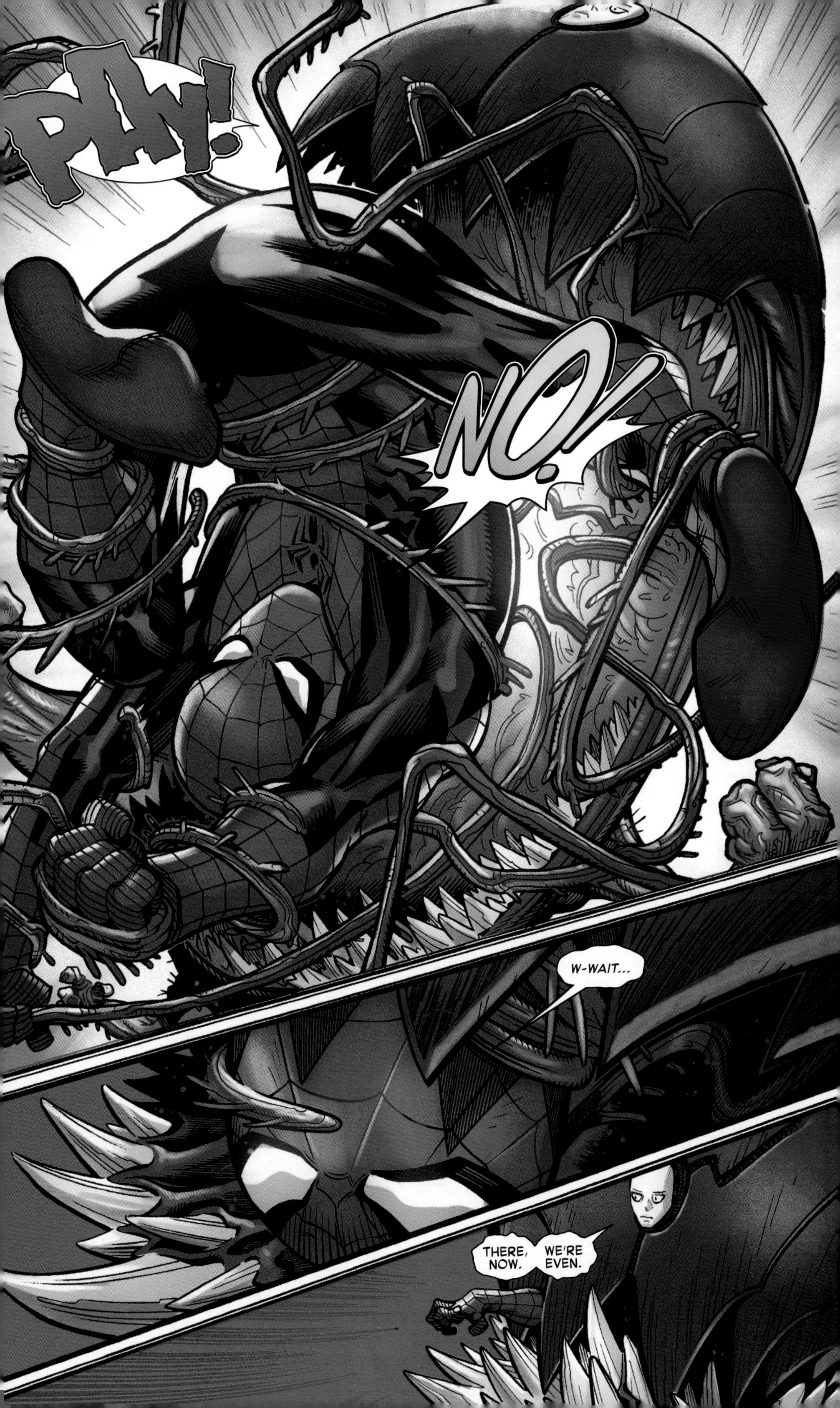
PAW!
NO!
W-WAIT...
THERE, NOW.
WE'RE EVEN.

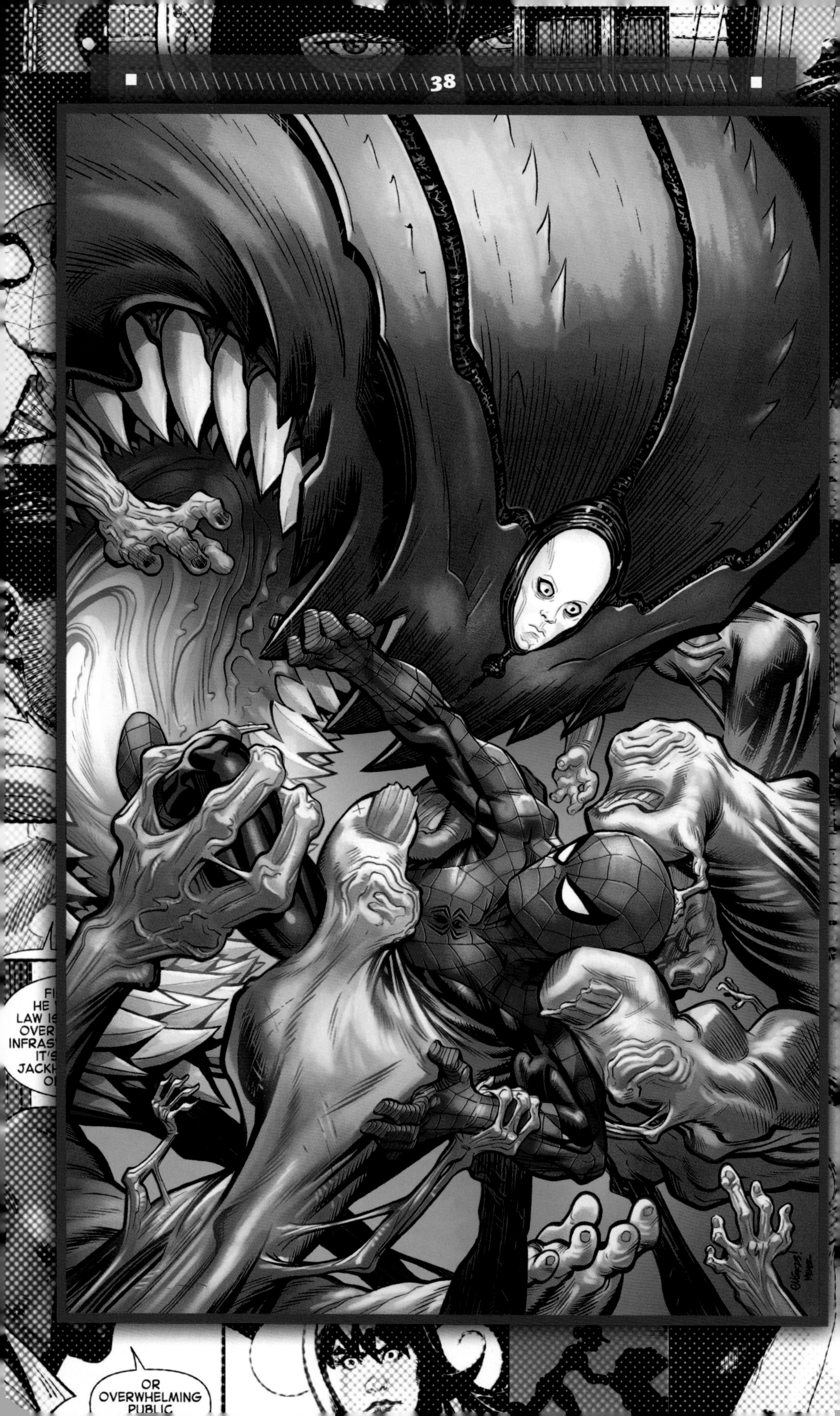
38
OR OVERWHELMING PUBLIC

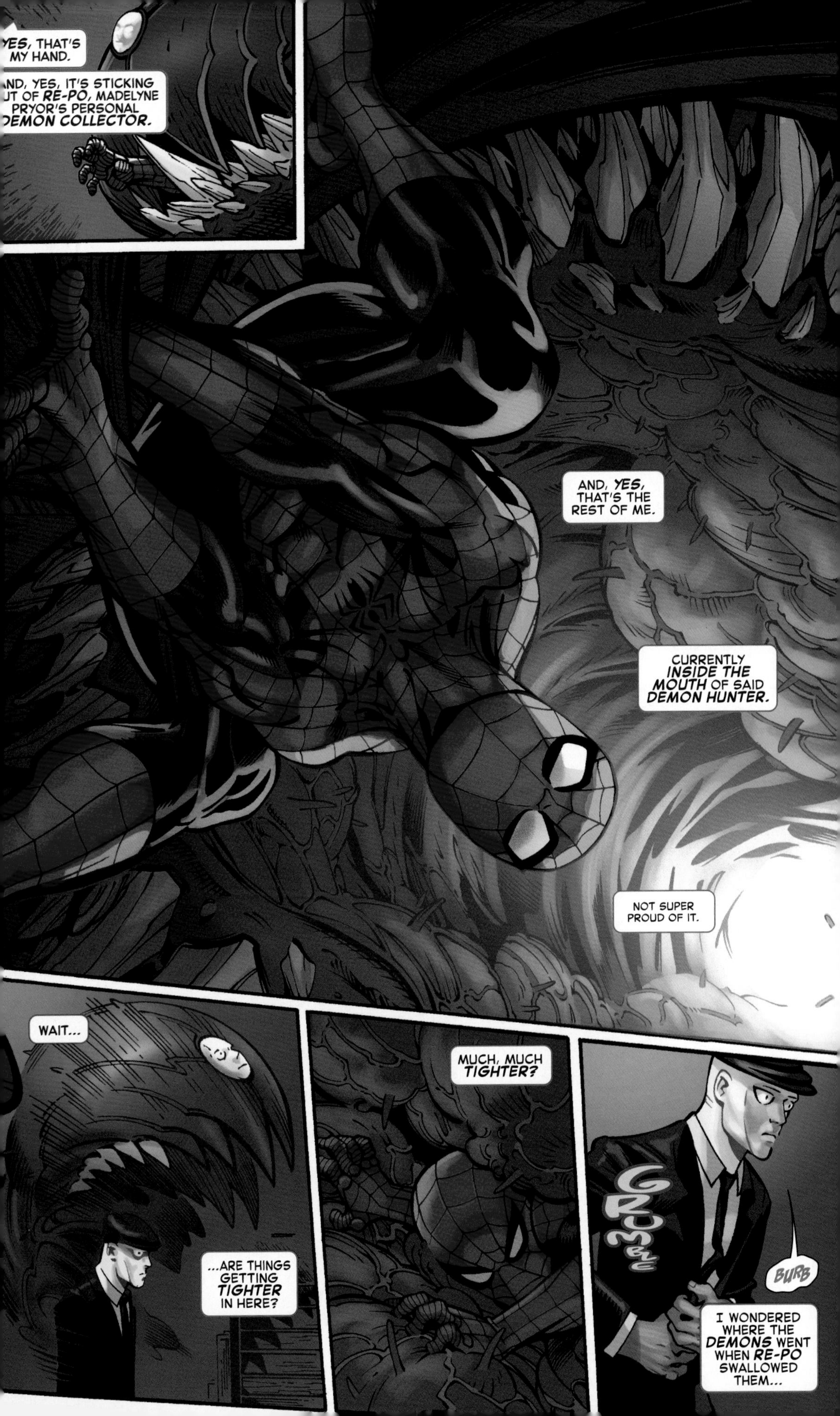
YES, THAT'S MY HAND.
AND, YES, IT'S STICKING OUT OF RE-PO, MADELYNE PRYOR'S PERSONAL DEMON COLLECTOR.
AND, YES, THAT'S THE REST OF ME.
CURRENTLY INSIDE THE MOUTH OF SAID DEMON HUNTER.
NOT SUPER PROUD OF IT.
WAIT...
...ARE THINGS GETTING TIGHTER IN HERE?
MUCH, MUCH TIGHTER?
GRUMBLE
BURB
I WONDERED WHERE THE DEMONS WENT WHEN RE-PO SWALLOWED THEM...

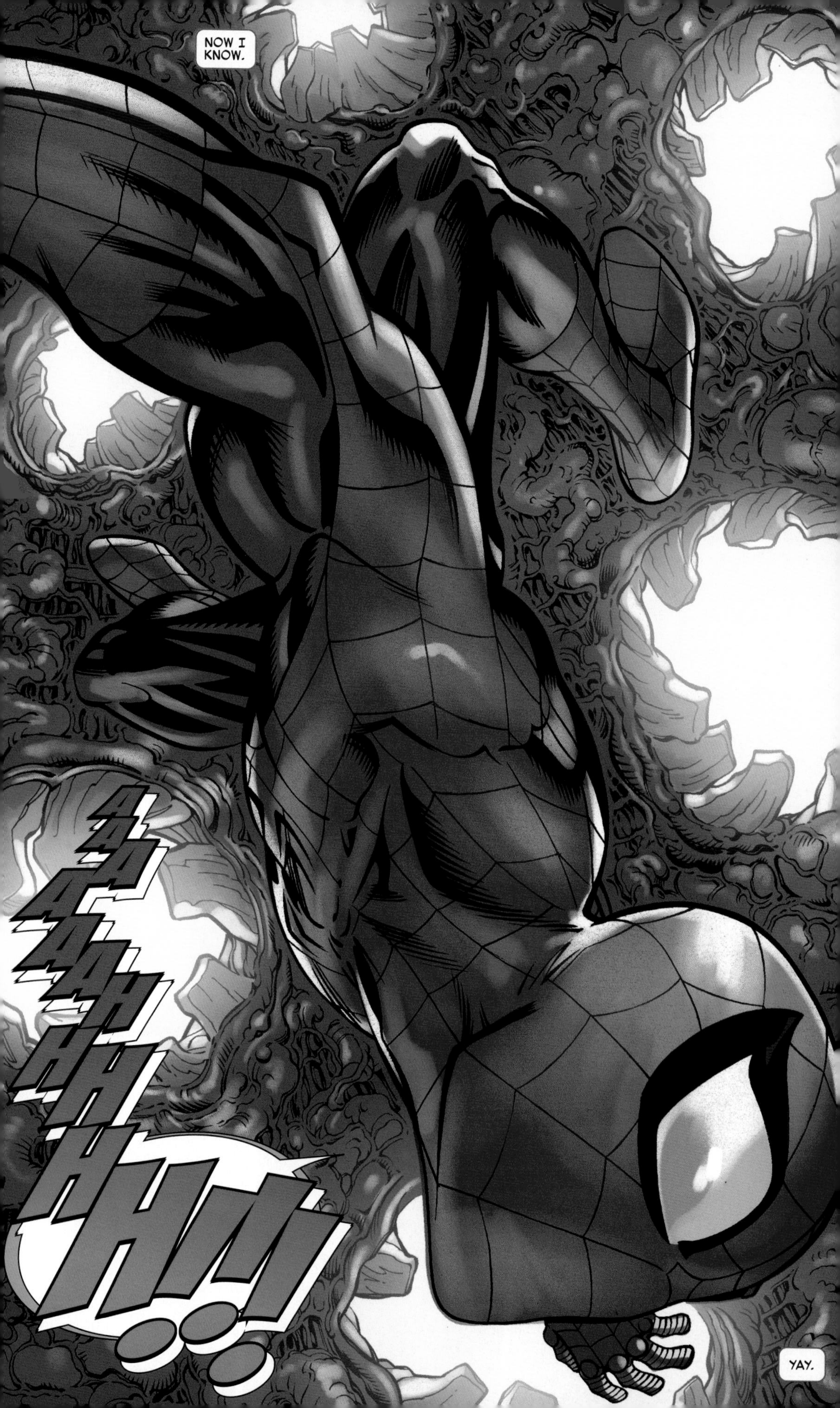
NOW I KNOW.
AAAAAAHHHHH!!...
YAY.

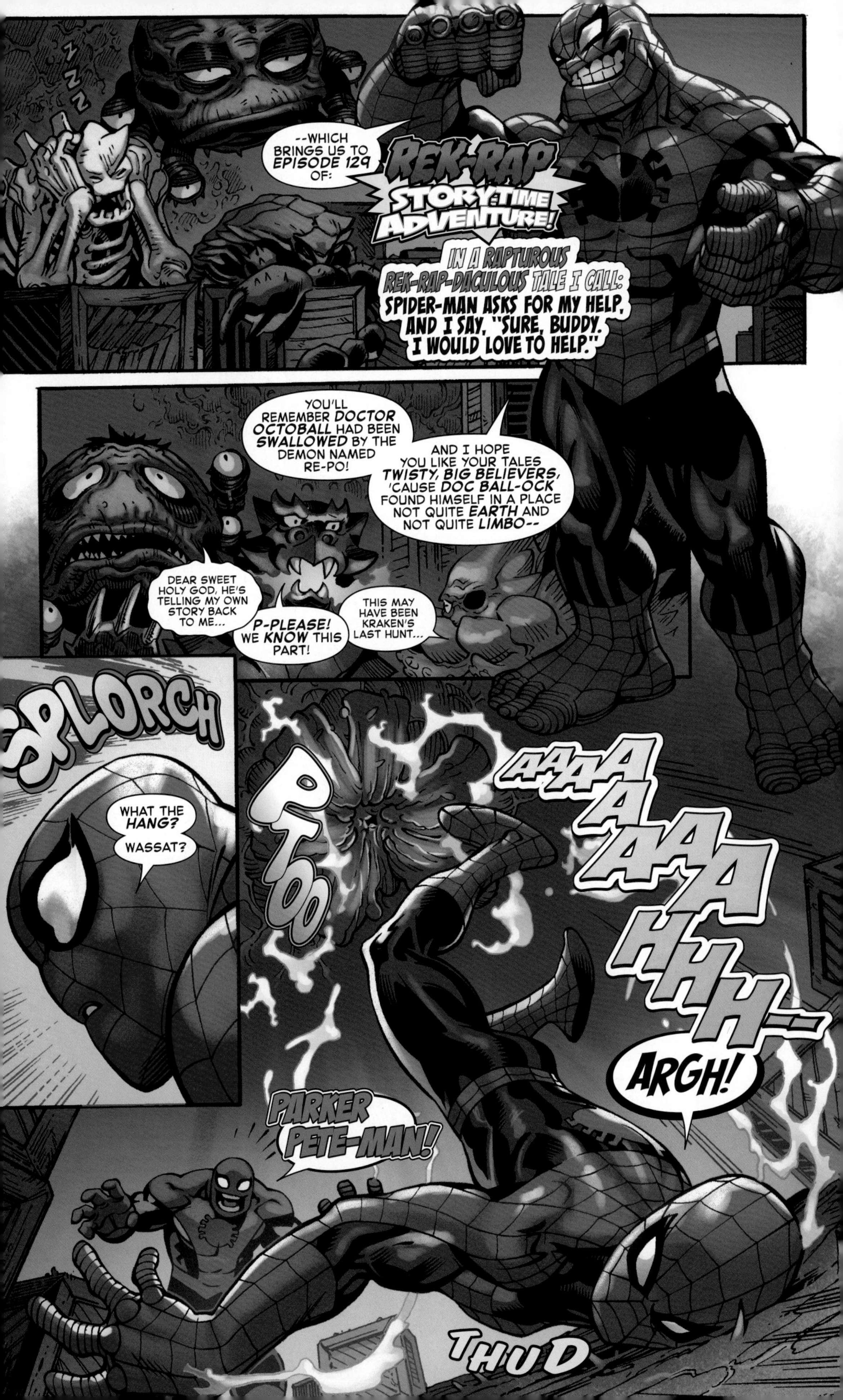

Z Z Z
--WHICH BRINGS US TO EPISODE 129 OF:
REK-RAP STORY-TIME ADVENTURE!
IN A RAPTUROUS REK-RAP-DACULOUS TALE I CALL:
SPIDER-MAN ASKS FOR MY HELP, AND I SAY, "SURE, BUDDY. I WOULD LOVE TO HELP."
YOU'LL REMEMBER DOCTOR OCTOBALL HAD BEEN SWALLOWED BY THE DEMON NAMED RE-PO!
AND I HOPE YOU LIKE YOUR TALES TWISTY, BIG BELIEVERS, 'CAUSE DOC BALL-OCK FOUND HIMSELF IN A PLACE NOT QUITE EARTH AND NOT QUITE LIMBO--
DEAR SWEET HOLY GOD, HE'S TELLING MY OWN STORY BACK TO ME...
P-PLEASE! WE KNOW THIS PART!
THIS MAY HAVE BEEN KRAKEN'S LAST HUNT...
SPLORCH
WHAT THE HANG?
WASSAT?
PTOO
AAAAAAAAHHHH--
ARGH!
PARKER PETE-MAN!
THUD

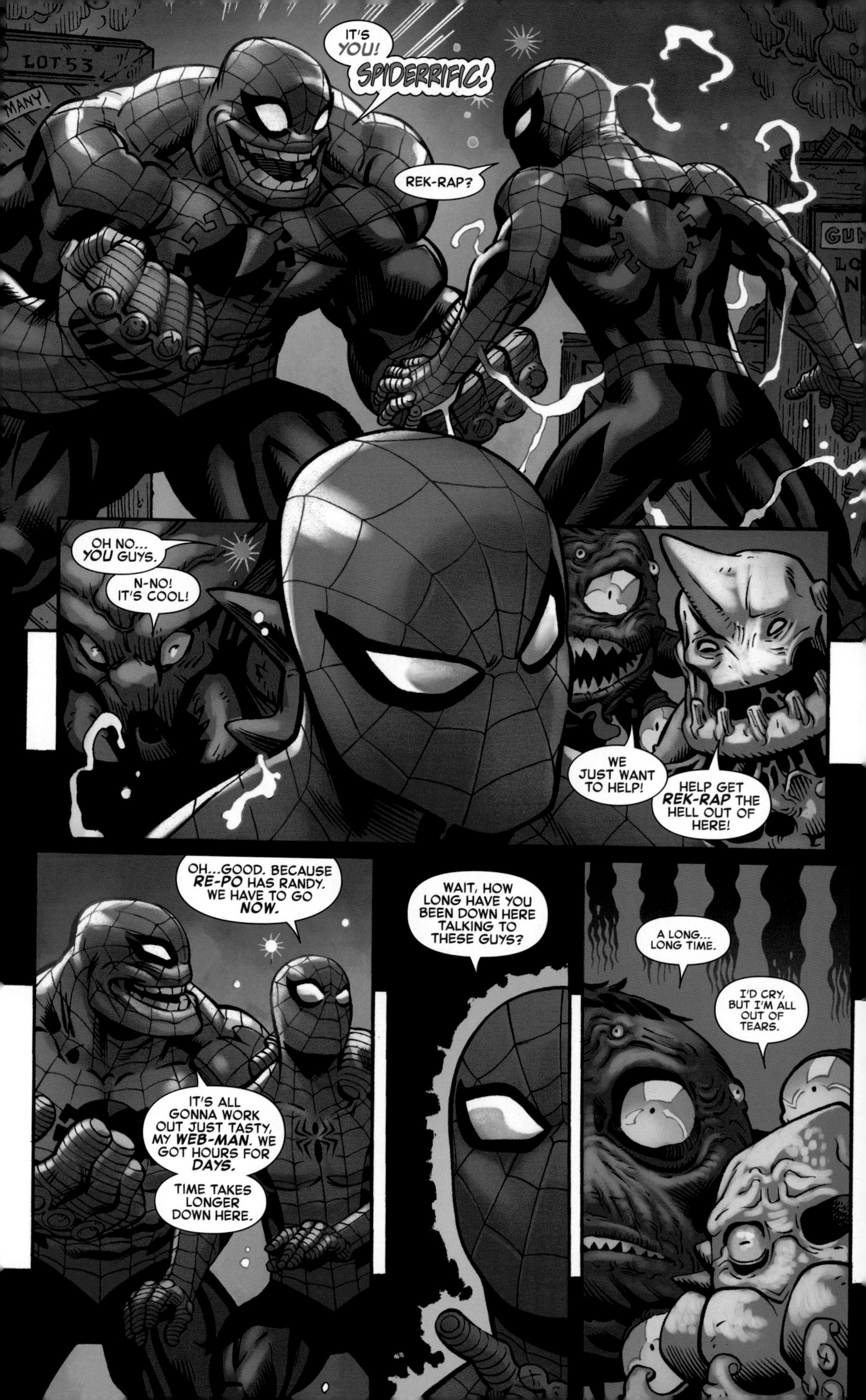

LOT 53
MANY
IT'S YOU! SPIDERRIFIC!
REK-RAP?
GUN
OH NO... YOU GUYS.
N-NO! IT'S COOL!
WE JUST WANT TO HELP!
HELP GET REK-RAP THE HELL OUT OF HERE!
OH...GOOD. BECAUSE RE-PO HAS RANDY. WE HAVE TO GO NOW.
IT'S ALL GONNA WORK OUT JUST TASTY, MY WEB-MAN. WE GOT HOURS FOR DAYS.
TIME TAKES LONGER DOWN HERE.
WAIT, HOW LONG HAVE YOU BEEN DOWN HERE TALKING TO THESE GUYS?
A LONG... LONG TIME.
I'D CRY, BUT I'M ALL OUT OF TEARS.

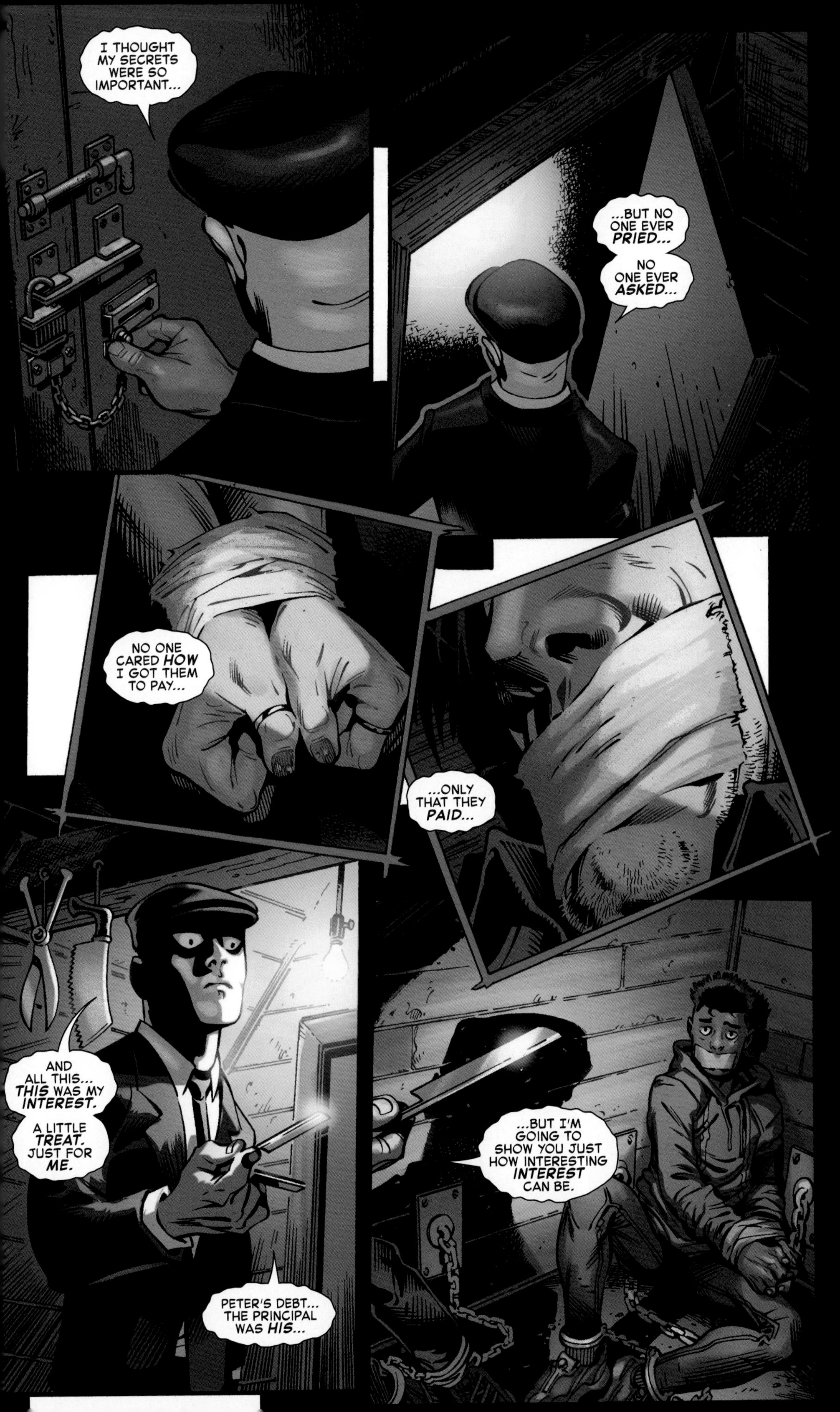

I THOUGHT MY SECRETS WERE SO IMPORTANT...
...BUT NO ONE EVER PRIED...
NO ONE EVER ASKED...
NO ONE CARED HOW I GOT THEM TO PAY...
...ONLY THAT THEY PAID...
AND ALL THIS... THIS WAS MY INTEREST.
A LITTLE TREAT. JUST FOR ME.
PETER'S DEBT... THE PRINCIPAL WAS HIS...
...BUT I'M GOING TO SHOW YOU JUST HOW INTERESTING INTEREST CAN BE.

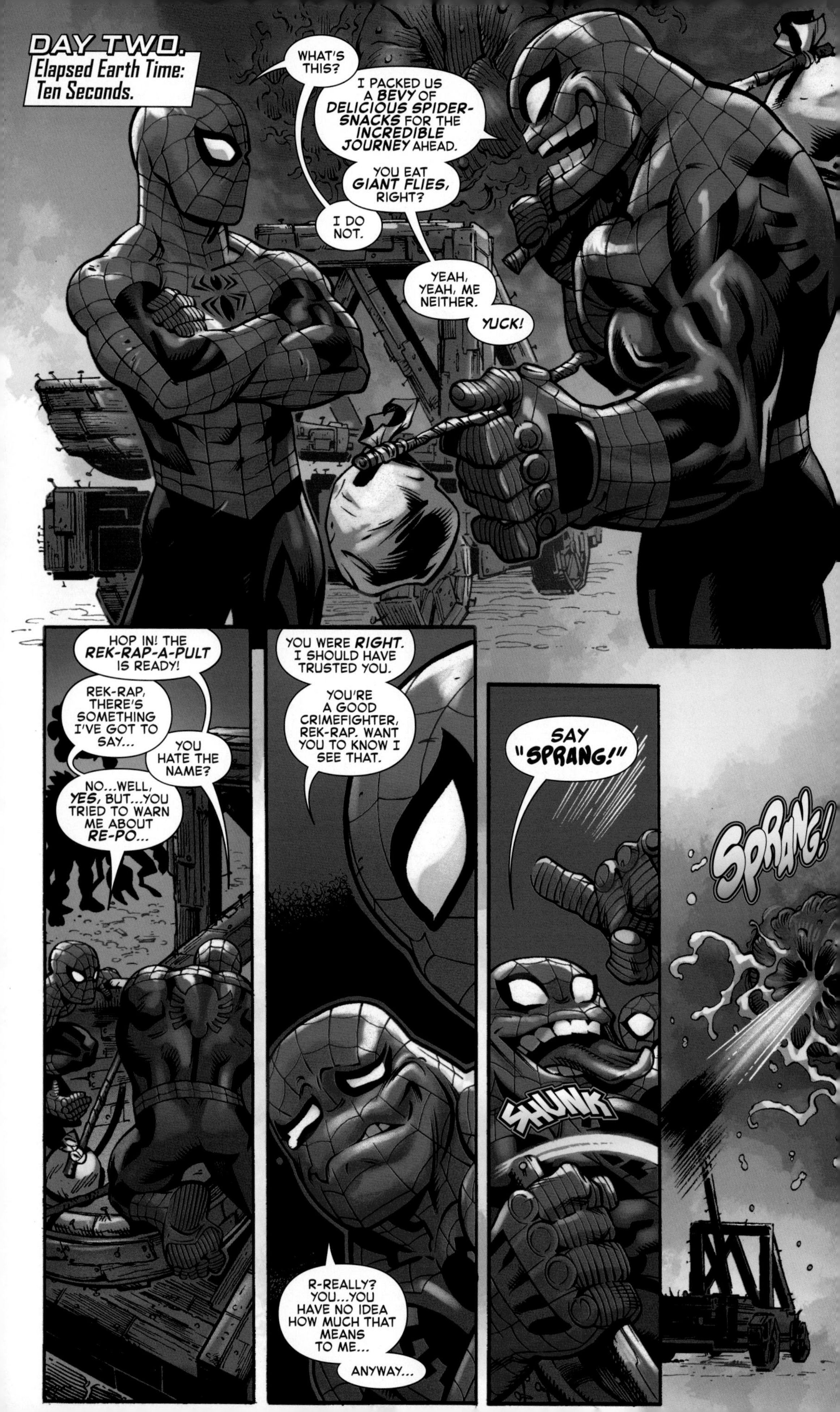
DAY TWO.
Elapsed Earth Time: Ten Seconds.
WHAT'S THIS?
I PACKED US A BEVY OF DELICIOUS SPIDER-SNACKS FOR THE INCREDIBLE JOURNEY AHEAD.
YOU EAT GIANT FLIES, RIGHT?
I DO NOT.
YEAH, YEAH, ME NEITHER.
YUCK!
HOP IN! THE REK-RAP-A-PULT IS READY!
REK-RAP, THERE'S SOMETHING I'VE GOT TO SAY...
YOU HATE THE NAME?
NO...WELL, YES, BUT...YOU TRIED TO WARN ME ABOUT RE-PO...
YOU WERE RIGHT. I SHOULD HAVE TRUSTED YOU.
YOU'RE A GOOD CRIMEFIGHTER, REK-RAP. WANT YOU TO KNOW I SEE THAT.
R-REALLY? YOU...YOU HAVE NO IDEA HOW MUCH THAT MEANS TO ME...
ANYWAY...
SAY "SPRANG!"
SHUNK
SPRANG!

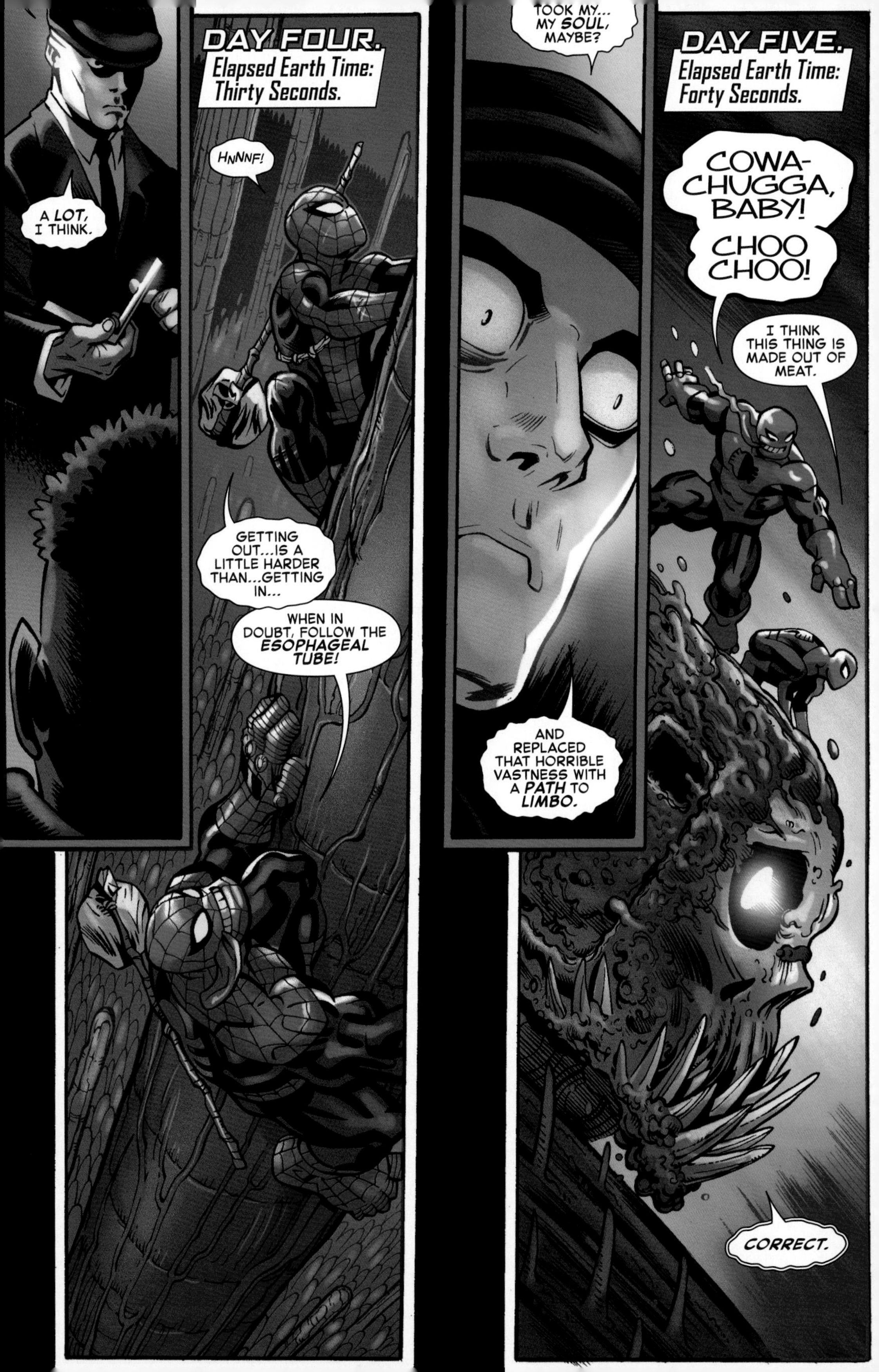
A LOT, I THINK.
DAY FOUR.
Elapsed Earth Time: Thirty Seconds.
HNNNF!
GETTING OUT...IS A LITTLE HARDER THAN...GETTING IN...
WHEN IN DOUBT, FOLLOW THE ESOPHAGEAL TUBE!
TOOK MY... MY SOUL, MAYBE?
AND REPLACED THAT HORRIBLE VASTNESS WITH A PATH TO LIMBO.
DAY FIVE.
Elapsed Earth Time: Forty Seconds.
COWA-CHUGGA, BABY!
CHOO CHOO!
I THINK THIS THING IS MADE OUT OF MEAT.
CORRECT.

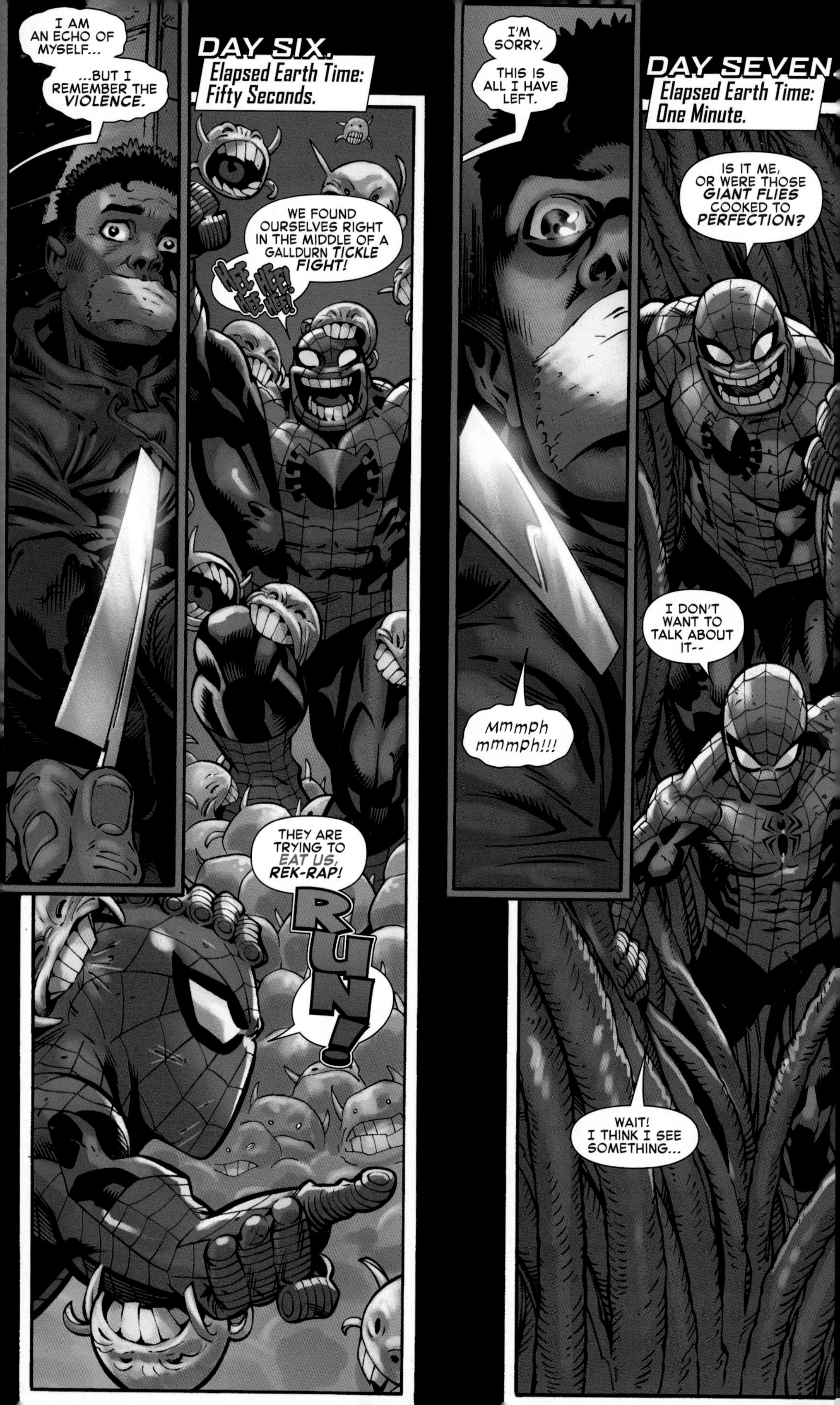

I AM AN ECHO OF MYSELF...
...BUT I REMEMBER THE VIOLENCE.
DAY SIX.
Elapsed Earth Time: Fifty Seconds.
WE FOUND OURSELVES RIGHT IN THE MIDDLE OF A GALLDURN TICKLE FIGHT!
HEE HEE! HEE HEE!
THEY ARE TRYING TO EAT US, REK-RAP!
RUN!
I'M SORRY.
THIS IS ALL I HAVE LEFT.
Mmmph mmmph!!!
DAY SEVEN
Elapsed Earth Time: One Minute.
IS IT ME, OR WERE THOSE GIANT FLIES COOKED TO PERFECTION?
I DON'T WANT TO TALK ABOUT IT--
WAIT! I THINK I SEE SOMETHING...

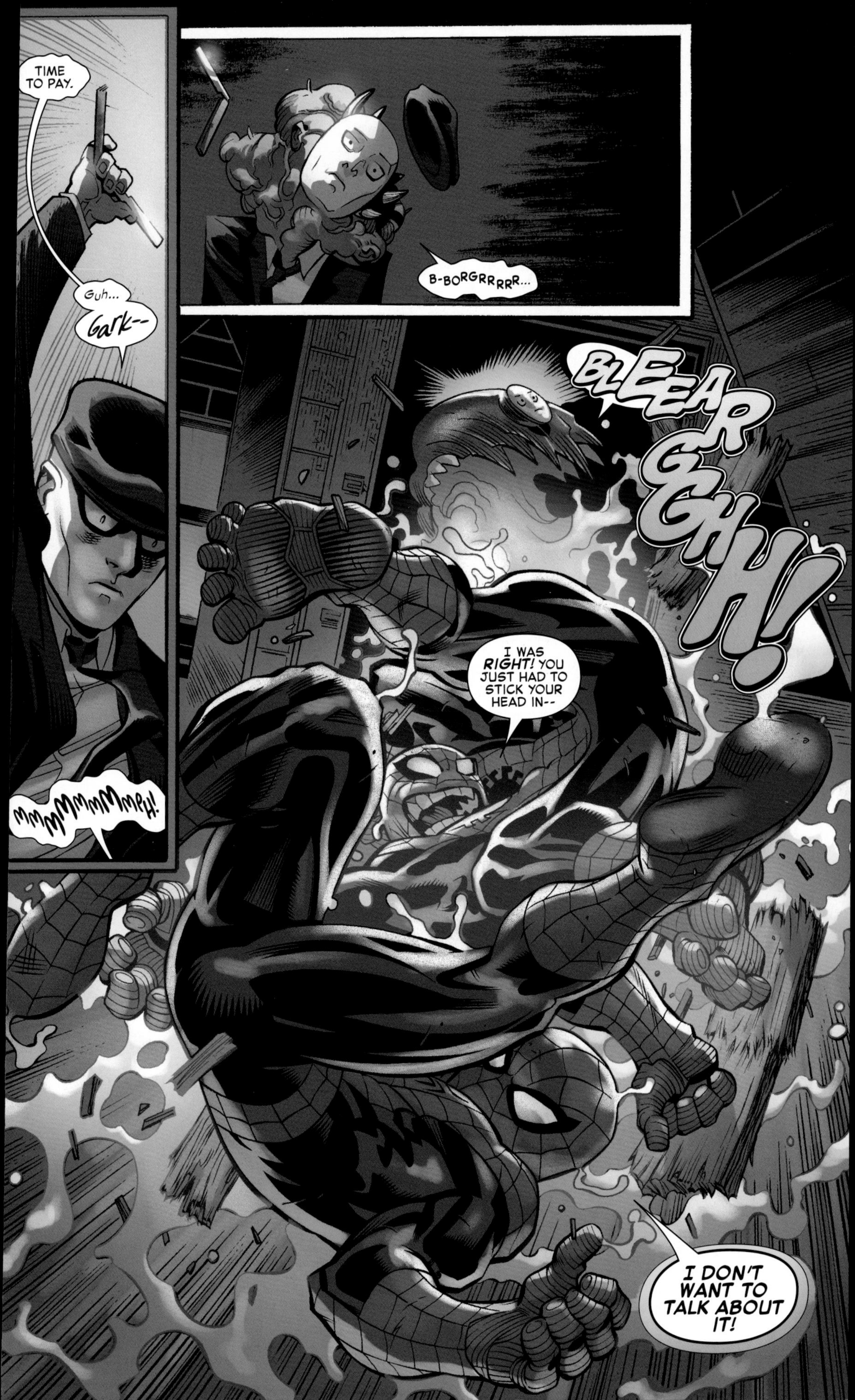
TIME TO PAY.
Guh...
Gark--
MMMMMMMMMEH!
B-BORGRRRRR...
BLEEARGGHH!
I WAS RIGHT! YOU JUST HAD TO STICK YOUR HEAD IN--
I DON'T WANT TO TALK ABOUT IT!

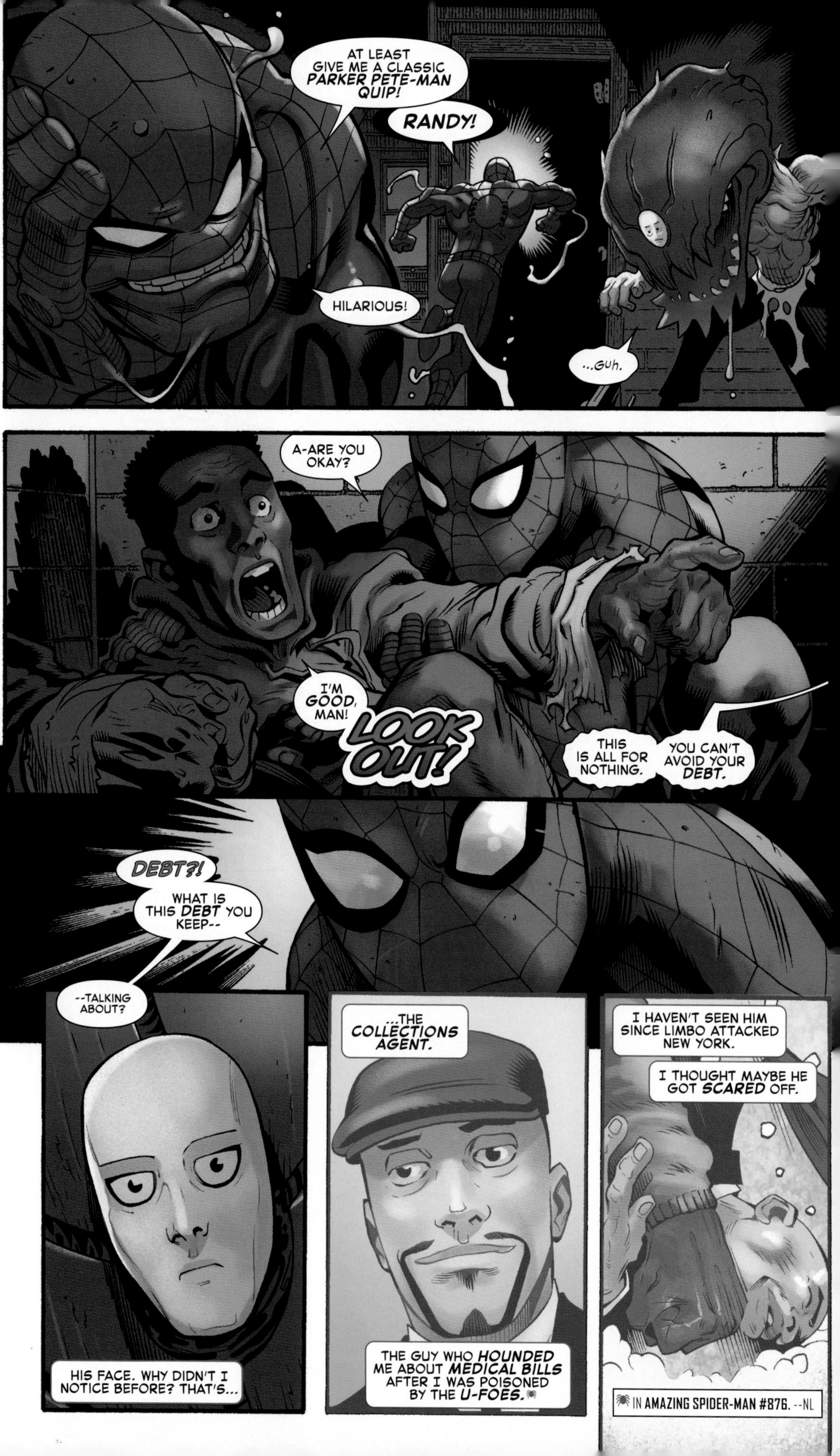

AT LEAST GIVE ME A CLASSIC PARKER PETE-MAN QUIP!
RANDY!
HILARIOUS!
...Guh.
A-ARE YOU OKAY?
I'M GOOD, MAN!
LOOK OUT!
THIS IS ALL FOR NOTHING.
YOU CAN'T AVOID YOUR DEBT.
DEBT?!
WHAT IS THIS DEBT YOU KEEP--
--TALKING ABOUT?
HIS FACE. WHY DIDN'T I NOTICE BEFORE? THAT'S...
...THE COLLECTIONS AGENT.
THE GUY WHO HOUNDED ME ABOUT MEDICAL BILLS AFTER I WAS POISONED BY THE U-FOES.
I HAVEN'T SEEN HIM SINCE LIMBO ATTACKED NEW YORK.
I THOUGHT MAYBE HE GOT SCARED OFF.
IN AMAZING SPIDER-MAN #876. --NL

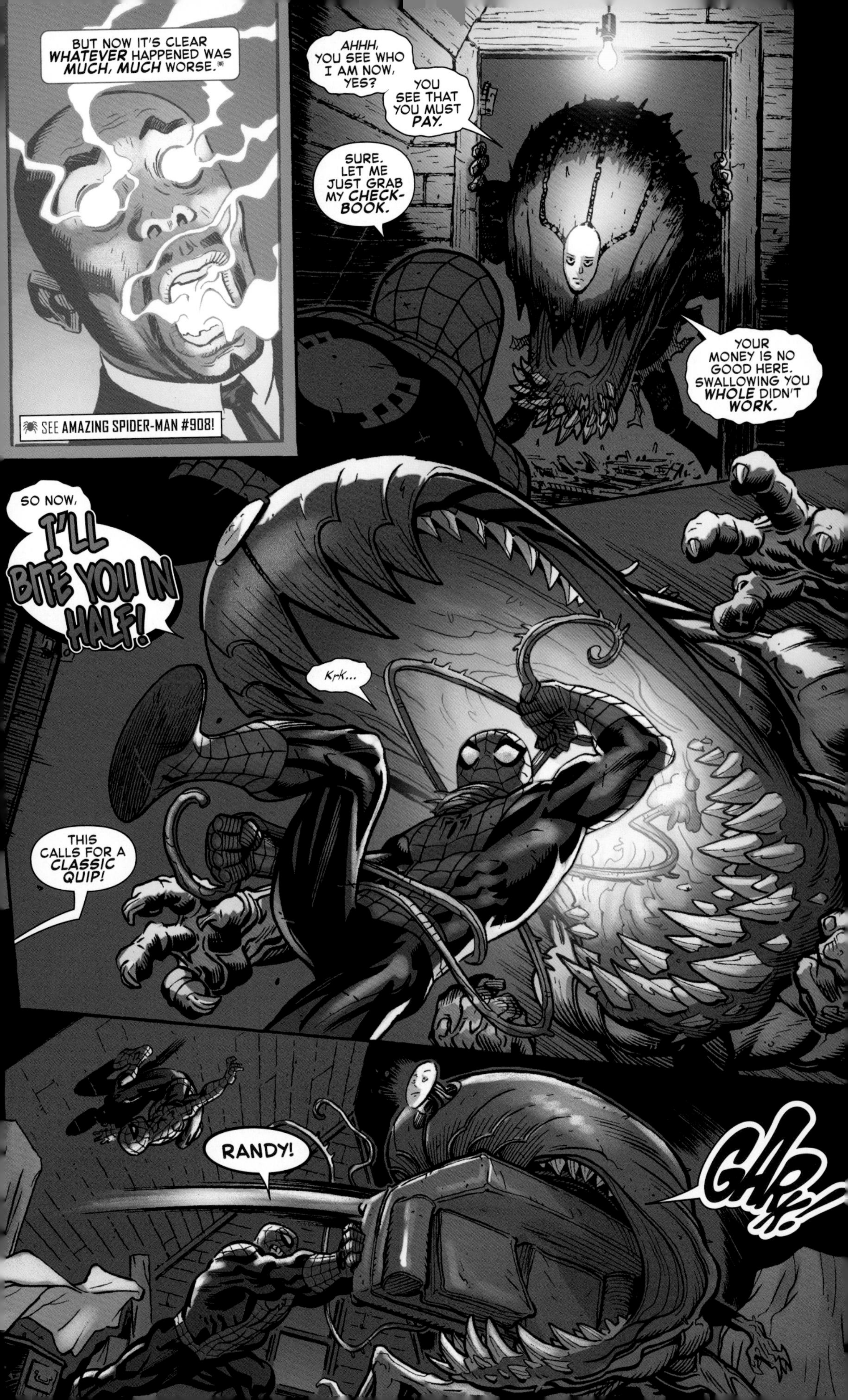

BUT NOW IT'S CLEAR WHATEVER HAPPENED WAS MUCH, MUCH WORSE.*
SEE AMAZING SPIDER-MAN #908!
AHHH, YOU SEE WHO I AM NOW, YES?
YOU SEE THAT YOU MUST PAY.
SURE. LET ME JUST GRAB MY CHECK-BOOK.
YOUR MONEY IS NO GOOD HERE. SWALLOWING YOU WHOLE DIDN'T WORK.
SO NOW, I'LL BITE YOU IN HALF!
Krk...
THIS CALLS FOR A CLASSIC QUIP!
RANDY!

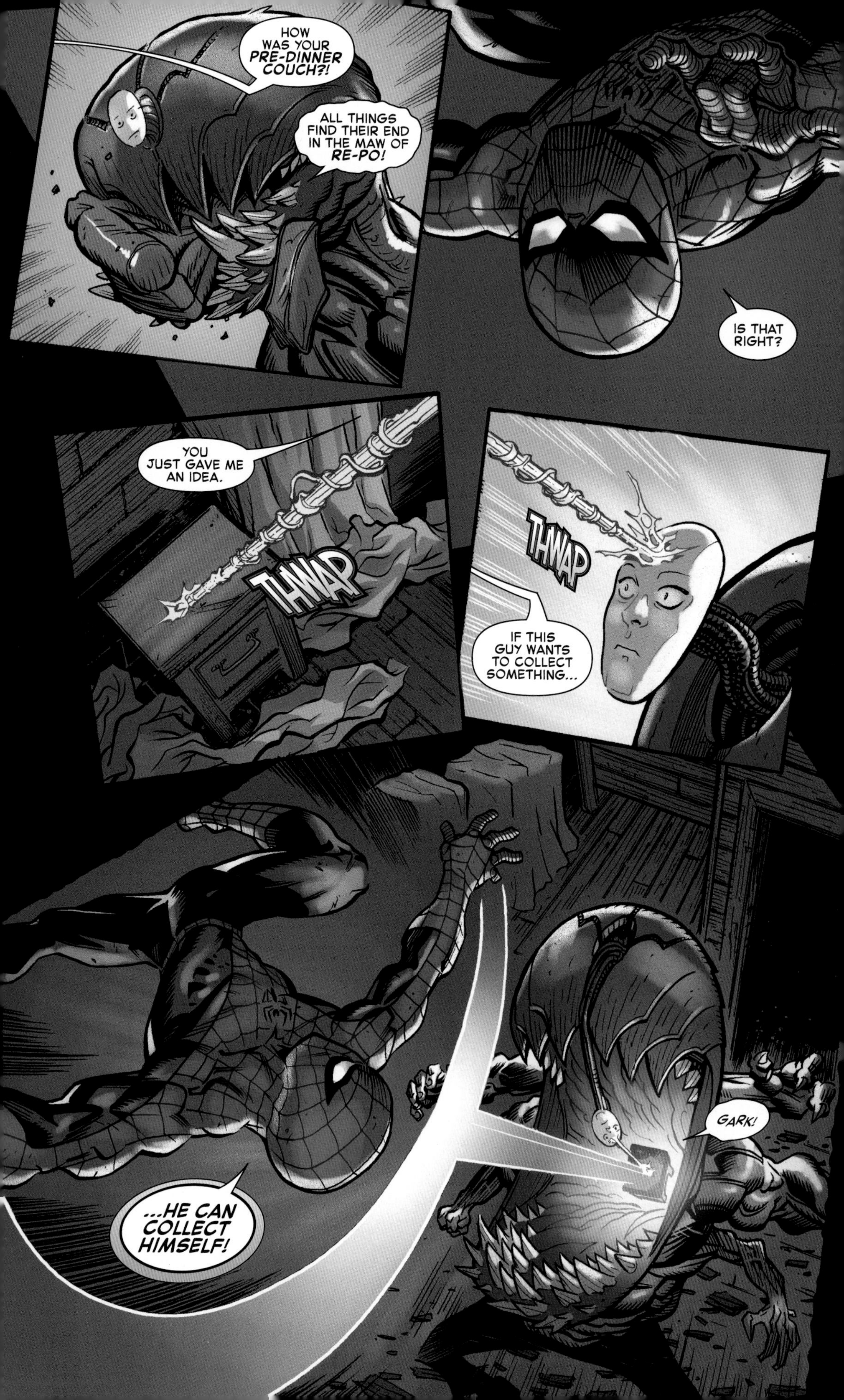
HOW WAS YOUR PRE-DINNER COUCH?!
ALL THINGS FIND THEIR END IN THE MAW OF RE-PO!
IS THAT RIGHT?
YOU JUST GAVE ME AN IDEA.
THWAP
THWAP
IF THIS GUY WANTS TO COLLECT SOMETHING...
GARK!
...HE CAN COLLECT HIMSELF!

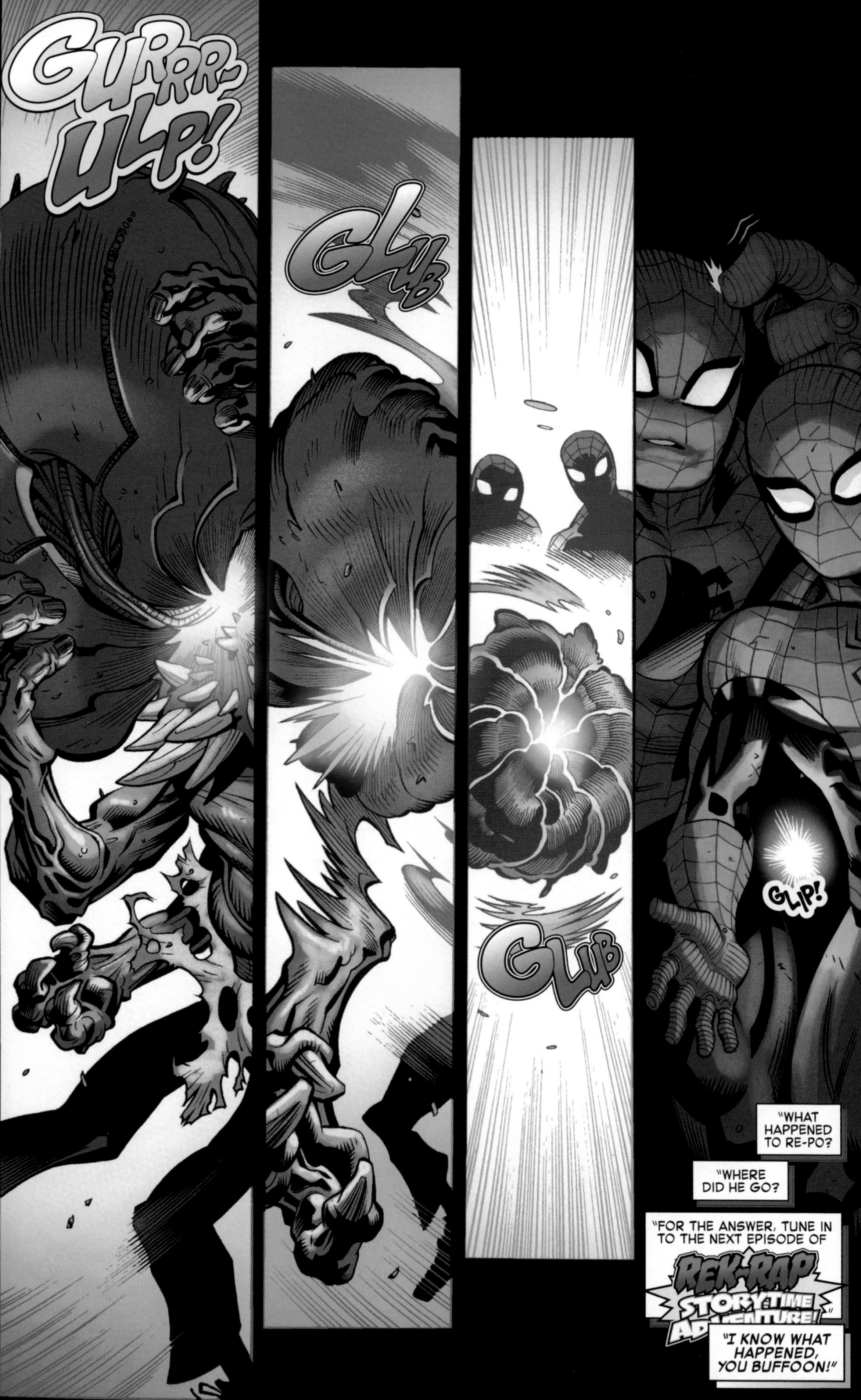
GURRR-ULP!
GLUB
GLUB
GLIP!
"WHAT HAPPENED TO RE-PO?
"WHERE DID HE GO?
"FOR THE ANSWER, TUNE IN TO THE NEXT EPISODE OF
REK-RAP STORYTIME ADVENTURE!"
"I KNOW WHAT HAPPENED, YOU BUFFOON!"

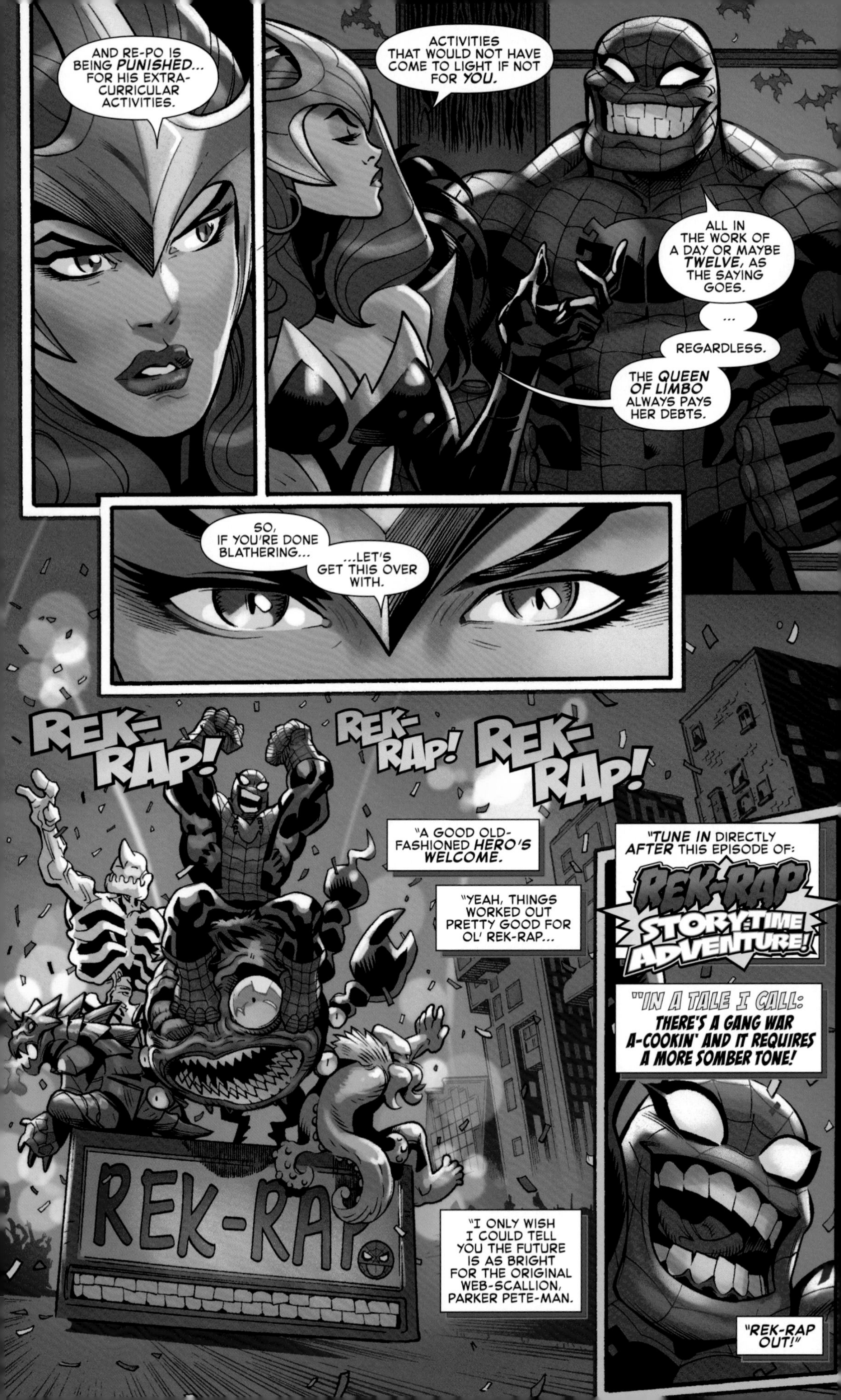
AND RE-PO IS BEING *PUNISHED*... FOR HIS EXTRA-CURRICULAR ACTIVITIES.
ACTIVITIES THAT WOULD NOT HAVE COME TO LIGHT IF NOT FOR *YOU.*
ALL IN THE WORK OF A DAY OR MAYBE *TWELVE*, AS THE SAYING GOES.
...
REGARDLESS.
THE *QUEEN OF LIMBO* ALWAYS PAYS HER DEBTS.
SO, IF YOU'RE DONE BLATHERING...
...LET'S GET THIS OVER WITH.
REK-RAP! REK-RAP! REK-RAP!
"A GOOD OLD-FASHIONED *HERO'S WELCOME.*
"YEAH, THINGS WORKED OUT PRETTY GOOD FOR OL' REK-RAP...
REK-RAP
"I ONLY WISH I COULD TELL YOU THE FUTURE IS AS BRIGHT FOR THE ORIGINAL WEB-SCALLION, PARKER PETE-MAN.
"*TUNE IN* DIRECTLY *AFTER* THIS EPISODE OF:
REK-RAP STORYTIME ADVENTURE!
"IN A TALE I CALL:
THERE'S A GANG WAR A-COOKIN' AND IT REQUIRES A MORE SOMBER TONE!
"REK-RAP OUT!"

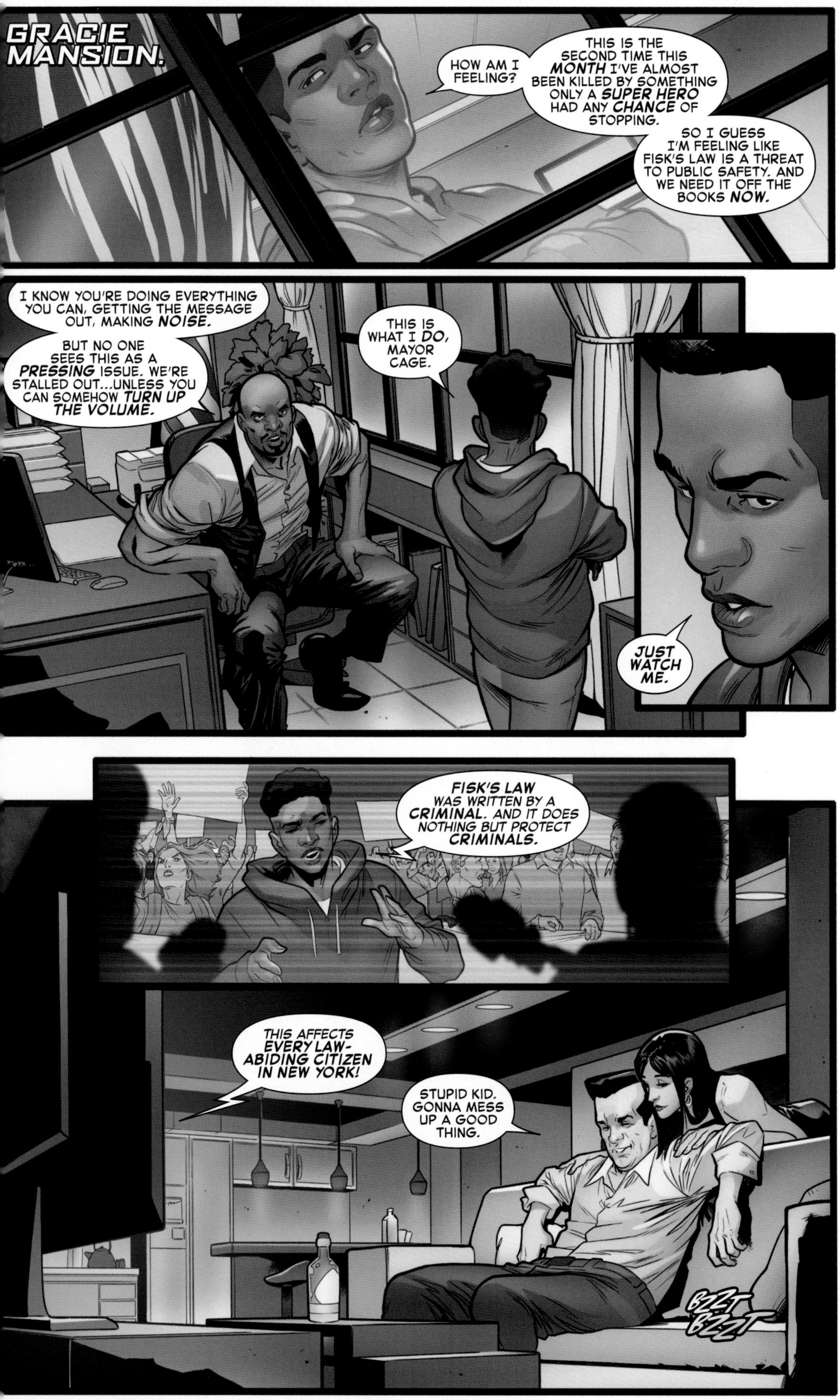
GRACIE MANSION.
HOW AM I FEELING?
THIS IS THE SECOND TIME THIS MONTH I'VE ALMOST BEEN KILLED BY SOMETHING ONLY A SUPER HERO HAD ANY CHANCE OF STOPPING.
SO I GUESS I'M FEELING LIKE FISK'S LAW IS A THREAT TO PUBLIC SAFETY. AND WE NEED IT OFF THE BOOKS NOW.
I KNOW YOU'RE DOING EVERYTHING YOU CAN, GETTING THE MESSAGE OUT, MAKING NOISE.
BUT NO ONE SEES THIS AS A PRESSING ISSUE. WE'RE STALLED OUT...UNLESS YOU CAN SOMEHOW TURN UP THE VOLUME.
THIS IS WHAT I DO, MAYOR CAGE.
JUST WATCH ME.
FISK'S LAW WAS WRITTEN BY A CRIMINAL. AND IT DOES NOTHING BUT PROTECT CRIMINALS.
THIS AFFECTS EVERY LAW-ABIDING CITIZEN IN NEW YORK!
STUPID KID. GONNA MESS UP A GOOD THING.
BZZT BZZT

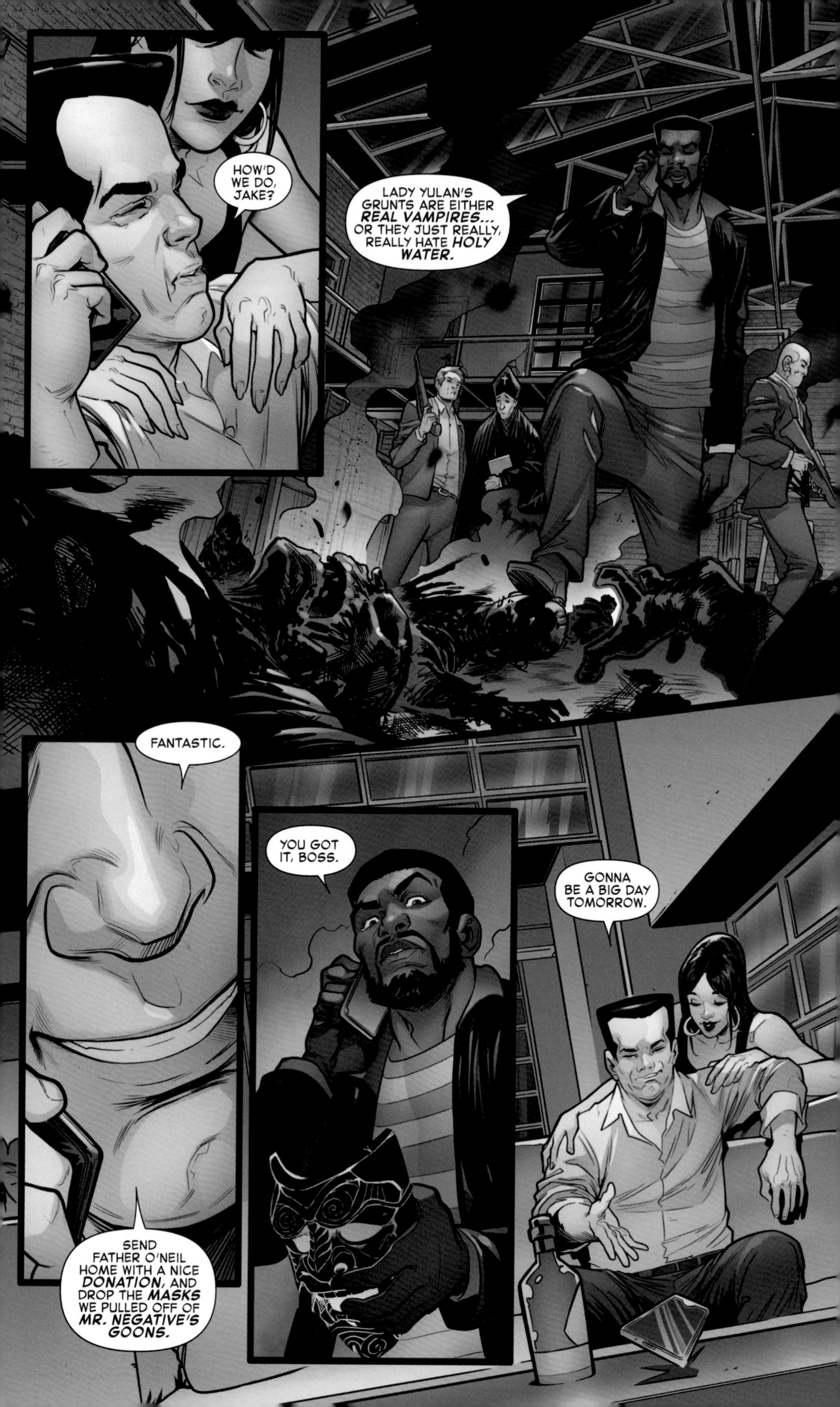

HOW'D WE DO, JAKE?
LADY YULAN'S GRUNTS ARE EITHER REAL VAMPIRES... OR THEY JUST REALLY, REALLY HATE HOLY WATER.
FANTASTIC.
SEND FATHER O'NEIL HOME WITH A NICE DONATION, AND DROP THE MASKS WE PULLED OFF OF MR. NEGATIVE'S GOONS.
YOU GOT IT, BOSS.
GONNA BE A BIG DAY TOMORROW.

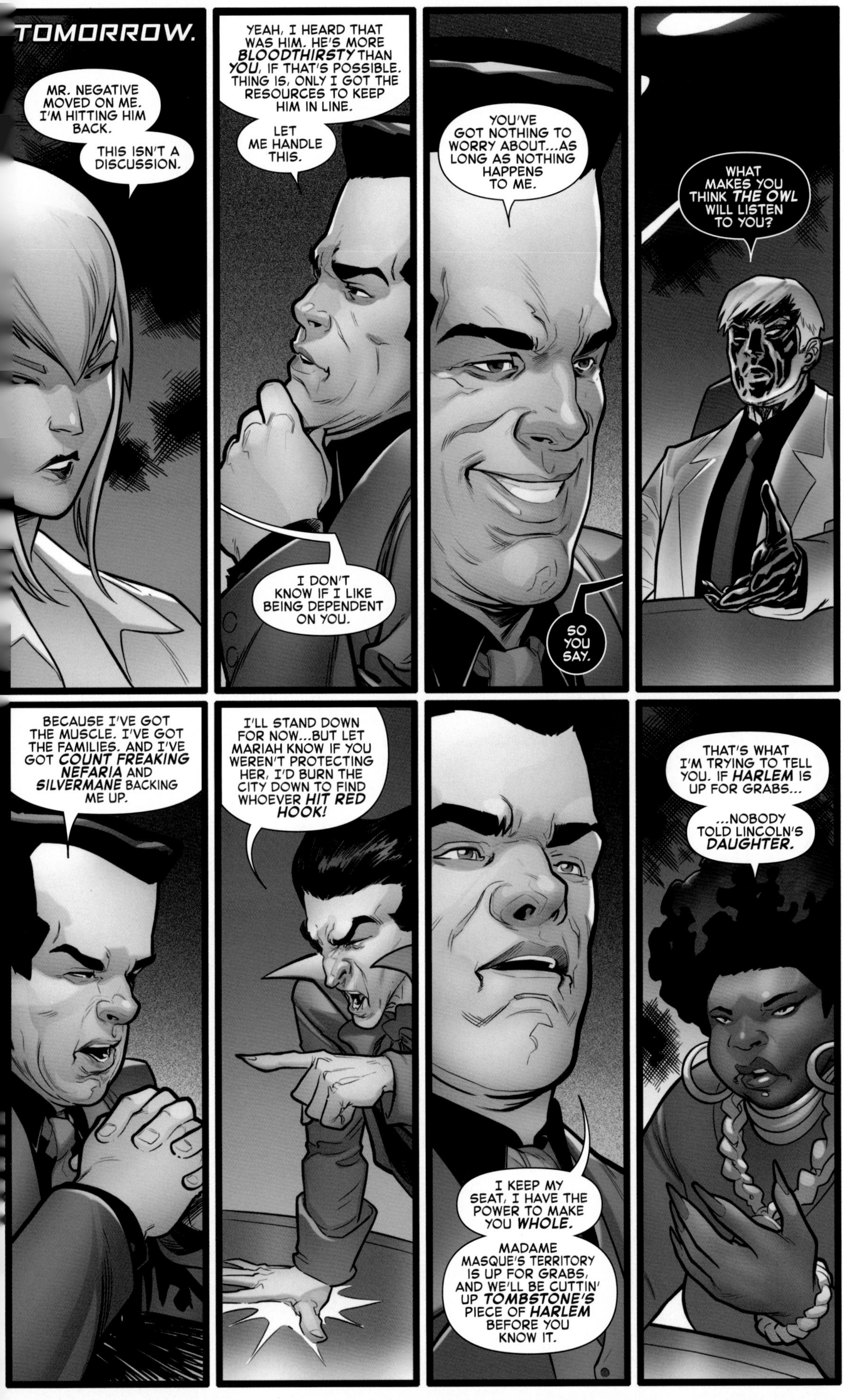
TOMORROW.
MR. NEGATIVE MOVED ON ME. I'M HITTING HIM BACK.
THIS ISN'T A DISCUSSION.
YEAH, I HEARD THAT WAS HIM. HE'S MORE BLOODTHIRSTY THAN YOU, IF THAT'S POSSIBLE. THING IS, ONLY I GOT THE RESOURCES TO KEEP HIM IN LINE.
LET ME HANDLE THIS.
I DON'T KNOW IF I LIKE BEING DEPENDENT ON YOU.
YOU'VE GOT NOTHING TO WORRY ABOUT...AS LONG AS NOTHING HAPPENS TO ME.
SO YOU SAY.
WHAT MAKES YOU THINK THE OWL WILL LISTEN TO YOU?
BECAUSE I'VE GOT THE MUSCLE. I'VE GOT THE FAMILIES. AND I'VE GOT COUNT FREAKING NEFARIA AND SILVERMANE BACKING ME UP.
I'LL STAND DOWN FOR NOW...BUT LET MARIAH KNOW IF YOU WEREN'T PROTECTING HER, I'D BURN THE CITY DOWN TO FIND WHOEVER HIT RED HOOK!
I KEEP MY SEAT, I HAVE THE POWER TO MAKE YOU WHOLE.
MADAME MASQUE'S TERRITORY IS UP FOR GRABS, AND WE'LL BE CUTTIN' UP TOMBSTONE'S PIECE OF HARLEM BEFORE YOU KNOW IT.
THAT'S WHAT I'M TRYING TO TELL YOU. IF HARLEM IS UP FOR GRABS...
...NOBODY TOLD LINCOLN'S DAUGHTER.

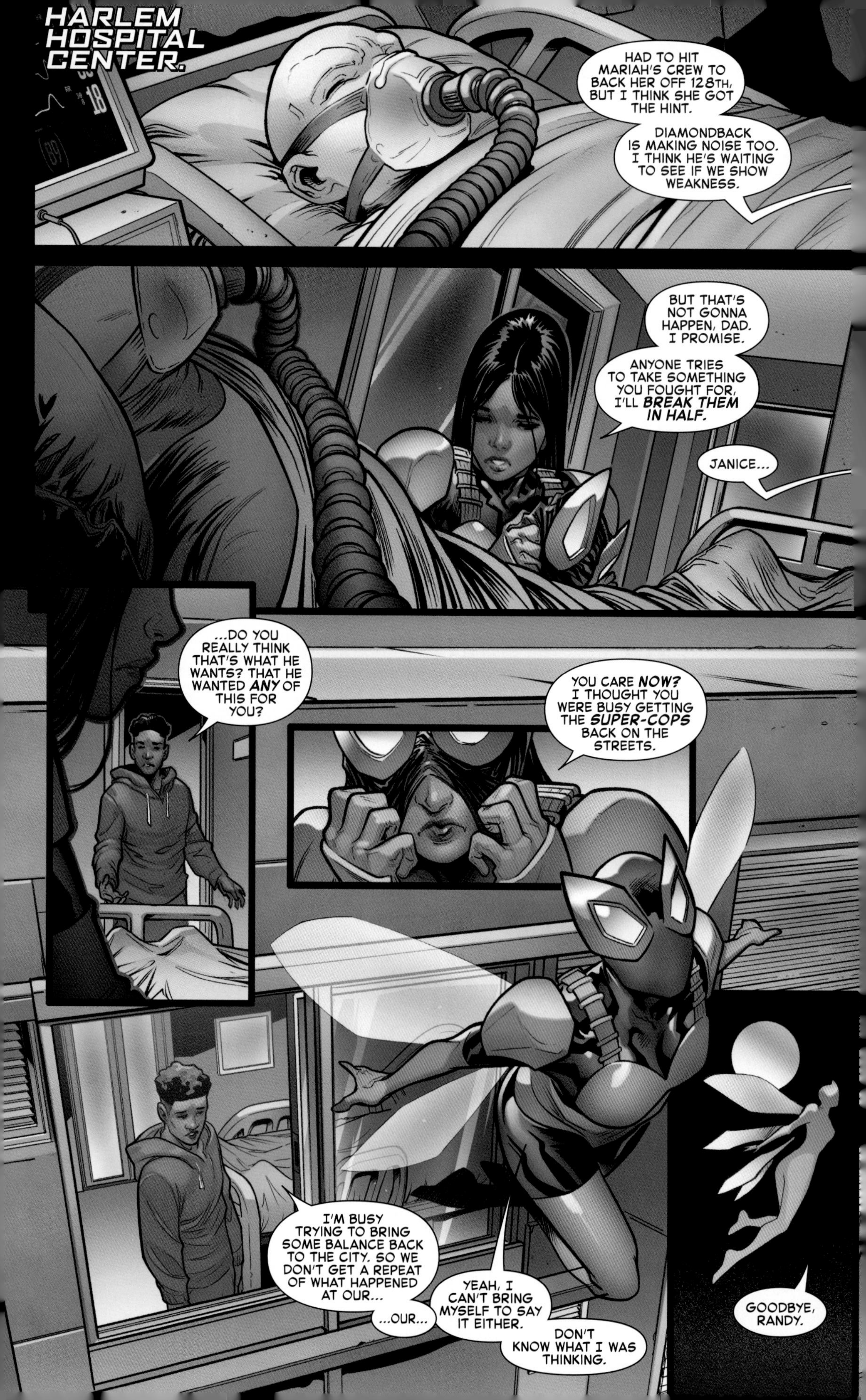
HARLEM HOSPITAL CENTER.
HAD TO HIT MARIAH'S CREW TO BACK HER OFF 128TH, BUT I THINK SHE GOT THE HINT.
DIAMONDBACK IS MAKING NOISE TOO. I THINK HE'S WAITING TO SEE IF WE SHOW WEAKNESS.
BUT THAT'S NOT GONNA HAPPEN, DAD. I PROMISE.
ANYONE TRIES TO TAKE SOMETHING YOU FOUGHT FOR, I'LL BREAK THEM IN HALF.
JANICE...
...DO YOU REALLY THINK THAT'S WHAT HE WANTS? THAT HE WANTED ANY OF THIS FOR YOU?
YOU CARE NOW? I THOUGHT YOU WERE BUSY GETTING THE SUPER-COPS BACK ON THE STREETS.
I'M BUSY TRYING TO BRING SOME BALANCE BACK TO THE CITY. SO WE DON'T GET A REPEAT OF WHAT HAPPENED AT OUR...
...OUR...
YEAH, I CAN'T BRING MYSELF TO SAY IT EITHER.
DON'T KNOW WHAT I WAS THINKING.
GOODBYE, RANDY.

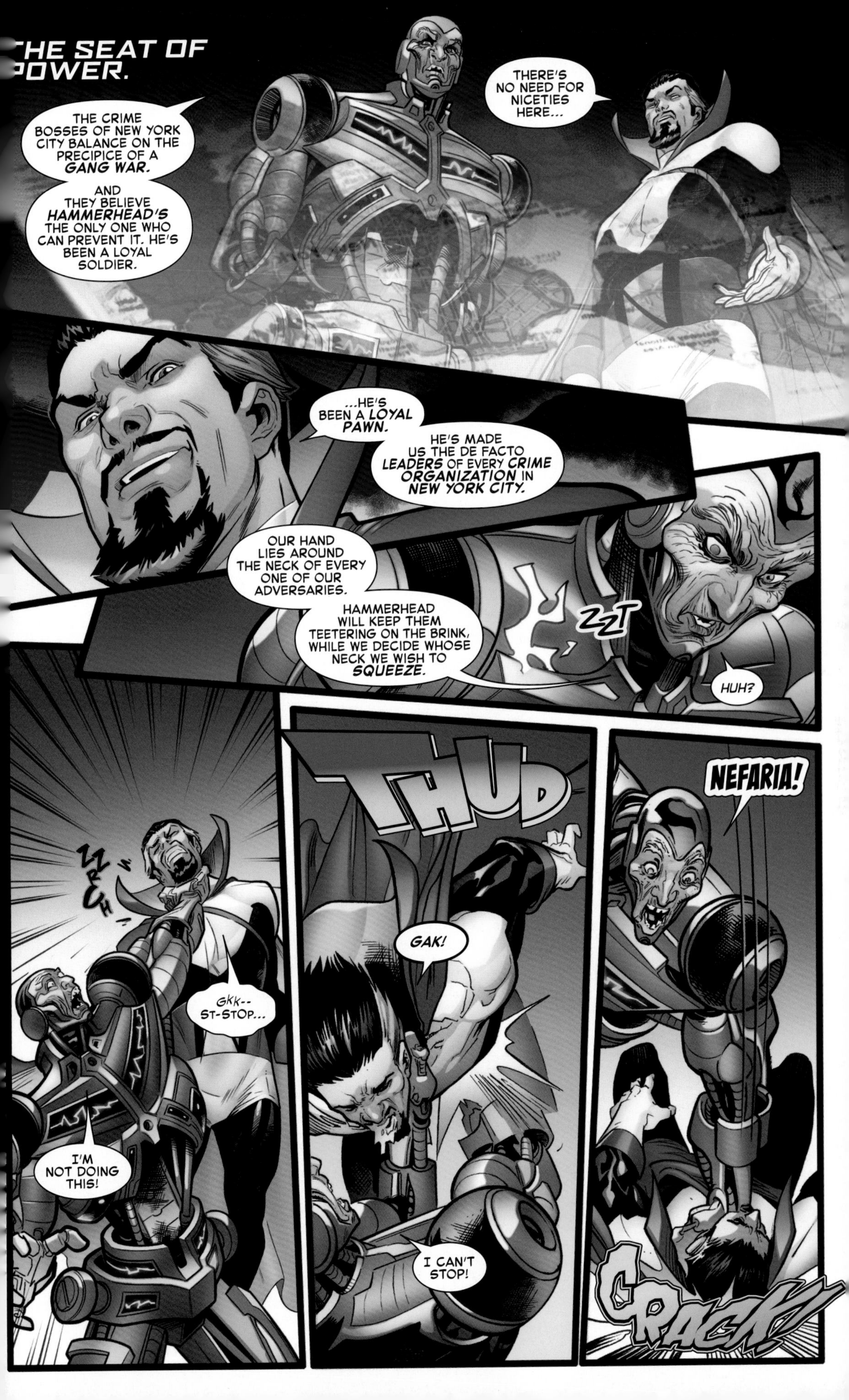
THE SEAT OF POWER.
THE CRIME BOSSES OF NEW YORK CITY BALANCE ON THE PRECIPICE OF A GANG WAR.
AND THEY BELIEVE HAMMERHEAD'S THE ONLY ONE WHO CAN PREVENT IT. HE'S BEEN A LOYAL SOLDIER.
THERE'S NO NEED FOR NICETIES HERE...
...HE'S BEEN A LOYAL PAWN.
HE'S MADE US THE DE FACTO LEADERS OF EVERY CRIME ORGANIZATION IN NEW YORK CITY.
OUR HAND LIES AROUND THE NECK OF EVERY ONE OF OUR ADVERSARIES.
HAMMERHEAD WILL KEEP THEM TEETERING ON THE BRINK, WHILE WE DECIDE WHOSE NECK WE WISH TO SQUEEZE.
ZZT
HUH?
ZZRCH
GKK-- ST-STOP...
I'M NOT DOING THIS!
THUD
GAK!
I CAN'T STOP!
NEFARIA!
CRACK!

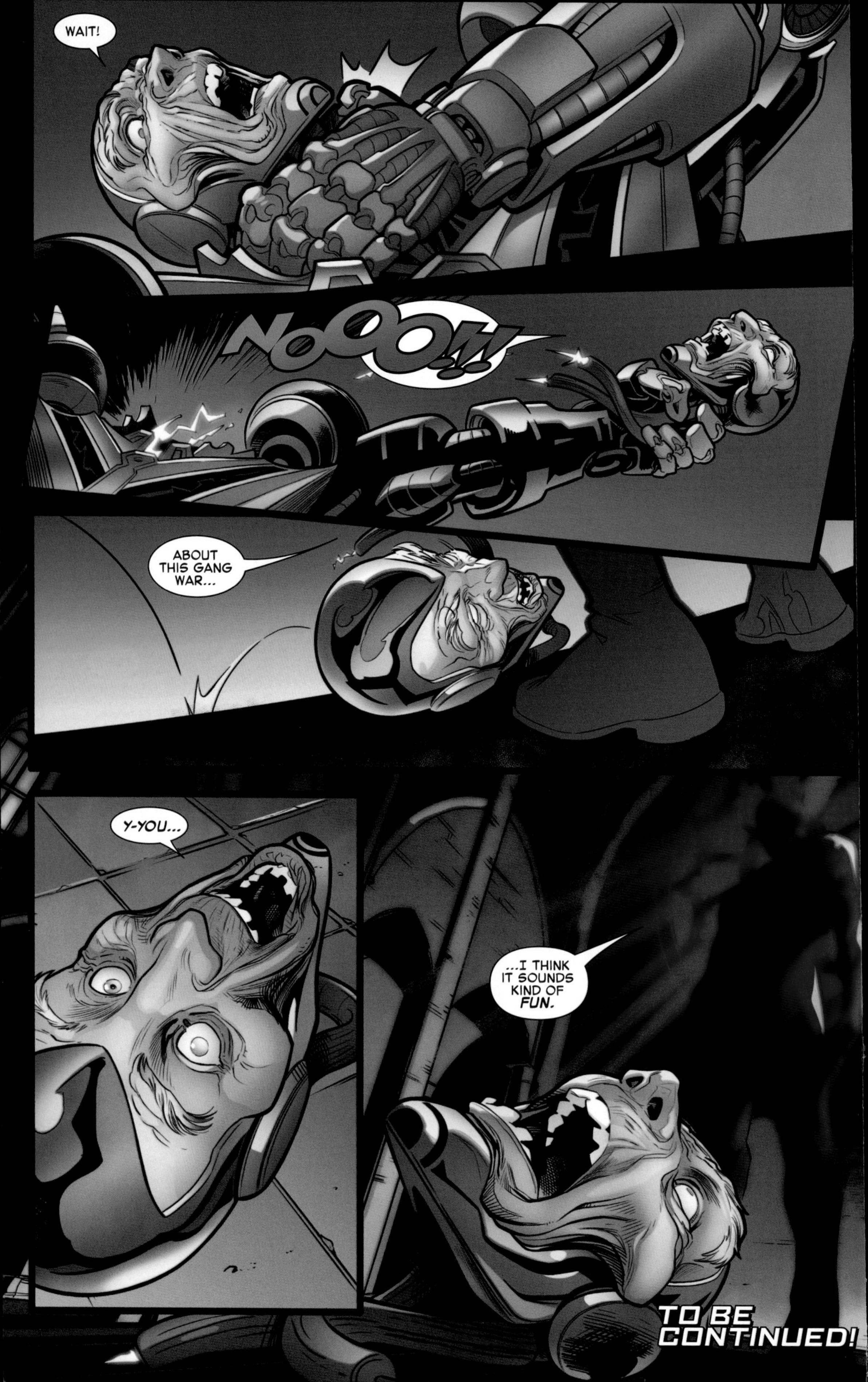
WAIT!
NOOOO...!!
ABOUT THIS GANG WAR...
Y-YOU...
...I THINK IT SOUNDS KIND OF FUN.
TO BE CONTINUED!

Patrick Gleason & Marte Gracia #32 VARIANT

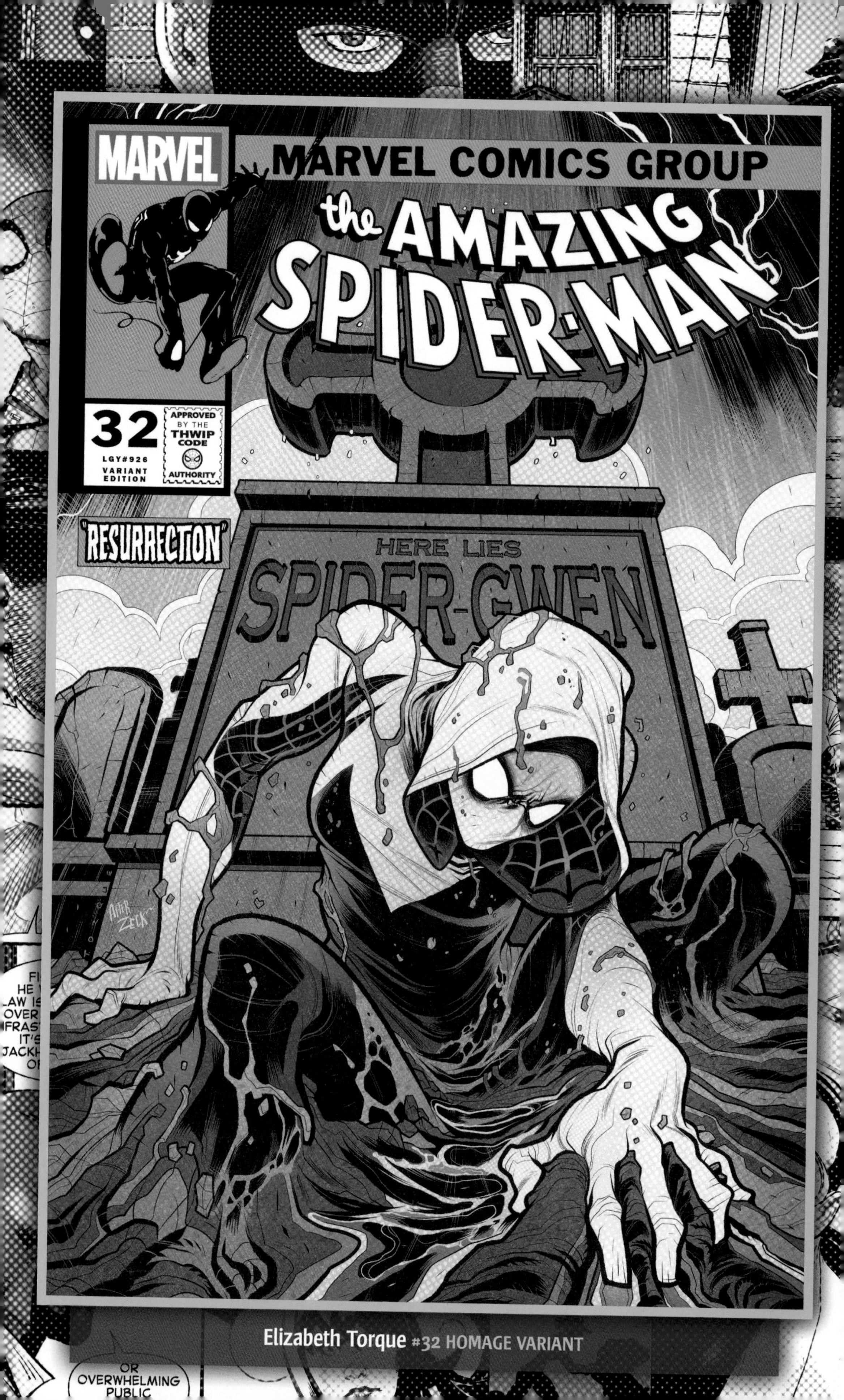
MARVEL
MARVEL COMICS GROUP
the AMAZING SPIDER-MAN
32
LGY#926
VARIANT EDITION
APPROVED BY THE THWIP CODE AUTHORITY
"RESURRECTION"
HERE LIES
SPIDER-GWEN

Elizabeth Torque #32 HOMAGE VARIANT

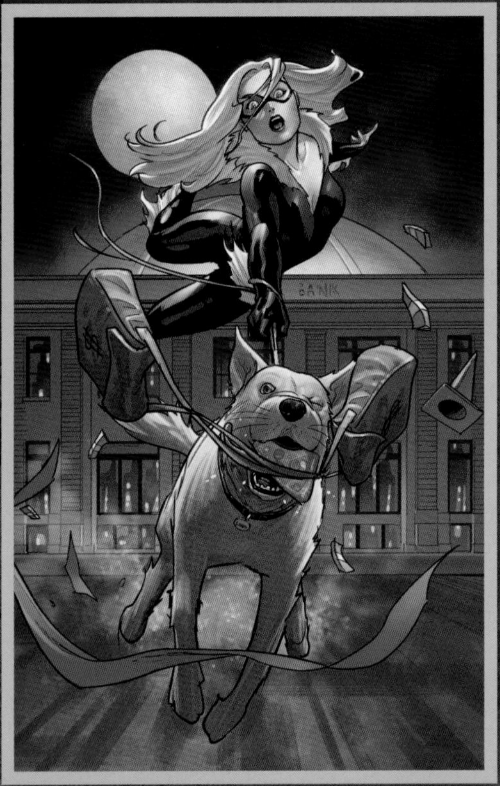

Jan Bazaldua & Jesus Aburtov
#32 STORMBREAKERS VARIANT

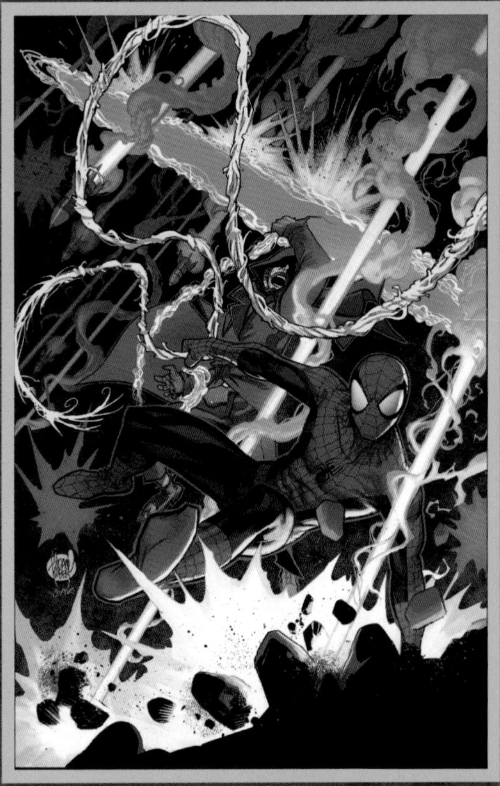

Adam Kubert & Brad Anderson
#32 G.O.D.S. VARIANT

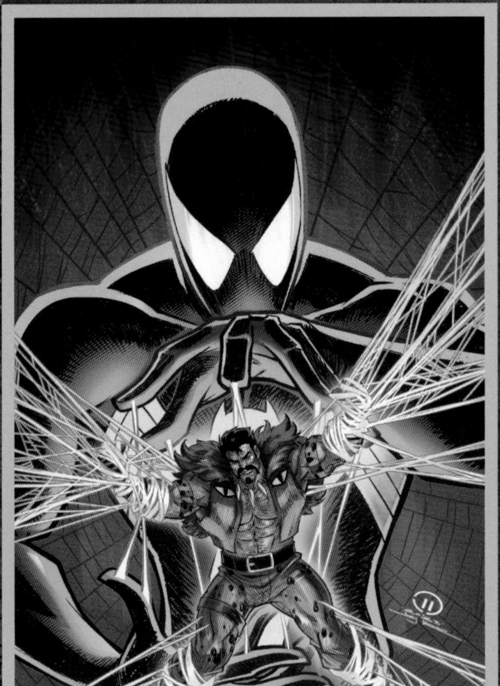

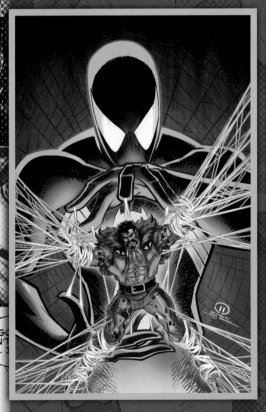

Joey Vazquez
#33 VARIANT

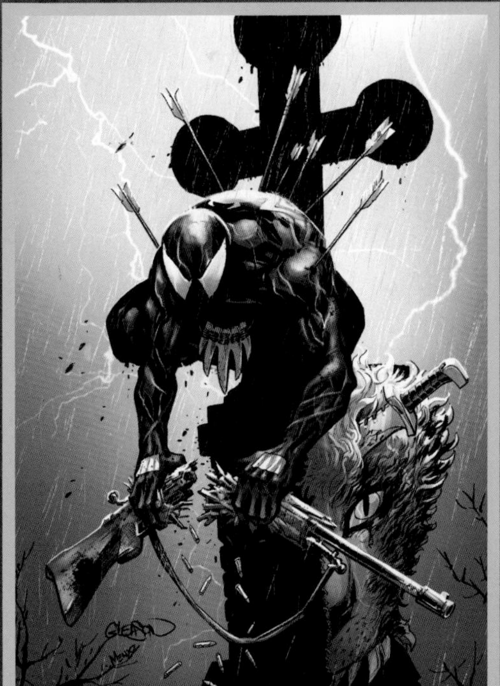

Patrick Gleason & Marcio Menyz
#33 VARIANT

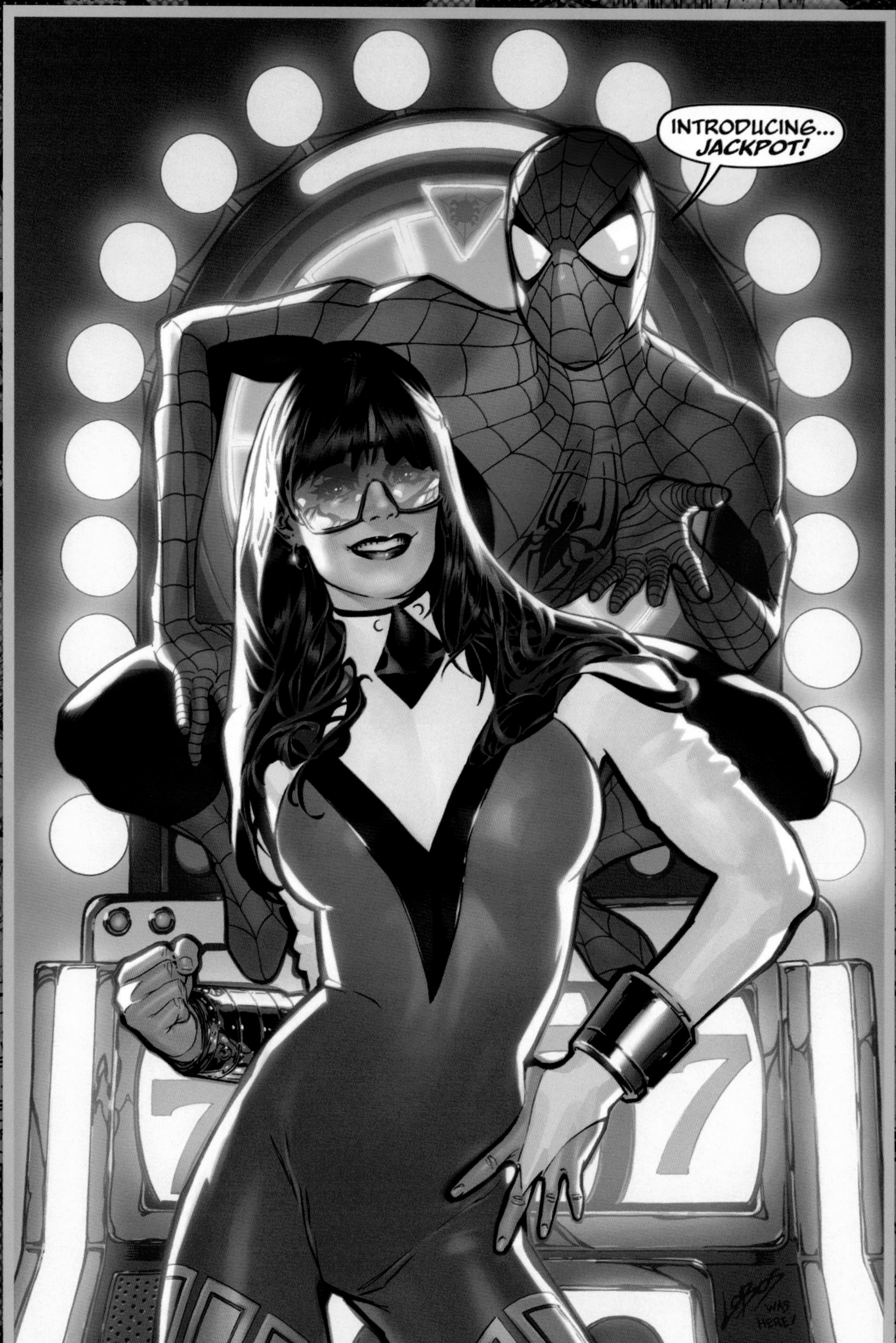
INTRODUCING... JACKPOT!

Pablo Villalobos & Romulo Fajardo Jr. #34 NYCC GIVEAWAY VARIANT

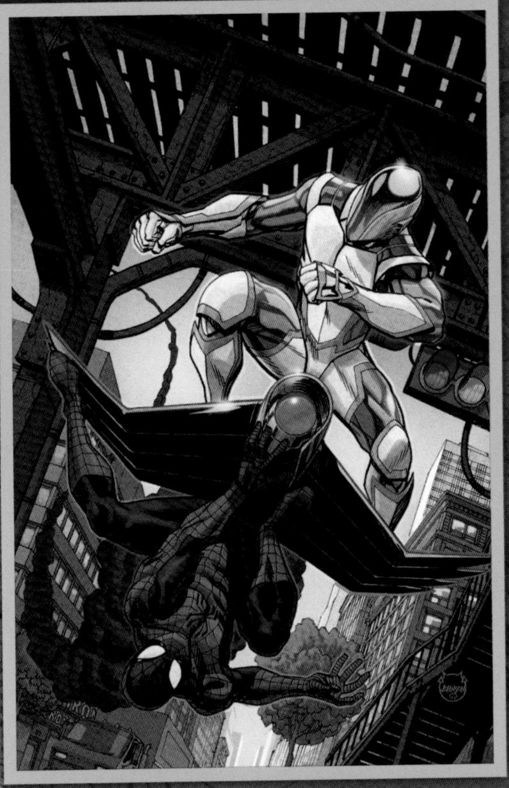

Dave Johnson
#34 VARIANT

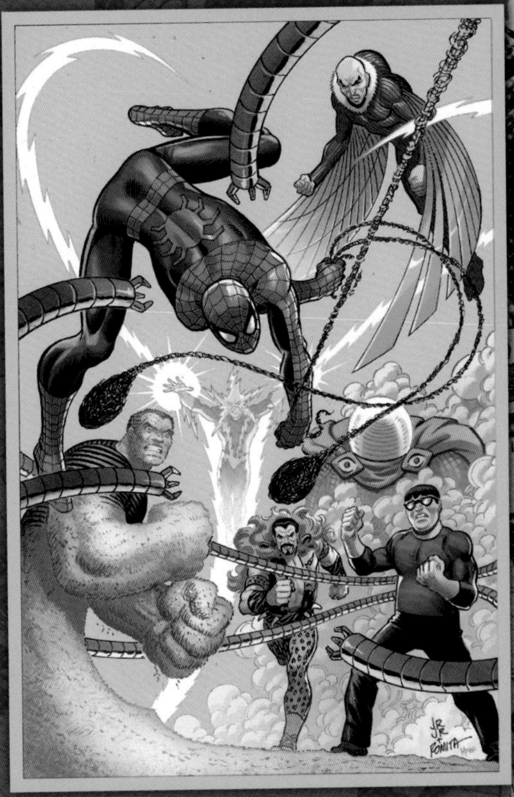

John Romita Jr., John Romita Sr. & Marcio Menyz #34 VARIANT

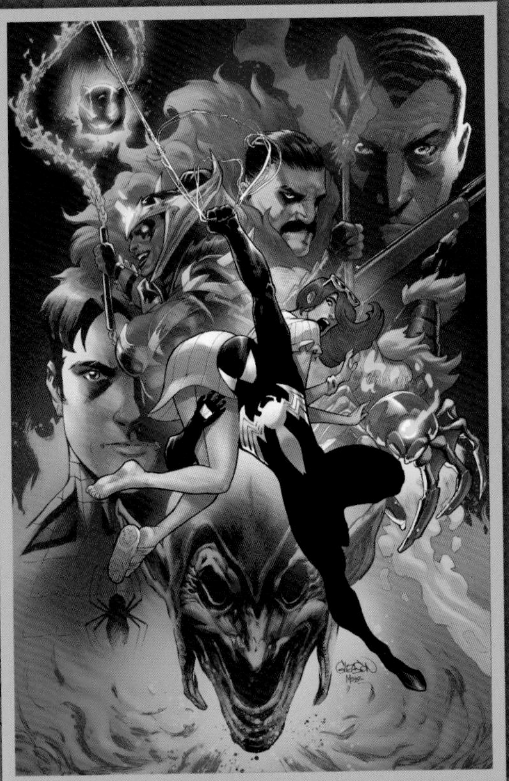

Patrick Gleason & Marcio Menyz
#34 VARIANT

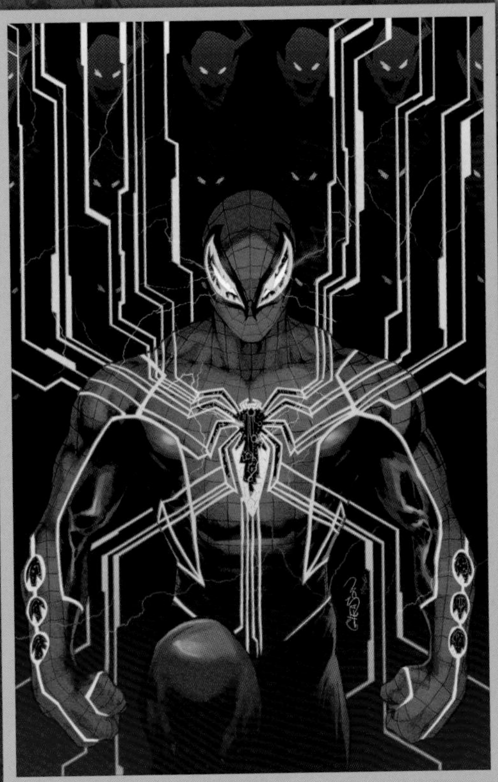

Patrick Gleason & Marcio Menyz
#35 VARIANT

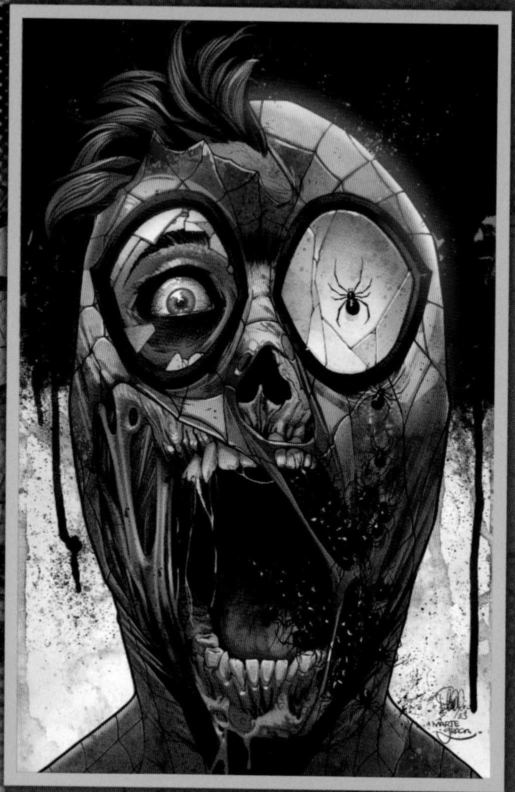

Elena Casagrande & Marte Gracia
#35 STORMBREAKERS VARIANT

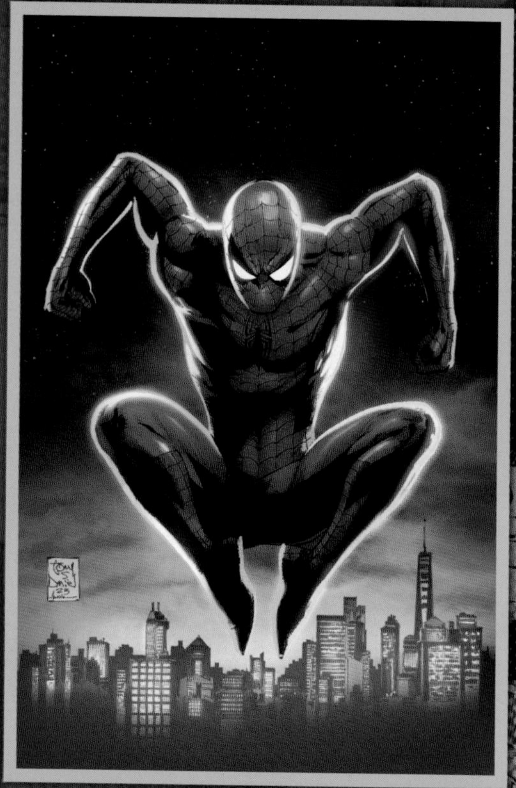

Tony Daniel & Marcelo Maiolo
#35 VARIANT

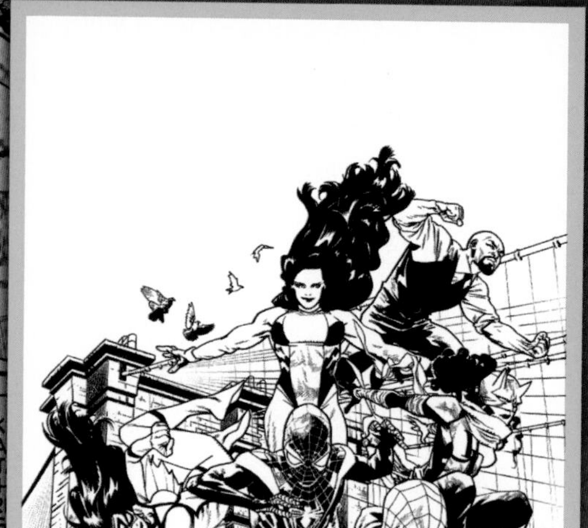

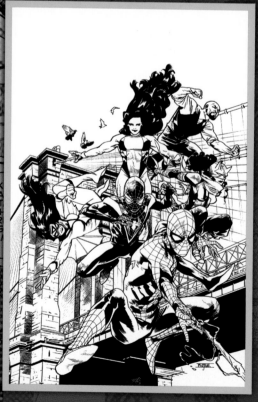

Mahmud Asrar
#35 NYCC GIVEAWAY SKETCH VARIANT

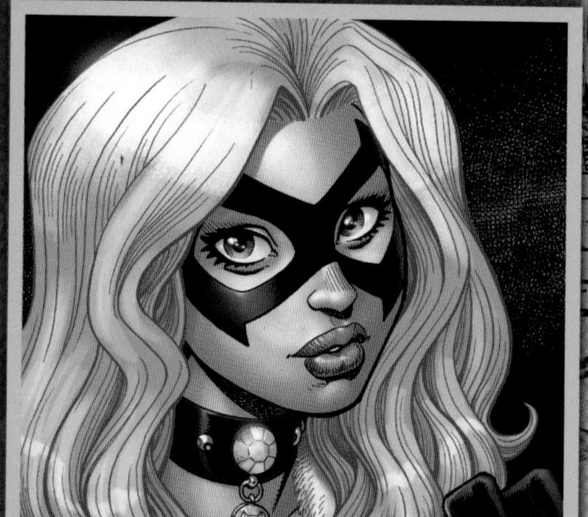

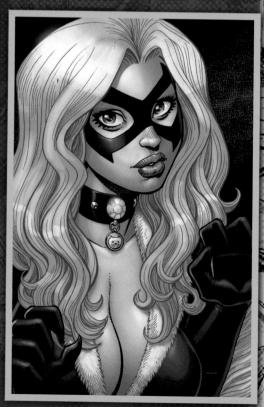

Arthur Adams & Alejandro Sánchez
#36 VARIANT

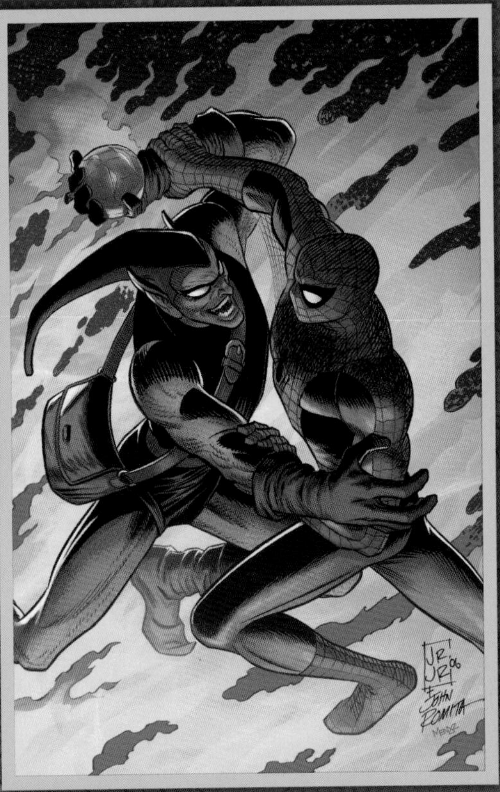

John Romita Jr., John Romita Sr. & Marcio Menyz #36 VARIANT

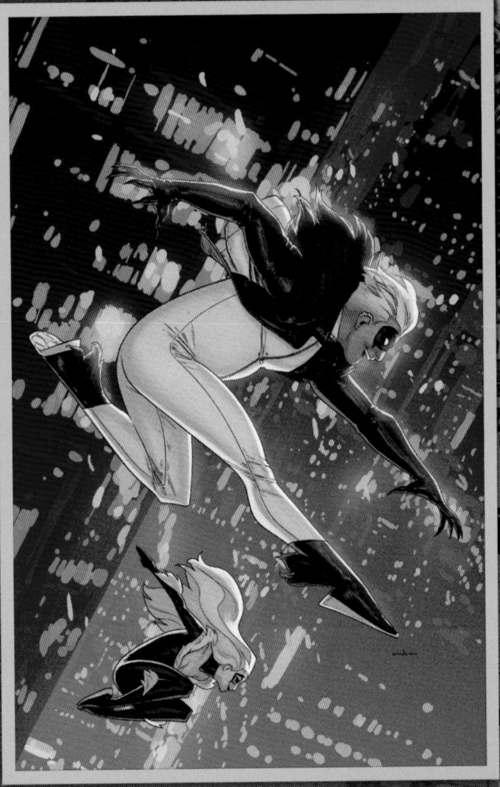

Kris Anka
#36 NEW CHAMPIONS VARIANT

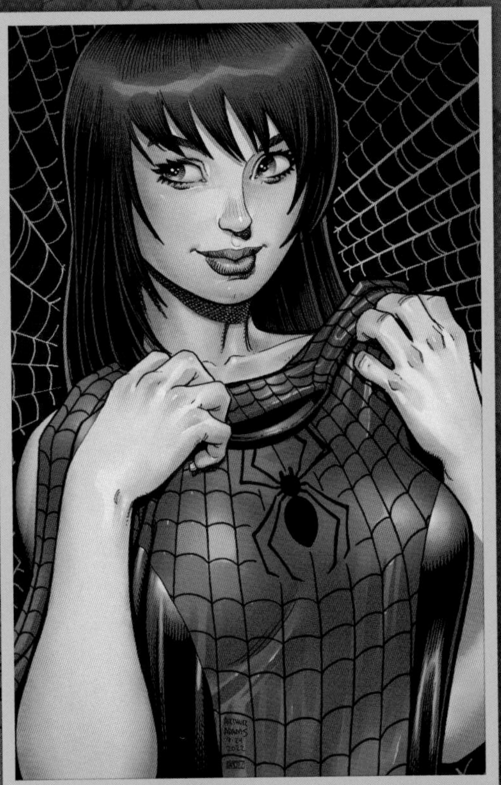

Arthur Adams & Alejandro Sánchez
#37 VARIANT

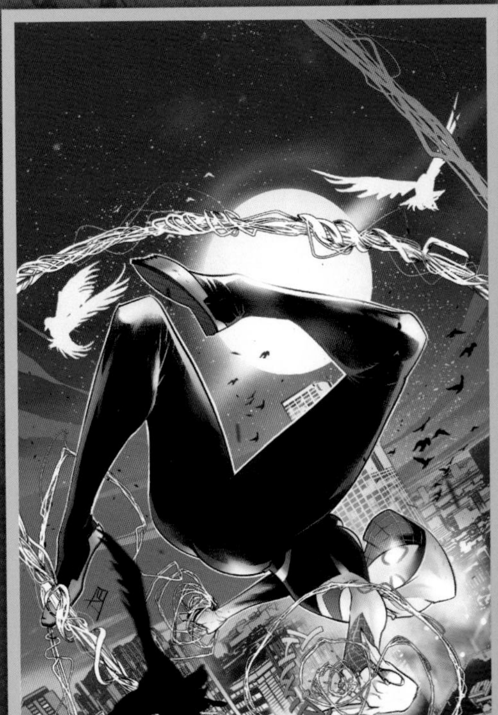

Federico Vicentini & Matt Milla
#37 STORMBREAKERS VARIANT

Kaare Andrews
#37 VARIANT

Steve Skroce & **Richard Isanove**
#38 VARIANT

Dike Ruan & **Alejandro Sánchez**
#38 VARIANT

Valerio Giangiordano & **Mattia Iacono**
#38 KNIGHT'S END VARIANT